BASIC LEGAL RESEARCH

ASPEN PUBLISHERS

BASIC LEGAL RESEARCH

TOOLS AND STRATEGIES

FOURTH EDITION

AMY E. SLOAN

Associate Professor of Law
and Co-Director, Legal Skills Program
University of Baltimore School of Law

Wolters Kluwer

Law & Business

AUSTIN   BOSTON   CHICAGO   NEW YORK   THE NETHERLANDS

Aspen Publishers
Attn: Permissions Department
76 Ninth Avenue, 7th Floor
New York, NY   10011-5201

To contact Customer Care, e-mail customer.care@aspenpublishers.com, call 1-800-234-1660, fax 1-800-901-9075, or mail correspondence to:

Aspen Publishers
Attn: Order Department
PO Box 990
Frederick, MD 21705

Printed in the United States of America.

1 2 3 4 5 6 7 8 9 0

ISBN 978-0-7355-7672-8

Library of Congress Cataloging-in-Publication Data

Sloan, Amy E., 1964-
    Basic legal research : tools and strategies / Amy E. Sloan—4th ed.
        p. cm.
    Includes index.
    ISBN 978-0-7355-7672-8
1.   Legal research—United States. I. Title.

KF240.S585 2009
340.072′073—dc22

2008055530

About Wolters Kluwer Law & Business

Wolters Kluwer Law & Business is a leading provider of research information and workflow solutions in key specialty areas. The strengths of the individual brands of Aspen Publishers, CCH, Kluwer Law International and Loislaw are aligned within Wolters Kluwer Law & Business to provide comprehensive, in-depth solutions and expert-authored content for the legal, professional and education markets.

CCH was founded in 1913 and has served more than four generations of business professionals and their clients. The CCH products in the Wolters Kluwer Law & Business group are highly regarded electronic and print resources for legal, securities, antitrust and trade regulation, government contracting, banking, pension, payroll, employment and labor, and healthcare reimbursement and compliance professionals.

Aspen Publishers is a leading information provider for attorneys, business professionals and law students. Written by preeminent authorities, Aspen products offer analytical and practical information in a range of specialty practice areas from securities law and intellectual property to mergers and acquisitions and pension/benefits. Aspen's trusted legal education resources provide professors and students with high-quality, up-to-date and effective resources for successful instruction and study in all areas of the law.

Kluwer Law International supplies the global business community with comprehensive English-language international legal information. Legal practitioners, corporate counsel and business executives around the world rely on the Kluwer Law International journals, loose-leafs, books and electronic products for authoritative information in many areas of international legal practice.

Loislaw is a premier provider of digitized legal content to small law firm practitioners of various specializations. Loislaw provides attorneys with the ability to quickly and efficiently find the necessary legal information they need, when and where they need it, by facilitating access to primary law as well as state-specific law, records, forms and treatises.

Wolters Kluwer Law & Business, a unit of Wolters Kluwer, is headquartered in New York and Riverwoods, Illinois. Wolters Kluwer is a leading multinational publisher and information services company.

For Bebe

SUMMARY OF CONTENTS

Contents   *xi*
Preface   *xv*
Acknowledgments   *xix*

CHAPTER 1   Introduction to Legal Research   1
CHAPTER 2   Generating Search Terms   25
CHAPTER 3   Secondary Source Research   29
CHAPTER 4   Case Research   77
CHAPTER 5   Research with Citators   129
CHAPTER 6   Statutory Research   157
CHAPTER 7   Federal Legislative History Research   199
CHAPTER 8   Federal Administrative Law Research   237
CHAPTER 9   Subject-Matter Service Research   259
CHAPTER 10   Electronic Legal Research   269
CHAPTER 11   Developing a Research Plan   305
APPENDIX A   Selected Internet Research Resources   333

Index   339

Contents

Preface xv
Acknowledgments xix

1. INTRODUCTION TO LEGAL RESEARCH 1

    A. Introduction to the legal system 2
    B. Introduction to the process of legal research 9
    C. Overview of print and electronic search strategies 12
    D. Introduction to legal citation 15
    E. Overview of this text 22

2. GENERATING SEARCH TERMS 25

    A. Generating search terms based on categories of information 25
    B. Expanding the initial search 27

3. SECONDARY SOURCE RESEARCH 29

    A. Introduction to secondary sources 29
    B. Researching secondary sources in print 31
    C. Researching secondary sources electronically 50
    D. Citing secondary sources 53
    E. Sample pages for print secondary source research 59
    F. Checklist for secondary source research 74

4. CASE RESEARCH 77

    A. Introduction to cases 77
    B. Researching cases in print 84

C. Researching cases electronically 99
D. Citing cases 105
E. Sample pages for researching cases using
   a print digest 108
F. Checklist for case research 126

5. RESEARCH WITH CITATORS 129

A. Introduction to citators 129
B. Using Shepard's in LexisNexis for case research 132
C. Using KeyCite in Westlaw for case research 140
D. Using Shepard's Citations in print for case research 145
E. Sample pages for case research with Shepard's and
   KeyCite 148
F. Checklist for case research with citators 155

6. STATUTORY RESEARCH 157

A. Introduction to statutory law 157
B. Researching statutes in print 163
C. Researching statutes electronically 174
D. Citing statutes 184
E. Sample pages for print statutory research 186
F. Checklist for statutory research 198

7. FEDERAL LEGISLATIVE HISTORY RESEARCH 199

A. Introduction to federal legislative history 199
B. Researching federal legislative history in print 206
C. Researching federal legislative history electronically 214
D. Citing federal legislative history 222
E. Sample pages for federal legislative history research 224
F. Checklist for federal legislative history research 233

8. FEDERAL ADMINISTRATIVE LAW RESEARCH 237

A. Introduction to federal administrative law 237
B. Researching federal regulations in print 242
C. Researching federal regulations electronically 244
D. Citing federal regulations 252
E. Sample pages for federal administrative law
   research 252
F. Checklist for federal administrative law research 257

9. SUBJECT-MATTER SERVICE RESEARCH   259

A. Introduction to subject-matter services   259
B. Researching subject-matter services in print, CD-ROM, and Internet formats   261
C. Subject-matter research in LexisNexis and Westlaw   262
D. Citing subject-matter services   263
E. Sample pages for subject-matter service research   264
F. Checklist for subject-matter service research   268

10. ELECTRONIC LEGAL RESEARCH   269

A. Introduction to electronic legal research   270
B. Conducting effective electronic legal research   275
C. Additional electronic research resources   292
D. Citing authority obtained from electronic legal research services   296
E. Sample pages for electronic legal research   299
F. Checklist for electronic legal research   303

11. DEVELOPING A RESEARCH PLAN   305

A. Introduction to research planning   305
B. Creating a research plan   305
C. Finding help   318
D. Sample research plans   320
E. Research checklists   325

Appendix A. Selected Internet Research Resources   333

Index   339

PREFACE

The fourth edition of *Basic Legal Research: Tools and Strategies* contains the following updated material:

An electronic version of the text on TeachingLaw.com—The fourth edition is available electronically through TeachingLaw.com, Aspen Publishers' electronic coursebook platform. The complete text is available online, along with interactive exercises, animated graphics, PowerPoint slides, and other teaching materials. Contact Aspen Publishers at www.teachinglaw.com to review the online version of the text.

Fully updated sample pages and research explanations—All sample pages have been updated. Discussions of print and electronic research have been updated to reflect the latest information on source coverage and the research process.

Coverage of print and electronic research that reflects both teaching needs and actual practice—The fourth edition has greater emphasis on electronic research than prior editions of the text to reflect changes in actual research practice and reduced print collections at many law libraries. At the same time, it maintains coverage of print sources necessary to give students a strong foundation in print research. Each chapter is organized to allow professors to tailor the degree of print and electronic coverage to fit their pedagogical approach.

New research process material—Chapter 1, Introduction to Legal Research, discusses locating authority by citation, subject, and word—search methods common to many authorities. Later chapters build on this introduction by explaining citation, subject, and word searching options for individual sources of authority. This approach more fully integrates instruction in print and electronic research and adds even more process orientation to the text.

Secondary sources—Chapter 3, Secondary Source Research, includes new material on nontraditional secondary sources, including Internet sources such as Wikipedia.

Citators—Chapter 5, Research with Citators, focuses almost exclusively on electronic citators.

The philosophy and the format of the fourth edition remain the same as those of earlier editions. The genesis of this book was a conversation I had with Todd Petit, a student in my Lawyering Skills class at Catholic University, in the fall of 1994. Todd was working on a research project, and he came to me in frustration and bewilderment over the research process. Over the course of the year, Todd ultimately mastered the skill of legal research. Nevertheless, our conversation that fall caused me to start thinking about how I could teach research more effectively, a process that ultimately culminated in this book.

I do not believe Todd's experience was unique. Mastering a skill is a form of experiential learning—learning that can be done only by doing. And the "doing" aspect necessarily involves periods of trial and error until a person grasps the skill. It is not surprising that this can be frustrating and even bewildering at times.

Having said that, however, even experiential learning has to be built on a base of information. My goal with this book is to provide two kinds of information necessary for students to learn the process of legal research: basic information about a range of research sources and a framework for approaching research projects.

This text provides instruction in a variety of legal research sources, including secondary sources, cases and digests, citators, statutes, federal legislative history, federal administrative regulations, and subject-matter ("looseleaf") services. Each of these sources is described in a separate chapter that includes the following components:

■ introductory information about the source
■ step-by-step instructions for print research
■ an explanation of electronic research tools available for the source
■ an explanation of citation rules for the source
■ an annotated set of sample pages and screen shots illustrating the research process for the source
■ a checklist summarizing both the research process and the key features of the source.

The range of material in each of these chapters is intended to accommodate a variety of teaching and learning styles. These chapters contain textual explanations, charts, and checklists that can be used for in-class discussions and for out-of-class reference as students are conducting research. In addition, the sample pages and screen shots illustrating the research process provide both instructional material and a useful summary synthesizing the information on the source from the rest of the chapter.

This text does more, however, than simply explain the bibliographic features of various research sources. It also provides instruction in research as a process, and it does this in two ways. First, Chapter 1 provides an overview of research sources and the research process. By providing a framework for understanding the relationships among different types of legal authority, this chapter sets the stage for a process-oriented introduction to research instruction. Second, Chapter 11 provides a framework for creating a research plan. By setting out a process based on a series of questions students can ask to define the contours of any type of research project, it provides a flexible approach that can be adapted to a variety of assignments. Although Chapter 11 is the last chapter in the text, it can be used whenever students are required to develop a strategy for approaching a research project.

Of course, a comprehensive understanding of legal research requires students to be familiar with both print and electronic research sources. This text explains electronic research in a way that will allow students to develop their electronic research skills regardless of whether they learn about electronic research along with print research or as a separate component of the curriculum. Each chapter devoted to an individual research source includes information on the types of electronic research options available for that source. General techniques for conducting electronic research, however, appear in a separate chapter, Chapter 10. Chapter 10 can be used in conjunction with other chapters at any point in the course when students begin learning about electronic legal research.

Moreover, the text provides instruction in a wide range of electronic research sources. It discusses research using commercial services such as Westlaw and LexisNexis. But it also covers a range of other electronic research options, including subscription services and material available for free via the Internet. As part of this instruction, the text discusses cost considerations in a way not addressed in other texts so that students can learn to make informed decisions about when to use electronic sources and how to select the best electronic source for any research project.

This text seeks to provide students with not only the bibliographic skills to locate the legal authorities necessary to resolve a research issue, but also an understanding of research process that is an integral component of students' training in problem-solving skills. I hope this text will prove to be a useful guide to students as they undertake this intellectual challenge.

Amy E. Sloan

January 2009

Acknowledgments

Many people contributed to the fourth edition of this book. My thanks here will not be adequate for the assistance they provided. I want to thank my research assistant, Jessica Thompson, and the reference librarians at the University of Baltimore Law Library, especially Joanne Dugan. I extend special thanks to Lynn Farnan for her invaluable assistance with a variety of tasks both large and small. A number of my colleagues at other schools contributed to this project by sharing their experiences in teaching with earlier editions, both by communicating with me directly and through anonymous reviews. I am indebted to them for their suggestions. I am grateful to Professor Diana Donahoe for her generous assistance. In addition, I want to thank the University of Baltimore School of Law for financial support of this project.

The people at Aspen Publishers have been incredibly generous with their time and talents. John Chatelaine, Melody Davies, Troy Froebe, Elizabeth Kenny, Carol McGeehan, Richard Mixter, Barbara Roth, Mark Scalise, and their colleagues provided everything from moral support to editorial advice to production assistance. Their guidance and expertise contributed greatly to the content, organization, and layout of the text, and I am grateful for their assistance.

I want to thank my family and friends for their support, especially Peggy Metzger and Jack and Drew Metzger-Sloan.

I would be remiss if I limited my acknowledgments to those who assisted with the fourth edition of the text because much of what appears here originated in the earlier editions. In particular, I would like to acknowledge Susan Dunham, Lauren Dunnock, Susan B. Koonin, Carli Masia, Herb Somers, Robert Walkowiak III, and Michelle Wu for their work on earlier editions of the text.

I would also like to acknowledge the publishers who permitted me to reprint copyrighted material in this text:

Figure 3.1 Index to Am. Jur. 2d
Reprinted with permission from Thomson Reuters/West, *American Jurisprudence*, 2d Ed., General Index (2008 edition), p. 404. ©2007 Thomson Reuters/West.

Figure 3.2   Am. Jur. 2d main volume entry under False Imprisonment
Reprinted with permission from Thomson Reuters/West, *American Jurisprudence*, 2d Ed., Vol. 32 (2007), p. 46. ©2007 Thomson Reuters/West.

Figure 3.3   Am. Jur. 2d pocket part entry for False Imprisonment
Reprinted with permission from Thomson Reuters/West, *American Jurisprudence*, 2d Ed., Vol. 32 Cumulative Supplement (2008), p. 1. ©2008 Thomson Reuters/West.

Figure 3.4   Treatise main volume entry for False Imprisonment
Reprinted with permission from Thomson Reuters/West. Dan B. Dobbs, *The Law of Torts* (2001), p. 67. ©2000 by Thomson Reuters/West.

Figure 3.5   ILP electronic citation list
From The H.W. Wilson Co., WilsonWeb, *Index to Legal Periodicals*. ©2002-2008 The H.W. Wilson Co.

Figure 3.6   LegalTrac citation list
From Gale. *Screenshot from LegalTrac.* ©Gale, a part of Cengage Learning, Inc. Reproduced by permission. www.cengage.com/permissions

Figure 3.7   Starting page of an A.L.R. Annotation
Reprinted with permission from Thomson Reuters/West, *American Law Reports*, 3d Ser., Vol. 97 (1980), p. 688. ©1980 Thomson Reuters/West.

Figure 3.8   Later page of an A.L.R. Annotation
Reprinted with permission from Thomson Reuters/West, *American Law Reports*, 3d Ser., Vol. 97 (1980), p. 693. ©1980 Thomson Reuters/West.

Figure 3.9   Section 35 of the *Restatement (Second) of Torts*
©1965 by The American Law Institute. Reproduced with permission. All rights reserved. *Restatement (Second) of the Law of Torts*, 2d Ed., Vol. 1, § 35 (1965), p. 52.

Figure 3.10   Entry under § 35 in the Appendix to the *Restatement (Second) of Torts*
©2005 by The American Law Institute. Reproduced with permission. All rights reserved. *Restatement (Second) of the Law of Torts*, 2d Ed., Appendix through June 2004, §§ 1–309 (2005), p. 119.

Figure 3.11   ULA entry for the Uniform Single Publication Act
Reprinted with permission from Thomson Reuters/West and National Conference of Commissioners on Uniform State Laws (NCCUSL), *Uniform Laws Annotated*, Vol. 14 (2005), pp. 471-472. ULA ©2005 Thomson Reuters/West. The text of the Act and any comments are copyright 1952 by NCCUSL.

Figure 3.12   HeinOnLine display of a legal periodical article
From HeinOnLine. ©2008 HeinOnLine.

Figure 3.14   A.L.R. Index
Reprinted with permission from Thomson Reuters/West, *American Law Reports*, Index E–H (1999), p. 350. ©1999 Thomson Reuters/West.

Figure 3.15   A.L.R. Annotation
Reprinted with permission from Thomson Reuters/West, *American Law Reports*, 3d Ser., Vol. 97 (1980), pp. 688–689. ©1980 Thomson Reuters/West.

Figure 3.16   A.L.R. Annotation
Reprinted with permission from Thomson Reuters/West, *American Law Reports*, 3d Ser., Vol. 97 (1980), pp. 690–692. ©1980 Thomson Reuters/West.

Figure 3.17   A.L.R. Annotation
Reprinted with permission from Thomson Reuters/West, *American Law Reports*, 3d Ser., Vol. 97 (1980), p. 693. ©1980 Thomson Reuters/West.

Figure 3.18   Pocket part accompanying an A.L.R. volume
Reprinted with permission from Thomson Reuters/West, *American Law Reports Supplement*, 3d Ser., Insert in Back of Vol. 97 (2008), pp. 92–93. ©2008 Thomson Reuters/West.

Figure 3.19   Table of Contents, *Restatement (Second) of Torts*
©1965 by The American Law Institute. Reproduced with permission. All rights reserved. *Restatement (Second) of the Law of Torts*, 2d Ed., Vol. 1, §§ 1–280 (1965), p. XII.

Figure 3.20   Restatement (Second) of Torts § 35
©1965 by The American Law Institute. Reproduced with permission. All rights reserved. *Restatement (Second) of the Law of Torts*, 2d Ed., Vol. 1, §§ 1–280 (1965), pp. 52–53.

Figure 3.21   Appendix volume, *Restatement (Second) of Torts*
©2005 by The American Law Institute. Reproduced with permission. All rights reserved. *Restatement (Second) of the Law of Torts*, 2d Ed., Appendix Volume through June 2004, §§ 1–309 (2005), title page.

Figure 3.22   Appendix volume, *Restatement (Second) of Torts*
©2005 by The American Law Institute. Reproduced with permission. All rights reserved. *Restatement (Second) of the Law of Torts*, 2d Ed., Appendix through June 2004, §§ 1–309 (2005), p. 119.

Figure 4.2   Excerpt from *Popkin v. New York State*
Reprinted with permission from Thomson Reuters/West, West's *Federal Reporter*, 2d Ser., *Popkin v. New York State*, 547 F.2d 18–19 (2d Cir. 1976). ©1976 Thomson Reuters/West.

Figure 4.3 Beginning of the West topic for "Abandoned and Lost Property"
Reprinted with permission from Thomson Reuters/West, *West's Federal Practice Digest*, 4th Ser., Vol. 1 (2006), p. 1. ©2006 Thomson Reuters/West.

Figure 4.4 Case summary under the "Abandoned and Lost Property" topic, key number 10
Reprinted with permission from Thomson Reuters/West, *West's Federal Practice Digest*, 4th Ser., Vol. 1 (2006), p. 7. ©2006 Thomson Reuters/West.

Figure 4.9 Excerpt from the Descriptive-Word Index
Reprinted with permission from Thomson Reuters/West, *West's Federal Practice Digest*, 4th Ser., Descriptive-Word Index, Vol. 98 (2002), p. 437. ©2002 Thomson Reuters/West.

Figure 4.10 Interim pamphlet closing table
Reprinted with permission from Thomson Reuters/West, *West's Federal Practice Digest*, 4th Ser., October 2007 Pamphlet (2007), inside cover. ©2007 Thomson Reuters/West.

Figure 4.11 Excerpt from the Table of Cases
Reprinted with permission from Thomson Reuters/West, *West's Federal Practice Digest*, 4th Ser., Vol. 103B (2000), p. 377. ©2000 Thomson Reuters/West.

Figure 4.12 Words and Phrases
Reprinted with permission from Thomson Reuters/West, *West's Federal Practice Digest*, 4th Ser., Vol. 108 (1999), p. 442. ©1999 Thomson Reuters/West.

Figure 4.13 Example of a case in Westlaw
Reprinted with permission of Thomson Reuters/West, from Westlaw, 16 F. Supp. 2d 1369. ©2008 Thomson Reuters/West.

Figure 4.14 Example of a case in LexisNexis
Reprinted with permission of LexisNexis, from LexisNexis, 16 F. Supp. 2d 1369.

Figure 4.16 Descriptive-Word Index
Reprinted with permission from Thomson Reuters/West, *West's Federal Practice Digest*, 4th Ser., Vol. 99 (2002), p. 82. ©2002 Thomson Reuters/West.

Figure 4.17 Descriptive-Word Index
Reprinted with permission from Thomson Reuters/West, *West's Federal Practice Digest*, 4th Ser., Vol. 98 (2002), p. 437 ©2002 Thomson Reuters/West.

Figure 4.18 Descriptive-Word Index, pocket part
Reprinted with permission from Thomson Reuters/West, *West's Federal Practice Digest*, 4th Ser., Cumulative Annual Pocket Part, Vol. 98 (2007), p. 151. ©2007 Thomson Reuters/West.

Figure 4.19 Key number outline, "Abandoned and Lost Property" topic
Reprinted with permission from Thomson Reuters/West, *West's Federal Practice Digest*, 4th Ser., Vol. 1 (2006), pp. 1–2. ©2006 Thomson Reuters/West.

Figure 4.20 Case summaries under "Abandoned and Lost Property" topic
Reprinted with permission from Thomson Reuters/West, *West's Federal Practice Digest*, 4th Ser., Vol. 1 (2006), pp. 11–12. ©2006 Thomson Reuters/West.

Figure 4.21 Digest volume, pocket part
Reprinted with permission from Thomson Reuters/West, *West's Federal Practice Digest*, 4th Ser., Pocket Part, Vol. 1 (2007), p. 1. ©2007 Thomson Reuters/West.

Figure 4.22 Noncumulative interim pamphlet
Reprinted with permission from Thomson Reuters/West, *West's Federal Practice Digest*, 4th Ser., October 2007 Pamphlet (2007), p. 1. ©2007 Thomson Reuters/West.

Figure 4.23 Noncumulative interim pamphlet, closing table
Reprinted with permission from Thomson Reuters/West, *West's Federal Practice Digest*, 4th Ser., October 2007 Pamphlet (2007), inside cover. ©2007 Thomson Reuters/West.

Figure 4.24 502 F. Supp. 2d, mini-digest
Reprinted with permission from Thomson Reuters/West, West's *Federal Supplement*, 2d Ser., Vol. 502 (2007), p. (1) (key number digest). ©2007 Thomson Reuters/West.

Figure 4.25 Sea Services of the Keys, Inc. v. The Abandoned 29' Midnight Express Vessel, 16 F. Supp. 2d 1369 (S.D. Fla. 1998).
Reprinted with permission from Thomson Reuters/West, West's *Federal Supplement*, 2d Ser., Vol. 16 (1998), pp. 1369–1374. ©1998 Thomson Reuters/West.

Figure 5.1 Shepard's® Entry Excerpt for 748 N.E.2d 41
Reprinted with permission of LexisNexis. Shepard's entry for 748 N.E.2d 41.

Figure 5.3 Headnote 11 from the original case, *Bennett v. Stanley*
Reproduced by permission of LexisNexis. LexisNexis, from LexisNexis 748 N.E.2d 41.

Figure 5.4 SHEPARD'S® entry for *Bennett v. Stanley*.
Reproduced by permission of LexisNexis. LexisNexis. SHEPARD's entry for 748 N.E.2d 41.

Figure 5.5 *Kiracofe v. Ketcham*, citing *Bennett v. Stanley*
LexisNexis, from LexisNexis 2005 Ohio 5271.

Figure 5.6   Shepard's® Focus™-RESTRICT BY Options
Reproduced by permission of LexisNexis. LexisNexis, Shepard's Focus™-Restrict By Options.

Figure 5.8   Keycite Full History Entry for 748 N.E.2d 41
Reprinted with permission from Thomson Reuters/West, from Westlaw, KeyCite entry for 748 N.E.2d 41. ©2008 Thomson Reuters/West.

Figure 5.9   Graphical Keycite Display for 748 N.E.2d 41.
Reprinted with permission from Thomson Reuters/West, from Westlaw, KeyCite entry for 748 N.E.2d 41. ©2008 Thomson Reuters/West.

Figure 5.10   KeyCite Citing References entry for 748 N.E.2d 41
Reprinted with permission from Thomson Reuters/West, from Westlaw, KeyCite entry for 748 N.E.2d 41. ©2008 Thomson Reuters/West.

Figure 5.12   KeyCite Limited Display Options
Reprinted with permission from Thomson Reuters/West, from Westlaw, Limit KeyCite Display options. ©2008 Thomson Reuters/West.

Figure 5.13   Shepard's® Entry for *Kenney v. Scientific, Inc.*
Reproduced by permission of LexisNexis. Further reproduction of any kind is strictly prohibited.
From *Shepard's Atlantic Report Citations*, 2005 Bound Volume, Part 8, p. 521.

Figure 5.14   Shepard's for Validation (KWIC) Display
Reproduced by permission of LexisNexis. From LexisNexis, Shepard's entry for 748 N.E.2d 41.

Figure 5.15   Shepard's Citing Case
Reproduced by permission of LexisNexis. From LexisNexis, 165 Ohio App. 699.

Figure 5.16   KeyCite Full History Entry for 748 N.E.2d 41
Reprinted with permission from Thomson Reuters/West, from Westlaw, KeyCite entry for 748 N.E.2d 41. ©2008 Thomson Reuters/West.

Figure 5.17   KeyCite Limited Display Options
Reprinted with permission from Thomson Reuters/West, from Westlaw, Limit KeyCite Display Options. ©2008 Thomson Reuters/West

Figure 5.18   KeyCite Limited Citing References Entry for 748 N.E.2d 41
Reprinted with permission from Thomson Reuters/West, from Westlaw, KeyCite entry for 748 N.E.2d 41. ©2008 Thomson Reuters/West.

Figure 5.19   KeyCite Citing Case Display
Reprinted with permission from Thomson Reuters/West, from Westlaw, KeyCite entry for 748 N.E.2d 41. ©2008 Thomson Reuters/West.

Figure 6.2   10 U.S.C.A. § 816
Reprinted with permission from Thomson Reuters/West, *United States Code Annotated*, Title 10 (1998), p. 202. ©1998 Thomson Reuters/West.

Figure 6.4   Excerpt from the U.S.C.A. General Index
Reprinted with permission from Thomson Reuters/West, *United States Code Annotated*, 2008 General Index J-R, p. 345. ©2008 Thomson Reuters/West.

Figure 6.6   Annotations accompanying 10 U.S.C.A. § 816
Reprinted with permission from Thomson Reuters/West, *United States Code Annotated*, Title 10 (1998), p. 203. ©1998 Thomson Reuters/West.

Figure 6.7   Pocket part update for 10 U.S.C.A. § 816
Reprinted with permission from Thomson Reuters/West, *United States Code Annotated*, 2008 Cumulative Annual Pocket Part, Title 10, p. 28. ©2008 Thomson Reuters/West.

Figure 6.8   FACE Act entry, popular name table
Reprinted with permission from Thomson Reuters/West, *United States Code Annotated*, 2008 Popular Name Table, p. 571. ©2008 Thomson Reuters/West.

Figure 6.9   Conversion table entry for Pub. L. No. 103-259, the FACE Act
Reprinted with permission from Thomson Reuters/West, Tables Vol. II, *United States Code Annotated*, 2008, p. 655. ©2008 Thomson Reuters/West.

Figure 6.10   Excerpt from 10 U.S.C.A. § 816 In Westlaw
Reprinted with permission from Thomson Reuters/West, from Westlaw, 10 U.S.C.A. § 816. ©2008 Thomson Reuters/West.

Figure 6.11   Westlaw U.S.C.A. Table of Contents Search Screen
Reprinted with permission from Thomson Reuters/West, from Westlaw, U.S.C.A. Table of Contents search screen. ©2008 Thomson Reuters/West.

Figure 6.12   KeyCite History Entry for 10 U.S.C.A. § 816
Reprinted with permission from Thomson Reuters/West, KeyCite entry for 10 U.S.C.A. § 816 ©2008 Thomson Reuters/West.

Figure 6.13   Excerpt From 10 U.S.C.S. § 816 in LexisNexis
Reprinted with permission of LexisNexis. From LexisNexis, 10 U.S.C.S. § 816.

Figure 6.14   LexisNexis U.S.C.S. search screen
Reprinted with permission of LexisNexis. From LexisNexis, U.S.C.S. search screen.

Figure 6.15   Shepard's Entry for 10 U.S.C.S. § 816
Reprinted with permission of LexisNexis. From LexisNexis, Shepard's entry for 10 U.S.C.S. § 816.

Figure 6.16   Excerpt from U.S.C.A. General Index
Reprinted with permission from Thomson Reuters/West, *United States Code Annotated*, 2008 General Index J-R, p. 345. ©2008 Thomson Reuters/West.

Figure 6.17   10 U.S.C.A. § 816
Reprinted with permission from Thomson Reuters/West, *United States Code Annotated*, Title 10 (1998), p. 202. ©1998 Thomson Reuters/West.

Figure 6.18   Annotations accompanying 10 U.S.C.A. § 816
Reprinted with permission from Thomson Reuters/West, *United States Code Annotated*, Title 10 (1998), pp. 203-204. ©1998 Thomson Reuters/West.

Figure 6.19   Pocket part entry for 10 U.S.C.A. § 816
Reprinted with permission from Thomson Reuters/West, *United States Code Annotated*, 2008 Cumulative Annual Pocket Part, Title 10, pp. 28-29. ©2008 Thomson Reuters/West.

Figure 6.20   Vernon's Texas Statutes and Codes Annotated General Index
Reprinted with permission from Thomson Reuters/West, Vernon's *Texas Statutes and Codes Annotated*, 2008 General Index P-Z, p. 278. ©2007 Thomson Reuters/West.

Figure 6.21   Texas Civil Practice and Remedies Code Chapter 82
Reprinted with permission from Thomson Reuters/West, Vol. 4 Vernon's *Texas Codes Annotated*, Civil Practice and Remedies Code, Chapter 82, p. 249 (2005). ©2005 Thomson Reuters/West.

Figure 6.22   Texas Civil Practice and Remedies Code § 82.004
Reprinted with permission from Thomson Reuters/West, Vol. 4 Vernon's *Texas Codes Annotated*, Civil Practice and Remedies Code, pp. 258–259 (2005). ©2005 Thomson Reuters/West.

Figure 6.23   Pocket part entry for Texas Civil Practice and Remedies Code § 82.004
Reprinted with permission from Thomson Reuters/West, Vol. 4 Vernon's *Texas Codes Annotated*, Civil Practice and Remedies Code, Cumulative Annual Pocket Part, p. 77 (2007). ©2007 Thomson Reuters/West.

Figure 7.1   How a Bill Becomes a Law
Reprinted with permission from Congressional Quarterly Inc., *Congressional Quarterly's Guide to Congress*, CQ Press, 5th Ed. (2000), p. 1093. Copyright ©2000 CQ Press, a division of SAGE Publications, Inc.

Figure 7.2   Excerpt from annotations accompanying 18 U.S.C.A. § 2441
Reprinted with permission from Thomson Reuters/West, *United States Code Annotated*, Vol. 18 (2000), p. 14. ©2000 Thomson Reuters/West.

Figure 7.3   Starting page, House Judiciary Committee Report on the War Crimes Act of 1996
Reprinted with permission from Thomson Reuters/West, *United States Code Congressional and Administrative News*, 104th Congress-Second Session 1996, Vol. 5 (1997), p. 2166. ©1997 Thomson Reuters/West.

Figure 7.4   CIS Legislative Histories entry for Pub. L. No. 104–192
Reprinted from *CIS/Annual* with permission of LexisNexis. Copyright 1997 LexisNexis Academic and Library Solutions, a division of Reed Elsevier Inc. All Rights Reserved. *CIS/Annual 1996*, Legislative Histories of U.S. Public Laws (1997), p. 315.

Figure 7.8   HeinOnLine Sources of Compiled Legislative Histories Entry
Reproduced with permission of HeinOnline. ©2008 HeinOnline.

Figure 7.9   Search Options for Congressional Publications In LexisNexis Congressional
Reprinted with permission of LexisNexis, LexisNexis Congressional search options.

Figure 7.10   18 U.S.C.A. § 2441 and Accompanying Annotations
Reprinted with permission from Thomson Reuters/West, *United States Code Annotated*, Vol. 18 (2000), pp. 13–14. ©2000 Thomson Reuters/West.

Figure 7.11   House Judiciary Committee report reprinted in U.S.C.C.A.N.
Reprinted with permission from Thomson Reuters/West, *United States Code Congressional and Administrative News*, 104th Congress-Second Session 1996, Vol. 5 (1997), p. 2166. ©1997 Thomson Reuters/West.

Figure 7.14   Search options, LexisNexis Congressional
Reprinted with permission of LexisNexis, LexisNexis Congressional search options.

Figure 7.15   Search results, LexisNexis Congressional
Reprinted with permission of LexisNexis, LexisNexis Congressional search options.

Figure 7.16   *Congressional Record* Excerpt from LexisNexis Congressional
Reprinted with permission of LexisNexis, LexisNexis Congressional abstract entries.

Figure 8.2   Annotations to 15 U.S.C.S. § 2063
Reprinted from *United States Code Service, Lawyer's Edition* with permission of LexisNexis. Copyright 1996 by Lawyer's Cooperative Publishing. *United States Code Service*, Title 15 Commerce and Trade §§ 1701-2800 (1996), p. 104.

Figure 9.1   Introductory Screen, BNA Labor and Employment Law Library
Reproduced with permission from BNA's Labor & Employment Law Library,

Introductory Screen. Copyright 2008 by The Bureau of National Affairs, Inc. (800-372-1033), http://www.bna.com.

Figure 9.2   Excerpt from 49 C.F.R. 38.161 from BNA Labor and Employment Law Library
Reproduced with permission from BNA's Labor & Employment Law Library, excerpt from 49 C.F.R. 38.161. Copyright 2008 by The Bureau of National Affairs, Inc. (800-372-1033), http://www.bna.com.

Figure 9.3   Excerpt from E.E.O.C. Technical Assistance for Employers from BNA Labor and Employment Law Library
Reproduced with permission from BNA's Labor & Employment Law Library, excerpt from E.E.O.C. Technical Assistance for Employers. Copyright 2008 by The Bureau of National Affairs, Inc. (800-372-1033), http://www.bna.com.

Figure 9.4   Classification Number Outline by Topic from BNA Labor and Employment Law Library
Reproduced with permission from BNA's Labor & Employment Law Library, Classification Number Outline By Topic. Copyright 2008 by The Bureau of National Affairs, Inc. (800-372-1033), http://www.bna.com.

Figure 9.5   Classification Number Digest and Full Text of a Case from BNA Labor and Employment Law Library
Reproduced with permission from BNA's Labor & Employment Law Library, Classification Number Digest and Full Text of a Case. Copyright 2008 by The Bureau of National Affairs, Inc. (800-372-1033), http://www.bna.com.

Figure 10.1   Westlaw search screen
Reprinted with permission from Thomson Reuters/West, from Westlaw, search screen. ©2008 Thomson Reuters/West.

Figure 10.2   LexisNexis search screen
Reprinted with permission of LexisNexis, from LexisNexis, search screen.

Figure 10.4   Westlaw Search Results
Reprinted with permission from Thomson Reuters/West, from Westlaw, search results display. ©2008 Thomson Reuters/West.

Figure 10.5   LexisNexis search results
Reprinted with permission of LexisNexis, from LexisNexis, search results display.

Figure 10.6   Legal Resources, Wrightslaw Web Site
Reprinted with the permission of wrightslaw.com. IDEA 2004 Legal Information Resources from wrightslaw.com. ©1998-2008, Peter D. Wright and Pamela Dan Wright. All rights reserved.

Figure 10.7   Entry from the CAMLaw blog
Reprinted with permission from Complementary and Alternative Medicine
Law Blog (CAMLaw Blog), www.camlawblog.com, ©2008, lexBlog, Inc.

Figure 10.8   Search options in FindLaw
Reprinted with permission. ©2008 FindLaw, a Thomson Reuters business, from
Findlaw for Legal Professionals, http://lp.findlaw.com.

Figure 10.9   Introductory screen, Legal Information Institute
Reprinted with permission. ©2008 Cornell Law School, from http://www.law.
cornell.edu.

Figure 10.10   Search Options in Legal Information Institute
Reprinted with permission. ©2008 Cornell Law School, from http://www.law.
cornell.edu.

BASIC LEGAL RESEARCH

CHAPTER 1

Introduction to Legal Research

A. Introduction to the legal system
B. Introduction to the process of legal research
C. Overview of print and electronic search strategies
D. Introduction to legal citation
E. Overview of this text

What is legal research and why do you need to learn about it? Researching the law means finding the rules that govern conduct in our society. To be a successful lawyer, you need to know how to research the law. Lawyers are often called upon to solve problems and give advice, and to do that accurately, you must know the rules applicable to the different situations you and your clients will face. Clients may come to you after an event has occurred and ask you to pursue a remedy for a bad outcome, or perhaps defend them against charges that they have acted wrongfully. You may be asked to help a client accomplish a goal like starting a business or buying a piece of property. In these situations and many others, you will need to know your clients' rights and responsibilities, as defined by legal rules. Consequently, being proficient in legal research is essential to your success in legal practice.

As a starting point for learning about how to research the law, it is important to understand some of the different sources of legal rules. This chapter discusses what these sources are and where they originate within our legal system. It also provides an introduction to the process of legal research, an overview of some of the research tools you will learn to use, and an introduction to legal citation. Later chapters explain how to locate legal rules using a variety of resources.

A. INTRODUCTION TO THE LEGAL SYSTEM

1. SOURCES OF LAW

There are four main sources of law, which exist at both the state and federal levels:

- constitutions
- statutes
- court opinions (also called cases)
- administrative regulations.

A constitution establishes a system of government and defines the boundaries of authority granted to the government. The United States Constitution is the preeminent source of law in our legal system, and all other rules, whether promulgated by a state or the federal government, must comply with its requirements. Each state also has its own constitution. A state's constitution may grant greater rights than those secured by the federal constitution, but because a state constitution is subordinate to the federal constitution, it cannot provide lesser rights than the federal constitution does. All of a state's legal rules must comport with both the state and federal constitutions.

Since grade school, you have been taught that the United States Constitution created three branches of government: the legislative branch, which makes the laws; the judicial branch, which interprets the laws; and the executive branch, which enforces the laws. State governments are also divided into these three branches. Although this is elementary civics, this structure truly does define the way government authority is divided in our system of government.

The legislative branch of government creates statutes, which must be approved by the executive branch (the president, for federal statutes; the governor, for state statutes) to go into effect. The executive branch also makes rules. Administrative agencies, such as the federal Food and Drug Administration or a state's department of motor vehicles, are part of the executive branch. They execute the laws passed by the legislature and create their own regulations to carry out the mandates established by statute.

The judicial branch is the source of court opinions. Courts interpret rules created by the legislative and executive branches of government. If a court determines that a rule does not meet constitutional requirements, it can invalidate the rule. Otherwise, however, the court must apply the rule to the case before it. Court opinions can also be an independent source of legal rules. Legal rules made by courts are called "common-law" rules. Although courts are empowered to make these rules, legislatures can adopt legislation that changes or abolishes a common-law rule, as long as the legislation is constitutional.

FIGURE 1.1   BRANCHES OF GOVERNMENT AND LEGAL RULES

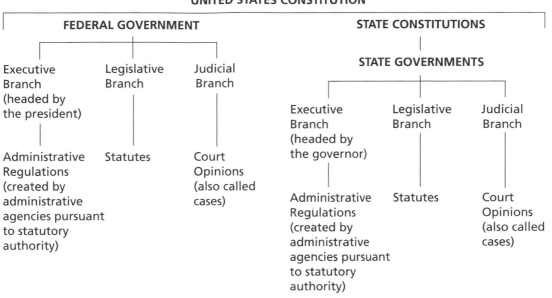

Figure **1.1** shows the relationships among the branches of government and the types of legal rules they create.

An example may be useful to illustrate the relationships among the rules created by the three branches of the federal government. As you know, the United States Constitution, through the First Amendment, guarantees the right to free expression. Congress could pass legislation requiring television stations to provide educational programming for children. The Federal Communications Commission (FCC) is the administrative agency within the executive branch that would have responsibility for carrying out Congress's will. If the statute were not specific about what constitutes educational programming or how much educational programming must be provided, the FCC would have to create administrative regulations to enforce the law. The regulations would provide the information not detailed in the statute, such as the definition of educational programming. A television station could challenge the statute and regulations by arguing to a court that prescribing the content of material that the station must broadcast violates the First Amendment. The court would then have to interpret the statute and regulations and decide whether they comply with the Constitution.

Another example illustrates the relationship between courts and legislatures in the area of common-law rules. The rules of negligence have been largely created by the courts. Therefore, liability for negligence is usually determined by common-law rules. A state supreme court could decide that a plaintiff who sues a defendant for negligence cannot recover any damages if the plaintiff herself was negligent and contributed to her own injuries. This decision would create a common-law rule governing future cases of negligence within that state. The state legislature could step in and pass a statute that changes the rule. For example, the legislature could enact a statute providing that juries are to determine the percentage of negligence attributable to either party and to apportion damages accordingly, instead of completely denying recovery to the plaintiff. Courts in that state would then be obligated to apply the rule from the statute, not the former common-law rule.

Although these examples are simplified, they demonstrate the basic roles of each of the branches of government in enunciating the legal rules governing the conduct of society. They also demonstrate that researching a legal issue may require you to research several different types of legal authority. The answer to a research question may not be found exclusively in statutes or court opinions or administrative regulations. Often, these sources must be researched together to determine all of the rules applicable to a factual scenario.

2. TYPES AND WEIGHT OF AUTHORITY

One term used to describe the rules that govern conduct in society is "legal authority." Rules, however, are only one type of legal authority, and some types of legal authority are more authoritative than others. To understand how legal authority is categorized, you must be able to differentiate "primary" authority from "secondary" authority and "mandatory" authority from "persuasive" authority. Making these distinctions will help you determine the weight, or authoritative value, a legal authority carries with respect to the issue you are researching.

a. Primary vs. Secondary Authority and Mandatory vs. Persuasive Authority

Primary authority is the term used to describe rules of law. Primary authority includes all of the types of rules discussed so far in this chapter. Constitutional provisions, statutes, court opinions, and administrative regulations contain legal rules, and as a consequence, are primary authority. Because "the law" consists of legal rules, primary authority is sometimes described as "the law."

Secondary authority, by contrast, refers to commentary on the law or analysis of the law, but not "the law" itself. An opinion from the United States Supreme Court is primary authority, but an article written by a private party explaining and analyzing the opinion is secondary authority. Secondary authority is often quite useful in legal research because its analysis can help you understand complex legal issues and refer you to primary authority. Nevertheless, secondary authority is not "the law" and therefore is distinguished from primary authority.

Mandatory and persuasive authority are terms courts use to categorize the different sources of law they use in making their decisions. Mandatory authority, which can also be called binding authority, refers to authority that the court is obligated to follow. Mandatory authority contains rules that you must apply to determine the correct answer to the issue you are researching. Persuasive authority, which can also be called nonbinding authority, refers to authority that the court may follow if it is persuaded to do so, but is not required to follow. Persuasive authority, therefore, will not dictate the answer to an issue, although it may help you figure out the answer. Whether an authority is mandatory or persuasive depends on several factors, as discussed in the next section.

b. Weight of Authority

The degree to which an authority controls the answer to a legal issue is called the weight of the authority. Not all authorities have the same weight. The weight of a legal authority depends on its status as primary or secondary authority and as mandatory or persuasive authority. Some primary authorities are mandatory, and others are persuasive. Secondary authority, by contrast, is always persuasive authority. You must be able to distinguish among these categories of authority, therefore, to determine how much weight a particular legal authority has in the resolution of the issue you are researching.

(1) Secondary authority: Always persuasive
A legal authority's status as a primary or secondary authority is fixed. An authority is either part of "the law," or it is not. Because secondary authority is always persuasive authority, it is not binding. Once you identify an authority as secondary, you can be certain that it will not control the outcome of the issue you are researching.

Although secondary authority is not binding, some secondary authorities are more persuasive than others. Some are so respected that a court, while not technically bound by them, would need a good reason to depart from or reject their statements of legal rules. Others do not enjoy the same degree of respect, leaving a court free to ignore or reject such authorities if it is not persuaded to follow them. Further discussion of the persuasive value of various secondary authorities appears in Chapter 3, on secondary source research. The important thing to remember for now is that secondary authority is always categorized as persuasive or nonbinding authority.

(2) Primary authority: Sometimes mandatory; sometimes persuasive
Sometimes primary authority is mandatory, or binding, authority, and sometimes it is not. You must be able to evaluate the authority to determine whether it is binding on the issue you are researching. One factor affecting whether a primary authority is mandatory is jurisdiction. The rules

contained in primary authority apply only to conduct occurring within the jurisdiction in which the authority is in force. For example, all laws in the United States must comport with the federal constitution because it is primary authority that is mandatory, or binding, in all United States jurisdictions. The New Jersey constitution is also primary authority because it contains legal rules establishing the scope of state government authority, but it is mandatory authority only in New Jersey. The New Jersey constitution's rules do not apply in Illinois or Michigan.

Determining the weight of court opinions is a little more complex. All court opinions are primary authority. Whether a particular opinion is mandatory or persuasive is a function not only of jurisdiction, but also level of court. To understand how these factors work together, it is easiest to consider level of court first and jurisdiction second.

(i) Determining the weight of court opinions: Level of court

The judicial branches of government in all states and in the federal system have multiple levels of courts. Trial courts are at the bottom of the judicial hierarchy. In the federal system, the United States District Courts are trial-level courts, and each state has at least one federal district court. Intermediate appellate courts hear appeals of trial court cases. Most, but not all, states have intermediate appellate courts. In the federal system, the intermediate appellate courts are called United States Courts of Appeals, and they are divided into thirteen separate circuits: eleven numbered circuits (First through Eleventh), the District of Columbia Circuit, and the Federal Circuit. The highest court or court of last resort is often called the supreme court. It hears appeals of cases from the intermediate appellate courts or directly from trial courts in states that do not have intermediate appellate courts. In the federal system, of course, the court of last resort is the United States Supreme Court.

Trial court opinions, including those from federal district courts, are not mandatory authority. These opinions bind the parties to the cases but do not bind other courts considering similar cases. They are persuasive authority.

The opinions of intermediate appellate courts bind the courts below them. In other words, intermediate appellate opinions are mandatory authority for the trial courts subordinate to them in the court structure. The weight of intermediate appellate opinions on the intermediate appellate courts themselves varies. In jurisdictions with multiple appellate divisions, the opinions of one division may or may not be binding on other divisions. In addition, in some circumstances, intermediate appellate courts have the ability to overrule their own prior opinions, but in others, they do not. Intermediate appellate opinions are persuasive authority for the court of last resort.

The court of last resort may, but is not required to, follow the opinions of the courts below it. The opinions of the court of last resort, however, are mandatory authority for both intermediate appellate courts and trial courts subordinate to it in the court structure. The court of last resort is not bound by its own prior opinions but will be reluctant to change an earlier ruling without a compelling justification.

Figure 1.2 illustrates the structures of federal and state court systems and shows how level of court affects the weight of opinions.

FIGURE 1.2   STRUCTURE OF THE FEDERAL COURT SYSTEM AND MOST STATE COURT SYSTEMS

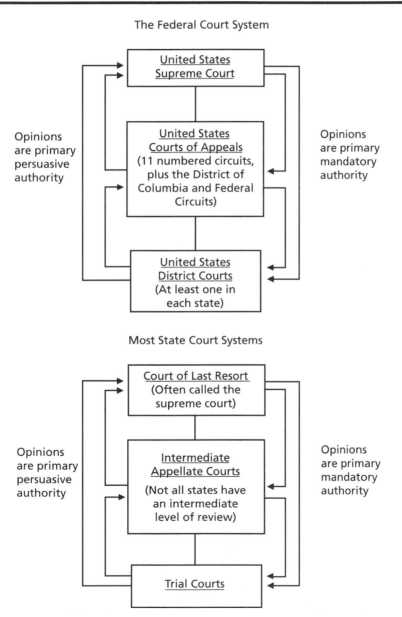

(ii) Determining the weight of court opinions: Jurisdiction

The second factor affecting the weight of court opinions is jurisdiction. As with other forms of primary authority, rules stated in court opinions are mandatory authority only within the court's jurisdiction. An opinion from the Texas Supreme Court is mandatory only for a court applying Texas law. A California court deciding a question of California law would consider the Texas opinion persuasive authority. If the California court had to decide a new issue not previously addressed by mandatory California authority (a "question of first impression"), it might choose to follow the Texas Supreme Court's opinion if it found the opinion persuasive.

On questions of federal law, opinions of the United States Supreme Court are mandatory authority for all other courts because it has nationwide jurisdiction. An opinion from a circuit court of appeals is mandatory only within the circuit that issued the opinion and is persuasive everywhere else. Thus, a decision of the United States Court of Appeals for the Eleventh Circuit would be binding within the Eleventh Circuit, but not within the Seventh Circuit. **Figure 1.3** shows the geographic boundaries of the federal circuit courts of appeal.

In considering the weight of a court opinion, it is important to remember that the federal government and each state constitute different jurisdictions. On questions of state law, each state's courts get the last word, and on questions of federal law, the federal courts get the last word. For an issue governed by state law, the opinions of the courts within the relevant state are mandatory authority. For an issue governed by federal law, the opinions of the relevant federal courts are mandatory authority.

Ordinarily, understanding how jurisdiction affects weight of authority is fairly intuitive. When a Massachusetts trial court is resolving a case arising out of conduct that took place in Massachusetts, it will treat the opinions of the Massachusetts Supreme Judicial Court as mandatory authority. Sometimes, however, a court has to resolve a case governed by the law of another jurisdiction. State courts sometimes decide cases governed by the law of another state or by federal law. Federal courts sometimes decide cases governed by state law. When that happens, the court deciding the case will treat the law of the controlling jurisdiction as mandatory authority.

For example, assume that the United States District Court for the Western District of Texas, a federal trial court, had to decide a case concerning breach of a contract to build a house in El Paso, Texas. Contract law is, for the most part, established by the states. To resolve this case, the federal court would apply the contract law of the state where the dispute arose, in this case, Texas. The Texas Supreme Court's opinions on contract law would be mandatory authority for resolving the case. Now assume that the same court had to decide a case concerning immigration

FIGURE 1.3   GEOGRAPHIC BOUNDARIES OF THE FEDERAL COURTS OF APPEALS

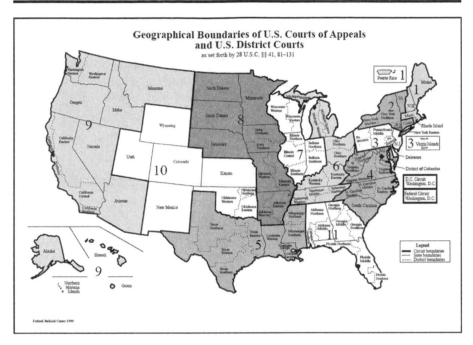

law. Immigration law is established by the federal government. To resolve the case, the court would apply federal law. The opinions of the United States Supreme Court and the United States Court of Appeals for the Fifth Circuit would be mandatory authority for resolving the case.

This discussion provides an overview of some common principles governing the weight of authority. These principles are subject to exceptions and nuances not addressed here. Entire fields of study are devoted to resolving questions of jurisdiction, procedure, and conflicts regarding which legal rules apply to various types of disputes. As you begin learning about research, however, these general principles will be sufficient to help you determine the weight of the authority you locate to resolve a research issue.

Figure 1.4 illustrates the relationships among the different types of authority.

B. INTRODUCTION TO THE PROCESS OF LEGAL RESEARCH

Legal research is not a linear process. Most research projects do not have an established series of steps that must be followed sequentially until the

FIGURE 1.4   TYPES OF AUTHORITY

TYPE OF AUTHORITY	MANDATORY (BINDING)	PERSUASIVE (NONBINDING)
PRIMARY (legal rules)	Constitutional provisions, statutes, and regulations in force within a jurisdiction are mandatory authority for courts within the same jurisdiction. Decisions from higher courts within a jurisdiction are mandatory authority for lower courts within the same jurisdiction.	Decisions from courts within one jurisdiction are persuasive authority for courts within another jurisdiction. Decisions from lower courts within a jurisdiction are persuasive authority for higher courts within the same jurisdiction.
SECONDARY (anything that is not primary authority; usually commentary on the law)	Secondary authority is *not* mandatory authority.	Secondary authority is persuasive authority.

answer to your question is uncovered. Although there are certain steps that you will ordinarily take with any research project, the starting, middle, and ending points will vary. When you know little or nothing about the issue you are researching, you will begin your research differently than if you were working on an issue about which you already had substantial background knowledge. One of the goals of this book is to help you learn to assess the appropriate starting, middle, and ending points for your research.

With most research projects, there are two preliminary steps that you will want to take before heading out on your search for authority: defining the scope of your project and generating search terms. In the first step, you will want to think about what you are being asked to do. Are you being asked to spend three weeks locating all information from every jurisdiction on a particular subject, or do you have a day to find out how courts in one state have ruled on an issue? Will you write an extensive analysis of your research, or will you summarize the results orally to the person who made the assignment? Evaluating the type of work product you are expected to produce, the amount of time you have, and the scope of the project will help you determine the best way to proceed. The second step is generating search terms to use to search for information in various research tools. Chapter 2 discusses different ways to do this. In general, however, you will need to construct a list of words or concepts to look up in an index, table of contents, or electronic database to locate information relevant to your issue.

Once you have accomplished these preliminary steps, you need to decide which research tool to use as the starting point for your research. You will also need to think about other probable sources of information and the sequence in which you plan to research those sources. The more you know about your research issue going in, the easier it will be to plan the steps. The less you know, the more flexible you will need to be in your approach. If you do not find any information, or find too much information, you may need to backtrack or rethink your approach.

To plan your research path, it may be useful for you to think about three categories of authority: secondary authority, primary mandatory authority, and primary persuasive authority. Your goal in most research projects will be to locate primary mandatory authority, if it exists, on your research issue. If primary mandatory authority is not available or does not directly answer your research question, persuasive authority (either primary or secondary) may help you analyze the issue. For any given research project, you will need to determine the order in which you will research these three types of authority.

Because your goal will usually be to locate primary mandatory authority, you might think that you should begin your research with those sources. In fact, sometimes you will begin by researching primary mandatory authority, but that is not always the case. Secondary authorities that cite, analyze, and explain the law can provide a very efficient way to obtain background information and references to primary authority. Although they are not controlling in your analysis, they are invaluable research tools and can be a good starting point for your project. Persuasive primary authority will rarely provide a good starting place because it provides neither the controlling rules nor analysis explaining the law. **Figure 1.5** shows the relationships among these three categories of authority.

Once you determine which category of authority to begin with, you need to decide which individual sources within the category to consult. In making this decision, it is important to bear in mind that many research sources are linked together. Once you find information in one source, research notes within that source may refer you to other relevant sources. Thus, there may be more than one source that would be an appropriate starting point for your research. The trick is to be able to determine for any given research project which source is most likely to lead you in the right direction the most quickly. This book will explain the features of a wide range of research sources so you can learn to make this assessment for different types of research projects.

FIGURE 1.5   WHERE TO BEGIN YOUR RESEARCH PROJECT

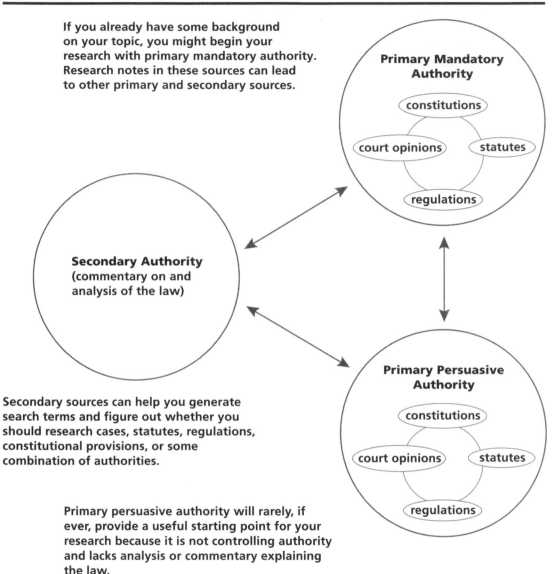

If you already have some background on your topic, you might begin your research with primary mandatory authority. Research notes in these sources can lead to other primary and secondary sources.

Secondary sources can help you generate search terms and figure out whether you should research cases, statutes, regulations, constitutional provisions, or some combination of authorities.

Primary persuasive authority will rarely, if ever, provide a useful starting point for your research because it is not controlling authority and lacks analysis or commentary explaining the law.

C. OVERVIEW OF PRINT AND ELECTRONIC SEARCH STRATEGIES

Most, if not all, of the primary and secondary authorities you will learn to research are available from a variety of sources. They may be published in one or more books. Most are now also available in electronic form. Electronic research services may include commercial databases that charge each user a fee for access; Internet and CD-ROM subscription services that libraries pay to access, but that are free to library patrons; and Internet sources available to anyone. As noted earlier, legal research often requires research into several different types of legal authority. Therefore, you will need to learn how to use a variety of tools to be able to research effectively.

The chapters that follow explain how to use both print and electronic research tools to locate various types of legal authority. Sometimes print sources will provide the easiest and most efficient means of accessing the information you need. In other circumstances, electronic sources may provide a better avenue for research. The tools you use will depend on a number of factors, including the resources available in your library, the amount of time you have for your project, the depth of research you need to do, and the amount of money your client can spend. Often, you will find that the best way to accomplish your research is to use some combination of print and electronic tools.

The finding tools available in a source, or stated differently, the ways you are able to search for information, will be one consideration that affects whether you use print or electronic research tools. Three common search methodologies are locating documents from their citations, searching for material within a source by subject, and, for electronic sources, word searching.

All legal authorities have citations assigned to them. The citation is the identifying information you can use to retrieve a document from a book or electronic database. Thus, if you have the citation to an authority, you can locate it using that identifying information. In print research, the citation generally includes the name of the book in which the source is published, the volume of the book containing the specific item, and the page or section number where the item begins. Although it would be possible for electronic sources to be organized differently, by and large, electronic sources are identified by the same citations used for print research. As a result, understanding how print resources are organized can be helpful to you even if you conduct the majority of your research electronically.

Print research tools are generally organized by type of authority and jurisdiction. Thus, court opinions from Maryland will be in one set of books (called "reporters"), and those from Massachusetts will be in another set of reporters. The same holds true for print collections of statutes and other types of legal authority. Within each set of books, individual authorities, such as a case or statutory provision, can be located by citation. For example, each court opinion is identified by a citation containing the volume number of the reporter in which it is published, the name of the reporter, and the starting page of the opinion. If you had the citation for a case, you could go to the library and locate it within a matter of minutes.

Of course, with most research projects, you will not know the citations to the authorities you need to find. You will have been assigned the project to find out which legal authorities, if any, pertain to the subject of your research issue. In those situations, you will often find that searching for information by subject is an effective strategy. In a print resource, the most commonly used subject searching tools are the index and table of contents, although some specialized subject searching tools are also available.

One challenge in researching with print sources is making sure the information is current. Most print research sources consist of hardcover books that can be difficult to update when the law changes. Some print resources are published in chronological order. For those resources, new books are published periodically as new material is compiled. Many, however, are organized by subject. For those resources, publishers cannot print new books every time the law changes. This would be prohibitively expensive, and because the law can change at any time, the new books would likely be out of date as soon as they were printed. To keep the books up to date, therefore, many print sources are updated with softcover pamphlets containing new information that became available after the hardcover book was published. These supplementary pamphlets are often called "pocket parts" because many of them fit into a "pocket" in the inside back cover of the hardcover book. You will see pocket parts mentioned throughout this text in reference to print research tools.

Electronic research tools are organized somewhat differently. Not all electronic resources are divided by jurisdiction and type of authority. Some provide access to only one type of authority from only one jurisdiction, while others provide access to multiple types of authority from many different jurisdictions. Most electronic resources provide the full text of the authorities in their databases. The two most commonly used full text services are Westlaw and LexisNexis. These are commercial databases that allow you to access all of the types of legal authority discussed in this chapter. They charge subscribers for use of their services, although your law school undoubtedly subsidizes the cost of student research while you are in school. Other commercial and government-operated research services also provide access to legal authority. LexisNexis, Westlaw, and other electronic research services are discussed throughout this text.

Like print resources, full text electronic services allow you to retrieve a document from its citation. If the service categorizes information by subject category, you can search by subject as well. Most fee-based or subscription services provide subject searching capabilities; free services may or may not. Electronic services may also permit you to browse the tables of contents of documents in a database, which provides another method of subject searching. Only a few electronic services reproduce the print indices of the sources in their databases, but index searching is occasionally an option. For example, electronic periodical indices are available for locating legal periodicals, a type of secondary source described in more detail in Chapter 3.

Word searching may be the form of electronic searching that is most familiar to you. You have probably conducted countless word searches in Internet search engines. Virtually all electronic search services offer word searching, either as a stand alone search option or in conjunction with subject searching functions. Word searching is a powerful research strategy because it allows you to specify the terms to search, unlike an index or table of contents search that requires you to figure out an author's or editor's method of categorizing concepts. It also allows you to search using unique criteria not incorporated into tables of contents or print indices. Word searching also has some limitations. One is that some concepts are expressed with many different terms and with varying degrees of abstraction, which can make it hard to locate the full range of relevant documents with word searches. Another is that sometimes very general terms, such as "right to privacy," make good subject headings but occur too frequently in individual documents to be useful as a word search. Although all concepts must ultimately be expressed in words, word searching alone will not always be the best research strategy; it is often most effective when combined with other search methodologies.

D. INTRODUCTION TO LEGAL CITATION

When you present the results of your research in written form, you will need to include citations to the legal authorities you have found. One place to find the rules for citing legal authority is *The Bluebook: A Uniform System of Citation* (18th ed. 2005). Another source for rules on citation is the *ALWD Citation Manual: A Professional System of Citation* (3d ed. 2006). The citation rules in these two sources overlap to a large degree, but they are not identical. You should use whichever citation manual your professor directs you to use.

This text provides information on citations in both *Bluebook* and *ALWD Manual* format. This section provides a brief overview of the organization of both citation manuals and will make the most sense if you have your citation manual in front of you as you read. Later chapters contain instructions for citing individual sources of legal authority. In many cases, the citation rules in the *Bluebook* and the *ALWD Manual* will be identical. Where there are differences, this text will alert you to that fact.

1. THE *BLUEBOOK*

The *Bluebook* is available in both print and electronic form. Both versions contain the same citation rules. The electronic version offers search options unavailable in the print version. Additionally, it allows you to bookmark commonly used rules and add your own annotations to the rules, tasks you would otherwise need to do manually with a print *Bluebook*. The electronic version also requires an annual subscription fee, whereas a print *Bluebook* requires only a single purchase. Most of the discussion in this section applies equally to the print and electronic versions of the *Bluebook*, but a few variations are noted.

The first part of the *Bluebook* that you should review is the Introduction. This section explains how the *Bluebook* is organized. As you will see when you review the Introduction, the *Bluebook* contains two sets of instructions for citing authority: "basic" citation rules used in legal practice and more complex rules used for citations in law journals. The "basic" citation rules apply to the types of documents most students write in their first year of law school, such as briefs and memoranda. The remainder of the citation rules apply primarily to law journals, a type of secondary source discussed in more detail in Chapter 3, although some aspects of these rules may also apply to practice documents. You are unlikely to write documents in law journal format at the beginning of your legal studies; therefore, you will want to focus your attention on the format for citations in briefs, memoranda, and other similar legal documents.

Learning to cite authority in *Bluebook* format requires you to become familiar with five items.

- the Bluepages and corresponding Bluepages Tables
- the text of the citation rules in the Rules section of the *Bluebook*
- the Tables
- the finding tools for locating individual citation rules (i.e., Table of Contents and Index; Quick Reference guides in print; search features in the electronic version)
- Blue Tips and *Bluebook* updates

THE BLUEPAGES AND CORRESPONDING BLUEPAGES TABLES. The Bluepages section summarizes the rules for citing legal authority in briefs, memoranda, and legal documents other than law journals. This section contains general information applicable to any type of citation, such as the uses of citations in legal writing. It also contains specific instructions for citing cases, statutes, secondary sources, and other forms of authority, as well as examples of many types of citations. The Bluepages Table BT.1 contains the abbreviations for words commonly found in the titles of court documents. In addition, because some jurisdictions have their own "local" citation rules that supplement or supersede the *Bluebook* rules, Table BT.2 refers you to sources for local citation rules. In print, the Bluepages appear at the beginning of the *Bluebook*. In the electronic version, use the Bluepages link to review the outline of the Bluepages rules.

THE TEXT OF THE CITATION RULES. Most of the *Bluebook* is devoted to explaining the rules for citing different types of authority. In print, the Rules section appears in the white pages in the middle of the *Bluebook*. In the electronic version, you can access the Rules section from the Rules link. These rules can be divided into five categories:

1. Rules 1 through 9 are general rules applicable to a citation to any type of authority. For example, Rule 5 discusses the proper format for quotations.
2. Rules 10 through 17 contain rules for citing various primary and secondary authorities published in print. For example, Rule 10 explains how to cite a court opinion, and Rule 12 explains how to cite a statute.
3. Rule 18 contains rules for citing authorities published in electronic format.
4. Rule 19 contains rules for citing authorities published in subject-matter services. Subject-matter services are explained in Chapter 9 of this text.
5. Rules 20 and 21 contain rules for citing foreign and international materials. This text does not discuss foreign or international materials.

Some of the material contained in the Rules section is summarized in the Bluepages. If the information you need for the authority you are citing is contained in the Bluepages, you may not need to consult the individual rules in the Rules section. If you face a citation question not addressed in the Bluepages, however, you should consult the individual rules for more detailed guidance. Most of the rules for citing specific types of legal authority begin with a description of the elements necessary for a full citation. The remainder of the rule will explain each component in greater detail.

Frequently, a rule will be accompanied by examples. Although this might seem like it would simplify things, in fact, sometimes it just complicates the citation. This is because the examples in the Rules section are in the typefaces (e.g., italics, large and small capital letters) required for law journals. These typefaces are not always used in other types of legal documents. Therefore, although the examples in the Rules section will be somewhat useful to you in understanding how to cite legal authority, you cannot rely on them exclusively. The instructions in Bluepages B13 explain the differences between typeface conventions for citations in law journal and other documents.

THE TABLES. In print, the Tables appear in the white pages with blue borders at the back of the *Bluebook*. In the electronic version, you can access them from the Tables link. The citation rules in the Bluepages and Rules sections of the *Bluebook* explain the general requirements for different types of citations. Often they require that certain words be abbreviated. The Tables contain abbreviations necessary for proper citations.[1] For example, Table T.1 lists each jurisdiction in the United States, and under each jurisdiction, it shows the proper abbreviations for citations to that jurisdiction's cases and statutes. Whenever you have a citation that includes an abbreviation, you will need to check the appropriate Table to find the precise abbreviation required for a proper citation. You should note, however, that the type styles of some of the abbreviations in the Tables are in law journal format and may need to be modified according to Bluepages B13 for the work you will produce in your first year of law school.

THE FINDING TOOLS FOR LOCATING INDIVIDUAL RULES. As noted above, the Bluepages should be your starting point for determining how to construct a citation in *Bluebook* format. If you cannot find what you need in the Bluepages, you can find individual citation rules in the Rules section using the Table of Contents or the Index. In the print version of the *Bluebook*, the Index references in black type refer to the pages with relevant rules. Those in blue type refer to examples of citations. The Index in the electronic version refers only to rule numbers, not page numbers.

In the print version, you can also refer to the Quick Reference examples of different types of citations on the inside front and back covers. The examples on the inside front cover are in the format for law review and journal footnotes and will be of little or no use to you in your first year of law school. The examples on the inside back cover are in the proper format for the types of documents you are likely to draft in your first year.

The electronic version does not contain the Quick Reference examples, but it offers additional search options. The search box at the top of the screen allows you to do a basic search for rules. The advanced search options allow you to tailor your search more specifically. As noted above, you can bookmark frequently used rules and add annotations to the rules. The search functions in the electronic version allow you to search your bookmarked rules and annotations in addition to the text of the rules themselves.

BLUE TIPS AND *BLUEBOOK* UPDATES. You will find citation tips and updates to the *Bluebook* on the *Bluebook* web site. This material is available without a subscription, so you will want to take advantage of these

---

[1]Citations in *ALWD Manual* format also require abbreviations. The *Bluebook* and the *ALWD Manual* use identical abbreviations for many words. Some abbreviations vary, however, depending on which format you use.

resources whether you use the *Bluebook* in print or electronic form. The web address for the *Bluebook*'s online resources appears in Appendix A at the end of this text.

All of the pieces of the *Bluebook* work together to help you determine the proper citation format for a legal authority:

1. Use the Bluepages to find citation instructions governing the authority you want to cite.
2. If the Bluepages do not contain all the information you need for the citation, use the Index, Table of Contents, Quick Reference guides (in print) or search functions (in the electronic version) to find the relevant rule in the Rules section.
3. Use the Tables to find abbreviations and other information necessary for a complete citation.
4. If necessary, convert the typefaces in the examples and Tables into the proper format for briefs and memoranda according to Bluepages B13.

As you read the remaining chapters in this book, you will find more specific information about citing individual legal authorities. In general, however, you will be able to figure out how to cite almost any type of authority in *Bluebook* format by following these five steps.

2. THE *ALWD MANUAL*

The first part of the *ALWD Manual* that you should review is Part 1, Introductory Material. This section explains what citations are and how to use them, how to use the *ALWD Manual*, how local citation rules can affect citation format, and how your word processor's settings may affect citations. It explains the *ALWD Manual*'s organization clearly, so it would be redundant to repeat all of that information here. Nevertheless, a few comments on the *ALWD Manual* may be useful as you begin learning about it.

Perhaps the biggest difference between the *ALWD Manual* and the *Bluebook* is that the *ALWD Manual* uses the same citation format for all documents. The *Bluebook*, by contrast, uses one format for citations in law journal footnotes and another for practice documents like briefs and memoranda. When you are using the *ALWD Manual*, you do not need to convert any of the citations into different formats for different documents.

As you will see when you review Part 1, learning to cite authority in *ALWD Manual* format requires you to become familiar with five items:

■ the Table of Contents and Index
■ the text of the citation rules
■ the Appendices

- the "Fast Formats"
- the *ALWD Manual* web site.

THE TABLE OF CONTENTS AND INDEX. To locate individual citation rules, you can use the Table of Contents at the beginning of the *ALWD Manual* or the Index at the end. Unless otherwise indicated, the references in the Index are to rule numbers, not page numbers or specific examples.

THE TEXT OF THE CITATION RULES. Most of the *ALWD Manual* is devoted to explaining the rules for citing different types of authority. The rules are divided into the following Parts:

1. Part 2 (with Rules 1 through 11) contains general rules applicable to a citation to any type of authority. For example, Rule 3 discusses spelling and capitalization.
2. Part 3 (with Rules 12 through 37) contains rules for citing various primary and secondary authorities published in print. For example, Rule 12 explains how to cite a court opinion, and Rule 14 explains how to cite a statute.
3. Part 4 (with Rules 38 through 42) contains rules for citing authorities published in electronic format.
4. Part 5 (with Rules 43 through 46) contains rules for incorporating citations into documents.
5. Part 6 (with Rules 47 through 49) contains rules regarding quotations.

At the beginning of each citation rule in Parts 3 and 4, you will find a description of the elements necessary for a full citation, followed by an annotated example showing how all of the elements fit together to create a complete citation. You should read this part of the rule first. The remainder of the rule will explain each component in greater detail.

Within the text of each rule in the *ALWD Manual*, you will find cross-references to other citation rules and to Appendices containing additional information that you may need for a complete citation. An explanation of the Appendices appears below.

You will also find "Sidebars" in some rules. The "Sidebars" are literally asides on citation. They provide information about sources of legal authority, help you avoid common citation errors, and offer citation tips.

THE APPENDICES. The *ALWD Manual* contains eight Appendices that follow the Parts containing the citation rules. The citation rules in Parts 3 and 4 explain the general requirements for citations to different types of authority. Most of these rules require that certain words be abbreviated. Appendices 1, 3, 4, and 5 contain abbreviations necessary for proper citations. For example, Appendix 1 lists Primary Sources by Jurisdiction.

It lists each jurisdiction in the United States, and under each jurisdiction, it shows the proper abbreviations for citations to that jurisdiction's cases and statutes. Whenever you have a citation that includes an abbreviation, you will need to check the appropriate Appendix to find the precise abbreviation required for a proper citation.[2]

Appendix 2 contains local court citation rules. Some courts require special citation formats for authorities cited in documents filed with those courts. The *ALWD Manual* includes these rules in Appendix 2, so you do not have to look them up in another source if you need to use them.

Appendix 6 contains an example of a memorandum with citations included. This example can help you see how citations are integrated into a document.

Appendix 7 contains information on citations to federal taxation materials, and Appendix 8 contains information on selected federal administrative publications.

THE FAST FORMATS. Before the text of each rule for citing an individual type of authority in Parts 3 and 4, you will find a section called "Fast Formats." The "Fast Formats" provide citation examples for each rule, in addition to the examples interwoven with the text of the rule. A "Fast Formats Locator" appears on the inside front cover of the *ALWD Manual*. You can use this alphabetical list to find "Fast Formats" pages without going to the Table of Contents or Index.

THE *ALWD MANUAL* WEB SITE. Updates to the *ALWD Manual* are posted on the Internet. The Internet address for the *ALWD Manual* web site is listed in Appendix A at the end of this text.

All of the pieces of the *ALWD Manual* work together to help you determine the proper citation format for a legal authority:

1. Use the Table of Contents or Index to find the rule governing the authority you want to cite.
2. Read the rule, beginning with the components of a full citation at the beginning of the rule.
3. Use the Appendices to find additional information necessary for a correct citation.
4. Use the "Fast Formats" preceding the rule for additional examples of citations.
5. If necessary, check the web site for any updates.

---

[2]Citations in *Bluebook* format also require abbreviations. The *ALWD Manual* and the *Bluebook* use identical abbreviations for many words. Some abbreviations differ, however, depending on which format you use.

As you read the remaining chapters in this book, you will find more specific information about citing individual legal authorities. In general, however, you will be able to figure out how to cite almost any type of authority in *ALWD Manual* format by following these five steps.

E. OVERVIEW OF THIS TEXT

Because different research projects have different starting and ending points, it is not necessary that you follow the chapters in this book in order. The sequence of assignments in your legal research class will determine the order in which you need to cover the material in this book.

Although you may not cover the chapters in order, a brief overview of the organization of this text may provide useful context for the material that follows. As noted earlier, Chapter 2 discusses how to generate search terms, one of the first steps in any research project. Secondary sources are covered next in Chapter 3. Chapters 4 through 8 explain how to research different types of primary authority, and Chapter 9 discusses how to use specialized research tools to locate both secondary and primary authority in specific subject areas of the law.

Chapters 3 through 9 are organized in a similar way. They all begin with an overview of the type of authority discussed. Then you will find an explanation of the print research process, followed by a description of electronic research sources. The material on print and electronic research will include excerpts from various research tools to highlight some of their key features. After the discussion of the research process, you will find information on citation format. The next item in each of these chapters is a section of sample pages. The sample pages contain step-by-step illustrations of the research process described earlier in the chapter. As you read through the text, you may find it helpful to review both the excerpts within the chapter and the sample pages section to get a sense of the research process for each type of authority. These chapters conclude with research checklists that summarize the research process and may be helpful as you conduct research.

Chapter 10 discusses general techniques for electronic research. The process of using print research sources varies according to the type of authority you are researching, which is why the preceding chapters largely focus on individual types of authority. With electronic research, however, there are certain common search techniques that can be used to research many types of authority. As a consequence, the discussion of electronic research in Chapters 3 through 9 focuses on where to locate legal authority using electronic resources, leaving most of the "how" of electronic research to Chapter 10. If you are learning about print and electronic research simultaneously, you should read Chapter 10 early in your studies. If you are learning about print research first, save

Chapter 10 until you begin instruction in electronic research. When you begin learning about electronic research, you may also want to review Appendix A at the end of the text, which lists a number of Internet research sites.

The final chapter, Chapter 11, discusses research strategy and explains how to create a research plan. You do not need to read all of the preceding chapters before reading Chapter 11, although you may find Chapter 11 easier to follow after you have some background on a few research sources. Learning about research involves more than simply learning how to locate individual types of authority. You must also be able to plan a research strategy that will lead to accurate research results, and you must be able to execute your research strategy efficiently and economically. Chapter 11 sets out a process that will help you achieve these goals in any research project, whether in your legal research class or in legal practice.

GENERATING SEARCH TERMS

A. Generating search terms based on categories of information

B. Expanding the initial search

All research sources, whether print or electronic, are indexed in some way. With print resources, you might use a subject index or a table of contents to locate information. With electronic resources, you might use an electronic subject index if one is available, a table of contents, or a word search to find documents containing particular terms. No matter where you begin your search for authority, one of the first steps in the research process is generating a list of words that are likely to lead you through each resource's indexing system. This chapter discusses how to generate a useful list of search terms.

A. GENERATING SEARCH TERMS BASED ON CATEGORIES OF INFORMATION

When presented with a set of facts, you could generate a list of search terms by constructing a random list of words that seem relevant to the issue. But a more structured approach—working from a set of categories, instead of random terms that sound relevant—will help ensure that you are covering all of your bases in conducting your research.

There are a number of ways that you could categorize the information in your research issue to create a list of search terms. Some people prefer to use the six questions journalists ask when covering a story: who, what, when, where, why, and how. Another way to generate search terms is to categorize the information presented by the facts as follows.

■ **THE *PARTIES* INVOLVED IN THE PROBLEM, DESCRIBED ACCORDING TO THEIR RELATIONSHIPS TO EACH OTHER.**
Here, you might be concerned not only with parties who are in direct conflict with each other, but also any other individuals, entities, or

groups involved. These might include fact witnesses who can testify as to what happened, expert witnesses if appropriate to the situation, other potential plaintiffs (in civil cases), or other potential defendants (in criminal or civil cases).

In describing the parties, proper names will not ordinarily be useful search terms, although if one party is a public entity or corporation, you might be able to locate other cases in which the entity or corporation was a party. Instead, you will usually want to describe the parties in terms of their legal status or relationships to each other, such as landlords and tenants, parents and children, employers and employees, or doctors and patients.

■ **THE *PLACES AND THINGS* INVOLVED IN THE PROBLEM.**
In thinking about place, both geographical locale and type of location can be important. For example, the conduct at issue might have taken place in Pennsylvania, which would help you determine which jurisdiction's law applies. It might also have taken place at a school or in a church, which could be important for determining which legal rules apply to the situation.

"Things" can involve tangible objects or intangible concepts. In a problem involving a car accident, tangible things could include automobiles or stop signs. In other types of situations, intangible "things," such as a vacation or someone's reputation, could be useful search terms.

■ **THE *POTENTIAL CLAIMS AND DEFENSES* THAT COULD BE RAISED.**
As you become more familiar with the law, you may be able to identify claims or defenses that a research problem potentially raises. The facts could indicate to you that the problem potentially involves particular claims (such as breach of contract, defamation, or bribery) or particular defenses (such as consent, assumption of the risk, or self-defense). When that is the case, you can often use claims and defenses effectively as search terms.

If you are dealing with an unfamiliar area of law, however, you might not know of any claims or defenses potentially at issue. In that situation, you can generate search terms by thinking about the conduct and mental states of the parties, as well as the injury suffered by the complaining party. Claims and defenses often flow from these considerations, and as a result, these types of terms can appear in a research tool's indexing system. When considering conduct, consider what was not done, as well as what was done. The failure to do an act might also give rise to a claim or defense.

For example, you could be asked to research a situation in which one person published an article falsely asserting that another person was guilty of tax evasion, knowing that the accusation was not true. You might recognize this as a potential claim for the tort of defamation, which occurs when one person publishes false information that is damaging to another person's reputation. Even if you were unfamiliar with this tort, however, you could still generate search terms relevant to the claim by considering the defendant's conduct (publication) or mental state (intentional actions), or the plaintiff's injury (to reputation). These search terms would likely lead you to authority on defamation.

■ **THE *RELIEF* SOUGHT BY THE COMPLAINING PARTY.**
Indexing systems often categorize information according to the relief a party is seeking. Damages, injunction, specific performance, restitution, attorneys' fees, and other terms relating to the relief sought can lead you to pertinent information.

As an example of how you might go about using these categories to generate search terms, assume you have been asked to research the following situation: Your client recently went to Illinois on vacation. While waiting to meet a friend in the lobby of the hotel where she was staying, she decided to use the ladies' room. The lobby restrooms were unlocked and accessible to the public. Upon entering the ladies' room, she was surprised by a man who tackled her to the ground and grabbed her purse. Just then, another woman entered the ladies' room. The man ran out the door, dropping the purse as he ran. He was never caught. Your client recovered her purse after the incident but suffered a broken wrist. She wants to know if the hotel is liable for her injury.

- PARTIES: hotel, guest, robber.
- PLACES AND THINGS: hotel, vacation, Illinois, purse, restroom.
- POTENTIAL CLAIMS AND DEFENSES: negligence, strict liability, assumption of the risk, contributory negligence. Additional terms could be generated according to conduct ("robbery" or "failure to protect"), mental state ("knowledge," regarding the hotel's awareness of criminal activity in the area), or injury ("broken wrist").
- RELIEF: damages, restitution for expenses, physical pain and suffering, mental or emotional distress.

This is not an exhaustive list of search terms for this problem, but it illustrates how you can use these categories of information to develop useful search terms.

B. EXPANDING THE INITIAL SEARCH

Once you have developed an initial set of search terms for your issue, the next task is to try to expand that list. The terms you originally generated may not appear in a print index or electronic database. Therefore, once you have developed your initial set of search terms, you should try to increase both the breadth and the depth of the list. You can increase the breadth of the list by identifying synonyms and terms related to the initial

FIGURE 2.1   EXPANDING THE BREADTH OF SEARCH TERMS

Increasing breadth with synonyms and related terms: motel ↔ hotel ↔ inn

FIGURE 2.2   INCREASING THE DEPTH OF SEARCH TERMS

Increasing depth with varying levels of abstraction: robbery
⇕
theft
⇕
crime

search terms, and you can increase the depth by expressing the concepts in your search terms both more abstractly and more concretely.

Increasing the breadth of your list with synonyms and related terms is essential to your research strategy. This is especially true for word searches in electronic research. In a print index, if you get close to the correct term, a cross-reference might refer you to an entry with relevant information. An electronic word search, however, searches only for the specific terms you identify. Therefore, to make sure you locate all of the pertinent information on your issue, you need to have a number of synonyms for the words and concepts in your search. In the research scenario described above, there are a number of synonyms and related terms for one of the initial search terms: hotel. As **Figure 2.1** illustrates, you might also search for terms such as motel or inn.

You are also more likely to find useful research material if you increase the depth of your list by varying the level of abstraction at which you express the terms you have included. For example, while the research scenario above involves a robbery, which is taking another's property by force or threat of force, you might find relevant information if you expressed the term more abstractly: theft or crime. See **Figure 2.2**. In the same vein, if you were researching a problem involving "transportation equipment," you would want to consider search terms that are more concrete: automobile, train, airplane, etc.

Once you have developed a list of search terms, you are ready to begin looking for authority in print or electronic legal research tools. The chapters that follow explain the indexing tools in a variety of legal research sources. Regardless of where you begin your research, you will be able to use the techniques described in this chapter to access information using the indexing tools in each resource you use.

SECONDARY SOURCE RESEARCH

A. Introduction to secondary sources

B. Researching secondary sources in print

C. Researching secondary sources electronically

D. Citing secondary sources

E. Sample pages for print secondary source research

F. Checklist for secondary source research

A. INTRODUCTION TO SECONDARY SOURCES

As you read in Chapter 1, primary authority refers to sources of legal rules, such as cases, statutes, and administrative regulations. Secondary sources, by contrast, provide commentary on the law. Although they are not binding on courts and are not cited as frequently as primary sources, secondary sources are excellent research tools. Because they often summarize or collect authorities from a variety of jurisdictions, they can help you find mandatory or persuasive primary authority on a subject. They also often provide narrative explanations of complex concepts that would be difficult for a beginning researcher to grasp thoroughly simply from reading primary sources. Equipped with a solid understanding of the background of an area of law, you will be better able to locate and evaluate primary authority on your research issue.

1. WHEN SECONDARY SOURCES WILL BE MOST USEFUL

Secondary sources will be most useful to you in the following situations:

(1) WHEN YOU ARE RESEARCHING AN AREA OF LAW WITH WHICH YOU ARE UNFAMILIAR. Secondary sources can give you the necessary background to generate search terms. They can also lead you directly to primary authorities.

(2) WHEN YOU ARE LOOKING FOR PRIMARY PERSUASIVE AUTHORITY BUT DO NOT KNOW HOW TO NARROW THE JURISDICTIONS THAT ARE LIKELY TO HAVE USEFUL INFORMATION. If you need to find primary persuasive authority on a subject, conducting a nationwide survey of the law on the topic is not likely to be an efficient research strategy. Secondary sources can help you locate persuasive authority relevant to your research issue.

(3) WHEN YOU ARE RESEARCHING AN UNDEVELOPED AREA OF THE LAW. When you are researching a question of first impression, commentators may have analyzed how courts should rule on the issue.

(4) WHEN AN INITIAL SEARCH OF PRIMARY SOURCES YIELDS EITHER NO AUTHORITY OR TOO MUCH AUTHORITY. If you are unable to find any authority at all on a topic, you may not be looking in the right places. Secondary sources can educate you on the subject in a way that may allow you to expand or refocus your research efforts. When your search yields an unmanageable amount of information, secondary sources can do two things. First, their citations to primary authority can help you identify the most important authorities pertaining to the research issue. Second, they can provide you with information that may help you narrow your search or weed out irrelevant sources.

2. LIMITS ON THE APPROPRIATE USE OF SECONDARY SOURCES

Knowing when *not* to use secondary sources is also important. As noted above, secondary sources are not binding on courts. Therefore, you will not ordinarily cite them in briefs or memoranda. This is especially true if you use secondary sources to lead you to primary authority. It is important never to rely exclusively on a discussion of a primary authority that appears in a secondary source. If you are discussing a primary authority in a legal analysis, you must read that authority yourself and update your research to make sure it is current.

This is true for two reasons. First, a summary of a primary authority might not include all of the information necessary to your analysis. It is important to read the primary authority for yourself to make sure you represent it correctly and thoroughly in your analysis.

Second, the information in the secondary source might not be completely current. Although most secondary sources are updated on a regular basis, the law can change at any time. The source may contain incomplete information simply because of the inevitable time lag between changes to the law and the publication of a supplement. One mistake some beginning researchers make is citing a secondary source for the text of a case or statute without checking to make sure that the case has not been overturned or that the statute has not been changed. Another potential error is citing a secondary source for a proposition about the state of the law generally, such as, "Forty-two states now recognize a cause of action for invasion of privacy based on disclosure of private facts." While statements of that nature were probably true when the secondary source was written, other states may have acted, or some of those noted may have changed their law, in the intervening time period. Accordingly, secondary sources should only be used as a starting point for locating primary authority, not an ending point.

3. METHODS OF LOCATING SECONDARY SOURCES

The first step in researching with secondary sources is deciding which type(s) of source(s) to use. There are many types of secondary sources, and you may need to use several of them to complete a research project. The features of the most commonly used legal secondary sources—legal encyclopedias, treatises, legal periodicals, *American Law Reports*, Restatements of the law, and uniform laws and model acts—are described in the next section. Once you know which types of secondary sources are likely to meet your research needs, you will need to locate relevant information within each source. Three common search techniques are searching by citation, by subject, and by words in the document. Some secondary sources are only published in print. Few of the ones published electronically are available on the Internet. Therefore, you will use these search techniques most often either in print or in a commercial database such as Westlaw or LexisNexis.

If you are just beginning your research, searching by subject is often a good strategy. Most secondary sources other than legal periodicals have subject indices (in print) and tables of contents (in print and online). To locate legal periodicals, you can use a separate periodical index that organizes periodical citations by subject. Word searching is another search option for locating secondary sources in a full-text database and may be an option in a periodical index as well. Many secondary sources cross reference other secondary sources. Therefore, once you have located one secondary source on your research issue, it may refer you to other secondary sources that you can locate by citation in print, or if they are available electronically, in an electronic database.

Sections B and C, below, explain how to research secondary sources in print and electronically. Not all law libraries maintain print collections of all of the secondary sources discussed in this chapter. Even if you will be accessing these sources primarily (or exclusively) electronically, you may want to read the section on print research for two reasons. First, the description of the print research process includes general information about the coverage and content of each source that will be useful to you whether you conduct print or electronic research. Second, the citation rules for these sources flow from their print formats and may make more sense to you if you understand how secondary sources are organized in print.

B. RESEARCHING SECONDARY SOURCES IN PRINT

This section discusses the following commonly used secondary sources: legal encyclopedias, treatises, legal periodicals, *American Law Reports*,

Restatements of the law, and uniform laws and model acts. It first sets out the typical print research process and then provides specifics for researching the individual types of secondary sources.

The print research process generally involves three steps: (1) using an index or table of contents to find references to material on the topic you are researching; (2) locating the material in the main text of the source; and (3) updating your research.

The first step is using an index or table of contents to find out where information on a topic is located within the secondary source. As with the index or table of contents in any other book, those in a secondary source will refer you to volumes, chapters, pages, or sections where you will find text explaining the topic you are researching. Some secondary sources consist only of a single volume. In those situations, you need simply to look up the table of contents or index references within the text. Often, however, the information in a secondary source is too comprehensive to fit within a single volume. In those cases, the source will consist of a multivolume set of books, which may be organized alphabetically by topic or numerically by volume number. The references in the index or table of contents will contain sufficient information for you to identify the appropriate book within the set, as well as the page or section number specifically relating to the topic you are researching. Locating material in the main text of the source is the second step in the process.

The final step in your research is updating the information you have located. Most secondary sources are updated with pocket parts, as described in Chapter 1. The pocket part will be organized the same way as the main volume of the source. Thus, to update your research, you need to look up the same provisions in the pocket part that you read in the main text to find any additional information on the topic. If you do not find any reference to your topic in the pocket part, there is no new information to supplement the main text.

As you will see below, there are some variations on this technique that apply to some secondary sources. For the most part, however, you will be able to use this three-step process to research a variety of secondary sources.

1. LEGAL ENCYCLOPEDIAS

Legal encyclopedias are just like the general subject encyclopedias you have used in the past, except they are limited in scope to legal subjects. Legal encyclopedias provide a general overview of the law on a variety of topics. They do not provide analysis or suggest solutions to conflicts in the law. Instead, they simply report on the general state of the law. Because encyclopedias cover the law in such a general way, you will usually use them to get background information on your research topic and, to a lesser extent, to locate citations to primary authority. You will rarely, if ever, cite a legal encyclopedia.

There are two general legal encyclopedias, *American Jurisprudence*, Second Edition (Am. Jur. 2d) and *Corpus Juris Secundum* (C.J.S.). Each is a multivolume set organized alphabetically by topic. These sources can be researched using the three-step process described above. The indices for these encyclopedias are contained in separate softcover volumes that are usually shelved at the end of the set. The index volumes are published annually, so be sure to use the most current set. You can also find information by scanning the table of contents at the beginning of each topic. Am. Jur. 2d and C.J.S. cover material in such a general way that they are useful primarily for background information. Many of the citations to primary authority are relatively old and, as a consequence, may not provide you with much useful information.

In addition to Am. Jur. 2d and C.J.S., your library may also have encyclopedias for individual states. For example, state encyclopedias are published for California, Maryland, New York, and Ohio, among other states. State encyclopedias can be researched using the same process you would use with Am. Jur. 2d or C.J.S. When you are researching a question of state law, state encyclopedias are often more helpful than the general encyclopedias for two reasons. First, the summary of the law will be tailored to the rules and court decisions within that state, and therefore is likely to be more helpful. Second, the citations to primary authority will usually be more up to date and will, of course, be from the controlling jurisdiction. Consequently, state encyclopedias can be more useful for leading you to primary sources.

The examples in **Figures 3.1** through **3.3** are taken from Am. Jur. 2d.

2. TREATISES

Treatises have a narrower focus than legal encyclopedias. Where legal encyclopedias provide a general overview of a broad range of topics, treatises generally provide in-depth treatment of a single subject, such as torts or constitutional law. A treatise may consist of a single volume.[1] Many, however, consist of multiple volumes. Most treatises provide both an overview of the topic and some analysis or commentary. They also usually contain citations to many primary and secondary authorities. If a treatise is widely respected and considered a definitive source in an area of law, you might cite the treatise in a brief or memorandum. Ordinarily, however, you will use treatises for research purposes and will not cite them in your written analysis.

Using a treatise once you have located it ordinarily is not difficult. With most treatises, you can use the three-step process described at the beginning of this section. The more difficult aspect of using treatises is finding one on your research topic. The online catalog in your library is the first place to

---

[1]One type of single-volume source with which you may already be familiar is a "hornbook." A hornbook provides a clear and straightforward statement of the law on a topic. Because a hornbook is a single volume, however, it usually is not an exhaustive source of information.

FIGURE 3.1   INDEX TO AM. JUR. 2d

Cross-reference

AMERICAN JURISPRUDENCE 2d

FALLS
Admiralty jurisdiction, falling from land into water, **Admiralty § 78**
Attractive Nuisances (this index)
Automobiles and Highway Traffic (this index)
Aviation, falling from plane, **FedTort § 63**
Boats and boating, falling overboard, **Boats § 55**
Carriers (this index)
Federal Tort Claims Act (this index)
Highways, Streets, and Bridges (this index)
Laundries, dyers, and dry cleaners, self-service laundries, **Laundries § 23**
Premises Liability (this index)
Ships and Shipping (this index)
Sidewalks (this index)
Slippery Conditions (this index)
Water, falls into
      generally, **Admiralty § 78**
      boats and boating, **Boats § 55**
Workers' compensation, **Workers § 358**

FALSE AND FALSITY
Advertising (this index)
Annulment of Marriage (this index)
Aviation, **Aviation § 211, 215, 221**
Bomb threats, prosecution for, admissibility to establish identity or modus operandi, **Evidence § 453**
Conflict of laws, **ConflictLw § 85, 135**
Contempt (this index)
Credibility of Witnesses (this index)
Credit Reporting Agencies (this index)
Estoppel and Waiver (this index)
Fair Housing Act (this index)
Fictitious Matters (this index)
Honesty or Dishonesty (this index)
Housing discrimination. **Fair Housing Act** (this index)
Impersonation (this index)
Injunctions (this index)
...
...-16
Records and recording, **Records § 11-16**
Secured Transactions (this index)
Wrongful Discharge (this index)

FALSE CLAIMS ACT
False Pretenses (this index)

FALSE ENTRIES
Criminal liability of bank officers and directors, **Banks § 444-446**

FALSE IMPERSONATION
Impersonation (this index)

FALSE IMPRISONMENT
Generally, **FalseImp § 1-163**
Abduction and kidnapping, **Abduction § 2**

Index entry for
False imprisonment

Reference to
multiple sections

FALSE IMPRISONMENT—Cont'd
Abuse of process, **Abuse § 4**
Acquittal or discharge, subsequent, **FalseImp § 23**
Actual malice, punitive damages, **FalseImp § 147**
Advice of counsel, acting on, **FalseImp § 61**
Affidavits
      generally, **Arrest § 20**
      acting without sufficient affidavit or complaint, **FalseImp § 93**
Agency. Vicarious liability, *below*
Answers, **FalseImp § 117**
Apportionment of damages, **FalseImp § 136**
Apprehension, necessity of, **FalseImp § 17**
Arraignment, damages, **FalseImp § 138**
Arrests
      false arrest, *below*
      legal process, *below*
Assisting officer on request, private persons, **FalseImp § 42**
Attorneys
      civil litigation, liability of attorneys or parties in, **FalseImp § 46**
      justification, acting on advice of counsel, **FalseImp § 61**
Attorney's fees, **FalseImp § 145**
Awareness of confinement, **FalseImp § 12**
Bail, denial of opportunity to post, **FalseImp § 31**
Carriers (this index)
Character or reputation, evidence as to, **FalseImp § 126**
Children, confinement of, **FalseImp § 161**
Circumstantial evidence, **FalseImp § 126**
Clerks of court, immunity, **FalseImp § 99**
Commitment of mentally ill persons
      generally, **FalseImp § 33**
      immunity of judicial officers, **FalseImp § 96**
      improper commitment, **FalseImp § 34**
      persons initiating commitment proceedings, **FalseImp § 44**
      warrant of commitment, **FalseImp § 79**
Common law, shoplifters, **FalseImp § 64, 65**
Complainant
      legal process, protection of complainant, **FalseImp § 77**
      liability of complainant, **FalseImp § 43**
Conditional restraint, **FalseImp § 14**
Conduct of officer in seeking warrant, **FalseImp § 82**
Confinement. Detention or restraint, *below*
Conflict of laws, **ConflictLw § 138**
Consent
      defense of consent, **FalseImp § 53**
      ratification. Vicarious liability, *below*
Contempt proceedings, immunity of judicial officers, **FalseImp § 95**
Continuing offense, **FalseImp § 157**
Contributory negligence, defense of, **FalseImp § 54**

FALSE IMPRISONMENT—Cont'd
Conviction of plaintiff, evidence as to
      generally, **FalseImp § 125**
      weight and sufficiency of evidence, **FalseImp § 127**
Court of Federal Claims (this index)
Criminal liability
      generally, **FalseImp § 154-163**
      acceptance of criminal disposition, **FalseImp § 57**
      children, confinement of, **FalseImp § 161**
      continuing offense, **FalseImp § 157**
      defenses, **FalseImp § 160**
      degree of offense, **FalseImp § 159**
      elements of offense, **FalseImp § 155**
      evidence, **FalseImp § 162**
      guilty plea, *below*
      nature of restraint, **FalseImp § 156**
      other offenses, relation to, **FalseImp § 158**
      penalties, **FalseImp § 163**
      relation to other offenses, **FalseImp § 158**
      sentence and punishment, **FalseImp § 163**
      sufficiency of evidence, **FalseImp § 162**
Damages
      generally, **FalseImp § 135-153**
      amount of compensatory damages, **FalseImp § 142-145**
      apportionment of damages, **FalseImp § 136**
      arraignment, **FalseImp § 138**
      attorney's fees, **FalseImp § 145**
      emotional distress, **FalseImp § 143**
      evidence
            enha...
            mitig...
            excessi...
      foreseeable consequences, **FalseImp § 137**
      future damages, **FalseImp § 144**
      inadequate damages, **FalseImp § 140**
      legal process, **FalseImp § 138**
      mental suffering, **FalseImp § 143**
      natural consequences, **FalseImp § 137**
      nominal damages, **FalseImp § 139**
      pleadings, **FalseImp § 116**
      punitive damages, *below*
      remittitur, **FalseImp § 141**
Defamation, **FalseImp § 5**
Defective on its face, process, **FalseImp § 81**
Defenses
      generally, **FalseImp § 52-107**
      consent, **FalseImp § 53**
      contributory negligence, **FalseImp § 54**
      criminal liability, **FalseImp § 160**
      immunity, *below*
      justification, *below*

Reference to an
individual section

...stance using this Index, call 1-800-328-4880

404

Reprinted with permission from Thomson Reuters/West, *American Jurisprudence*, 2d Ed., General Index (2008 edition), p. 404 © 2007 Thomson Reuters/West.

FIGURE 3.2   AM. JUR. 2d MAIN VOLUME ENTRY UNDER FALSE IMPRISONMENT

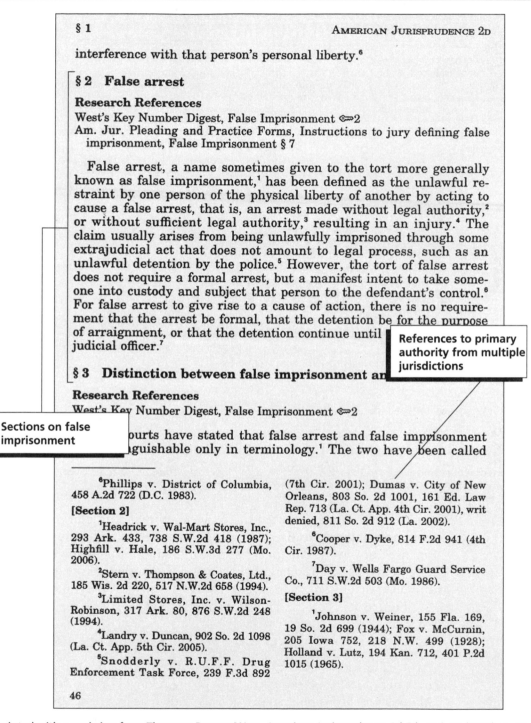

§ 1

AMERICAN JURISPRUDENCE 2D

interference with that person's personal liberty.[6]

§ 2   **False arrest**

Research References

West's Key Number Digest, False Imprisonment ⊕2
Am. Jur. Pleading and Practice Forms, Instructions to jury defining false imprisonment, False Imprisonment § 7

False arrest, a name sometimes given to the tort more generally known as false imprisonment,[1] has been defined as the unlawful restraint by one person of the physical liberty of another by acting to cause a false arrest, that is, an arrest made without legal authority,[2] or without sufficient legal authority,[3] resulting in an injury.[4] The claim usually arises from being unlawfully imprisoned through some extrajudicial act that does not amount to legal process, such as an unlawful detention by the police.[5] However, the tort of false arrest does not require a formal arrest, but a manifest intent to take someone into custody and subject that person to the defendant's control.[6] For false arrest to give rise to a cause of action, there is no requirement that the arrest be formal, that the detention be for the purpose of arraignment, or that the detention continue until judicial officer.[7]

§ 3   **Distinction between false imprisonment an**

Research References

West's Key Number Digest, False Imprisonment ⊕2

ourts have stated that false arrest and false imprisonment guishable only in terminology.[1] The two have been called

[Boxed annotation: References to primary authority from multiple jurisdictions]

[Boxed annotation: Sections on false imprisonment]

[6]Phillips v. District of Columbia, 458 A.2d 722 (D.C. 1983).

[Section 2]

[1]Headrick v. Wal-Mart Stores, Inc., 293 Ark. 433, 738 S.W.2d 418 (1987); Highfill v. Hale, 186 S.W.3d 277 (Mo. 2006).

[2]Stern v. Thompson & Coates, Ltd., 185 Wis. 2d 220, 517 N.W.2d 658 (1994).

[3]Limited Stores, Inc. v. Wilson-Robinson, 317 Ark. 80, 876 S.W.2d 248 (1994).

[4]Landry v. Duncan, 902 So. 2d 1098 (La. Ct. App. 5th Cir. 2005).

[5]Snodderly v. R.U.F.F. Drug Enforcement Task Force, 239 F.3d 892

(7th Cir. 2001); Dumas v. City of New Orleans, 803 So. 2d 1001, 161 Ed. Law Rep. 713 (La. Ct. App. 4th Cir. 2001), writ denied, 811 So. 2d 912 (La. 2002).

[6]Cooper v. Dyke, 814 F.2d 941 (4th Cir. 1987).

[7]Day v. Wells Fargo Guard Service Co., 711 S.W.2d 503 (Mo. 1986).

[Section 3]

[1]Johnson v. Weiner, 155 Fla. 169, 19 So. 2d 699 (1944); Fox v. McCurnin, 205 Iowa 752, 218 N.W. 499 (1928); Holland v. Lutz, 194 Kan. 712, 401 P.2d 1015 (1965).

46

FIGURE 3.3   AM. JUR. 2d POCKET PART ENTRY FOR FALSE IMPRISONMENT

FALSE IMPRISONMENT

®: Cases and other legal materials listed in KeyCite Scope can be ~~hed~~ through the KeyCite service on Westlaw®. Use KeyCite to check ~~s~~ for form, parallel references, prior and later history, and comprehensive ~~information~~, including citations to other decisions and secondary materials.

> No new research references are listed for § 2.

I. CIVIL ACTIONS

D. DEFENSES

2. *Justification*

b. Detention of Suspected Shoplifters

(2) Under Statute

§ 70 Reasonable manner and time of detention

Cases

Department store's detention of customer, on suspicion of theft of merchandise, did not constitute malicious prosecution or false imprisonment, absent evidence that the manner and length of customer's detention by the store was unreasonable under statute governing the defense of lawful detention. Conteh v. Sears, Roebuck and Co., 38 A.D.3d 314, 831 N.Y.S.2d 408 (1st Dep't 2007).

c. Arrest Without Warrant

§ 74 Probable cause justifying arrest

Cases

Police officers had probable cause to arrest

bank robbery suspect, and, since arrestee's detention was lawful, arrestee had no cause of action against officers for false imprisonment under Massachusetts law. Godette v. Stanley, 490 F. Supp. 2d 72 (D. Mass. 2007).

E. PROCEDURE

6. *Judgment*

§ 134 Summary judgment

Cases

Material issues of fact, as to whether elementary school principal, assistant principal and teacher were acting in good faith in attempting to have another teacher arrested for allegedly jabbing accusing teacher with pencil, precluded summary judgment that they were not state actors, capable of participating in false arrest in violation of Fourth Amendment. Weintraub v. Board of Educ. of City of New York, 423 F. Supp. 2d 38, 208 Ed. Law Rep. 435 (E.D. N.Y. 2006), on reconsideration in part, 2007 WL 1549138 (E.D. N.Y. 2007).

Reprinted with permission from Thomson Reuters/West, *American Jurisprudence*, 2d Ed., Vol. 32 Cumulative Supplement (2008), p. 1. © 2008 Thomson Reuters/West.

look. Treatises will be listed there by call number with all other library holdings. Because treatises do not usually have titles identifying them as treatises, however, sometimes it can be difficult figuring out which listings refer to treatises. The reference librarians in your library are a great asset in this area; they should be able to recommend treatises on your subject.

Figure 3.4 is an example from a treatise on torts.

3. LEGAL PERIODICALS

Articles in legal periodicals can be very useful research tools. You may hear periodical articles referred to as "law review" or "journal" articles. Many law schools publish periodicals known as law reviews or journals that collect articles on a wide range of topics. Many other types of legal periodicals also exist, however, including commercially published journals, legal newspapers, and magazines.

Articles published in law reviews or journals are thorough, thoughtful treatments of legal issues by law professors, practitioners, judges, and even

FIGURE 3.4   TREATISE MAIN VOLUME ENTRY FOR FALSE IMPRISONMENT

TOPIC E.   FALSE IMPRISONMENT

§ 36.   Simple False Imprisonment

Textual explanation of false imprisonment

Elements of the tort. Courts protect personal freedom of movement by imposing liability for false imprisonment. False imprisonment in its simple form[1] is established by proof that the defendant intentionally confined[2] or instigated[3] the confinement of the plaintiff. Confinement implies that the plaintiff is constrained against her will.[4] A third element, according to the Restatement and some authority, is that the plaintiff must have been aware of the confinement at the time.[5]

"False arrest." False arrest is a term that describes the setting for false imprisonment when it is committed by an officer or by one who claims the power to make an arrest. Although false arrest is not essentially different from false imprisonment,[6] detention by an officer or one acting under color of law may also amount to a civil rights violation.[7]

Burden of proof. When intent, confinement, and awareness are established, the plaintiff is entitled to recover unless the defendant can establish an affirmative defense. Many false imprisonment cases actually

ing reasonable fear by the plaintiff for herself or an immediate family member. In [...] must either make a [...] a restraining or- [...]

Reference to another secondary source

§ 36

1. As to false imprisonment secondary to some other tort, see § 40.

2. Restatement § 35. Confinement, detention, restraint are all terms used; they appear to refer to the same underlying idea.

3. Deadman v. Valley Nat. Bank of Arizona, 154 Ariz. 452, 743 P.2d 961 (Ct. App. 1987); Desai v. SSM Health Care, 865 S.W.2d 833 (Mo.App.1993); Restatement § 45A. This rule explains why a physician who testifies that he examined the plaintiff and found her mentally ill when in fact he never examined her at all may be held for the plaintiff's false imprisonment when she is later confined as a mentally ill person. See Crouch v. Cameron, 414 S.W.2d 408, 30 A.L.R.3d 520 (Ky. 1967). The rule is presumably the basis for imposing liability upon one who makes a false report of crime to police in the expectation that police will arrest the plaintiff. Washington v. Farlice, 1 Cal.App.4th 766, 2 Cal.Rptr.2d 607 (1991) (defendant reported her car stolen, knowing it was rightfully in possession of plaintiff's family; plaintiff was subjected to a humiliating arrest for which defendant was liable). When the defendant instigates an inappropriate *warrant* for prosecution, however, the action must be for malicious prosecu-

tion. See Montgomery Ward v. Wilson, 339 Md. 701, 664 A.2d 916 (1995) . Nor does a mere report of facts to [...] instigation of the arre[...] Watson Company, 1[...] S.E.2d 630 (1991).

References to primary authority from multiple jurisdictions

4. A plaintiff who [...] apparent confinement is not confined if she can leave at any time. See Pounders v. Trinity Court Nursing Home, 265 Ark. 1, 576 S.W.2d 934, 4 A.L.R.4th 442 (1979). In other cases the plaintiff consents in advance to a confinement from which she cannot escape, in which case the confinement is real but the consent is a defense until it is properly revoked. See Day v. Providence Hospital, 622 So.2d 1273 (Ala.1993) (consent to stay overnight in locked psychiatric ward).

5. Douthit v. Jones, 619 F.2d 527 (5th Cir.1980); Parvi v. City of Kingston, 41 N.Y.2d 553, 362 N.E.2d 960, 394 N.Y.S.2d 161 (1977); Restatement §§ 35, 42; but cf. Scofield v. Critical Air Medicine, Inc., 45 Cal.App.4th 990, 52 Cal.Rptr.2d 915 (1996) (seemingly, liability without actual knowledge or actual harm). Consciousness of confinement is required only for the purely dignitary tort; the plaintiff can recover for actual harm without consciousness of confinement.

6. See, e.g., Asgari v. City of Los Angeles, 15 Cal.4th 744, 937 P.2d 273, 63 Cal. Rptr.2d 842 (1997).

7. §§ 44–48.

students. The articles are usually focused fairly narrowly on specific issues, although they often include background or introductory sections that provide a general overview of the topic. They are generally well researched and contain citations to many primary and secondary authorities. In addition, they often address undeveloped areas in the law and propose solutions for resolving problems in the law. As a result, periodical articles can be useful for obtaining an overview of an area of law, finding references to primary and secondary authority, and developing ideas for analyzing a question of first impression or resolving a conflict in the law.

Although law review and journal articles will be useful to you for research, you would not ordinarily cite one if you can support your analysis with primary authority. If you cannot find primary support, however, you might cite a persuasive article. An article's persuasive value depends on a number of factors, including the author's expertise, the reputation of the journal in which it is published, the article's age, and the depth of the article's research and analysis. For example, an article written by a recognized expert in a field would be more persuasive than a note or comment on the same topic written by a student.

Researching legal periodicals is somewhat different from researching the other secondary sources discussed in this chapter. Thousands of articles in hundreds of periodicals are published each year. Because each periodical is an independent publication, trying to find articles through the indices or tables of contents within individual publications would be impossible. Instead, you need to use an indexing service that collects references to a wide range of legal periodicals. Two print indices, the *Index to Legal Periodicals and Books* and the *Current Law Index*, will lead you to periodical articles, but they are cumbersome to use. Electronic indexing services are a better research option. The electronic version of the *Index to Legal Periodicals* (ILP) and LegalTrac, another popular indexing service, are available in through most law libraries.

ILP is available as an indexing-only service, but many law libraries subscribe to ILP in a format that provides full text of some articles. ILP is divided into two separate databases: *Index to Legal Periodicals Retrospective*, which indexes articles from 1908 to 1980, and *Index to Legal Periodicals Full-Text*, which covers articles from 1980 to the present and includes the full text of selected articles. LegalTrac indexes articles from 1980 to present and also provides access to the full text of some articles. Both services allow you to search for legal periodicals in a variety of ways, including by author, subject, or keyword. When you execute the search, you will retrieve a list of citations to articles that fit the specifications of your search. If the document is available in full text, you can access it from the appropriate link. If the search results include articles that are not available electronically, you can print a list of citations and locate the articles in print.

Figures 3.5 and **3.6** show portions of the results of subject searches for false imprisonment in ILP and LegalTrac, respectively.

FIGURE 3.5 ILP CITATION LIST

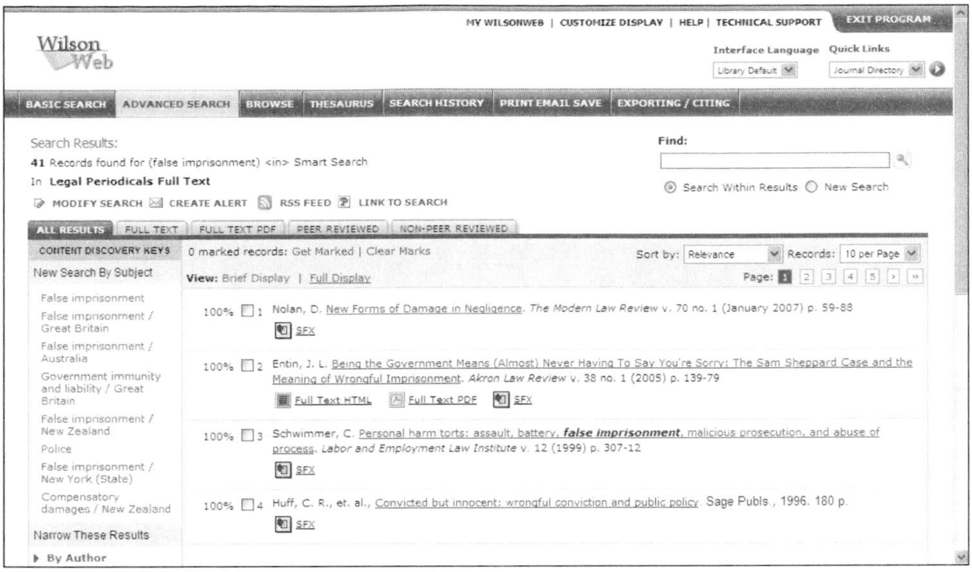

From The H.W. Wilson Co., WilsonWeb, *Index to Legal Periodicals.* © 2002-2008 The H.W. Wilson Co.

FIGURE 3.6   LEGALTRAC CITATION LIST

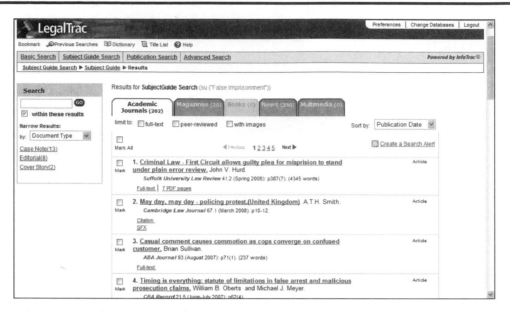

From Gale. *Screenshot from LegalTrac.* © Gale, a part of Cengage Learning, Inc. Reproduced by permission. www.cengage.com/permissions

The citations in ILP and LegalTrac will typically appear as follows: ***Publication Name*** volume (date) starting page.

Thus, a reference to *Valparaiso University Law Review* v.25 (Spring 1991) p. 407 tells you to locate the *Valparaiso University Law Review*, locate volume 25, and turn to page 407. You can locate the periodical on the shelves by checking the online catalog for the call number of the publication.

With most legal research tools, the next step in the process would be to update your research. Periodical articles are one exception to this rule. There is no way to update an individual periodical article, short of locating later articles that add to or criticize an earlier article. As a consequence, it is important to note the date of any periodical article you use. If the article is more than a few years old, you may want to supplement your research with more current material. In addition, as noted earlier, if you use the article to lead you to primary authority, you will need to update your research using the updating tools available for those primary sources to make sure your research is completely current.

4. AMERICAN LAW REPORTS

American Law Reports, or A.L.R., contains articles called "Annotations." Annotations collect summaries of cases from a variety of jurisdictions to provide an overview of the law on a topic. A.L.R. combines the breadth of topic coverage found in an encyclopedia with the depth of discussion in a treatise or legal periodical. Nevertheless, A.L.R. is different from these other secondary sources in significant ways. Because A.L.R. Annotations provide summaries of individual cases, they are more detailed than encyclopedias. Unlike treatises or legal periodicals, however, they mostly report the results of the cases without much analysis or commentary. A.L.R. Annotations are especially helpful at the beginning of your research to give you an overview of a topic. Because Annotations collect summaries of cases from many jurisdictions, they can also be helpful in directing you toward mandatory or persuasive primary authority. More recent Annotations also contain references to other research sources, such as other secondary sources and tools for conducting additional case research. Although A.L.R. is a useful research tool, you will rarely, if ever, cite an A.L.R. Annotation.

There are eight series of A.L.R.: A.L.R., A.L.R.2d, A.L.R.3d, A.L.R.4th, A.L.R.5th, A.L.R.6th, A.L.R. Fed., and A.L.R. Fed. 2d. Each series contains multiple volumes organized by volume number. A.L.R. Fed. and Fed. 2d cover issues of federal law. The remaining series usually cover issues of state law, although they do bring in federal law as appropriate to the topic. A.L.R. and A.L.R.2d are, for the most part, out of date and will not be useful to you. They are also updated using special tools not applicable to any of the other A.L.R. series. Generally, you will find A.L.R.3d, 4th, 5th, 6th, Fed., and Fed. 2d to be the most useful.

A.L.R. Annotations can be researched using the three-step process described earlier in this chapter. Annotations can be located using the A.L.R. Index.[2] The A.L.R. Index is a separate set of index volumes usually shelved near the A.L.R. sets. It contains references to Annotations in A.L.R.2d, 3d, 4th, 5th, 6th, Fed., and Fed. 2d. The A.L.R. Index and the individual volumes in A.L.R.3d, 4th, 5th, 6th, Fed. and Fed. 2d are updated with pocket parts.

Figures 3.7 and **3.8** illustrate some of the features of an A.L.R. Annotation.

5. RESTATEMENTS

The American Law Institute publishes what are called Restatements of the law in a variety of fields. You may already be familiar with the Restatements for contracts or torts from your other classes. Restatements essentially "restate" the common-law rules on a subject. Restatements have been published in the following fields:

- Agency
- Conflicts of Laws

---

[2]A.L.R. also publishes "digests," which are separate finding tools from the A.L.R. Index. You do not need to use the A.L.R. digests to locate Annotations. Annotations can be located directly from the A.L.R. Index.

FIGURE 3.7   STARTING PAGE OF AN A.L.R. ANNOTATION

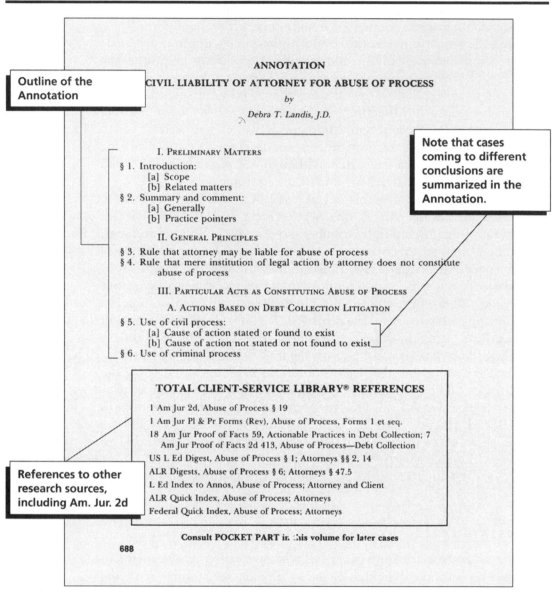

Reprinted with permission from Thomson Reuters/West, *American Law Reports*, 3d Ser., Vol. 97 (1980), p. 688.
© 1980 Thomson Reuters/West.

FIGURE 3.8 LATER PAGE OF AN A.L.R. ANNOTATION

97 ALR3d   Liability of Attorney for Abuse of Process   § 3
97 ALR3d 688

and another statute governed "injuries to the rights of others," the court held that an action for abuse of process was controlled by the latter statute.[16]

II. General principles

§ 3. Rule that attorney may be liable [for] abuse of process

[The fo]llowing cases support the [rule that] an attorney may be held [liable in] a civil action for abuse of [process w]here the acts complained of [are his o]wn personal acts, or the acts of others instigated and carried on by him.

US—For federal cases involving state law, see state headings infra.

Ga—Walker v Kyser (1967) 115 Ga App 314, 154 SE2d 457 (by implication).

Kan—Little v Sowers (1949) 167 Kan 72, 204 P2d 605.

Me—Lambert v Breton (1929) 127 Me 510, 144 A 864 (recognizing rule).

Minn—Hoppe v Klapperich (1937) 224 Minn 224, 28 NW2d 780, 173 ALR 819.

NJ—Ash v Cohen (1937) 119 NJL 54, 194 A 174.

Voytko v Ramada Inn of Atlantic City (1978, DC NJ) 445 F Supp 315 (by implication; applying New Jersey law).

NY—Board of Education v Farmingdale Classroom Teachers Asso. (1975) 38 NY2d 397, 380 NYS2d 635, 343 NE2d 278 (by implication).

Dishaw v Wadleigh (1897) 15 App Div 205, 44 NYS 207.

Cote v Knickerbocker Ice Co. (1936) 160 Misc 658, 290 NYS 483 (recognizing rule); Rothbard v Ringler (1947, Sup) 77 NYS2d 351 (by

implication); Weiss v Hunna (1963, CA2 NY) 312 F2d 711, cert den 374 US 853, 10 L Ed 2d 1073, 83 S Ct 1920, reh den 375 US 874, 11 L Ed 2d 104, 84 S Ct 37 (by implication; applying New York law).

Pa—Haggerty v Moyerman (1936) 321 Pa 555, 184 A 654 (by implication).

Adelman v Rosenbaum (193[8] Pa Super 386, 3 A2d 15; Sachs (1963, ED Pa) 216 F Supp [ ] implication; applying Penns[ylvania] law).

Wash—Fite v Lee (1974) 1[1 Wash] App 21, 521 P2d 964, 97 ALR3d 678, (by implication).

An attorney is personally liable to a third party if he maliciously participates with others in an abuse of process, or if he maliciously encourages and induces another to act as his instrumentality in committing an act constituting an abuse of process, the court held in Hoppe v Klapperich (1947) 224 **Minn** 224, 28 NW2d 780, 173 ALR 819. The court reversed the order of the trial court which had sustained the demurrers of an attorney and other defendants in a proceeding for abuse of process and malicious prosecution. The plaintiff had alleged, as to the cause of action for abuse of process, that it was the intent of the defendants, an attorney, his client, a sheriff, and a municipal judge, to force her to part with certain bonds, negotiable instruments, and other valuable papers by threatening her with arrest and prosecution on a criminal charge of theft of a watch. The plaintiff's subsequent arrest and confinement on the charge of theft were alleged to constitute a continuing abuse of process. The court noted that in the performance

16. See 7 Am Jur Proof of Facts 2d, Abuse of Process—Debt Collection § 4.

693

Citations to cases from multiple jurisdictions

Discussion of the law with a more detailed case summary

- Contracts
- Foreign Relations Law of the United States
- Judgments
- Law Governing Lawyers
- Property
- Restitution
- Security
- Suretyship and Guaranty
- Torts
- Trusts
- Unfair Competition

In determining what the common-law rules are, the Restatements often look to the rules in the majority of United States jurisdictions. Sometimes, however, the Restatements will also state emerging rules where the rules seem to be changing, or proposed rules in areas where the authors believe a change in the law would be appropriate. Although the Restatements are limited to common-law doctrines, the rules in the Restatements are set out almost like statutes, breaking different doctrines down into their component parts. In addition to setting out the common-law rules for a subject, the Restatements also provide commentary on the proper interpretations of the rules, illustrations demonstrating how the rules should apply in certain situations, and summaries of cases applying and interpreting the Restatement.

Although a Restatement is a secondary source, it is one with substantial weight. Courts can decide to adopt a Restatement's view of an issue, which then makes the comments and illustrations especially persuasive in that jurisdiction. If you are researching the law of a jurisdiction that has adopted a Restatement, you can use the Restatement volumes effectively to locate persuasive authority from other Restatement jurisdictions. As a result, a Restatement is an especially valuable secondary source.

Figures 3.9 and **3.10** show some of the features of one Restatement, the *Restatement (Second) of Torts*. There are two components to the *Restatement (Second) of Torts*: the Restatement volumes, which contain the Restatement rules, comments, and illustrations; and the Appendix volumes, which contain case summaries. To research the *Restatement (Second) of Torts*, you must follow two steps: (1) find relevant sections of the Restatement in the Restatement volumes; and (2) find case summaries interpreting the Restatement in the Appendix volumes.

In the first step, the subject index or table of contents in the Restatement volumes will direct you to individual rules within the Restatement. After the formal statement of the rule, the comments and illustrations will follow. **Figure 3.9** shows the text of § 35 of the *Restatement (Second) of Torts* on false imprisonment.

In the second step, you need to go to the separate Appendix volumes. The Appendix volumes are organized numerically by Restatement section

FIGURE 3.9 **SECTION 35 OF THE** *RESTATEMENT (SECOND) OF TORTS*

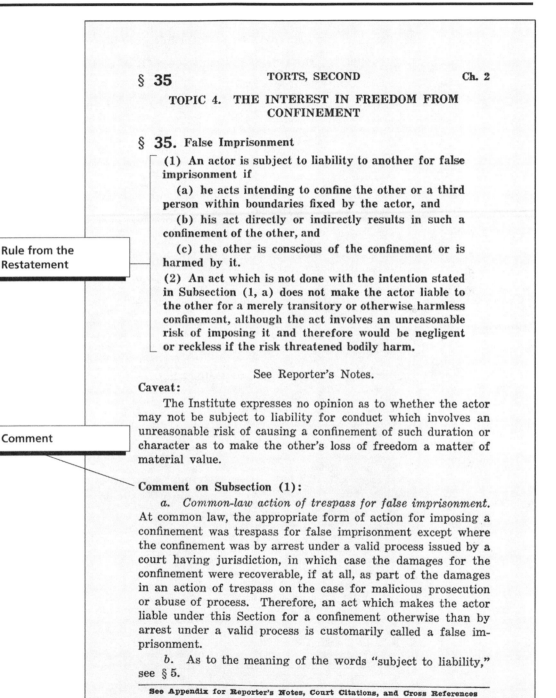

§ 35   TORTS, SECOND   Ch. 2

TOPIC 4. THE INTEREST IN FREEDOM FROM
CONFINEMENT

§ 35. False Imprisonment

(1) An actor is subject to liability to another for false imprisonment if

(a) he acts intending to confine the other or a third person within boundaries fixed by the actor, and

(b) his act directly or indirectly results in such a confinement of the other, and

(c) the other is conscious of the confinement or is harmed by it.

(2) An act which is not done with the intention stated in Subsection (1, a) does not make the actor liable to the other for a merely transitory or otherwise harmless confinement, although the act involves an unreasonable risk of imposing it and therefore would be negligent or reckless if the risk threatened bodily harm.

Rule from the Restatement

See Reporter's Notes.

Caveat:

The Institute expresses no opinion as to whether the actor may not be subject to liability for conduct which involves an unreasonable risk of causing a confinement of such duration or character as to make the other's loss of freedom a matter of material value.

Comment

Comment on Subsection (1):

a. Common-law action of trespass for false imprisonment. At common law, the appropriate form of action for imposing a confinement was trespass for false imprisonment except where the confinement was by arrest under a valid process issued by a court having jurisdiction, in which case the damages for the confinement were recoverable, if at all, as part of the damages in an action of trespass on the case for malicious prosecution or abuse of process. Therefore, an act which makes the actor liable under this Section for a confinement otherwise than by arrest under a valid process is customarily called a false imprisonment.

b. As to the meaning of the words "subject to liability," see § 5.

See Appendix for Reporter's Notes, Court Citations, and Cross References

52

FIGURE 3.10   ENTRY UNDER § 35 IN THE APPENDIX TO THE *RESTATEMENT (SECOND) OF TORTS*

Ch. 2   CITATIONS TO RESTATEMENT SECOND   § 35

TOPIC 4.   THE INTEREST IN FREEDOM FROM CONFINEMENT

C.A.1, 1995. §§ 35–45A, constituting all of Ch. 2, Topic 4, cit. in sup. and adopted. Puerto Rican resident was arrested by federal agents who mistakenly believed that she was the subject of a 1975 arrest warrant; following the dismissal of all proceedings against her, she sued the United States for false arrest. Affirming the district court's grant of summary judgment for the United States, this court held that the United States was not liable for the false arrest of plaintiff, since the name in the warrant, together with information contained in the arrest packet, provided ample basis for the arresting agents to form an objectively reasonable belief that plaintiff was the person named in the warrant. The court also held that the conduct of the federal agent responsible for instigating the errant arrest was conditionally privileged, since the arrestee was sufficiently named in the warrant and the agent reasonably believed that plaintiff was the subject of the warrant. Rodriguez v. U.S., 54 F.3d 41, 45.

Cases interpreting § 35

§ 35.   **False Imprisonment**

C.A.1, 1995. Cit. in ftn. Two men who were arrested and acquitted of selling cocaine sued police officers of Puerto Rico and their confidential informants for constitutional violations, alleging that defendants falsely identified them as sellers. District court held that the false-arrest claims were barred by the one-year statute of limitations and that the malicious-prosecution claims were not actionable under 42 U.S.C. § 1983. This court vacated and remanded, holding that, for purposes of determining the appropriate accrual rule, both the Fourth and Fourteenth Amendment claims more closely resembled the common law tort of malicious prosecution. Consequently, plaintiffs' § 1983 claims did not accrue until their respective criminal prosecutions ended in acquittals. Calero–Colon v. Betancourt–Lebron, 68 F.3d 1, 3.

C.A.1, 2000. Cit. in headnote, quot. in disc. After being detained by store employees who accused them of shoplifting on a prior occasion, two children and their mother sued the store for false imprisonment. District court entered judgment on jury verdict awarding plaintiffs damages. This court affirmed, holding, inter alia, that plaintiffs stated a viable false-imprisonment claim, because a reasonable jury could conclude that the store's employees intended to confine plaintiffs within boundaries fixed by the store, that the store's acts resulted in such confinement, and that plaintiffs were conscious of the confinement. Employees' direction to plaintiffs, their reference to the police, and their continued presence were enough to induce reasonable people to believe either that they would be restrained physically if they sought to leave, or that the store was claiming lawful authority to confine them until the police arrived, or both. McCann v. Wal–Mart Stores, Inc., 210 F.3d 51, 51, 53.

C.A.7, 2003. Quot. in sup. African–American store employee who was fired for allegedly stealing from a coemployee sued store for federal civil-rights violations and false imprisonment under Indiana law, alleging that store representatives locked her in her manager's office for several minutes while they investigated the theft charges. District court granted store summary judgment. This court affirmed, holding, inter alia, that plaintiff did not establish a claim of false imprisonment under Indiana law, because her several-minute confinement was accidental, and store established justification for the brief detention. No one told plaintiff that she could not leave, and store provided a reasonable explanation for having left her alone in the office so that she could draft her written statement without distraction. Adams v. Wal–Mart Stores, Inc., 324 F.3d 935, 941.

C.A.9, 2003. Com. (a) quot. in sup. California resident who had been director of Australian corporation was extradited to Australia for criminal trial. After Australian government dropped fraud charges and jury acquitted extraditee on other charge, he sued two instrumentalities and two employees of Australian government for malicious prosecution, abuse of process, and false imprisonment. District court granted motion to dismiss for employees, but denied motion as to instrumentalities. This court reversed in part, holding that plaintiff's claims of malicious prosecution and abuse of process were barred by Foreign Sovereign Immunities Act, since plaintiff could not overcome sovereign immu-

Cit.–cited; fol.–followed; quot.–quoted; sup.–support.
A complete list of abbreviations precedes page 1.

119

number. By looking up the appropriate section number, you will find cases from a variety of jurisdictions interpreting that section. The Appendix volumes are not cumulative; each volume covers only a specific period of time. Therefore, to find all of the cases interpreting a section, you would need to look it up in each Appendix volume. The latest Appendix volume will have a pocket part with the most recent references.

Figure 3.10 shows the Appendix entry under § 35, which lists several cases discussing this section of the Restatement.

6. UNIFORM LAWS AND MODEL ACTS

Uniform laws and model acts are proposed statutes that can be adopted by legislatures. Two examples with which you may already be familiar are the Uniform Commercial Code and the Model Penal Code. Uniform laws and model acts are similar to Restatements in that they set out proposed rules, followed by commentary, research notes, and summaries of cases interpreting the rules. Unlike Restatements, which are limited to common-law doctrines, uniform laws and model acts exist in areas governed by statutory law.

Although uniform laws and model acts look like statutes, they are secondary sources. Their provisions do not take on the force of law unless they are adopted by a legislature. When that happens, however, the commentary, research references, and case summaries become very useful research tools. They can help you interpret the law and direct you to persuasive authority from other jurisdictions that have adopted the law.

One of the best ways to locate uniform laws and model acts in print is through a publication entitled *Uniform Laws Annotated, Master Edition* (ULA). This is a multivolume set of books containing the text of a number of uniform laws and model acts. You can locate it through the online catalog in your library.

Once you have located the ULA set, you have several research options. To determine the best research option for your project, you should review the *Directory of Uniform Acts and Codes: Tables and Index*. This softcover booklet is published annually and explains the finding tools available in this resource. You can research uniform laws and model acts by subject, by the name of the law, or by adopting jurisdiction. Once you have located relevant information in the main volumes of the ULA set, use the pocket part to update your research.

You are most likely to research uniform laws and model acts when your project involves research into state statutes, and generally speaking, researching in the ULA set is similar to statutory research. As a consequence, if you decide to use this resource, you may also want to review Chapter 6, which discusses statutory research.

Figure 3.11 shows a uniform law as it appears in the ULA set.

FIGURE 3.11   ULA ENTRY FOR THE UNIFORM SINGLE PUBLICATION ACT

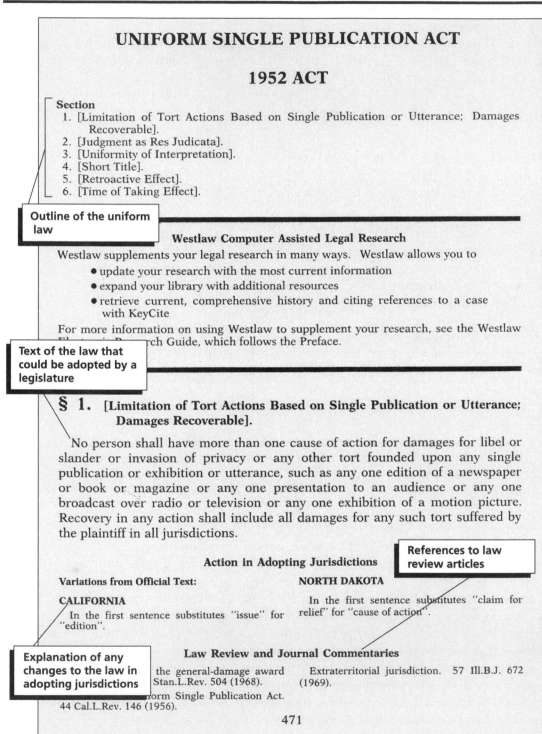

UNIFORM SINGLE PUBLICATION ACT

1952 ACT

Section
1. [Limitation of Tort Actions Based on Single Publication or Utterance; Damages Recoverable].
2. [Judgment as Res Judicata].
3. [Uniformity of Interpretation].
4. [Short Title].
5. [Retroactive Effect].
6. [Time of Taking Effect].

Outline of the uniform law

Westlaw Computer Assisted Legal Research

Westlaw supplements your legal research in many ways. Westlaw allows you to
- update your research with the most current information
- expand your library with additional resources
- retrieve current, comprehensive history and citing references to a case with KeyCite

For more information on using Westlaw to supplement your research, see the Westlaw Electronic Research Guide, which follows the Preface.

Text of the law that could be adopted by a legislature

§ 1.   [Limitation of Tort Actions Based on Single Publication or Utterance; Damages Recoverable].

No person shall have more than one cause of action for damages for libel or slander or invasion of privacy or any other tort founded upon any single publication or exhibition or utterance, such as any one edition of a newspaper or book or magazine or any one presentation to an audience or any one broadcast over radio or television or any one exhibition of a motion picture. Recovery in any action shall include all damages for any such tort suffered by the plaintiff in all jurisdictions.

References to law review articles

Action in Adopting Jurisdictions

Variations from Official Text: NORTH DAKOTA

CALIFORNIA   In the first sentence substitutes "claim for
    In the first sentence substitutes "issue" for   relief" for "cause of action".
"edition".

Explanation of any changes to the law in adopting jurisdictions

Law Review and Journal Commentaries

the general-damage award   Extraterritorial jurisdiction.   57 Ill.B.J. 672
Stan.L.Rev. 504 (1968).   (1969).
...orm Single Publication Act.
44 Cal.L.Rev. 146 (1956).

471

FIGURE 3.11   ULA ENTRY FOR THE UNIFORM SINGLE PUBLICATION ACT (Continued)

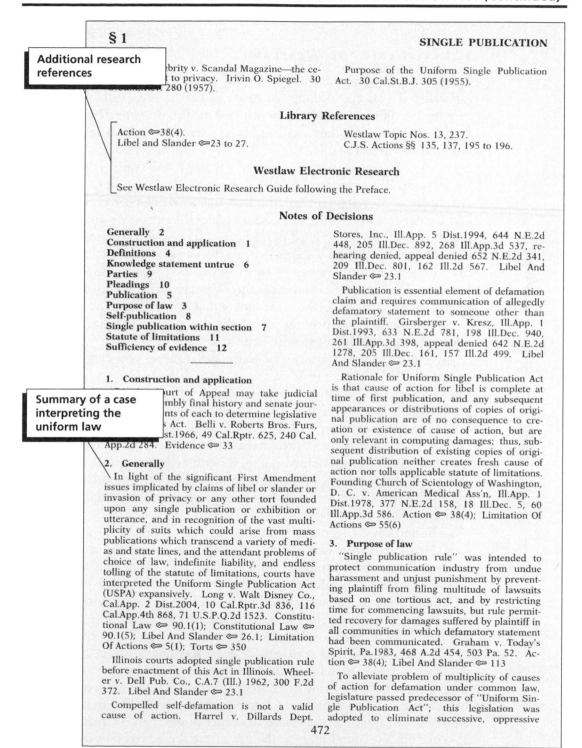

Additional research references

Summary of a case interpreting the uniform law

§ 1

SINGLE PUBLICATION

...brity v. Scandal Magazine—the ce... to privacy. Irivin O. Spiegel. 30 ...280 (1957).

Purpose of the Uniform Single Publication Act. 30 Cal.St.B.J. 305 (1955).

Library References

Action ☞38(4).
Libel and Slander ☞23 to 27.

Westlaw Topic Nos. 13, 237.
C.J.S. Actions §§ 135, 137, 195 to 196.

Westlaw Electronic Research

See Westlaw Electronic Research Guide following the Preface.

Notes of Decisions

Generally 2
Construction and application 1
Definitions 4
Knowledge statement untrue 6
Parties 9
Pleadings 10
Publication 5
Purpose of law 3
Self-publication 8
Single publication within section 7
Statute of limitations 11
Sufficiency of evidence 12

1. **Construction and application**
...urt of Appeal may take judicial ...mbly final history and senate jour-...nts of each to determine legislative ...s Act. Belli v. Roberts Bros. Furs, ...st.1966, 49 Cal.Rptr. 625, 240 Cal. App.2d 284. Evidence ☞ 33

2. **Generally**
In light of the significant First Amendment issues implicated by claims of libel or slander or invasion of privacy or any other tort founded upon any single publication or exhibition or utterance, and in recognition of the vast multiplicity of suits which could arise from mass publications which transcend a variety of medias and state lines, and the attendant problems of choice of law, indefinite liability, and endless tolling of the statute of limitations, courts have interpreted the Uniform Single Publication Act (USPA) expansively. Long v. Walt Disney Co., Cal.App. 2 Dist.2004, 10 Cal.Rptr.3d 836, 116 Cal.App.4th 868, 71 U.S.P.Q.2d 1523. Constitutional Law ☞ 90.1(1); Constitutional Law ☞ 90.1(5); Libel And Slander ☞ 26.1; Limitation Of Actions ☞ 5(1); Torts ☞ 350

Illinois courts adopted single publication rule before enactment of this Act in Illinois. Wheeler v. Dell Pub. Co., C.A.7 (Ill.) 1962, 300 F.2d 372. Libel And Slander ☞ 23.1

Compelled self-defamation is not a valid cause of action. Harrel v. Dillards Dept.

Stores, Inc., Ill.App. 5 Dist.1994, 644 N.E.2d 448, 205 Ill.Dec. 892, 268 Ill.App.3d 537, rehearing denied, appeal denied 652 N.E.2d 341, 209 Ill.Dec. 801, 162 Ill.2d 567. Libel And Slander ☞ 23.1

Publication is essential element of defamation claim and requires communication of allegedly defamatory statement to someone other than the plaintiff. Girsberger v. Kresz, Ill.App. 1 Dist.1993, 633 N.E.2d 781, 198 Ill.Dec. 940, 261 Ill.App.3d 398, appeal denied 642 N.E.2d 1278, 205 Ill.Dec. 161, 157 Ill.2d 499. Libel And Slander ☞ 23.1

Rationale for Uniform Single Publication Act is that cause of action for libel is complete at time of first publication, and any subsequent appearances or distributions of copies of original publication are of no consequence to creation or existence of cause of action, but are only relevant in computing damages; thus, subsequent distribution of existing copies of original publication neither creates fresh cause of action nor tolls applicable statute of limitations. Founding Church of Scientology of Washington, D. C. v. American Medical Ass'n, Ill.App. 1 Dist.1978, 377 N.E.2d 158, 18 Ill.Dec. 5, 60 Ill.App.3d 586. Action ☞ 38(4); Limitation Of Actions ☞ 55(6)

3. **Purpose of law**
"Single publication rule" was intended to protect communication industry from undue harassment and unjust punishment by preventing plaintiff from filing multitude of lawsuits based on one tortious act, and by restricting time for commencing lawsuits, but rule permitted recovery for damages suffered by plaintiff in all communities in which defamatory statement had been communicated. Graham v. Today's Spirit, Pa.1983, 468 A.2d 454, 503 Pa. 52. Action ☞ 38(4); Libel And Slander ☞ 113

To alleviate problem of multiplicity of causes of action for defamation under common law, legislature passed predecessor of "Uniform Single Publication Act"; this legislation was adopted to eliminate successive, oppressive

472

C. RESEARCHING SECONDARY SOURCES ELECTRONICALLY

1. LexisNexis and Westlaw

LexisNexis and Westlaw can be useful in locating secondary sources, especially if you are looking for material that is not available in print in your law library. As of this writing, Am. Jur. 2d is available in both LexisNexis and Westlaw, and C.J.S. is available in Westlaw. A.L.R. Annotations are available only in Westlaw. Westlaw also contains electronic A.L.R. Annotations ("e-annos") that are not available in print or LexisNexis. E-annos are identified by year and number, e.g., 2005 A.L.R.6th 1. Restatements of the law and a number of uniform laws and model acts are available in both services. LexisNexis and Westlaw provide access to many legal periodicals, but not all of them, and their periodical databases go back only until the early to mid-1980s. In addition, only a limited number of treatises can be accessed through these services. Thus, while LexisNexis and Westlaw are very good sources of secondary material, they are not exhaustive. You may find that these services do not provide all of the secondary material you need and must be supplemented with print research.

If you have the citation to a secondary source, you can retrieve it using the Find function in Westlaw or the Get A Document function in LexisNexis. You can also execute word searches to locate secondary authority. In general, if you know which type of secondary authority you want to research, you can execute a word search in the database for that type of authority, e.g., the database for Am. Jur. 2d. LexisNexis and Westlaw also offer combined databases containing multiple secondary sources. Furthermore, you can limit your research to secondary sources covering a particular jurisdiction or subject area by searching in jurisdictional or subject area databases.

The indices to secondary sources are not available in Westlaw or LexisNexis, but you can search by subject by browsing the table of contents for some secondary sources. This will allow you to retrieve sections of the publication by selecting them from the table of contents without having to execute a word search. Table of contents searching is available for legal encyclopedias, treatises, Restatement rules, and many uniform laws but not for A.L.R. Annotations or legal periodicals.

To view the table of contents for most secondary sources, select the database for the source you want to search. In LexisNexis, if you select a source for which the table of contents is available, the table of contents will be displayed with the search screen. In Westlaw, a link to the table of contents will appear in the top right corner of the search screen. You can also use the Site Map link near the top of the screen to browse a table of contents. Under the list of Westlaw search features, select the Table of

Contents option to view a list of publications for which tables of contents are available.

To research Restatements in LexisNexis and Westlaw, remember that the Restatement rules, comments, and illustrations are separate from the annotations summarizing cases interpreting the rules. In LexisNexis, the Restatement rules and the case citations are in separate databases. You can execute word searches or browse the table of contents in the rules databases, but word searching is the only option in the databases with case annotations. You have the option to execute a word search in both rules and case annotation databases simultaneously, with search results divided between those from the rules database and those from the case annotation database.

In Westlaw, the rules and case annotations for individual Restatements are combined together. Therefore, when you view a Restatement section, the case annotations will follow the comments and illustrations in a single document. This means that any word search you execute in a Restatement database will search for the terms in both the rules and the case annotations (unless you specifically limit the search). To browse a Restatement's table of contents, you must pay attention to how you access the database. As of this writing, you can view the table of contents for Restatement rules from the Table of Contents option under the Site Map or by selecting a Restatement database from the Directory. You will also find a link to Restatements on the Resources page under the Law Schools tab, but if you use that link, word searching is the only option; the option to view the table of contents does not appear.

The process of researching in LexisNexis and Westlaw is explained in more detail in Chapter 10.

2. SUBSCRIPTION SERVICES FOR LEGAL PERIODICALS

As noted earlier in this chapter, two electronic periodical indices, the *Index to Legal Periodicals* (ILP) and LegalTrac, provide access to some legal periodicals. These services index a wide range of periodicals, but their full text access is more limited. Articles in either of these services may be available in html format, .pdf format, or both, depending on the publication. For information about the search options available in ILP and LegalTrac, you may want to refer back to the discussion of these services in Section B, above.

HeinOnline is another service that provides electronic access to legal periodicals, among other types of authority. Many law libraries subscribe to this service; users generally access it through the library network. HeinOnline's holdings go back further in time than those of ILP, Legal-Trac, LexisNexis, or Westlaw, often dating back to the inception of the periodicals in its database. You can search for legal periodical articles in HeinOnline in several ways. You can retrieve an article from its citation,

FIGURE 3.12   HEINONLINE DISPLAY OF A LEGAL PERIODICAL ARTICLE

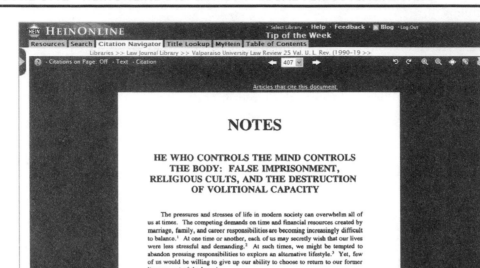

From HeinOnline. © 2008 HeinOnline.

search by title or author, or conduct word searches in the full text of the articles in HeinOnline's database. You can also browse the table of contents of individual publications. HeinOnline displays articles in .pdf format.

Figure 3.12 shows the HeinOnline display of a legal periodical article.

3. INTERNET SOURCES

You undoubtedly use publicly accessible Internet sites on a daily basis for news, entertainment, shopping, and many other purposes. It is natural, therefore, to think of using the Internet for legal research as well. Although there is certainly nothing wrong with using general Internet sources as one component of your research strategy, you would not want that to be your sole approach for locating secondary material on an issue.

Legal encyclopedias, treatises, and A.L.R. Annotations are not available via publicly accessible Internet sites. You may be able to find some uniform laws or model acts and selected sections of Restatements on the Internet, but you will not generally find complete compilations of these sources, nor will you find the comments, illustrations, or annotations.

Although most legal periodicals are not yet available on the Internet, an increasing number of law reviews, journals, and other legal periodicals are beginning to publish their articles on the web. To locate periodical articles on the Internet, you could use a general or law-related search engine. General legal research web sites may also contain links to legal periodicals. Another approach is viewing individual law school web sites to see if their publications are accessible on the Internet. Some of these sites will allow you to execute word or subject searches. Others will list the tables of contents for periodicals available electronically.

If you have the citation or title of an article that is available on the Internet, this can be a quick and economical way to obtain it. Nevertheless, the number of periodicals accessible on the Internet is still small relative to the total number of publications available, and limitations on searching capabilities can make it difficult to locate pertinent material.

The secondary sources discussed so far in this chapter are the traditional sources used for legal research, but many non-traditional secondary sources are now available on the Internet. Sources such as Wikipedia contain information about the law. Free legal research sites like FindLaw often include articles written by lawyers or legal commentators. Using a search engine such as Google could retrieve a pathfinder or bibliography compiled by a law librarian that lists sources on an area of law. These non-traditional Internet sources are secondary sources, and all of the caveats regarding appropriate uses of traditional legal secondary sources apply to them with equal force. Lawyers do not consider these sources authoritative, and it is difficult to imagine circumstances under which you would cite one.

Using publicly available Internet sites can be both easier and harder than using more traditional legal research tools. It can be easier in the sense that Internet sources are cost effective to use and can provide easy access to information relevant to your research. It can be harder in the sense that you cannot assume that a non-traditional secondary source is reliable. It is important to remember that any person with a message and the appropriate equipment can publish material on the Internet. Because electronic sources can be updated at any time, they may be perceived as providing current information even if they have not been updated for a long period of time. Therefore, you must take special care to evaluate any secondary information you find on the Internet. Chapter 10, on electronic legal research, discusses publically available web sites, blogs, and other Internet-based research sources. You may want to review that chapter before using the Internet to locate non-traditional secondary sources. In addition, Appendix A lists Internet sites that may be useful for secondary source research.

D. CITING SECONDARY SOURCES

The chart in **Figure 3.13** lists the rules in the *ALWD Manual* and the *Bluebook* governing citations to secondary sources. Citations to each of these sources are discussed in turn.

FIGURE 3.13   RULES FOR CITING SECONDARY SOURCES

SECONDARY SOURCE	ALWD MANUAL	BLUEBOOK
Legal encyclopedias	Rule 26	Bluepages B8
Treatises	Rule 22	Bluepages B8
Legal periodicals	Rule 23	Bluepages B9
A.L.R. Annotations	Rule 24	Rule 16.6.6
Restatements	Rule 27	Bluepages B6.1.3
Uniform laws & Model acts	Rule 27	Uniform laws— Bluepages B6.1.3; see also Rule 12.8.4 Model acts—Rule 12.8.5

1. LEGAL ENCYCLOPEDIAS

Citations to legal encyclopedias are covered in *ALWD Manual* Rule 26 and *Bluebook* Bluepages B8 and are the same using either format. The citation consists of five elements: (1) the volume number; (2) the abbreviated name of the encyclopedia; (3) the name of the topic, underlined or italicized; (4) the section cited (with a space between the section symbol (§) and the section number); and (5) a parenthetical containing the date of the book, including, if appropriate, the date of the pocket part or supplement. Here is an example:

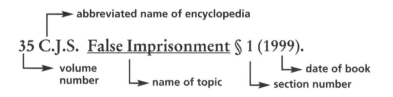

Sometimes determining which date or dates to include in the parenthetical can be confusing. The answer is always a function of where a reader would have to look to find all of the text and footnote information on the section you are citing. If all of the information appears in the main volume of the encyclopedia, the date in the parenthetical should refer only to the main volume. If the section is a new section that appears only in the pocket part, the date should refer only to the pocket part. If the reader must refer both to the main volume and to the pocket part, the parenthetical should list both dates. Here are several examples:

35 C.J.S. <u>False Imprisonment</u> § 1 (1999).

In this example, the reference is only to the main volume.

35 C.J.S. <u>False Imprisonment</u> § 1 (1999 & Supp. 2009).

In this example, the reference is both to the main volume and to the pocket part.

32 Am. Jur. 2d <u>False Imprisonment</u> § 1 (Supp. 2009).

In this example, the reference is only to the pocket part.

2. TREATISES

Citations to treatises contain roughly the same elements in both *ALWD Manual* and *Bluebook* formats. There are a few differences between them, however, and the order of the elements varies in minor respects.

In the *ALWD Manual*, citations to treatises are covered in Rule 22 and consist of four elements: (1) the author's full name (if the treatise has more than two authors, you may list the first, followed by et al.); (2) the title of the treatise, underlined or italicized; (3) a pinpoint reference containing the volume of the treatise (in a multivolume treatise), the section cited (with a space between the section symbol (§) and the section number), and the specific page or pages cited; and (4) a parenthetical containing the edition (if more than one edition has been published), the publisher, and the date, including, if appropriate, the date of the pocket part. Here is an example in *ALWD Manual* format:

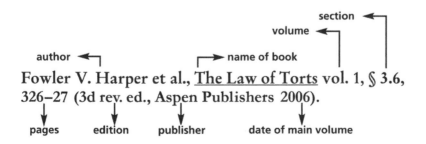

In the *Bluebook*, citations to treatises are covered in Bluepages B8 and consist of five elements: (1) the volume number of the treatise (in a multivolume set); (2) the author's full name (if the treatise has more than two authors, list the first, followed by et al.); (3) the title of the treatise, underlined or italicized; (4) the section cited (with a space between the section symbol (§) and the section number); and (5) a parenthetical containing the edition (if more than one edition has been published)

and the date, including, if appropriate, the date of the pocket part. Here is an example in *Bluebook* format:

volume ←┐   ┌→ author   ┌→ name of book   ┌→ section

1 Fowler V. Harper et al., <u>The Law of Torts</u> § 3.6 (3d ed. 1996).

edition ←┘   └→ date of main volume

Note that in both citation formats, a comma separates the part of the citation identifying the author or authors from the title of the treatise. No other commas appear in a *Bluebook* citation. In an *ALWD Manual* citation, commas also separate the components of the pinpoint reference, as well as the edition and publisher's name in the parenthetical.

Both the *ALWD Manual* and the *Bluebook* have additional requirements for books with editors or translators.

3. LEGAL PERIODICALS

Legal periodicals are published in two formats. Some publications begin the first issue within each volume with page one and continue numbering the pages of subsequent issues within that volume consecutively. These are called consecutively paginated publications. Most law reviews and journals are consecutively paginated. Other publications, such as monthly magazines, begin each new issue with page one, regardless of where the issue falls within the volume. These are called nonconsecutively paginated publications.

There are some differences in the citations to articles published in consecutively and nonconsecutively paginated periodicals. The explanation in this section focuses on citations to articles published in consecutively paginated law reviews, which are covered in *ALWD Manual* Rule 23 and *Bluebook* Bluepages B9.

A citation to a law review article in both *ALWD Manual* and *Bluebook* formats consists of seven elements: (1) the author's full name; (2) the title of the article, underlined or italicized; (3) the volume number of the publication; (4) the abbreviated name of the publication; (5) the starting page of the article; (6) the pinpoint citation to the specific page or pages cited; and (7) a parenthetical containing the date of the publication. Here is an example:

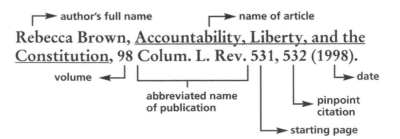

Note that the author's name, the name of the article, and the starting page of the article are followed by commas. The comma following the name of the article is not underlined or italicized.

Publication abbreviations can be found in *ALWD Manual* Appendix 5 and *Bluebook* Table T.13. Notice that the periodical abbreviations in *Bluebook* Table T.13 appear in large and small capital letters. According to Bluepages B13, however, you should not use large and small capitals when citing authority in a brief or memorandum. Use ordinary roman type for the publication's name. Both the *ALWD Manual* and the *Bluebook* have additional rules for citing articles appearing in nonconsecutively paginated publications, articles written by students, and articles with more than one author.

4. A.L.R. ANNOTATIONS

Citations to A.L.R. Annotations are covered in *ALWD Manual* Rule 24 and *Bluebook* Rule 16.6.6. They are almost identical in both formats, with only one minor difference between them. A citation to an A.L.R. Annotation consists of seven elements: (1) the author's full name (in a *Bluebook* citation, the author's name is followed by the notation "Annotation"); (2) the title of the Annotation, underlined or italicized; (3) the volume number; (4) the A.L.R. series; (5) the starting page of the Annotation; (6) the pinpoint citation to the specific page or pages cited; and (7) a parenthetical containing the date, including, if appropriate, the date of the pocket part. Here is an example in *ALWD Manual* format:

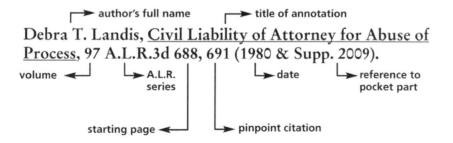

Here is an example in *Bluebook* format:

Although the example in *Bluebook* Rule 16.6.6 shows A.L.R. Fed. in large and small capital letters, use ordinary roman type pursuant to Bluepages B13 for a citation in a memorandum or brief.

5. RESTATEMENTS

Citations to Restatements are covered in *ALWD Manual* Rule 27 and *Bluebook* Bluepages B6.1.3. They contain three elements using either format: (1) the name of the Restatement; (2) the section cited (with a space between the section symbol (§) and the section number); and (3) a parenthetical containing the date. The only difference is that the name of the Restatement is underlined or italicized in *ALWD Manual* format, but not in *Bluebook* format. Here is an example in *ALWD Manual* format:

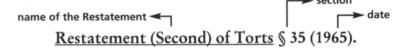

Here is an example in *Bluebook* format:

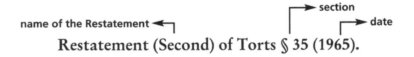

6. UNIFORM LAWS AND MODEL ACTS

The citation format for a uniform law depends on whether the law has been adopted by a jurisdiction. If a jurisdiction adopts a uniform law, the law will be published with all of the other statutes for that jurisdiction. In that situation, cite directly to the jurisdiction's statute. The requirements for statutory citations are explained in Chapter 6.

Citations to uniform laws published in the ULA set are governed by *ALWD Manual* Rule 27. In the *Bluebook*, Bluepages B6.1.3 gives an example of a citation to a uniform law; additional information on citing laws published in the ULA set appears in Rule 12.8.4. The citation is the same using either format and consists of six elements: (1) the abbreviated title of the act; (2) the section cited (with a space between the section symbol (§) and section number); (3) the ULA volume number; (4) the abbreviation "U.L.A."; (5) the page of the ULA on which the section appears; and (6) a parenthetical containing the date of the ULA volume, including, if appropriate, the date of the pocket part. Here is an example:

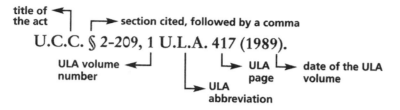

Citations to model acts are covered in *ALWD Manual* Rule 27 and *Bluebook* Rule 12.8.5. Model act citations are almost identical in both formats, with only one minor difference between them. The citation consists of three elements: (1) the name of the act; (2) the section cited (with a space between the section symbol (§) and the section number); and (3) a parenthetical.

In *ALWD Manual* citations, the parenthetical contains the name of the organization that issued the act, abbreviated according to Appendix 3, and the date. Here is an example in *ALWD Manual* format:

name of the act ←   section ←   → date

Model Penal Code § 5.03 (ALI 1985).

organization that issued the act ←

The *Bluebook* requires that the parenthetical include the name of the organization that issued the act for some model acts, but not others. In all model act citations, however, the *Bluebook* requires the date in the parenthetical. Here is an example in *Bluebook* format:

name of the act ←   section ←

Model Penal Code § 5.03 (1985).

date ←

The examples of citations to uniform laws and model acts in Rules 12.8.4 and 12.8.5 show the names of the laws in large and small capital letters. According to Bluepages B13, however, you should use ordinary roman type to cite these authorities in a memorandum or brief.

E. SAMPLE PAGES FOR PRINT SECONDARY SOURCE RESEARCH

Beginning on the next page, **Figures 3.14** through **3.22** are sample pages from A.L.R. and the *Restatement (Second) of Torts* showing what you would see in the books if you had researched false imprisonment and the related topic of abuse of process.

To locate an A.L.R. Annotation, begin by looking up your subject in the A.L.R. Index. The A.L.R. Index will refer you directly to applicable Annotations. The reference will tell you the volume number, series, and starting page of the Annotation.

FIGURE 3.14   A.L.R. INDEX

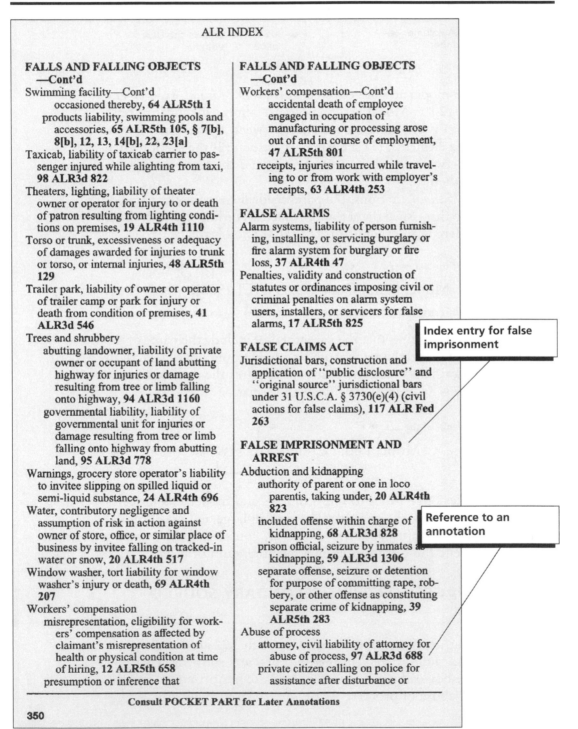

ALR INDEX

FALLS AND FALLING OBJECTS
—Cont'd
Swimming facility—Cont'd
   occasioned thereby, **64 ALR5th 1**
   products liability, swimming pools and
   accessories, **65 ALR5th 105, § 7[b],**
   8[b], 12, 13, 14[b], 22, 23[a]
Taxicab, liability of taxicab carrier to passenger injured while alighting from taxi,
   98 ALR3d 822
Theaters, lighting, liability of theater
   owner or operator for injury to or death
   of patron resulting from lighting conditions on premises, **19 ALR4th 1110**
Torso or trunk, excessiveness or adequacy
   of damages awarded for injuries to trunk
   or torso, or internal injuries, **48 ALR5th**
   129
Trailer park, liability of owner or operator
   of trailer camp or park for injury or
   death from condition of premises, **41**
   ALR3d 546
Trees and shrubbery
   abutting landowner, liability of private
      owner or occupant of land abutting
      highway for injuries or damage
      resulting from tree or limb falling
      onto highway, **94 ALR3d 1160**
   governmental liability, liability of
      governmental unit for injuries or
      damage resulting from tree or limb
      falling onto highway from abutting
      land, **95 ALR3d 778**
Warnings, grocery store operator's liability
   to invitee slipping on spilled liquid or
   semi-liquid substance, **24 ALR4th 696**
Water, contributory negligence and
   assumption of risk in action against
   owner of store, office, or similar place of
   business by invitee falling on tracked-in
   water or snow, **20 ALR4th 517**
Window washer, tort liability for window
   washer's injury or death, **69 ALR4th**
   207
Workers' compensation
   misrepresentation, eligibility for work-
      ers' compensation as affected by
      claimant's misrepresentation of
      health or physical condition at time
      of hiring, **12 ALR5th 658**
   presumption or inference that

FALLS AND FALLING OBJECTS
—Cont'd
Workers' compensation—Cont'd
   accidental death of employee
   engaged in occupation of
   manufacturing or processing arose
   out of and in course of employment,
   47 ALR5th 801
   receipts, injuries incurred while travel-
      ing to or from work with employer's
      receipts, **63 ALR4th 253**

FALSE ALARMS
Alarm systems, liability of person furnish-
   ing, installing, or servicing burglary or
   fire alarm system for burglary or fire
   loss, **37 ALR4th 47**
Penalties, validity and construction of
   statutes or ordinances imposing civil or
   criminal penalties on alarm system
   users, installers, or servicers for false
   alarms, **17 ALR5th 825**

FALSE CLAIMS ACT
Jurisdictional bars, construction and
   application of "public disclosure" and
   "original source" jurisdictional bars
   under 31 U.S.C.A. § 3730(e)(4) (civil
   actions for false claims), **117 ALR Fed**
   263

FALSE IMPRISONMENT AND
ARREST
Abduction and kidnapping
   authority of parent or one in loco
      parentis, taking under, **20 ALR4th**
      823
   included offense within charge of
      kidnapping, **68 ALR3d 828**
   prison official, seizure by inmates as
      kidnapping, **59 ALR3d 1306**
   separate offense, seizure or detention
      for purpose of committing rape, rob-
      bery, or other offense as constituting
      separate crime of kidnapping, **39**
      ALR5th 283
Abuse of process
   attorney, civil liability of attorney for
      abuse of process, **97 ALR3d 688**
   private citizen calling on police for
      assistance after disturbance or

Index entry for false imprisonment

Reference to an annotation

Consult POCKET PART for Later Annotations

350

Reprinted with permission from Thomson Reuters/West, *American Law Reports*, Index E-H (1999), p. 350.
© 1999 Thomson Reuters/West.

The Annotation will begin with an outline and references to related research sources. After the outline, an alphabetical index of topics within the Annotation will appear.

FIGURE 3.15   A.L.R. ANNOTATION

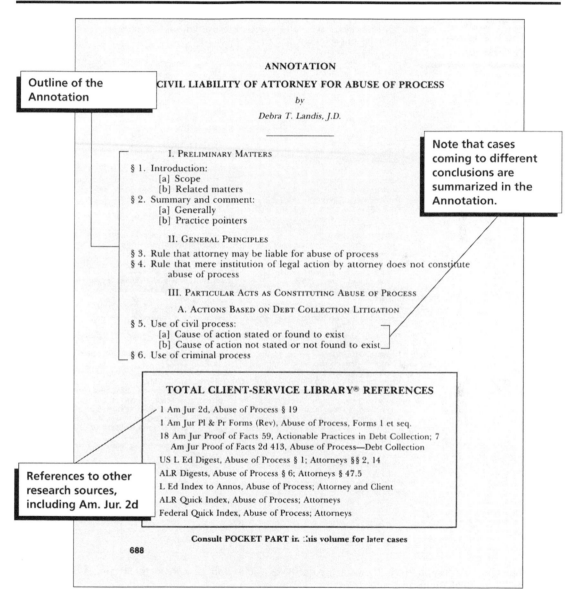

Outline of the Annotation

ANNOTATION

CIVIL LIABILITY OF ATTORNEY FOR ABUSE OF PROCESS

by

Debra T. Landis, J.D.

I. PRELIMINARY MATTERS

§ 1. Introduction:
    [a] Scope
    [b] Related matters
§ 2. Summary and comment:
    [a] Generally
    [b] Practice pointers

II. GENERAL PRINCIPLES

§ 3. Rule that attorney may be liable for abuse of process
§ 4. Rule that mere institution of legal action by attorney does not constitute abuse of process

III. PARTICULAR ACTS AS CONSTITUTING ABUSE OF PROCESS

A. ACTIONS BASED ON DEBT COLLECTION LITIGATION

§ 5. Use of civil process:
    [a] Cause of action stated or found to exist
    [b] Cause of action not stated or not found to exist
§ 6. Use of criminal process

Note that cases coming to different conclusions are summarized in the Annotation.

TOTAL CLIENT-SERVICE LIBRARY® REFERENCES

1 Am Jur 2d, Abuse of Process § 19

1 Am Jur Pl & Pr Forms (Rev), Abuse of Process, Forms 1 et seq.

18 Am Jur Proof of Facts 59, Actionable Practices in Debt Collection; 7 Am Jur Proof of Facts 2d 413, Abuse of Process—Debt Collection

US L Ed Digest, Abuse of Process § 1; Attorneys §§ 2, 14

ALR Digests, Abuse of Process § 6; Attorneys § 47.5

L Ed Index to Annos, Abuse of Process; Attorney and Client

ALR Quick Index, Abuse of Process; Attorneys

Federal Quick Index, Abuse of Process; Attorneys

References to other research sources, including Am. Jur. 2d

Consult POCKET PART in this volume for later cases

688

FIGURE 3.15   A.L.R. ANNOTATION (Continued)

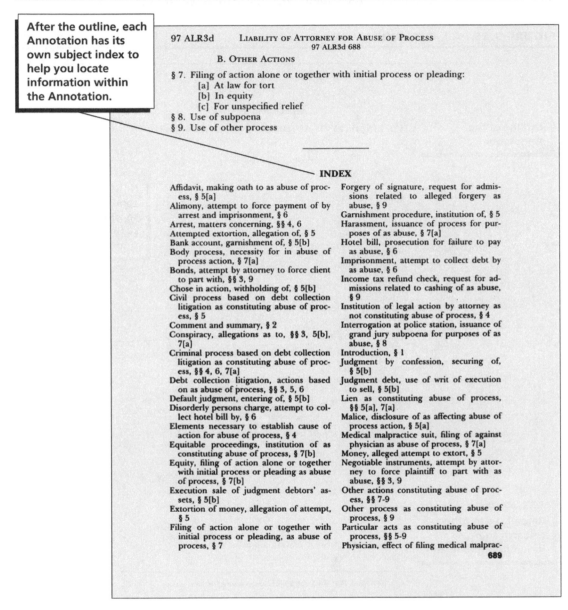

After the outline, each Annotation has its own subject index to help you locate information within the Annotation.

97 ALR3d   LIABILITY OF ATTORNEY FOR ABUSE OF PROCESS
97 ALR3d 688

B. OTHER ACTIONS

§ 7. Filing of action alone or together with initial process or pleading:
    [a] At law for tort
    [b] In equity
    [c] For unspecified relief
§ 8. Use of subpoena
§ 9. Use of other process

INDEX

Affidavit, making oath to as abuse of process, § 5[a]

Alimony, attempt to force payment of by arrest and imprisonment, § 6

Arrest, matters concerning, §§ 4, 6

Attempted extortion, allegation of, § 5

Bank account, garnishment of, § 5[b]

Body process, necessity for in abuse of process action, § 7[a]

Bonds, attempt by attorney to force client to part with, §§ 3, 9

Chose in action, withholding of, § 5[b]

Civil process based on debt collection litigation as constituting abuse of process, § 5

Comment and summary, § 2

Conspiracy, allegations as to, §§ 3, 5[b], 7[a]

Criminal process based on debt collection litigation as constituting abuse of process, §§ 4, 6, 7[a]

Debt collection litigation, actions based on as abuse of process, §§ 3, 5, 6

Default judgment, entering of, § 5[b]

Disorderly persons charge, attempt to collect hotel bill by, § 6

Elements necessary to establish cause of action for abuse of process, § 4

Equitable proceedings, institution of as constituting abuse of process, § 7[b]

Equity, filing of action alone or together with initial process or pleading as abuse of process, § 7[b]

Execution sale of judgment debtors' assets, § 5[b]

Extortion of money, allegation of attempt, § 5

Filing of action alone or together with initial process or pleading, as abuse of process, § 7

Forgery of signature, request for admissions related to alleged forgery as abuse, § 9

Garnishment procedure, institution of, § 5

Harassment, issuance of process for purposes of as abuse, § 7[a]

Hotel bill, prosecution for failure to pay as abuse, § 6

Imprisonment, attempt to collect debt by as abuse, § 6

Income tax refund check, request for admissions related to cashing of as abuse, § 9

Institution of legal action by attorney as not constituting abuse of process, § 4

Interrogation at police station, issuance of grand jury subpoena for purposes of as abuse, § 8

Introduction, § 1

Judgment by confession, securing of, § 5[b]

Judgment debt, use of writ of execution to sell, § 5[b]

Lien as constituting abuse of process, §§ 5[a], 7[a]

Malice, disclosure of as affecting abuse of process action, § 5[a]

Medical malpractice suit, filing of against physician as abuse of process, § 7[a]

Money, alleged attempt to extort, § 5

Negotiable instruments, attempt by attorney to force plaintiff to part with as abuse, §§ 3, 9

Other actions constituting abuse of process, §§ 7-9

Other process as constituting abuse of process, § 9

Particular acts as constituting abuse of process, §§ 5-9

Physician, effect of filing medical malprac-

689

Reprinted with permission from Thomson Reuters/West, *American Law Reports*, 3d Ser., Vol. 97 (1980), pp. 688-689. © 1980 Thomson Reuters/West.

Following the subject index, you will see a list of the jurisdictions from which authority is cited within the Annotation. The first part of the Annotation will set out the scope of coverage, list Annotations on related subjects, and summarize the law on the topic.

FIGURE 3.16   A.L.R. ANNOTATION

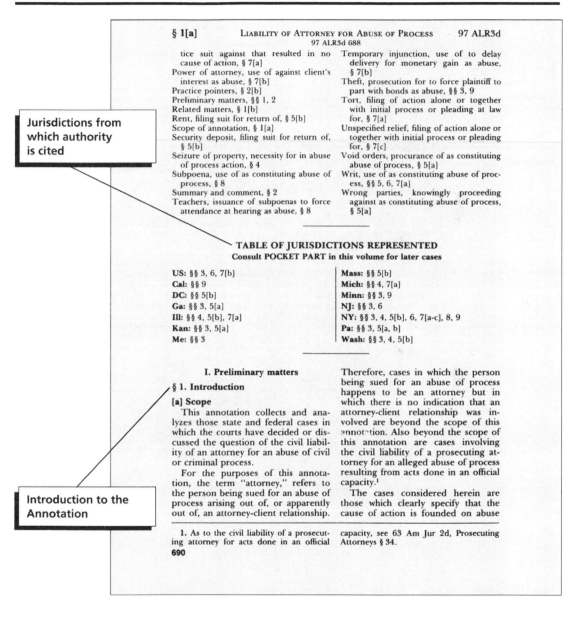

§ 1[a]   LIABILITY OF ATTORNEY FOR ABUSE OF PROCESS   97 ALR3d
                                    97 ALR3d 688

tice suit against that resulted in no cause of action, § 7[a]
Power of attorney, use of against client's interest as abuse, § 7[b]
Practice pointers, § 2[b]
Preliminary matters, §§ 1, 2
Related matters, § 1[b]
Rent, filing suit for return of, § 5[b]
Scope of annotation, § 1[a]
Security deposit, filing suit for return of, § 5[b]
Seizure of property, necessity for in abuse of process action, § 4
Subpoena, use of as constituting abuse of process, § 8
Summary and comment, § 2
Teachers, issuance of subpoenas to force attendance at hearing as abuse, § 8

Temporary injunction, use of to delay delivery for monetary gain as abuse, § 7[b]
Theft, prosecution for to force plaintiff to part with bonds as abuse, §§ 3, 9
Tort, filing of action alone or together with initial process or pleading at law for, § 7[a]
Unspecified relief, filing of action alone or together with initial process or pleading for, § 7[c]
Void orders, procurance of as constituting abuse of process, § 5[a]
Writ, use of as constituting abuse of process, §§ 5, 6, 7[a]
Wrong parties, knowingly proceeding against as constituting abuse of process, § 5[a]

Jurisdictions from which authority is cited

TABLE OF JURISDICTIONS REPRESENTED
Consult POCKET PART in this volume for later cases

US: §§ 3, 6, 7[b]
Cal: §§ 9
DC: §§ 5[b]
Ga: §§ 3, 5[a]
Ill: §§ 4, 5[b], 7[a]
Kan: §§ 3, 5[a]
Me: §§ 3

Mass: §§ 5[b]
Mich: §§ 4, 7[a]
Minn: §§ 3, 9
NJ: §§ 3, 6
NY: §§ 3, 4, 5[b], 6, 7[a-c], 8, 9
Pa: §§ 3, 5[a, b]
Wash: §§ 3, 4, 5[b]

I. Preliminary matters

§ 1. Introduction

[a] Scope

This annotation collects and analyzes those state and federal cases in which the courts have decided or discussed the question of the civil liability of an attorney for an abuse of civil or criminal process.

For the purposes of this annotation, the term "attorney," refers to the person being sued for an abuse of process arising out of, or apparently out of, an attorney-client relationship.

Therefore, cases in which the person being sued for an abuse of process happens to be an attorney but in which there is no indication that an attorney-client relationship was involved are beyond the scope of this annotation. Also beyond the scope of this annotation are cases involving the civil liability of a prosecuting attorney for an alleged abuse of process resulting from acts done in an official capacity.[1]

The cases considered herein are those which clearly specify that the cause of action is founded on abuse

Introduction to the Annotation

1. As to the civil liability of a prosecuting attorney for acts done in an official

capacity, see 63 Am Jur 2d, Prosecuting Attorneys § 34.

690

FIGURE 3.16   A.L.R. ANNOTATION *(Continued)*

Summary of the law on this topic

Related A.L.R. Annotations

97 ALR3d   LIABILITY OF ATTORNEY FOR ABUSE OF PROCESS
                            97 ALR3d 688

of process, as distinguished from those which, although involving alleged wrongful conduct similar to that found in an action for abuse of process, do not state that the action is based on that tort.

Thus, beyond the scope of this annotation is the liability of an attorney for wrongful execution or attachment of property unless the cause of action is specified to be that for an abuse of process.[2]

[b] Related matters

Institution of confessed judgment proceedings as ground of action for abuse of process or malicious prosecution. 87 ALR3d 554.

Action for breach of contract as basis of action for malicious prosecution or abuse of process. 87 ALR3d 580.

Civil liability of judicial officer for malicious prosecution or abuse of process. 64 ALR3d 1251.

What constitutes malice sufficient to justify an award of punitive damages in action for wrongful attachment or garnishment. 61 ALR3d 984.

Liability of attorney acting for client, for false imprisonment or malicious prosecution of third party. 27 ALR3d 1113.

Use of criminal process to collect debt as abuse of process. 27 ALR3d 1202.

What statute of limitations governs action for malicious use of process or abuse of process, in the absence of an express provision for such tort. 10 ALR3d 533.

When statute of limitations begins to run against action for abuse of process. 1 ALR3d 953.

§ 2. Summary and comment

[a] Generally

It has been generally stated that an abuse of legal process consists of the malicious misuse or misapplication of regularly issued civil or criminal process to accomplish some purpose not warranted or commanded by the writ.[3] The Restatement of Torts 2d § 682 similarly provides that one who uses legal process, either civil or criminal, against another person primarily to accomplish a purpose for which it was not designed is liable to the other for harm caused by the abuse of process.

The question whether an attorney, by virtue of the attorney-client relationship, enjoys exemption from civil liability for abuse of process, similar to that of a judicial officer, has arisen in some cases, and it has been held that an attorney may be held liable in an action for damages for abuse of process where the acts complained of are his own personal acts, or the acts of others wholly instigated and carried on by him.[4] However, courts have held that the mere institution of a legal action by an attorney does not constitute an abuse of process, absent other circumstances.[5]

Turning to particular allegations against attorneys in actions for abuse of process, courts have reached opposite results, under varying factual circumstances, in determining whether a cause of action was stated or existed

---

2. As to the liability of an attorney for wrongful attachment or execution, see 7 Am Jur 2d, Attorneys at Law § 197.

3. 1 Am Jur 2d, Abuse of Process § 1.
As to the distinction between an abuse of process and an action for malicious

prosecution, malicious use of process, or false imprisonment, see generally 1 Am Jur 2d, Abuse of Process §§ 2, 3.

4. § 3, infra.

5. § 4, infra.

691

FIGURE 3.16   A.L.R. ANNOTATION *(Continued)*

§ 2[a]   LIABILITY OF ATTORNEY FOR ABUSE OF PROCESS   97 ALR3d
                        97 ALR3d 688

against an attorney by virtue of the use of civil process to collect a debt for a client.[6] Some courts have also held that where it was alleged that an attorney used criminal process as a means of collecting a debt due a client, a cause of action against the attorney for abuse of process was stated.[7]

In cases involving the filing of a tort action by an attorney, where no acts were alleged against the attorney involving the improper use of process, it has been held that a cause of action against the attorney was not stated.[8] Likewise, in a case in which no facts were stated in a complaint for abuse of process against an attorney showing that he was the active and procuring cause of the institution by his client of civil actions, whose nature was not specified in the court's opinion, or showing interference with the plaintiff's personal property, the court held that no cause of action for abuse of process was stated.[9] However, where a complaint alleged that an attorney did not act in a bona fide effort to protect the interest of a client in filing equitable actions, but rather acted in the interest of other clients to prevent the plaintiff from delivering shares of stock before a contractual deadline, the court held that a cause of action for abuse of process against the attorney was stated.[10]

It has been held or recognized that a cause of action was stated or found to exist against an attorney where the attorney was alleged to have used subpoenas for other than their legitimate purpose.[11] However, in cases involving the use of other types of process, the courts, under the particular facts, found that the complaints failed to state a cause of action against the attorney.[12]

[b] Practice pointers

Counsel representing a plaintiff in an action for abuse of process against an attorney should be aware that the same facts which give rise to the action may also establish an action for malicious prosecution, false arrest, or false imprisonment, and that the causes may be joined in the same action, but not in the same count.[13] The attorney should, however, keep in mind that an action for abuse of process is based on the improper use of the process after it has been issued, while malicious prosecution is based on the wrongful intent or malice that caused the process to be issued initially.[14]

Counsel should note that an action for abuse of process has generally been held to accrue, and the statute of limitations to commence to run, from the termination of the acts which constitute the abuse complained of and not from the completion of the action in which the process issued.[15] Actions for abuse of process are generally governed by the statute of limitations applicable to actions for injury to the person. However, in a jurisdiction in which one statute governed injury to the person

Practice pointers

---

6. § 5[a], [b], infra.

7. § 6, infra.

8. § 7[a], infra.

9. § 7[c], infra.

10. § 7[b], infra.

11. § 8, infra.

692

12. § 9, infra.

13. As to pleading in actions for abuse of process, see generally 1 Am Jur 2d, Abuse of Process § 21.

14. 1 Am Jur 2d, Abuse of Process § 2.

15. 1 Am Jur 2d, Abuse of Process § 24.

After the introductory material, the Annotation will explain the law on the topic in greater detail, summarize key cases, and provide citations to additional cases on the topic.

FIGURE 3.17   A.L.R. ANNOTATION

97 ALR3d   LIABILITY OF ATTORNEY FOR ABUSE OF PROCESS   § 3
97 ALR3d 688

and another statute governed "injuries to the rights of others," the court held that an action for abuse of process was controlled by the latter statute.[16]

II. General principles

§ 3. Rule that attorney may be liable for abuse of process

[The fo]llowing cases support the [rule that] an attorney may be held [liable in] a civil action for abuse of [process w]here the acts complained of [are his o]wn personal acts, or the acts of others instigated and carried on by him.

US—For federal cases involving state law, see state headings infra.

Ga—Walker v Kyser (1967) 115 Ga App 314, 154 SE2d 457 (by implication).

Kan—Little v Sowers (1949) 167 Kan 72, 204 P2d 605.

Me—Lambert v Breton (1929) 127 Me 510, 144 A 864 (recognizing rule).

Minn—Hoppe v Klapperich (1937) 224 Minn 224, 28 NW2d 780, 173 ALR 819.

NJ—Ash v Cohen (1937) 119 NJL 54, 194 A 174.

Voytko v Ramada Inn of Atlantic City (1978, DC NJ) 445 F Supp 315 (by implication; applying New Jersey law).

NY—Board of Education v Farmingdale Classroom Teachers Asso. (1975) 38 NY2d 397, 380 NYS2d 635, 343 NE2d 278 (by implication).

Dishaw v Wadleigh (1897) 15 App Div 205, 44 NYS 207.

Cote v Knickerbocker Ice Co. (1936) 160 Misc 658, 290 NYS 483 (recognizing rule); Rothbard v Ringler (1947, Sup) 77 NYS2d 351 (by

implication); Weiss v Hunna (1963, CA2 NY) 312 F2d 711, cert den 374 US 853, 10 L Ed 2d 1073, 83 S Ct 1920, reh den 375 US 874, 11 L Ed 2d 104, 84 S Ct 37 (by implication; applying New York law).

Pa—Haggerty v Moyerman (1936) 321 Pa 555, 184 A 654 (by implication).

Adelman v Rosenbaum (1938) 133 Pa Super 386, 3 A2d 15; Sachs [v] (1963, ED Pa) 216 F Supp [4] implication; applying Pennsy[lvania] law).

Wash—Fite v Lee (1974) 11 [Wash] App 21, 521 P2d 964, 97 ALR3d 678, (by implication).

An attorney is personally liable to a third party if he maliciously participates with others in an abuse of process, or if he maliciously encourages and induces another to act as his instrumentality in committing an act constituting an abuse of process, the court held in Hoppe v Klapperich (1947) 224 **Minn** 224, 28 NW2d 780, 173 ALR 819. The court reversed the order of the trial court which had sustained the demurrers of an attorney and other defendants in a proceeding for abuse of process and malicious prosecution. The plaintiff had alleged, as to the cause of action for abuse of process, that it was the intent of the defendants, an attorney, his client, a sheriff, and a municipal judge, to force her to part with certain bonds, negotiable instruments, and other valuable papers by threatening her with arrest and prosecution on a criminal charge of theft of a watch. The plaintiff's subsequent arrest and confinement on the charge of theft were alleged to constitute a continuing abuse of process. The court noted that in the performance

16. See 7 Am Jur Proof of Facts 2d, Abuse of Process—Debt Collection § 4.

693

> Citations to cases from multiple jurisdictions

> Discussion of the law with a more detailed case summary

To update, check the pocket part. The pocket part is organized by the page numbers of the Annotations, not by their titles.

FIGURE 3.18 POCKET PART ACCOMPANYING AN A.L.R. VOLUME

97 A.L.R.3d 627 ALR3d

of plaintiff's injury (or indeed had any connection whatsoever with it). Garner v. Raven Industries, Inc., 732 F.2d 112 (**10th Cir.** 1984) (applying New Mexico law).

A motion by the plaintiff seeking a declaration that failure by the defendant manufacturer of a helicopter to comply with maintenance regulations constituted negligence per se was properly denied, since the purpose of such regulations was not to protect persons such as the plaintiff from loss of helicopters in crashes, but rather, was to ensure safety of persons both in the aircraft and on the ground. Erickson Air-Crane Co. v United Technologies Corp. (1987) 87 **Or App** 577, 743 P2d 747, review den 304 Or 680, 748 P2d 142.

Summary judgment was granted in favor of airline in strict liability and negligence action that was brought by passenger who, upon standing up from her seat to deplane American Airlines Boeing 727-200 operated by airline, hit her head on overhead bin compartment located over her seat and allegedly herniated several intervertebral discs. Civil engineer was not qualified to give expert testimony on behalf of plaintiff with regard to design of aircraft's overhead bin compartments, where civil engineer had no prior experience in design, manufacturing, or operation of aircraft and had never before analyzed ergonomics of seating and overhead compartment arrangements in aircraft interiors. Even if witness were qualified, his testimony that aircraft's overhead bin compartments were defectively designed because they were too rigid and that passengers sitting in seat located in emergency exit aisle, where plaintiff sat, have false sense of spaciousness such that airline should have warned passengers about low ceiling under bins was without scientific basis and was inadmissible. Former airline flight attendant was not qualified to render expert opinion as to whether airline should have warned passengers about existence of overhead bin compartments, even though flight attendant may have been qualified to state lay opinions, where flight attendant had no experience in design, manufacturing, or operation of aircraft that would have allowed him to determine what, if any, warning practices would have been appropriate. Flight attendant's testimony that placement of padding in overhead bin compartments would have minimized danger of serious injury thus amounted to simple speculation and was not admissible. Given fact that there was no competent scientific evidence of compartment or seating arrangement in question nor of how coach cabins and overhead bin compartments should be designed and that hazard posed to plaintiff by overhead bin

92

compartment was apparent and obvious, plaintiff's case was insufficient to survive airline's motion for summary judgment as to plaintiff's design defect and failure to warn claims. Silva v. American Airlines, Inc., 960 F. Supp. 528 (**D.P.R.** 1997) (applying Puerto Rico law).

In action brought by and on behalf of survivors of Army pilot who was killed in crash of Army Cobra AH-1 helicopter, in which it was alleged that civilian company which had at one time been responsible for maintenance of helicopter was negligent in using improper grease, using improper maintenance procedure, and failing to supply adequate information to Army of swashplate (bearing container) malfunction that occurred in helicopter prior to swashplate malfunction that occurred when helicopter crashed, judgment on jury verdict in favor of maintenance company was affirmed on appeal. Appellate court noted that Army report of accident made no final conclusions or recommendations regarding accident. Court further noted that in addition to developing evidence to rebut allegations of negligence, maintenance company presented evidence that product defect, and not improper maintenance, caused accident. Court stated that in its review of all evidence presented at trial, it could not find that verdict was s‹overwhelming weight of evide‹clearly wrong and unjust. Beave‹Worldwide Aircraft Services, In‹**App Amarillo**) 821 SW2d 669.

> **The pocket part is organized by page number.**

97 A.L.R.3d 688

Civil liability of attorney for abuse of process

Research References
A.L.R. Library

Necessity and permissibility of raising claim for abuse of process by reply or counterclaim in same proceeding in which abuse occurred—state cases, 82 A.L.R.4th 1115

Attorney's liability, to one other than immediate client, for negligence in connection with legal duties, 61 A.L.R.4th 615

Liability of attorney, acting for client, for malicious prosecution, 46 A.L.R.4th 249

Initiating, or threatening to initiate, criminal prosecution as ground for disciplining counsel, 42 A.L.R.4th 1000

Abuse of process action based on misuse of discovery or deposition procedures after commencement of civil action without seizure of person or property, 33 A.L.R.4th 650

For latest cases, call the toll free number appearing on the cover of this supplement.

FIGURE 3.18   POCKET PART ACCOMPANYING AN A.L.R. VOLUME *(Continued)*

SUPPLEMENT   97 A.L.R.3d 688

Authority of United States District Court, under 28 U.S.C.A. § 1651(a), to enjoin, sua sponte, a party from filing further papers in support of frivolous claim, 53 A.L.R. Fed. 651

Trial Strategy

Physicians' countersuits, 35 Am. Jur. Trials 225

Model Codes and Restatements

Restatement (Third) of the Law Governing Lawyers § 6 (2000), Judicial Remedies Available to a Client or Nonclient for Lawyer Wrongs.

Restatement (Third) of the Law Governing Lawyers § 56 (2000), Liability to a Client or Nonclient Under General Law.

I. PRELIMINARY MATTERS

§ 1[b] Introduction—Related matters

Supplemental related annotations, if any, are now located under the Research Reference heading of this annotation.

§ 2[a] Summary and comment—Generally

Allegations that attorneys obtained default judgment based on error, and demanded payment of fee for services rendered prior to agreeing to enter satisfaction of judgment to correct error, did not state cause of action for abuse of process. Varela v Investors Ins. Holding Corp. (1992, 2d Dept) 185 App Div 2d 309, 586 **NYS2d** 272.

II. GENERAL PRINCIPLES

§ 3 Rule that attorney may be liable for abuse of process

[Newer cases are summarized.] v Beck (1987) 204 **Conn** 490, 7[a].

v Auty (1989) 232 **NJ Super** 541, 557 A2d 1030, § 5[a].

Under New York law, elements for claim of abuse of process are (1) regularly issued process (civil or criminal), (2) an intent to do harm without excuse or justification, and (3) use of the process in a perverted manner to obtain a collateral objective. 3H Enterprises, Inc. v. Dwyre, 182 F. Supp. 2d 249 (**N.D. N.Y.** 2001) (applying New York law).

Under New York law, claim for abuse of process can be stated against attorney who prepares or causes abused process to be issued in bad faith and for purpose of gaining collateral advantage. Reisner v. Stoller, 51 F. Supp. 2d 430, R.I.C.O. Bus. Disp. Guide (CCH) ¶ 9760 (**S.D.N.Y.** 1999) (applying New York law).

Attorney is liable if he or she causes irregular process to be issued which occasions loss to party against whom it is enforced. ERA Realty

Co. v RBS Properties (1992, 2d Dept) 185 App Div 2d 871, 586 **NYS2d** 831.

Attorney who knowingly prosecutes a groundless action to accomplish a malicious purpose may be held accountable under the Dragonetti Act. 42 Pa. C.S.A. § 8351. Electronic Laboratory Supply Co. v. Cullen, 712 A.2d 304 (**Pa. Super. Ct.** 1998).

§ 4 Rule that mere institution of legal action by attorney does not constitute abuse of process

The courts in the following cases held or recognized that the plaintiff failed to state a cause of action against an attorney for an abuse of process by alleging that the attorney instituted a legal action against the plaintiff on behalf of the attorney's client, even where it was alleged that this was done with an improper purpose or motive.

Ala—Shoney's, Inc. v. Barnett, 773 So. 2d 1015 (Ala. Civ. App. 1999), cert. denied, (Aug. 27, 1999).

While simply bringing lawsuit may not be abuse of process under Puerto Rico law, obtaining search and arrest warrants by means of false testimony is proper basis for claim of abuse of process, at least for pleading purposes. Gonzalez Rucci v. U.S. I.N.S., 405 F.3d 45 (**1st Cir.** 2005).

Abuse of process contemplates some overt act done in addition to the initiating of the suit; thus, the mere filing or maintenance of a lawsuit, even for an improper purpose, is not a proper basis for an abuse of process action. Meidinger v. Koniag, Inc., 31 P.3d 77 (**Alaska** 2001).

The essence of the tort of abuse of process is the use of a legal proceeding primarily to accomplish a purpose that the proceeding was not designed to achieve. Yadon v. Lowry, 126 P.3d 332 (**Colo. Ct. App.** 2005).

Under Iowa law, a party sued for abuse of process is not liable if he or she has done no more than carry the process to its authorized conclusion, even with bad intentions. Jensen v. Barlas, 438 F. Supp. 2d 988 (**N.D. Iowa** 2006) (applying Iowa law).

See Tedards v Auty (1989) 232 **NJ Super** 541, 557 A2d 1030, § 5[a].

Trial court erred in denying summary judgment motion of defendant law firm in abuse of process action by former husband of firm's dissolution client, where fact that firm chose legally insufficient method of recovering fees ordered to be paid by husband (for techinical reason that submitted order did not expressly compel clerk to enter judgment on interim fee award) did not support conclusion that firm

93

For latest cases, call the toll free number appearing on the cover of this supplement.

To research in the *Restatement (Second) of Torts*, the first step is locating pertinent Restatement sections using either the subject index or the table of contents. This example shows a portion of the table of contents.

FIGURE 3.19   TABLE OF CONTENTS, *RESTATEMENT (SECOND) OF TORTS*

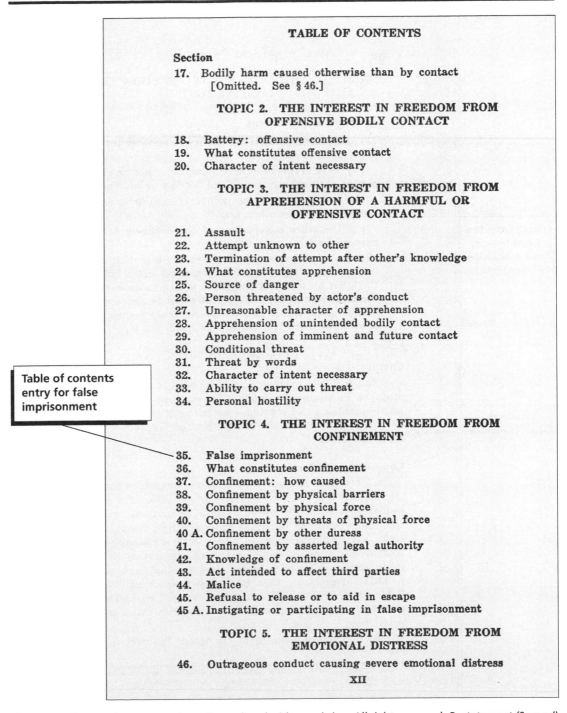

TABLE OF CONTENTS

Section
17. Bodily harm caused otherwise than by contact
    [Omitted. See § 46.]

TOPIC 2. THE INTEREST IN FREEDOM FROM
OFFENSIVE BODILY CONTACT

18. Battery: offensive contact
19. What constitutes offensive contact
20. Character of intent necessary

TOPIC 3. THE INTEREST IN FREEDOM FROM
APPREHENSION OF A HARMFUL OR
OFFENSIVE CONTACT

21. Assault
22. Attempt unknown to other
23. Termination of attempt after other's knowledge
24. What constitutes apprehension
25. Source of danger
26. Person threatened by actor's conduct
27. Unreasonable character of apprehension
28. Apprehension of unintended bodily contact
29. Apprehension of imminent and future contact
30. Conditional threat
31. Threat by words
32. Character of intent necessary
33. Ability to carry out threat
34. Personal hostility

TOPIC 4. THE INTEREST IN FREEDOM FROM
CONFINEMENT

35. False imprisonment
36. What constitutes confinement
37. Confinement: how caused
38. Confinement by physical barriers
39. Confinement by physical force
40. Confinement by threats of physical force
40 A. Confinement by other duress
41. Confinement by asserted legal authority
42. Knowledge of confinement
43. Act intended to affect third parties
44. Malice
45. Refusal to release or to aid in escape
45 A. Instigating or participating in false imprisonment

TOPIC 5. THE INTEREST IN FREEDOM FROM
EMOTIONAL DISTRESS

46. Outrageous conduct causing severe emotional distress

XII

> Table of contents entry for false imprisonment

The Restatement sections are organized numerically. Comments follow the Restatement section. If Illustrations are provided, they will follow the appropriate Comment. The Illustrations demonstrate how the Restatement section is intended to apply to hypothetical situations.

FIGURE 3.20 *RESTATEMENT (SECOND) OF TORTS § 35*

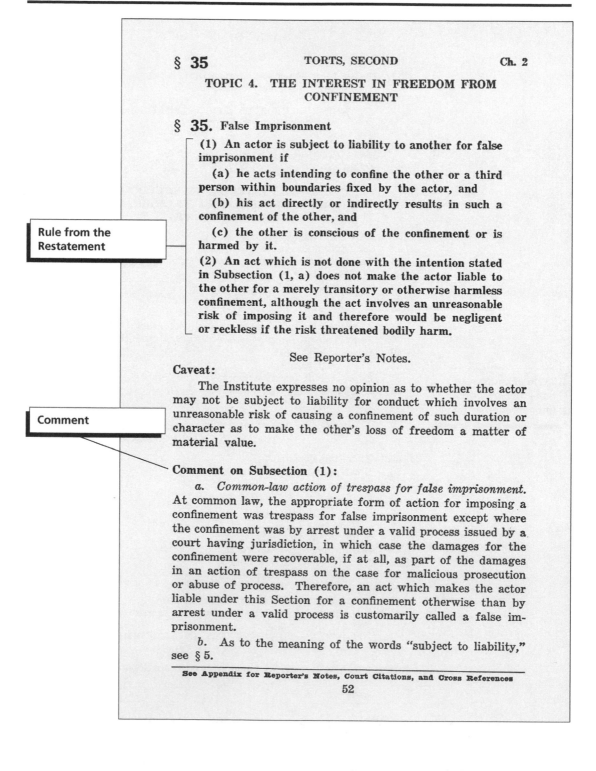

§ 35   TORTS, SECOND   Ch. 2

TOPIC 4. THE INTEREST IN FREEDOM FROM CONFINEMENT

§ 35. False Imprisonment

Rule from the Restatement

(1) An actor is subject to liability to another for false imprisonment if

(a) he acts intending to confine the other or a third person within boundaries fixed by the actor, and

(b) his act directly or indirectly results in such a confinement of the other, and

(c) the other is conscious of the confinement or is harmed by it.

(2) An act which is not done with the intention stated in Subsection (1, a) does not make the actor liable to the other for a merely transitory or otherwise harmless confinement, although the act involves an unreasonable risk of imposing it and therefore would be negligent or reckless if the risk threatened bodily harm.

See Reporter's Notes.

Caveat:

The Institute expresses no opinion as to whether the actor may not be subject to liability for conduct which involves an unreasonable risk of causing a confinement of such duration or character as to make the other's loss of freedom a matter of material value.

Comment

Comment on Subsection (1):

a. *Common-law action of trespass for false imprisonment.* At common law, the appropriate form of action for imposing a confinement was trespass for false imprisonment except where the confinement was by arrest under a valid process issued by a court having jurisdiction, in which case the damages for the confinement were recoverable, if at all, as part of the damages in an action of trespass on the case for malicious prosecution or abuse of process. Therefore, an act which makes the actor liable under this Section for a confinement otherwise than by arrest under a valid process is customarily called a false imprisonment.

b. As to the meaning of the words "subject to liability," see § 5.

See Appendix for Reporter's Notes, Court Citations, and Cross References

52

FIGURE 3.20 *RESTATEMENT (SECOND) OF TORTS § 35 (Continued)*

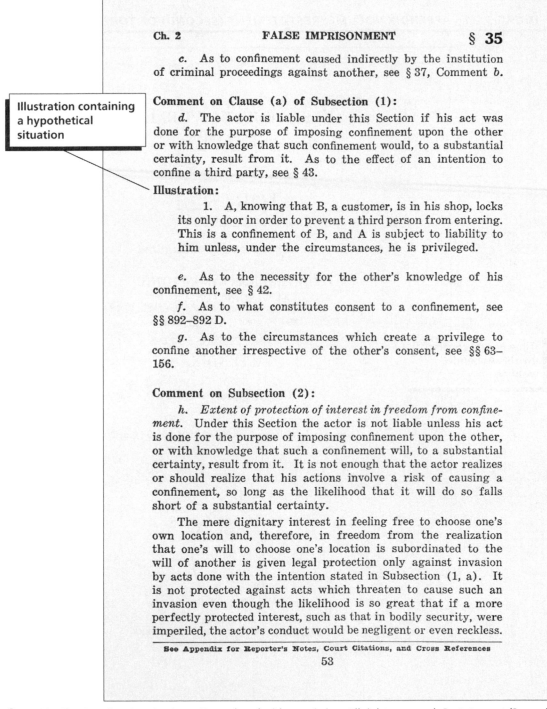

Illustration containing a hypothetical situation

Ch. 2   FALSE IMPRISONMENT   § 35

c. As to confinement caused indirectly by the institution of criminal proceedings against another, see § 37, Comment *b.*

Comment on Clause (a) of Subsection (1):

d. The actor is liable under this Section if his act was done for the purpose of imposing confinement upon the other or with knowledge that such confinement would, to a substantial certainty, result from it. As to the effect of an intention to confine a third party, see § 43.

Illustration:

    1. A, knowing that B, a customer, is in his shop, locks its only door in order to prevent a third person from entering. This is a confinement of B, and A is subject to liability to him unless, under the circumstances, he is privileged.

e. As to the necessity for the other's knowledge of his confinement, see § 42.

f. As to what constitutes consent to a confinement, see §§ 892–892 D.

g. As to the circumstances which create a privilege to confine another irrespective of the other's consent, see §§ 63–156.

Comment on Subsection (2):

h. Extent of protection of interest in freedom from confinement. Under this Section the actor is not liable unless his act is done for the purpose of imposing confinement upon the other, or with knowledge that such a confinement will, to a substantial certainty, result from it. It is not enough that the actor realizes or should realize that his actions involve a risk of causing a confinement, so long as the likelihood that it will do so falls short of a substantial certainty.

The mere dignitary interest in feeling free to choose one's own location and, therefore, in freedom from the realization that one's will to choose one's location is subordinated to the will of another is given legal protection only against invasion by acts done with the intention stated in Subsection (1, a). It is not protected against acts which threaten to cause such an invasion even though the likelihood is so great that if a more perfectly protected interest, such as that in bodily security, were imperiled, the actor's conduct would be negligent or even reckless.

See Appendix for Reporter's Notes, Court Citations, and Cross References

53

To locate cases interpreting the Restatement section, use the Appendix volume or volumes. Each volume is organized by section number and covers a specific period of time.

FIGURE 3.21   APPENDIX VOLUME, *RESTATEMENT (SECOND) OF TORTS*

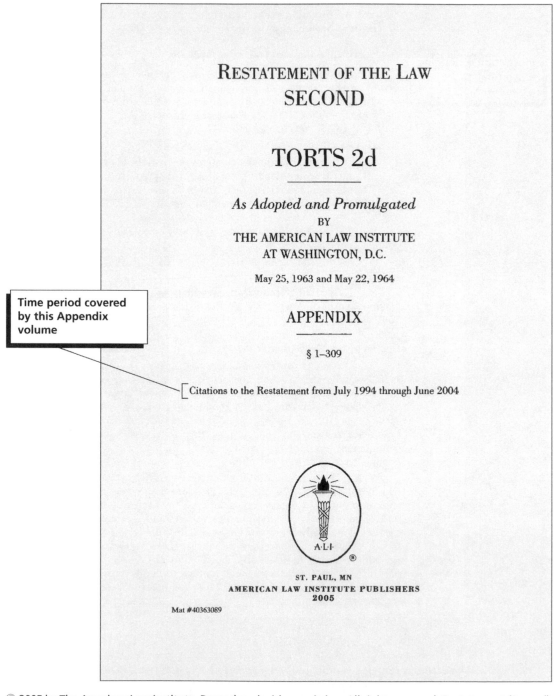

RESTATEMENT OF THE LAW
SECOND

TORTS 2d
————

As Adopted and Promulgated
BY
THE AMERICAN LAW INSTITUTE
AT WASHINGTON, D.C.

May 25, 1963 and May 22, 1964

————

APPENDIX
————

§ 1–309

Time period covered by this Appendix volume

Citations to the Restatement from July 1994 through June 2004

ST. PAUL, MN
AMERICAN LAW INSTITUTE PUBLISHERS
2005

Mat #40363089

The Appendix will list cases interpreting the Restatement section. The latest volume of the Appendix is updated with a pocket part containing references to the most current cases.

FIGURE 3.22 APPENDIX VOLUME, *RESTATEMENT (SECOND) OF TORTS*

Ch. 2   CITATIONS TO RESTATEMENT SECOND   § 35

TOPIC 4. THE INTEREST IN FREEDOM FROM CONFINEMENT

C.A.1, 1995. §§ 35–45A, constituting all of Ch. 2, Topic 4, cit. in sup. and adopted. Puerto Rican resident was arrested by federal agents who mistakenly believed that she was the subject of a 1975 arrest warrant; following the dismissal of all proceedings against her, she sued the United States for false arrest. Affirming the district court's grant of summary judgment for the United States, this court held that the United States was not liable for the false arrest of plaintiff, since the name in the warrant, together with information contained in the arrest packet, provided ample basis for the arresting agents to form an objectively reasonable belief that plaintiff was the person named in the warrant. The court also held that the conduct of the federal agent responsible for instigating the errant arrest was conditionally privileged, since the arrestee was sufficiently named in the warrant and the agent reasonably believed that plaintiff was the subject of the warrant. Rodriguez v. U.S., 54 F.3d 41, 45.

Cases interpreting § 35

§ 35. False Imprisonment

C.A.1, 1995. Cit. in ftn. Two men who were arrested and acquitted of selling cocaine sued police officers of Puerto Rico and their confidential informants for constitutional violations, alleging that defendants falsely identified them as sellers. District court held that the false-arrest claims were barred by the one-year statute of limitations and that the malicious-prosecution claims were not actionable under 42 U.S.C. § 1983. This court vacated and remanded, holding that, for purposes of determining the appropriate accrual rule, both the Fourth and Fourteenth Amendment claims more closely resembled the common law tort of malicious prosecution. Consequently, plaintiffs' § 1983 claims did not accrue until their respective criminal prosecutions ended in acquittals. Calero-Colon v. Betancourt-Lebron, 68 F.3d 1, 3.

C.A.1, 2000. Cit. in headnote, quot. in disc. After being detained by store employees who accused them of shoplifting on a prior occasion, two children and their mother sued the store for false imprisonment. District court entered judgment on jury verdict awarding plaintiffs damages. This court affirmed, holding, inter alia, that plaintiffs stated a viable false-imprisonment claim, because a reasonable jury could conclude that the store's employees intended to confine plaintiffs within boundaries fixed by the store, that the store's acts resulted in such confinement, and that plaintiffs were conscious of the confinement. Employees' direction to plaintiffs, their reference to the police, and their continued presence were enough to induce reasonable people to believe either that they would be restrained physically if they sought to leave, or that the store was claiming lawful authority to confine them until the police arrived, or both. McCann v. Wal-Mart Stores, Inc., 210 F.3d 51, 51, 53.

C.A.7, 2003. Quot. in sup. African-American store employee who was fired for allegedly stealing from a coemployee sued store for federal civil-rights violations and false imprisonment under Indiana law, alleging that store representatives locked her in her manager's office for several minutes while they investigated the theft charges. District court granted store summary judgment. This court affirmed, holding, inter alia, that plaintiff did not establish a claim of false imprisonment under Indiana law, because her several-minute confinement was accidental, and store established justification for the brief detention. No one told plaintiff that she could not leave, and store provided a reasonable explanation for having left her alone in the office: so that she could draft her written statement without distraction. Adams v. Wal-Mart Stores, Inc., 324 F.3d 935, 941.

C.A.9, 2003. Com. (a) quot. in sup. California resident who had been director of Australian corporation was extradited to Australia for criminal trial. After Australian government dropped fraud charges and jury acquitted extraditee on other charge, he sued two instrumentalities and two employees of Australian government for malicious prosecution, abuse of process, and false imprisonment. District court granted motion to dismiss for employees, but denied motion as to instrumentalities. This court reversed in part, holding that plaintiff's claims of malicious prosecution and abuse of process were barred by Foreign Sovereign Immunities Act, since plaintiff could not overcome sovereign immu-

Cit.–cited; fol.–followed; quot.–quoted; sup.–support.
A complete list of abbreviations precedes page 1.

119

F. CHECKLIST FOR SECONDARY SOURCE RESEARCH

1. LEGAL ENCYCLOPEDIAS

❑ Use legal encyclopedias for very general background information and limited citations to primary authority, but not for in-depth analysis of a topic.

❑ Use Am. Jur. 2d or C.J.S. for a general overview; look for a state encyclopedia for an overview of the law in an individual state.

❑ Locate material in a print encyclopedia by (1) using the subject index or table of contents; (2) locating relevant sections in the main subject volumes; and (3) updating with the pocket part.

❑ Locate material in legal encyclopedias in LexisNexis and Westlaw by executing word searches in the databases for individual publications or by viewing the table of contents.

2. TREATISES

❑ Use treatises for an in-depth discussion and some analysis of an area of law and for citations to primary authority.

❑ Locate treatises in print through the online catalog or by asking a reference librarian for a recommendation; locate material within a treatise by (1) using the subject index or table of contents; (2) locating relevant sections within the main text; and (3) updating with the pocket part.

❑ Locate material in treatises in LexisNexis and Westlaw by executing word searches in the databases for individual publications, multiple secondary sources, specific subject areas, or individual jurisdictions. View the table of contents for individual publications if available.

3. LEGAL PERIODICALS

❑ Use legal periodicals for background information, citations to primary authority, in-depth analysis of a narrow topic, or information on a conflict in the law or an undeveloped area of the law.

❑ Locate citations to periodical articles with the *Index to Legal Periodicals* (ILP) or LegalTrac periodical indices; execute a search to obtain a list of citations. Full text of some articles is available through these services.

❑ Locate citations to, or the full text of, legal periodicals in LexisNexis and Westlaw by searching in the databases for multiple or individual publications.

❑ Locate the full text of legal periodicals in .pdf format using HeinOnline.

❑ Selected periodicals may be available on the Internet.

4. *AMERICAN LAW REPORTS*

❐ Use A.L.R. Annotations for an overview of an area of law and citations to primary authority (especially to locate persuasive authority from other jurisdictions), but not for in-depth analysis of a topic.

❐ Use A.L.R.3d, A.L.R.4th, A.L.R.5th, A.L.R.6th, A.L.R. Fed., and A.L.R. Fed. 2d; avoid A.L.R. and A.L.R.2d as generally out-of-date sources.

❐ Locate material within A.L.R. in print by (1) using the A.L.R. Index; (2) locating relevant Annotations in the main volumes; and (3) updating with the pocket part.

❐ Locate A.L.R. Annotations in Westlaw by executing word searches in the ALR database.

5. RESTATEMENTS

❐ Use Restatements for research into common-law subjects and to locate mandatory and persuasive authority from jurisdictions that have adopted a Restatement.

❐ Locate Restatements in print through the online catalog.

❐ Locate information within a print Restatement by (1) using the subject index or table of contents to identify relevant sections within the Restatement volumes; (2) using the noncumulative Appendix volumes to find pertinent case summaries; and (3) using the pocket part in the latest Appendix volume to locate the most recent cases.

❐ Locate Restatements in LexisNexis and Westlaw by executing word searches or viewing the table of contents.

   ▪ In LexisNexis, Restatement rules and case annotations are in separate databases.

   ▪ In Westlaw, Restatement rules and case annotations are combined; case annotations will follow individual Restatement rules.

6. UNIFORM LAWS AND MODEL ACTS

❐ Use uniform laws and model acts to interpret a law adopted by a legislature and to locate persuasive authority from other jurisdictions that have adopted the law.

❐ Locate uniform laws and model acts in print using *Uniform Laws Annotated, Master Edition* (ULA).

❐ Locate information in the ULA set by (1) using the *Directory of Uniform Acts and Codes: Tables and Index* to search by subject, by the name of the law, or by adopting jurisdiction; (2) locating relevant provisions in the main volumes; and (3) updating with the pocket part.

❐ Locate selected uniform laws and model acts in LexisNexis and Westlaw by executing word searches in the appropriate database or viewing the table of contents.

CASE RESEARCH

A. Introduction to cases

B. Researching cases in print

C. Researching cases electronically

D. Citing cases

E. Sample pages for researching cases using a print digest

F. Checklist for case research

A. INTRODUCTION TO CASES

1. THE STRUCTURE OF THE COURT SYSTEM

The United States has more than fifty separate court systems, including the federal system, the fifty state systems, and the District of Columbia system. You may recall from Chapter 1 that there are three levels of courts in the federal system: the United States District Courts (the trial courts), the United States Courts of Appeals (the intermediate appellate courts), and the United States Supreme Court (the court of last resort). Most state court systems are structured the same way as the federal court system.

Judges from any of these courts can issue written decisions, and their decisions are one source of legal rules. This chapter focuses on where these decisions are published and how they are indexed.

2. CASE REPORTERS

Court opinions, or cases, are published in books called reporters. Reporters are sets of books collecting cases in chronological order. Many sets of reporters are limited to opinions from a single jurisdiction or level of court. Thus, for example, federal reporters contain opinions from federal courts, and state reporters contain opinions from state courts. In addition, each set of reporters may be subdivided into different series covering different time periods.

A reporter published under government authority is known as an official reporter.[1] Reporters published by commercial publishers are called unofficial reporters. Because these two types of reporters exist, the same opinion may be published in more than one reporter. The text of the opinion should be exactly the same in an official and an unofficial reporter; the only difference is that the former is published by the government, and the latter is not. When a case appears in more than one reporter, it is described as having parallel citations. This is because each set of reporters will have its own citation for the case.

The only federal court opinions published by the government are those of the United States Supreme Court; these are published in a reporter called *United States Reports*. State governments usually publish the decisions of their highest courts, and most also publish decisions from some of their lower courts.

Perhaps the largest commercial publisher of cases is Thomson Reuters/West, formerly West Publishing Company. West has created a network of unofficial reporters called the *National Reporter System*, which comprises reporters with decisions from almost every United States jurisdiction.

West publishes United States Supreme Court decisions in the *Supreme Court Reporter*. Decisions from the United States Courts of Appeals are published in the *Federal Reporter*, and those from United States District Courts are published in the *Federal Supplement*. West also publishes some specialized reporters that contain decisions from the federal courts. For example, *Federal Rules Decisions* (F.R.D.) contains federal district court decisions interpreting the Federal Rules of Civil and Criminal Procedure, and *Federal Appendix* (Fed. Appx. or F. App'x) contains non-precedential decisions from the federal courts of appeals. (Non-precedential decisions are discussed in more detail below.)

West publishes state court decisions in what are called regional reporters. West has divided the country into seven regions. The reporter for each region collects state court decisions from all of the states within that region.

Because West publishes reporters for almost every jurisdiction in a common format with common indexing features, this chapter will focus on research using West publications. The chart in **Figure 4.1** shows where cases from the various state and federal courts can be found.

---

[1]The government may publish the reporter itself, or it may arrange for the reporter to be published by a commercial publisher. As long as the government arranges for the publication, the reporter is official, even if it is physically produced by a commercial publisher.

FIGURE 4.1 REPORTERS

COURT OR JURISDICTION	REPORTER (followed by reporter abbreviation; multiple abbreviations denote multiple series)
United States Supreme Court	*United States Reports* (U.S.)* *Supreme Court Reporter* (S. Ct.) *United States Supreme Court Reports, Lawyer's Edition* (L. Ed., L. Ed. 2d)
United States Courts of Appeals	*Federal Reporter* (F., F.2d, F.3d) *Federal Appendix* (Fed. Appx. or F. App'x)
United States District Courts	*Federal Supplement* (F. Supp., F. Supp. 2d) *Federal Rules Decisions* (F.R.D.)
Atlantic Region States (Connecticut, Delaware, District of Columbia, Maine, Maryland, New Hampshire, New Jersey, Pennsylvania, Rhode Island, Vermont)	*Atlantic Reporter* (A., A.2d)
North Eastern Region States (Illinois, Indiana, Massachusetts, New York, Ohio)	*North Eastern Reporter* (N.E., N.E.2d) New York: *New York Supplement* (N.Y.S., N.Y.S.2d) Illinois: *Illinois Decisions* (Ill. Dec.)
South Eastern Region States (Georgia, North Carolina, South Carolina, Virginia, West Virginia)	*South Eastern Reporter* (S.E., S.E.2d)
Southern Region States (Alabama, Florida, Louisiana, Mississippi)	*Southern Reporter* (So., So. 2d)
South Western Region States (Arkansas, Kentucky, Missouri, Tennessee, Texas)	*South Western Reporter* (S.W., S.W.2d, S.W.3d)
North Western Region States (Iowa, Michigan, Minnesota, Nebraska, North Dakota, South Dakota, Wisconsin)	*North Western Reporter* (N.W., N.W.2d)
Pacific Region States (Alaska, Arizona, California, Colorado, Hawaii, Idaho, Kansas, Montana, Nevada, New Mexico, Oklahoma, Oregon, Utah, Washington, Wyoming)	*Pacific Reporter* (P., P.2d, P.3d) California: *California Reporter* (Cal. Rptr., Cal. Rptr. 2d, Cal. Rptr. 3d)

*Official reporter published by the federal government.

Decisions for most states can be found in the state's official reporter, as well as in the reporters listed in **Figure 4.1**.[2]

3. THE ANATOMY OF A PUBLISHED CASE

A case published in a West reporter has five components:

1. The heading containing the parallel citation (if any) to an official reporter, the case name, the court that rendered the decision, and the date of the decision.
2. A synopsis of the decision written by case editors, not by the court.
3. One or more paragraphs summarizing the key points within the decision. These summary paragraphs are called headnotes, and they are written by case editors, not by the court.
4. The names of the attorneys who represented the parties and the judge or judges who decided the case.
5. The opinion of the court. If the decision has any concurring or dissenting opinions, these will follow immediately after the majority or plurality opinion.

Only the fifth item on this list, the opinion of the court, constitutes legal authority. All of the remaining items are editorial enhancements. These editorial enhancements are very useful for locating cases, but they are not part of the court's opinion. Therefore, you should never rely on any part of a case other than the text of the opinion itself.[3]

Figure 4.2 shows an excerpt from a case published in a West reporter.

4. UNPUBLISHED, OR NON-PRECEDENTIAL, OPINIONS

Not all court decisions are published; only those designated by the courts for publication appear in print reporters. The decisions not designated for publication are called unpublished decisions. In the past, the only ways to obtain copies of unpublished decisions were from the parties

---

[2]West also publishes separate unofficial state reporters for New York, California, and Illinois. Thus, New York, California, and Illinois cases may appear in three places: (1) an official state reporter; (2) a West regional reporter; and (3) a West unofficial state reporter. Some lower court opinions published in West's New York and California reporters are not published in the regional reporters covering those states. By contrast, all of the cases in *West's Illinois Decisions* are included in the regional reporter covering Illinois.

[3]There are limited exceptions to this rule. For example, in Ohio, the text of the opinion is preceded by a "syllabus," or summary of the opinion, which is written by the court and which contains the holding of the decision. Ordinarily, however, everything other than the opinion itself is an editorial enhancement. Unless you see a notation indicating otherwise, you should assume that only the text of the opinion is authoritative.

FIGURE 4.2 EXCERPT FROM *POPKIN v. NEW YORK STATE*

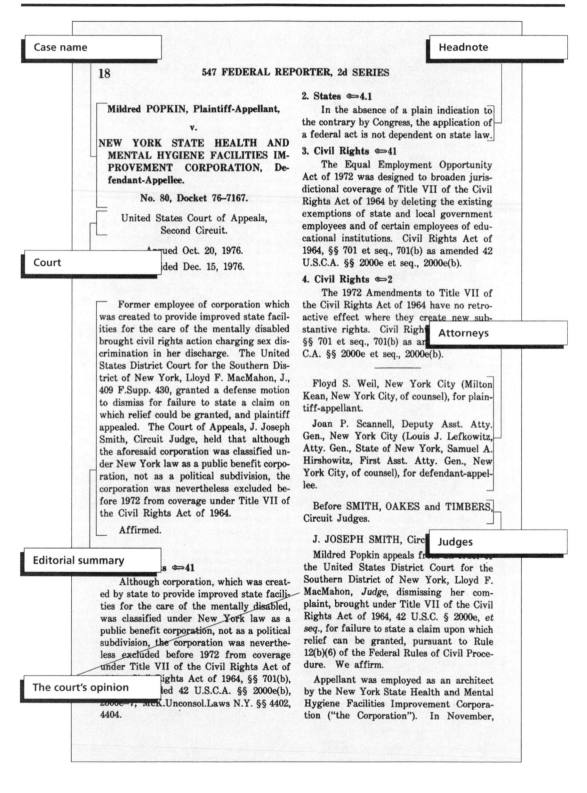

Case name

Headnote

18   547 FEDERAL REPORTER, 2d SERIES

Mildred POPKIN, Plaintiff-Appellant,

v.

NEW YORK STATE HEALTH AND MENTAL HYGIENE FACILITIES IMPROVEMENT CORPORATION, Defendant-Appellee.

No. 80, Docket 76–7167.

United States Court of Appeals, Second Circuit.

Argued Oct. 20, 1976.

Decided Dec. 15, 1976.

Court

Former employee of corporation which was created to provide improved state facilities for the care of the mentally disabled brought civil rights action charging sex discrimination in her discharge. The United States District Court for the Southern District of New York, Lloyd F. MacMahon, J., 409 F.Supp. 430, granted a defense motion to dismiss for failure to state a claim on which relief could be granted, and plaintiff appealed. The Court of Appeals, J. Joseph Smith, Circuit Judge, held that although the aforesaid corporation was classified under New York law as a public benefit corporation, not as a political subdivision, the corporation was nevertheless excluded before 1972 from coverage under Title VII of the Civil Rights Act of 1964.

Affirmed.

Editorial summary

s ⟨⟩ 41

Although corporation, which was created by state to provide improved state facilities for the care of the mentally disabled, was classified under New York law as a public benefit corporation, not as a political subdivision, the corporation was nevertheless excluded before 1972 from coverage under Title VII of the Civil Rights Act of 1964, §§ 701(b), as amended 42 U.S.C.A. §§ 2000e(b), 2000e–1, McK.Unconsol.Laws N.Y. §§ 4402, 4404.

The court's opinion

2. States ⟨⟩ 4.1

In the absence of a plain indication to the contrary by Congress, the application of a federal act is not dependent on state law.

3. Civil Rights ⟨⟩ 41

The Equal Employment Opportunity Act of 1972 was designed to broaden jurisdictional coverage of Title VII of the Civil Rights Act of 1964 by deleting the existing exemptions of state and local government employees and of certain employees of educational institutions. Civil Rights Act of 1964, §§ 701 et seq., 701(b) as amended 42 U.S.C.A. §§ 2000e et seq., 2000e(b).

4. Civil Rights ⟨⟩ 2

The 1972 Amendments to Title VII of the Civil Rights Act of 1964 have no retroactive effect where they create new substantive rights. Civil Rights, §§ 701 et seq., 701(b) as amended 42 U.S.C.A. §§ 2000e et seq., 2000e(b).

Attorneys

Floyd S. Weil, New York City (Milton Kean, New York City, of counsel), for plaintiff-appellant.

Joan P. Scannell, Deputy Asst. Atty. Gen., New York City (Louis J. Lefkowitz, Atty. Gen., State of New York, Samuel A. Hirshowitz, First Asst. Atty. Gen., New York City, of counsel), for defendant-appellee.

Before SMITH, OAKES and TIMBERS, Circuit Judges.

J. JOSEPH SMITH, Circ

Judges

Mildred Popkin appeals from an order of the United States District Court for the Southern District of New York, Lloyd F. MacMahon, *Judge*, dismissing her complaint, brought under Title VII of the Civil Rights Act of 1964, 42 U.S.C. § 2000e, *et seq.*, for failure to state a claim upon which relief can be granted, pursuant to Rule 12(b)(6) of the Federal Rules of Civil Procedure. We affirm.

Appellant was employed as an architect by the New York State Health and Mental Hygiene Facilities Improvement Corporation ("the Corporation"). In November,

FIGURE 4.2   EXCERPT FROM *POPKIN v. NEW YORK STATE* (Continued)

POPKIN v. N. Y. ST. HEALTH & MENTAL HYGIENE, ETC.   19
Cite as 547 F.2d 18 (1976)

1970 she was notified that her employment would be terminated as of January 15, 1971. Appellant instituted this action under Title VII alleging that the termination was an act of discrimination based on her sex. Jurisdiction was based on 42 U.S.C. § 2000e *et seq.* and 28 U.S.C. § 1332. The district court dismissed the complaint on the [ground that the] Corporation was a "political [subdivision of] New York State and was [exclude]d from coverage of 42 [U.S.C. § 2000e] *et seq.* prior to March 24, [1972. The] amendments to Title VII, [bringing] [coverag]e of the Act to political [subdivisions,] held by the district court not to have retroactive effect.

> **Bracketed numbers indicate the place in the opinion where material summarized in the headnotes appears.**

[1, 2] The Corporation was created by the Health and Mental Hygiene Facilities Improvement Act as a "corporate governmental agency constituting a public benefit corporation." McKinney's Unconsol.Laws §§ 4402, 4404. Appellant contends that because under New York law her employer is classified as a public benefit corporation and not as a political subdivision, the Corporation was not excluded from Title VII coverage before 1972 under 42 U.S.C. § 2000e(b). We disagree. Title VII does not provide that the terms of the federal statute are to be construed according to state law. Title 42 U.S.C. § 2000e–7 merely provides that state laws prohibiting employment discrimination will remain in effect. In the absence of a plain indication to the contrary by Congress, the application of a federal act is not dependent on state law. *Jerome v. United States*, 318 U.S. 101, 104,

63 S.Ct. 483, 87 L.Ed. 640 (1943). Congressional intent concerning coverage of Title VII and the actual nature of appellee's relationship to the state determine whether or not the Corporation was covered by Title VII before 1972.

[3] The Equal Employment Opportunity Act of 1972 was designed to broaden jurisdictional coverage of Title VII by deleting the existing exemptions of state and local government employees and of certain employees of educational institutions. The bill amended the Civil Rights Act of 1964 to include state and local governments, governmental agencies, and political subdivisions within the definition of "employer" in 42 U.S.C. § 2000e(b). H.R.Rep.No.92–238, 92nd Cong., 2d Sess., *reprinted in* 1972 U.S. Code Cong. & Ad.News 2137, 2152. The conference report of the Senate Amendment to H.R. 1746, which was adopted by the conference, stated explicitly that the Senate Amendment "expanded coverage to include: (1) State and local governments, governmental agencies, political subdivisions . . . ." *Id.* at 2180. The 1964 House Report on the Civil Rights Act of 1964, on the other hand, refers to the exclusion from the term "employer" of "all Federal, State, and local government agencies. . . ." 1964 U.S.Code Cong. & Ad. News 2402. Until 1972, state agencies as well as political subdivisions were exempt from Title VII. Under the terms of the Mental Hygiene Facilities Development Corporation Act, "state agencies" include public benefit corporations.[2]

---

1. Section 701(b) of Title VII, the Civil Rights Act of 1964, P.L. 88–352 as enacted provided in relevant part:

> (b) The term "employer" means a person engaged in an industry affecting commerce who has twenty-five or more employees for each working day in each of twenty or more calendar weeks in the current or preceding calendar year, and any agent of such a person, but such term does not include (1) the United States, a corporation wholly owned by the Government of the United States, an Indian tribe, or a State or political subdivision thereof. . . .

In 1972 § 701(b), 42 U.S.C. § 2000e(b) was amended as follows:

> (b) The term "employer" means a person engaged in an industry affecting commerce who has fifteen or more employees for each working day in each of twenty or more calendar weeks in the current or preceding calendar year, and any agent of such a person, but such term does not include (1) the United States, a corporation wholly owned by the Government of the United States, an Indian tribe, or any department or agency of the District of Columbia subject by statute to procedures of the competitive service (as defined in section 2102 of Title 5). . . .

2. McKinney's Unconsol.Laws § 4403(17) contains the following definition:

> "State agency" means any officer, department, board, commission, bureau division,

---

Reprinted with permission from Thomson Reuters/West, West's *Federal Reporter*, 2d Ser., *Popkin v. New York State*, 547 F.2d 18-19 (2d Cir. 1976). © 1976 Thomson Reuters/West.

to the case or from the clerk's office at the courthouse. This is still true today for some unpublished decisions, especially those issued by state courts. Many unpublished decisions, however, are available through electronic research services and on the Internet. The federal courts of appeals are in the process of making all their decisions, both published and unpublished, available on their web sites. In addition, unpublished decisions issued by the federal courts of appeals since 2001 are now available in print in the *Federal Appendix*, a West reporter.

Because these decisions are increasingly available electronically and in print, the term "unpublished" opinion has become a misnomer. A more accurate term is "non-precedential" opinion. Non-precedential decisions are often subject to special court rules. For example, unlike decisions published in the *Federal Reporter*, those appearing in the *Federal Appendix* are not treated as binding precedent by the courts, which is why they are described as "non-precedential" decisions. In the past, the federal courts of appeals often limited the circumstances under which non-precedential decisions could be cited in documents filed with the court, although all non-precedential opinions issued on or after January 1, 2007, may now be cited without restriction. Because of restrictions on citations to earlier non-precedential opinions, many decisions in the *Federal Appendix* contain notations indicating that they are not binding precedent and cautioning readers to check court rules before citing the opinions. Non-precedential decisions by other courts may also be subject to special rules.

Although courts have issued non-precedential opinions for many years, the practice is not without controversy. The authoritative value of non-precedential decisions is a subject of ongoing debate in the legal community. Regardless of the controversy, non-precedential decisions can be valuable research tools. Therefore, you should not disregard them when you are conducting case research.

5. METHODS OF LOCATING CASES

You can locate cases in many ways. Four common techniques are searching by citation, by subject, by words in the document, or by party name. If you have the citation to a case that you have obtained from another source, such as a secondary source, you can easily locate the case in a print reporter or retrieve it from an electronic database. If not, you will need to use other research tools to locate relevant cases.

Researching by subject is often a useful way to locate cases. Reviewing summaries of cases arranged by subject can help you identify those that address the topic of your research. You can search by subject in print using a research tool called a digest. You can also sort cases by subject categories in Westlaw, LexisNexis, and other electronic services. Word searching is another way to locate cases electronically. This option is available in free and fee-based commercial services as well as some court web sites.

One additional search option is locating a case by party name. In print, you can use a directory of cases organized by party name. In an electronic service, you can use a party name as a term in a word search; many services also have search templates that allow you to enter party names.

Sections B and C, below, explain how to research cases in print and electronically.

B. RESEARCHING CASES IN PRINT

1. LOCATING CASES BY SUBJECT USING A DIGEST

a. What Is a Digest?

Reporters are published in chronological order; they are not organized by subject. Trying to research cases in chronological order would be impossible. The research tool that organizes cases by subject is called a digest, and that is the finding tool you will ordinarily use to locate cases by topic.

The term "digest" literally means to arrange and summarize, and that is exactly what a digest does. In a digest, the law is arranged into different subject categories such as torts, contracts, or criminal law. Then, within each category, the digest provides summaries of cases that discuss the law on that subject. You can use the summaries to decide which cases you should read to find the answer to your research question.

The digest system created by West is the most commonly used digest in legal research. West has divided the law into more than 400 subject categories called topics. Under each topic, West provides summaries of cases relevant to the subject. Each topic is listed alphabetically in the digest. Because there are so many topics, a digest actually consists of a multivolume set of books. This is similar to a set of encyclopedias with multiple volumes covering topics in alphabetical order.

The West topics are quite broad. Subject areas such as torts or contracts generate thousands of cases. Therefore, the topics have been further subdivided into smaller categories. Each subdivision within a topic is assigned a number that West calls a key number. Thus, the case summaries within a West digest will appear under the relevant key number. Instead of requiring you to read summaries of all the cases on a very broad topic, the key number subdivisions allow you to focus more specifically on the precise issue you are researching.

The topic, key number, and case summary that you find in a West digest will correspond exactly to one of the headnotes at the beginning of an opinion published in a West reporter.

The following examples illustrate some of the features of a West digest. **Figure 4.3** shows the beginning of the West topic for Abandoned and Lost Property, including the outline of subtopics covered in each key number. **Figure 4.4** shows a summary of a case under key number 3.

Digests, like many other research tools, are updated with pocket parts, which are explained in Chapter 1. If the pocket part gets too big to fit in the back of the book, you may find a separate softcover pamphlet on the shelf next to the hardcover volume. Whenever you use any hardcover book in digest research, it is especially important to check the pocket part for new information because hardcover digest volumes are not reprinted frequently.

b. The Digest Research Process

The digest research process consists of four steps:

1. locating the correct digest set for the type of research you are doing
2. locating relevant topics and key numbers within the digest
3. reading the case summaries under the topics and key numbers
4. updating your research to make sure you find summaries of the most recent cases.

(1) Locating the correct digest set

Reporters and digests are similar in several ways. Just as there are different reporters containing cases from different jurisdictions, there are also different sets of digests for finding cases from these various jurisdictions. And just as a case may be published in more than one reporter, so also could a case be summarized in more than one digest. Thus, the first step in finding cases that will help you answer a research question is choosing the correct digest set.

Digest sets are organized by jurisdiction and by date. The four jurisdictional categories for digests are federal, state, regional, and combined. A federal digest, as you might imagine, summarizes federal cases. A state digest contains summaries of decisions from that state as well as opinions from the federal courts located in that state. A regional digest summarizes state court decisions from the states within the region, but it does not contain summaries of any federal cases. West publishes regional digests for some, but not all, of its regional reporters. A combined digest summarizes cases from all state and federal jurisdictions.

Within each category, the digest set may be divided into different series covering different time periods. For example, *West's Federal Practice Digest*, one of the federal digests, is currently in its Fourth Series. The Fourth Series contains cases from the early 1980s to the present. Earlier cases, from 1975 through the early 1980s, can be found in the

FIGURE 4.3 BEGINNING OF THE WEST TOPIC FOR "ABANDONED AND LOST PROPERTY"

Topic

ABANDONED AND LOST PROPERTY

SUBJECTS INCLUDED

General nature of relinquishment of property or other rights of any kind by abandonment, as distinguished from dedication, surrender, waiver, etc.

Effect of abandonment by way of extinguishment of the title or right

Finding and taking of possession of lost goods of another, whereby the finder may acquire title thereto

Nature, requisites and incidents of such finding and possession

Rights, duties and liabilities of finders of lost goods as to the owners or losers and as to others in general

SUBJECTS EXCLUDED AND COVERED BY OTHER TOPICS

Estrays, see ANIMALS

Lost instruments in writing, establishment of and action on, see LOST INSTRUMENTS

Negotiable paper, rights of finders, see BILLS AND NOTES

Particular persons or personal relations, abandonment of, see specific topics

Particular species of property, rights, remedies, or proceedings, abandonment of, see specific topics

Reversion of property to the state, see ESCHEAT

Rewards for recovery of lost goods, etc., see REWARDS

Sales of lost goods, see SALES

Wrecks and vessels and goods derelict at sea, see SHIPPING

For detailed references to other topics, see Descriptive-Word Index

Summary of the topic

Key number

Analysis

I. ABANDONMENT, ☞1–9.

II. FINDING LOST GOODS, ☞10–13.

I. ABANDONMENT.
    ☞1. Nature and elements.
        1.1. —— In general.
        2. —— Intent.
        3. —— Acts and omissions.
        4. Evidence and questions for jury.
        5. Operation and effect.

II. FINDING LOST GOODS.
    ☞10. In general; loss of property.
        11. Rights and liabilities of finder as to owner.

Outline of subtopics covered

FIGURE 4.4 CASE SUMMARY UNDER THE "ABANDONED AND LOST PROPERTY" TOPIC, KEY NUMBER 10

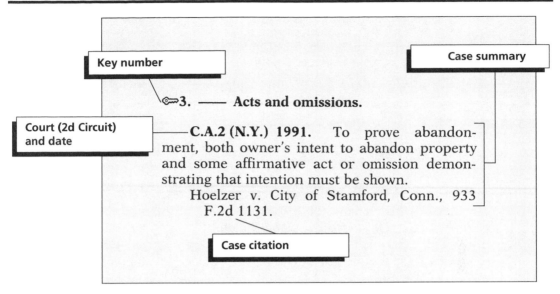

Reprinted with permission from Thomson Reuters/West, *West's Federal Practice Digest*, 4th Ser., Vol. (2006), p. 7. © 2006 Thomson Reuters/West.

Third Series of the digest. Ordinarily, you will want to begin your research in the most current series. If you are unable to find information in the most current series, however, you could locate older cases by looking in the earlier series.

Figures 4.5 through **4.7** summarize some of the characteristics of West digests.

To decide which digest is the best choice for your research, you will need to consider the nature and scope of the project. Usually, you will want to choose the narrowest digest that still has enough information for you to find relevant legal authority. Sometimes you will need to use more than one digest to find all of the cases you need.

West's Federal Practice Digest is the best place to start looking for federal cases. If you are researching case law from an individual state, the digest from that state is usually the best starting place. If you do not have access to the state digest, the regional digest is another good place to look. It is also a good place to find persuasive authority from surrounding jurisdictions. Remember, however, that regional digests summarize only state court decisions, not federal decisions. Therefore, if you also want to find cases from the federal courts located within an individual state, you will need to supplement your regional digest research by using *West's Federal Practice Digest*.

The combined digests have the most comprehensive coverage, but they are also the most difficult to use. You would probably begin with *West's General Digest*, Eleventh Series, which covers cases from 2004 to the present. The *General Digest* volumes are noncumulative. Thus, you would

FIGURE 4.5   FEDERAL DIGESTS

DESCRIPTION	WEST'S FEDERAL PRACTICE DIGEST, FOURTH SERIES	WEST'S UNITED STATES SUPREME COURT DIGEST
What is included	Summaries of cases from all federal courts	Summaries of cases from the United States Supreme Court
What is excluded	Summaries of state cases	Summaries of cases from lower federal courts and all state courts
Coverage	Includes summaries of cases from the early 1980s–present. Older cases are summarized in prior series of this set (e.g., West's Federal Practice Digest, Third Series).	Includes summaries of all United States Supreme Court cases

FIGURE 4.6   STATE AND REGIONAL DIGESTS

DESCRIPTION	STATE DIGESTS	REGIONAL DIGESTS
What is included	Summaries of cases from the state's courts and the federal courts within the state	Summaries of cases from the state courts within the region
What is excluded	Summaries of state and federal cases from courts outside the state	Summaries of state cases from states outside the region and all federal cases
Coverage	West publishes state digests for all states except Delaware, Nevada, and Utah. The Virginia Digest summarizes cases from both Virginia and West Virginia. The Dakota Digest summarizes cases from both North and South Dakota. Some state digests have multiple series.	West publishes Atlantic, North Western, Pacific, and South Eastern Digests. West does not publish North Eastern, Southern, or South Western Digests. All of the regional digests have multiple series.

FIGURE 4.7   COMBINED DIGESTS

DESCRIPTION	COMBINED DIGESTS
What is included	Summaries of state and federal cases from all jurisdictions across the United States
What is excluded	Nothing
Coverage	The combined digests are divided into the *General, Decennial*, and *Century Digests*, covering the following dates:

General Digest, 11th Series (Each volume in the *General Digest* set is noncumulative.)	2004–present
Eleventh Decennial Digest, Part 3	2001–2004
Eleventh Decennial Digest, Part 2	2001–2004
Eleventh Decennial Digest, Part 1	1996–2001
Tenth Decennial Digest, Part 2	1991–1996
Tenth Decennial Digest, Part 1	1986–1991
Ninth Decennial Digest, Part 2	1981–1986
Ninth Decennial Digest, Part 1	1976–1981
Eighth Decennial Digest	1966–1976
Seventh Decennial Digest	1956–1966
Sixth Decennial Digest	1946–1956
Fifth Decennial Digest	1936–1946
Fourth Decennial Digest	1926–1936
Third Decennial Digest	1916–1926
Second Decennial Digest	1907–1916
First Decennial Digest	1897–1906
Century Digest	1658–1896

need to begin by researching in each volume of the most recent series. For earlier cases, you would also need to use the *Eleventh Decennial Digest*, Part 3, and as many previous series as necessary to locate cases on your topic. Because this is a cumbersome process, the combined digests are usually only useful when you know the approximate time period you want to research or when you are conducting nationwide research.

Figure 4.8 summarizes when you might want to consider using each of these types of digests.

(2) Locating topics and key numbers

Once you have decided which set or sets of the digest to use, the next step is locating topics and key numbers relevant to your research issue. You can do this in three ways:

FIGURE 4.8   WHEN TO USE DIFFERENT DIGESTS

FEDERAL DIGESTS	STATE DIGESTS	REGIONAL DIGESTS	COMBINED DIGESTS
To research federal cases	To research state and federal cases from an individual state	To research state cases from an individual state within the region (may require additional research with the federal digest)	To research federal cases or cases from an individual state if you know the approximate time period you wish to research
To supplement regional digest research by locating federal cases within an individual state		To locate persuasive authority from surrounding jurisdictions	To research the law of all jurisdictions within the United States

   i.   using the headnotes in a case on point
   ii. using the index to the digest
   iii. going directly to topics relevant to your research.

(i) Using the headnotes in a case on point

The easiest way to find relevant topics and key numbers is to use the headnotes in a case that you have already determined is relevant to your research. If you have read other chapters in this book, you already know that the digest is not the only way to locate cases. Many other research sources, including secondary sources (covered in Chapter 3) and statutes (covered in Chapter 6), can lead you to relevant cases. Therefore, when another source has led you to a relevant case that is published in a West reporter, you can use the headnotes to direct you to digest topics and key numbers.

(ii) Using the Descriptive-Word Index

If you do not already have a case on point, you will need to use the index to find topics and key numbers in the digest. The index in a West digest is called the Descriptive-Word Index (DWI). The DWI actually consists of several volumes that may be located either at the beginning or at the end of the digest set, and it lists subjects in alphabetical order.

To use the DWI, all you need to do is look up the subjects you want to research. The subjects will be followed by abbreviations indicating the topics and key numbers relevant to each subject. A list of abbreviations appears at the beginning of the volume. You may also see cross-references to other index entries with additional information on the subject. An excerpt from a page in the DWI appears in **Figure 4.9**.

The DWI volumes, like all other hardcover volumes within the digest set, are updated with pocket parts. The next step in using the index is checking the pocket part. Because the hardcover DWI volumes are not reprinted frequently, many of the newer entries may be in the pocket part. Moreover, West sometimes uses information from specific cases to generate index entries. Therefore, it is important to check the pocket part for new material that may be relevant to your research. If you do not find anything listed in the pocket part, no new index entries on that subject are available.

Once you have identified relevant topics and key numbers, the next step is looking them up within the digest volumes. Remember that digest volumes are organized alphabetically. Therefore, you will need to look on the spines of the books until you locate the volume covering your topic. When you look up the topic, you will see that the key numbers follow in numerical order.

(iii) Going directly to relevant topics

Because digest topics are arranged alphabetically, you can bypass the DWI and go directly to the topic you are interested in researching. At the beginning of each topic, West provides an overview section that lists the subjects included and excluded, as well as an outline of all the key numbers under the topic. Case summaries, of course, follow the overview in key number order.

This can be a difficult way to start your research unless you are already familiar with an area of law and know which topics are likely to be relevant. For example, cases involving some types of real estate transactions are listed under the topic "Vendor and Purchaser," which might not be a topic you would have considered using.

Although you might not want to start your research by going directly to a digest topic, once you have identified useful topics through other means, you may want to review the overview section. The list of subjects included and excluded and outline of key numbers can provide additional helpful research leads.

(3) *Reading case summaries*

Once you have reviewed the topic overview, you are ready to begin reading case summaries. There is some inconsistency in the way West organizes its digest summaries, but in general, summaries are organized in descending order from highest to lowest court. If the digest contains summaries of both federal and state cases, federal cases will appear first. If the digest contains summaries of cases from multiple states, the states will be listed

FIGURE 4.9   EXCERPT FROM THE DESCRIPTIVE-WORD INDEX

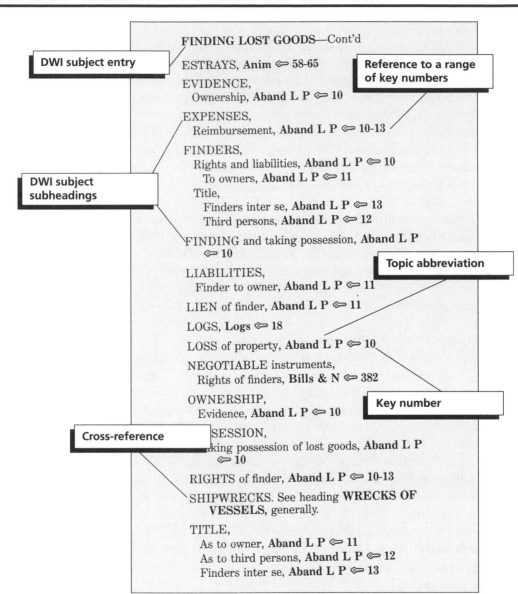

Reprinted with permission from Thomson Reuters/West, *West's Federal Practice Digest*, 4th Ser., Descriptive-Word Index, Vol. 98 (2002), p. 437. © 2002 Thomson Reuters/West.

alphabetically. Summaries of multiple decisions from the same level of court and the same jurisdiction are listed in reverse chronological order.

One of the most difficult aspects of digest research is deciding which cases to read based on the summaries. The court and date abbreviations at the beginning of each entry will help you decide which cases to review. If you are using a digest with cases from more than one jurisdiction, paying attention to the abbreviations will help you stay focused on the summaries of cases from the appropriate jurisdiction. The abbreviations will also help you figure out which cases are from the highest court in the jurisdiction and which are the most recent decisions. In addition, many case summaries include not only a synopsis of the rule the court applied in the case, but also a concise description of the facts. You can use the factual summaries to narrow down the cases applicable to your issue.

Even a fact-specific summary, however, does not provide the full context of the case. Using the digest is only the first step in researching cases; all the digest can do is point you toward cases that may help answer your research question. Digest summaries, like headnotes, are editorial enhancements designed to assist you with your research. They are not authoritative, and you should never rely on one as a statement of the law. Always read the case in full before relying on it to answer a research question.

(4) *Updating digest research*
The final step in digest research is updating. The updating process involves three steps:

i.   checking the pocket part for the subject volume covering your topic
ii. checking a separate set of interim pamphlets at the end of the digest set
iii. updating beyond the digest set for cases published after the supplements were printed.

It is very important to update your research for new cases. Newer cases may reflect a change in the law, or cases more factually relevant to your problem may have been decided since the hardcover books were published. Obviously, in legal practice you must find these cases for your research to be complete. In law school, professors love to assign research problems for which the best material is in the updating sources. Therefore, you should get in the habit now of updating your research thoroughly.

(i) Pocket parts
Each subject volume should have either a pocket part or a separate supplement on the shelf next to the hardcover book. This is the first place to look to update your research.

The pocket part is organized the same way as the main volume. The topics are arranged alphabetically, and the key numbers are arranged in numerical order within each topic. There are two pieces of information you will find in the pocket part. First, if any cases under the key number were decided after the main volume was published, you will find summaries of those cases in the pocket part. These case summaries will be organized in the same order as those in the main volume. If no reference to your topic and key number appears in the pocket part, no new decisions have been issued during the time period covered by the pocket part.

Second, you may find that West has created new key numbers or divided the key numbers from the main volume into a series of subsections. If that is the case, you will find a short outline of the new subsections at the beginning of the original key number, along with summaries of any cases categorized under the new subsections.

(ii) Interim pamphlets

The pocket part is not the only supplement you should check. Pocket parts are generally published only once a year. For some digest sets, West also publishes interim pamphlets to update for cases decided since the pocket part was published. These pamphlets are ordinarily softcover booklets, although occasionally you will see hardcover supplements. They are usually shelved at the end of the digest set. The pamphlets contain summaries of new decisions under all of the topics and key numbers within the digest set. Just as with pocket parts, the topics in the interim pamphlets are arranged alphabetically. And as with pocket parts, if no entry appears under your topic and key number, no new cases have been decided during the time period covered by the interim pamphlet.

Some interim pamphlets are cumulative, meaning you only need to look in the one book to update your research. Others, however, are noncumulative. If the pamphlets you are using are noncumulative, each one covers a specific time period, and you must check each one to update your research completely. To determine the dates covered by an interim pamphlet, check the dates on the spine or cover of the book.

(iii) Closing tables

Once you have checked the interim pamphlets accompanying the digest, you have updated your research as far as the digest will take you. The final step in the process is checking for cases decided after the last interim pamphlet was published.

To do this, you will need to refer to the chart on the inside front cover of the latest interim pamphlet. This chart is called a closing table. **Figure 4.10** contains an example of a closing table. If the digest set you are using does not have interim pamphlets, you should check the closing table on the inside front cover of the pocket part for the subject volume.

FIGURE 4.10   INTERIM PAMPHLET CLOSING TABLE

Closing with Cases Reported in

Supreme Court Reporter .... 127 S.Ct.
Federal Reporter, Third Series 494 F.3d 1026
Federal Appendix .... 231 Fed.Appx.
Federal Supplement, Second Series 496 F.Supp.2d
Federal Rules Decisions .... 242 F.R.D. 661
Bankruptcy Reporter .... 371 B.R. 570
Federal Claims Reporter .... 77 Fed.Cl. 709
Military Justice Reporter — U.S.Armed Forces .... 65 M.J. 248
Military Justice Reporter — A.F.Ct.Crim.App. .... 65 M.J. 745
Veterans Appeals Reporter .... 21 Vet.App. 359

Reprinted with permission from Thomson Reuters/West, *West's Federal Practice Digest*, 4th Ser., October 2007 Pamphlet (2007), inside cover. © 2007 Thomson Reuters/West.

The closing table lists the names of all of the reporters whose decisions are summarized within the digest set. For each of those reporters, the table lists the last volume with decisions summarized in the interim pamphlet. For example, the closing table in **Figure 4.10** lists the *Federal Supplement*, Second Series, closing with volume 496. That means that decisions through volume 496 of F. Supp. 2d are summarized within the interim pamphlet. Any cases reported in volume 497 and beyond came out too late to be included in the interim pamphlet.

To find out if any relevant cases are reported after volume 496, therefore, you will need to check the reporters on the shelves. Within each reporter, you will find a mini-digest in the back of the book. The mini-digest summarizes all of the decisions within that volume. You need to look up your topic and key number in each of the reporter volumes after volume 496 through the end of the set to make sure no new relevant decisions were issued after the interim pamphlet was published. Again, if nothing is listed under the topic and key number, no new decisions were issued, and your updating is complete.

Students often ask whether this last updating step is truly necessary. The answer largely depends on the progress of your research. If you have not been able to locate a sufficient amount of authority, you might want to use the closing table and mini-digests to expand your research results. This is especially true if the digest set does not have interim pamphlets and a number of months have passed since the pocket part was printed. If you are satisfied that you have located the pertinent cases on your issue and only need to verify that they still state the law accurately, the closing table and mini-digests are not the best tools for you to use. Chapter 5 discusses resources you can use to verify case research. These resources will allow you to check your research more efficiently than the closing table and mini-digests. As Chapter 5 explains, they can also be used to expand your research results, although you may still find the case summaries in the mini-digests helpful.

2. ADDITIONAL FEATURES OF DIGESTS

In addition to collecting case summaries under subject matter topics, digests have two other features you can use to locate cases: the Table of Cases and the Words and Phrases feature. All West digest sets have a Table of Cases, but not all have the Words and Phrases feature.

a. Table of Cases

The Table of Cases lists cases alphabetically by the name of both the plaintiff and the defendant.[4] Thus, if you know either party's name, you can find the case in the Table of Cases. In the Table of Cases, you will find the following items of information:

1. the full name of the case
2. the court that decided the case
3. the complete citation to the case, including the parallel citation (if any) to an official reporter
4. a list of the topics and key numbers appearing in the headnotes to the case.

   Figure 4.11 is an excerpt from the Table of Cases.
   The Table of Cases usually appears at the end of the digest set. Often, it is contained in a separate volume or set of volumes, but in smaller digest sets, it may be included in a volume containing other material.
   The Table of Cases is updated the same way as the subject volumes. The volumes containing the Table of Cases should have pocket parts. Some older digest sets also have hardcover supplements. If the digest set has interim pamphlets, one of those pamphlets will also contain a Table of Cases listing cases decided during the time period covered by the pamphlet.

---

[4]West used to divide the Table of Cases into two tables: the Table of Cases, which listed cases by the plaintiff's name, and the Defendant-Plaintiff Table, which listed cases by the defendant's name. West now consolidates these two tables into one, called the Table of Cases. In some older digest sets, however, you may still find a separate Defendant-Plaintiff Table.

FIGURE 4.11 EXCERPT FROM THE TABLE OF CASES

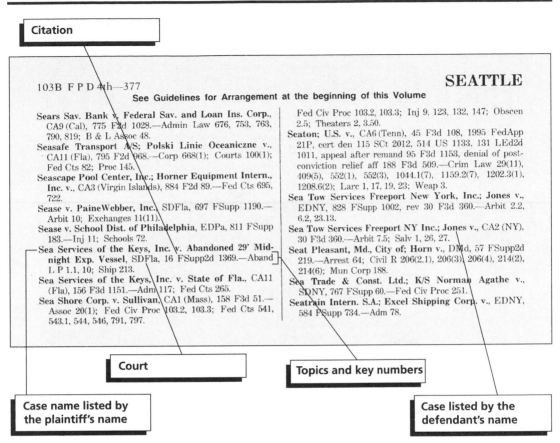

Reprinted with permission from Thomson Reuters/West, *West's Federal Practice Digest*, 4th Ser., Vol. 103B (2000), p. 377. © 2000 Thomson Reuters/West.

b. Words and Phrases

The Words and Phrases feature provides citations to cases that have defined legal terms or phrases. Because dictionary definitions are not legally binding on courts, Words and Phrases can help you find legally binding definitions from cases that have interpreted or construed a term. In a sense, Words and Phrases is the closest print equivalent to electronic word searching because it collects case summaries based on specific words in the opinion. Words and Phrases is organized much like a dictionary. To determine whether the courts have defined a term, you simply look up the term alphabetically. If the term is listed, you will find citations to cases construing it. Newer volumes also contain brief summaries of the cases.

Words and Phrases is usually located near the Table of Cases within the digest set and is updated the same way as that table.

Figure 4.12 illustrates the Words and Phrases feature.

FIGURE 4.12   WORDS AND PHRASES

FIND

108 F P D 4th—442

quate within meaning of the statute; in other words, it must at least make pass at conducting objective analysis of the data and its own rates. Social Security Act, § 1902(a)(13)(A), as amended, 42 U.S.C.A. § 1396a(a)(13)(A).—Memorial Hosp., Inc. v. Childers, 896 F.Supp. 1427.—Social S 241.66, 241.91.

W.D.Ky. 1995. Kentucky's Cabinet for Human Resources (CHR) failed to meet procedural requirement under Boren Amendment that it "find" that its Medicaid payment rates were reasonable and adequate; CHR did not submit any analyses of bona fact finding procedures, and, since the only findings that would be relevant would be current findings, earlier-conducted fiscal study could not be considered as "findings" for a year which was nearly completed. Social Security Act, § 1902(a)(13)(A), as amended, 42 U.S.C.A. § 1396a(a)(13)(A).—Memorial Hosp., Inc. v. Childers, 896 F.Supp. 1427.—Social S 241.66, 241.91.

FINDER

C.A.9 (Cal.) 1987. Seller of computer products, who provided test modem to computer company, arranged for its repair, and generally remained in contact with company, was "broker," rather than "finder," under California law and, therefore, was not required to establish bad-faith termination to recover damages from computer modem manufacturer for breach of contract.—LuMetta v. U.S. Robotics, Inc., 824 F.2d 768.—Brok 2, 11.

D.D.C. 1990. If "finder" takes any part in negotiations concerning real estate transaction, no matter how slight, he will be considered a "broker" and must be licensed to collect a commission.—Kassatly v. Yazbeck, 734 F.Supp. 13, reconsideration denied 739 F.Supp. 651.—Brok 2, 42.

D.D.C. 1990. Individual who personally negotiated the transaction for lease of hotel with option [...] was a "real estate broker" under District of [Colum]bia law, and not a mere "finder" or "business [servi]ce broker," and thus could not recover a commission in view of his failure to obtain a license.—Kassatly v. Yazbeck, 734 F.Supp. 13, reconsideration denied 739 F.Supp. 651.—Brok 2, 42.

FINDING A PURCHASER

S.D.Fla. 1987. Phrase "finding a purchaser" as used in exclusive listing agreement required actual sales contract to have been executed or a similar type of agreement to have been reached and it was not sufficient that the broker contacted the ultimate purchaser during the exclusive listing period.—Doran Jason Co. of Miami, Inc. v. Lou, 675 F.Supp. 635.—Brok 52.

FINDING OF REHABILITATION

C.A.2 (N.Y.) 1993. Evidence rule precluding admission of prior conviction if conviction had been a subject of a pardon, annulment, certificate of rehabilitation or other equivalent procedure, barred admission of a prior conviction only when there had been express finding that the person convicted had

been rehabilitated; community-mindedness and lawful conduct, standing alone, was not a "finding of rehabilitation" within the meaning of the rule. Fed.Rules Evid.Rule 609(c)(1), 28 U.S.C.A.—Zinman v. Black & Decker (U.S.), Inc., 983 F.2d 431.—Witn 345(8).

FINDING OF ULTIMATE FACT

C.A.9 (Ariz.) 1990. Neither original sentence nor substitute sentence by appellate court was "finding of ultimate fact" for purposes of collateral estoppel.—McDaniel v. State of Ariz., 921 F.2d 966, certiorari denied 111 S.Ct. 1426, 499 U.S. 952, 113 L.Ed.2d 478.—Judgm 751.

FINDINGS

W.D.Ky. 1995. Kentucky's Cabinet for Human Resources (CHR) failed to meet procedural requirement under Boren Amendment that it "find" that its Medicaid payment rates were reasonable and adequate; CHR did not submit any analyses of bona fact finding procedures, and, since the only findings that would be relevant would be current findings, earlier-conducted fiscal study could not be considered as "findings" for a year which was nearly completed. Social Security Act, § 1902(a)(13)(A), as amended, 42 U.S.C.A. § 1396a(a)(13)(A).—Memorial Hosp., Inc. v. Childers, 896 F.Supp. 1427.—Social S 241.66, 241.91.

FINDINGS OF FACT

N.D.Ind. 1995. State court's findings that counsel performed adequately, and that any shortcoming in representation did not prejudice defendant's case, are not "findings of fact" under federal habeas corpus statute but are instead "mixed questions of law and fact" subject to independent review by federal habeas court. 28 U.S.C.A. § 2254(d).—Bennett v. Duckworth, 909 F.Supp. 1169, affirmed 103 F.3d 133.—Hab Corp 773.

S.D.N.Y. 1997. In context of ascertaining extent of obligation of arbitrators to render written opinion, "findings of fact" and "conclusions of law" are familiar terms in legal parlance with reasonably plain meanings; touchstone is simply whether enough facts are found and enough legal principles stated so that reviewing tribunal can ascertain reasons for ultimate determination. 5 U.S.C.A. § 557(c); Fed.Rules Civ.Proc.Rule 52, 28 U.S.C.A.—New Elliott Corp. v. MAN Gutehoffnungshutte AG, 969 F.Supp. 13.—Arbit 52.5.

FINDINGS OF LIABILITY

D.R.I. 1995. Granting of motion for judgment on pleadings as well as bankruptcy court's granting of debtor's motion for determination of his tax liabilities are "findings of liability" and, thus, must be treated as "default," within meaning of federal civil rule governing entry of default when party against whom judgment for affirmative relief is sought has failed to plead or otherwise defend. Fed.Rules Civ.Proc.Rule 55(a), 28 U.S.C.A.; Fed. Rules Bankr.Proc.Rule 7055, 11 U.S.C.A.—Ga-

Entry for word defined

Summary of a case defining the word

Reprinted with permission from Thomson Reuters/West, *West's Federal Practice Digest*, 4th Ser., Vol. 108 (1999), p. 442. © 1999 Thomson Reuters/West.

C. RESEARCHING CASES ELECTRONICALLY

1. WESTLAW

a. The Format of a Case in Westlaw

The format of a case in Westlaw is the same as the format of a case in a West reporter, although the case will look different in electronic form. At the beginning of the document, you will see a caption with the name of the case and other identifying information. The caption will be followed by an editorial summary of the decision. In more recent cases, the summary is divided into two sections: background and holding. The summary will be followed by one or more numbered headnotes and then the full text of the opinion. Just as in the print version of a case, the editorial summary and headnotes, if any, are not part of the decision and are not authoritative.

In the body of the opinion, the pagination from the print version of the case will be indicated by starred numbers. For example, if a case begins on page 1369 of the print reporter, the transition to the next page will be indicated by *1370.

Figure 4.13 shows what a case looks like in Westlaw.

b. Search Options in Westlaw

You can search for cases in Westlaw by citation, by party name, by subject, or by words in the document. To retrieve a case from its citation, use the Find function. The Find screen contains a link to a template you can use to locate a case by party name if you do not have the citation.

Although the digests themselves are not accessible in exactly the same way they are in print, you can still search for cases by subject in Westlaw. Westlaw has two functions that allow you to search by subject using the digest topics and key numbers. One is the West Key Number Digest Outline (Custom Digest) function. You can access this function by choosing the Key Numbers option at the top of the Westlaw screen or from the Site Map. This will display a list of the digest topics. You can view individual key numbers by expanding the list under each topic, and you can select the topic(s) and key number(s) you want to search. If you locate a relevant case, you can also access the Custom Digest function by following the key number link. Using either approach brings up a search screen that allows you to customize your search. For example, you can select the jurisdiction in which to execute the search and add your own terms to further refine the search.

When you search using Custom Digest, the search results are displayed in a format similar to the print digest. That is, the document retrieved will contain a list of case summaries under the relevant key

FIGURE 4.13   EXAMPLE OF A CASE IN WESTLAW

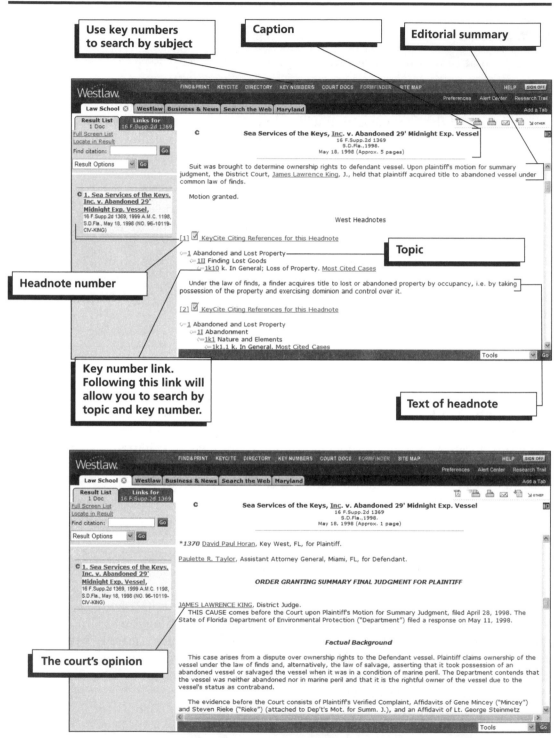

number, and a single case may be summarized multiple times if it contains multiple headnotes with the same key number. You can retrieve the full text of a case by following the link to the citation.

Another way to search using the West digest topics and key numbers is with the KeySearch function. You can access this function from the Key Numbers link or through the Site Map. This brings up an alphabetical list of search topics. Each topic contains multiple subtopics, and most subtopics are further subdivided into even narrower categories. You can find a subject to search by selecting a subject and browsing the subdivisions, or you can search for a subject using the search box on the left side of the screen. From the KeySearch search screen, you can further customize the search by selecting the jurisdiction and sources you wish to search, as well as by adding your own search terms.

The relationship between the KeySearch function and the West digest topics is not immediately apparent. Although KeySearch lists subjects alphabetically, the subject categories are not identical to the topics in a West digest. In a KeySearch search, the query consists of a combination of various topics and key numbers, plus additional search terms that West selects. Thus, although it is largely driven by the topic and key number system, it usually will not retrieve exactly the same results that a Custom Digest search will.

The search results in KeySearch are displayed like those from a word search, not like those from a Custom Digest search. KeySearch results display a list of case citations. Each case appears in the results only once, regardless of the number of relevant headnotes within the document.

You can also locate cases in Westlaw using word searches. To execute a word search, you must first select a database. Selecting a database is similar to selecting a print digest. You should use the narrowest one that still has enough information to answer your research question. Westlaw has databases with cases from federal courts or individual states, as well as combined databases with both federal and state decisions. In addition, Westlaw has subject-matter databases containing federal and state cases in specific subject areas such as products liability or family law.

Once you have selected a database, you are ready to construct and execute a word search. Chapter 10 contains more information on the process of word searching in Westlaw.

2. LexisNexis

a. The Format of a Case in LexisNexis

The format of a case in LexisNexis is similar to the format of a case in Westlaw. At the beginning of the document, you will see a caption with the name of the case and other identifying information. The caption will be followed by an editorial summary of the decision. The summary is divided into three components: procedural posture, overview, and outcome. No key number headnotes appear in the LexisNexis version of a case because the key number system is an editorial feature unique to West. LexisNexis has a similar editorial feature, however, called Lexis-Nexis Headnotes. These headnotes are summary paragraphs organized by subject and quoting passages from the case. Even though the Lexis-Nexis Headnotes usually quote the opinion verbatim, they are not part of the decision and are not authoritative.

In the body of the opinion, the pagination from the print version of the case will be indicated by starred numbers in brackets. For example, if a case begins on page 1369 of the print reporter, the transition to the next page will be indicated by [*1370].

Figure 4.14 shows what a case looks like in LexisNexis.

b. Search Options in LexisNexis

You can search for cases in LexisNexis by citation, by party name, by subject, or by words in the document. To retrieve a case from its citation, use the Get A Document function. Under the Get A Document tab, you will find a link to a template you can use to locate a case by party name if you do not have the citation.

Although the West topic and key number system is not available in LexisNexis, LexisNexis has its own subject searching capabilities. Under the Search tab in LexisNexis, you can choose the option to search by topic or headnote. Choosing this option brings up an alphabetical list of search topics. Each topic contains multiple subtopics, and most subtopics are further subdivided into even narrower categories. You can find a subject to search in three ways: You can select a subject you have searched before by browsing the last twenty topics you have selected. You can search for a subject using the search box. Or you can explore a general subject by expanding the list and browsing the subtopics.

After you select a search topic, LexisNexis displays a search screen. You can search in two ways. One option is to search across sources. With this option, you can choose to search for multiple types of authority (e.g., cases and statutes) simultaneously in the subject area you selected, or you can limit your search to a particular source. A second option is to search by headnote. A headnote search will retrieve cases containing the headnote topic you selected. You can select the jurisdiction to search, but the results will be limited to cases. If you locate a relevant case, you can also search by headnote by selecting the "more like this headnote" option. This brings up a slightly different search screen that will also allow you to

FIGURE 4.14   EXAMPLE OF A CASE IN LEXISNEXIS

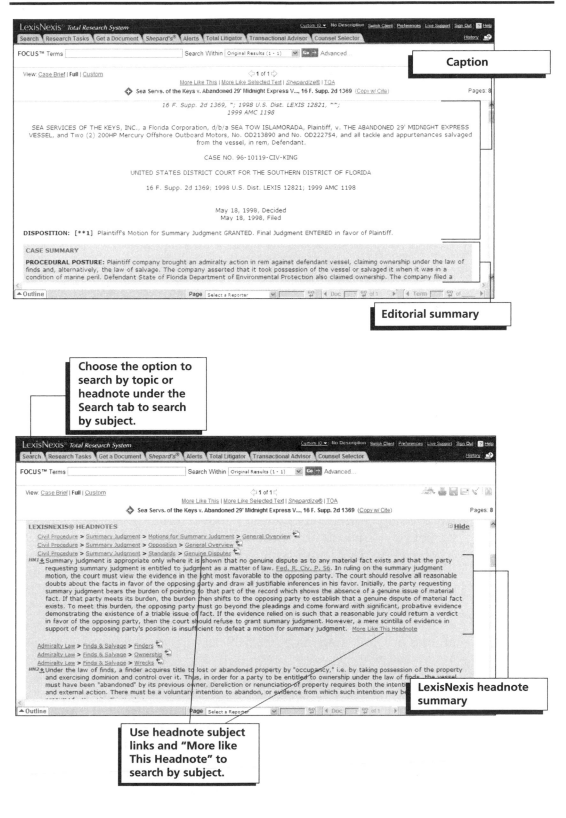

FIGURE 4.14 **EXAMPLE OF A CASE IN LEXISNEXIS** *(Continued)*

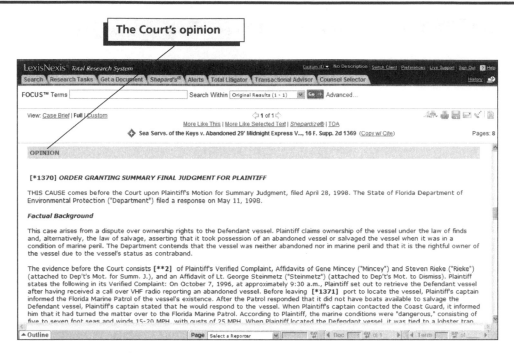

The Court's opinion

Reprinted with permission of LexisNexis, from LexisNexis, 16 F. Supp. 2d 1369.

search for cases with material relevant to the headnote you selected. Although the option to search across sources allows you to add search terms to the search, the search by headnotes and "more like this headnote" options do not.

You can also locate cases in LexisNexis using word searches. To execute a word search, you must first select a database from the source directory. As noted above, you should use the narrowest source that still has enough information to answer your research question. LexisNexis has sources with cases from federal courts or individual states, as well as combined databases with both federal and state decisions. In addition, LexisNexis has sources devoted to specific subject areas that contain federal and state cases on topics such as products liability or family law.

Once you have selected a source, you are ready to construct and execute a word search. Chapter 10 contains more information on the process of word searching in LexisNexis.

3. RESEARCHING CASES ON THE INTERNET

Judicial opinions are increasingly available on the Internet. To locate cases on the Internet, you can try two approaches. The first is to review the web site for the court whose decisions you are trying to locate. Many courts and government organizations maintain web sites with the full text of court opinions. The second is to go to general legal research sites. Many of these sites either include links to sites with court opinions or index their own databases of cases. Appendix A lists the Internet addresses for a number of legal research web sites that may be useful for case research.

Once you have located a source containing cases, several searching options may be available. You may be able to search by date, docket number, case name, or key word, depending on how the web site is organized.

Because comprehensive digesting tools are not yet available on the Internet, it is not likely to be an effective resource as your sole avenue for case research. It is almost impossible to search for cases by subject on the Internet, and the full-text search options available on many sites are limited. In addition, a number of databases only contain decisions going back a few years, so comprehensive research over time may not be possible. Once you have located a case, you will usually only see the text of the court's opinion. Internet sources generally lack the editorial enhancements available with commercial research services, which may hinder your research efforts.

Despite these difficulties, the Internet can be useful for targeted case research. If you know which jurisdiction's cases you want to research and the relevant court web sites offer full-text searching, searching court web sites is one way of gathering some citations to get started with your research. Internet sources are also useful for locating the most recent opinions and opinions from tribunals whose decisions are not published in print reporters or commercial databases. For example, United States Supreme Court decisions are available on the Internet almost immediately after issuance. Opinions of municipal courts or local agencies may only be available on the Internet. In addition, the Internet is a more cost-effective way to access cases otherwise available in LexisNexis, Westlaw, or other commercial services. Thus, although cases are not yet sufficiently accessible to make Internet research viable as your only strategy for case research, it may be a cost-effective way to supplement other research methods.

D. CITING CASES

As Chapter 1 explains, any time you report the results of your research in written form, you must cite your sources properly. This is especially important for cases because the information in the citation can help the reader assess the weight of the authority you are citing.

A case citation has three basic components:

1. the case name
2. information on the reporter in which the case is published
3. a parenthetical containing the jurisdiction, the level of court that decided the case, and the year of decision.

You can find rules for each component in the *ALWD Manual* and the *Bluebook*. Using the *ALWD Manual*, you should read Rule 12 and use Appendices 1, 3, and 4 for any necessary abbreviations. Using the *Bluebook*, you should begin with Bluepages B5 and use Tables T.1, T.6, and T.10 to find any necessary abbreviations. **Figure 4.15** directs you to the citation rules for cases.

The remainder of this section uses an example citation to illustrate each of these components. The example citation is to a fictional 1983 decision of the Delaware Court of Chancery in the case of Patricia Ellis and Sam Anson versus Acme Manufacturing Company, published in volume 327 of the *Atlantic Reporter*, Second Series, beginning on page 457.

1. THE CASE NAME

The name of the case appears first and must be underlined or *italicized*. The case name consists of the name of the first party on either side of the "v." In other words, if more than one plaintiff or defendant is listed in the full case name, give only the name of the first named plaintiff or first named defendant. In the example citation, Sam Anson would not be listed. Do not include "et al." when a case has multiple parties; simply refer to the first named party on both sides. If a person is named as a party, use only the person's last name, but if a company or other entity is listed, use the entity's full name.

Often, the case name will be abbreviated. The abbreviation rules vary slightly in the *ALWD Manual* and the *Bluebook*. You will need to read the rules and refer to the appropriate appendix or table to determine when words should be abbreviated and what the proper abbreviations are.

FIGURE 4.15 *ALWD MANUAL* **AND** *BLUEBOOK* **RULES GOVERNING CASE CITATIONS**

CITATION COMPONENT	*ALWD MANUAL*, RULE 12	*BLUEBOOK*, BLUEPAGES B5
Case name	Rule 12.2 & Appendix 3	Bluepages B5.1.1 & Tables T.6 & T.10
Reporter information	Rules 12.3-12.5 & Appendix 1	Bluepages B5.1.2, B5.1.3, & Table T.1
Parenthetical	Rules 12.6-12.7 & Appendices 1 & 4	Bluepages B5.1.3 & Table T.1

The case name should be followed by a comma, which is not underlined or italicized.

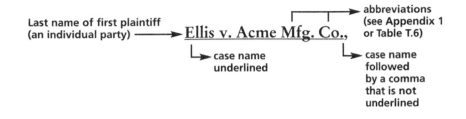

2. THE REPORTER

After the case name, the citation should list information on the reporter in which the case is published. If the case is published in more than one reporter, you will need to determine which reporter or reporters to cite, as explained in *ALWD Manual* Rule 12.4 and *Bluebook* Bluepages B5.1.3. In the citation, the name of the reporter will be abbreviated, so you must also determine the proper abbreviation. In the *ALWD Manual*, you can find this information in Appendix 1, which lists each jurisdiction in the United States alphabetically. For each jurisdiction, Appendix 1 lists reporter names and abbreviations. In the *Bluebook*, this same information appears in Table T.1.

Ordinarily, you will list the volume of the reporter, the reporter abbreviation, and the starting page of the case. If you are citing a specific page within the case, you will also usually cite to that page as well, using what is called a pinpoint citation. A comma should appear between the starting page and the pinpoint citation, but the pinpoint citation should not be followed by a comma.

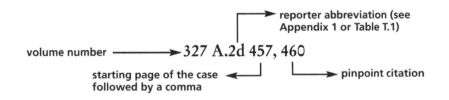

3. THE PARENTHETICAL

Following the information on the reporter, the case citation should include a parenthetical containing the abbreviated name of the jurisdiction, the abbreviated name of the level of court that decided the case, and the year the court issued its decision. This information is important because it can help the reader assess the weight of the authority you are citing.

The place to find the proper abbreviation for the jurisdiction and level of court is Appendix 1 in the *ALWD Manual* or Table T.1 in the *Bluebook*. Appendix 1 and Table T.1 list the levels of courts under each jurisdiction. Next to the name of each court, an abbreviation will appear in parentheses. This is the abbreviation for both the jurisdiction and the level of court, and this is what should appear in your parenthetical. You will notice that for the highest court in each state, the jurisdiction abbreviation is all that is necessary. This alerts the reader that the decision came from the highest court in the state; no additional court name abbreviation is necessary. Neither Appendix 1 nor Table T.1 lists the abbreviations for all courts. If you do not find the abbreviations you need in Appendix 1 in the *ALWD Manual*, consult Appendix 4, which contains court abbreviations. In the *Bluebook*, Table T.7 contains court names.

The last item to appear in the parenthetical is the year of the decision. The date when the court heard the case is not necessary in the citation; only the year of decision is required. No comma should appear before the year. After the year, the parenthetical should be closed.

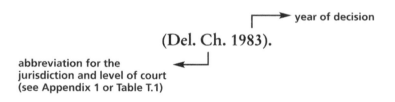

When all of the pieces are put together, the citation should look like this:

<u>Ellis v. Acme Mfg. Co.</u>, 327 A.2d 457, 460 (Del. Ch. 1983).

E. SAMPLE PAGES FOR RESEARCHING CASES USING A PRINT DIGEST

On the following pages, you will find sample pages illustrating the process of print digest research. For purposes of this illustration, assume that your client found a bag containing a large amount of money while swimming in the ocean off the Florida coast and wants to know whether she is now the legal owner of the money. If you were researching this issue, you might want to look for relevant federal cases. **Figures 4.16** through **4.23** show what you would see in *West's Federal Practice Digest*, Fourth Series. **Figure 4.24** shows the mini-digest in the back of an individual reporter volume. **Figure 4.25** contains sample pages from a case published in West's *Federal Supplement*, Second Series.

The first step is using the Descriptive-Word Index to lead you to relevant topics and key numbers. One search term you might have used is "Lost Goods." This entry directs you to another index entry: "Finding Lost Goods." Because digests are organized by subject, other terms in the DWI could have referred you to the "Finding Lost Goods" entry as well.

FIGURE 4.16   DESCRIPTIVE-WORD INDEX

LOSS

99 F P D 4th–82

References are to Digest Topics and Key Numbers

LOSS—Cont'd
MORTGAGES—Cont'd
  Redemption right—Cont'd

    Waiver, **Mtg** ⟋ 596

OIL and gas lien, **Mines** ⟋ 115

PARTNERSHIP. See heading
  PARTNERSHIP, LOSSES.

PERSONAL property, trespass, damages,
  Tresp ⟋ 49

PRIORITIES of claims and liens,
  Marshaling assets and securities, **Debtor &**
    C ⟋ 18

PROFITS, damages for loss of. See heading
  PROFITS, DAMAGES for loss of profits.

RECORD,
  Equitable relief against judgment, **Judgm**
    ⟋ 407(5)

RECORD on appeal. See heading **RECORD**
  ON APPEAL, LOST or destroyed
  records.

RECORDS. See heading **LOST RECORDS**,
  generally.

SALVAGE lien, **Salv** ⟋ 41

SAVINGS banks, **Banks** ⟋ 304

SEALS, **Seals** ⟋ 7

SEAMEN'S clothing and effects, **Seamen**
  ⟋ 31

SEAMEN'S lien, **Seamen** ⟋ 27(11)

SERVICES of,
  Child,
    Generally, **Parent & C** ⟋ 5(4), 7
    Evidence of damages for, **Damag**
      ⟋ 172(2)
  Damages for loss of,
    Amount, **Damag** ⟋ 133
    Element of compensation, generally,
      Damag ⟋ 37
    Evidence, **Damag** ⟋ 172, 186
    Instructions, **Damag** ⟋ 216(8)
    Jury questions, **Damag** ⟋ 208(4)
    Personal injuries, measure of damages,
      Damag ⟋ 99
    Pleading, **Damag** ⟋ 144
    Proof at variance with pleading, **Damag**
      ⟋ 159(2)
  Employee. See heading **EMPLOYMENT**
    LAW, INTERFERENCE with employ-
    ment relationship.
  Ground for action for seduction, **Seduct**
    ⟋ 8

LOSS—Cont'd

SHERIFF or constable, liability, **Sheriffs**
  ⟋ 119

SUBROGATION, loss of right to, **Subrog**
  ⟋ 35

SURETYSHIP, securities, as discharging
  surety, **Princ & S** ⟋ 115(1, 2)

TAX liens, **Tax** ⟋ 514

TAXATION-FEDERAL. See heading
  TAXATION-FEDERAL, generally.

UNITED States. See heading **UNITED**
  STATES, LOSS.

VESSEL,
  Chartered vessel or equipment, **Ship** ⟋ 54
  Effect on respondentia or bottomry bond,
    Ship ⟋ 98
  General average contribution, **Ship** ⟋ 192

WILLS. See heading **WILLS**, LOSS.

WORKERS' compensation, [DWI subject entry]
  heading **WORKERS' C**
  generally.

ZONING. See heading **ZONING**, LOSS.

LOST GOODS

FINDING lost goods. See heading **FINDING**
  LOST GOODS, generally.

LARCENY,
  Property subject to, **Larc** ⟋ 10
  Taking, element and requisites of, **Larc**
    ⟋ 16

LOST INSTRUMENTS

ACTIONS on lost instruments,
  Generally, **Lost Inst** ⟋ 13
  Affidavit of loss, **Lost Inst** ⟋ 17
  Attorney fees, **Lost Inst** ⟋ 25
  Burden of proof, **Lost Inst** ⟋ 23(1)
  Costs, **Lost Inst** ⟋ 25
  Defenses, **Lost Inst** ⟋ 19
  Evidence,
    Generally, **Lost Inst** ⟋ 23
    Admissibility, **Lost Inst** ⟋ 23(2)
    Sufficiency, **Lost Inst** ⟋ 23(3)
  Indemnity, **Lost Inst** ⟋ 18
  Judgment, **Lost Inst** ⟋ 24
  Jurisdiction, **Lost Inst** ⟋ 20
  Nature and form, **Lost Inst** ⟋ 14
  Parties, **Lost Inst** ⟋ 21
  Pleading, **Lost Inst** ⟋ 22
  Presumptions, **Lost Inst** ⟋ 23(1)
  Review, **Lost Inst** ⟋ 24

[Cross-reference to another entry]

Under "Finding Lost Goods," the entry for "Finders" refers to relevant topics and key numbers. The abbreviation "Aband L P" refers to the "Abandoned and Lost Property" topic, and the numbers refer to key numbers under that topic. Several relevant index entries refer you to key number 10.

FIGURE 4.17   DESCRIPTIVE-WORD INDEX

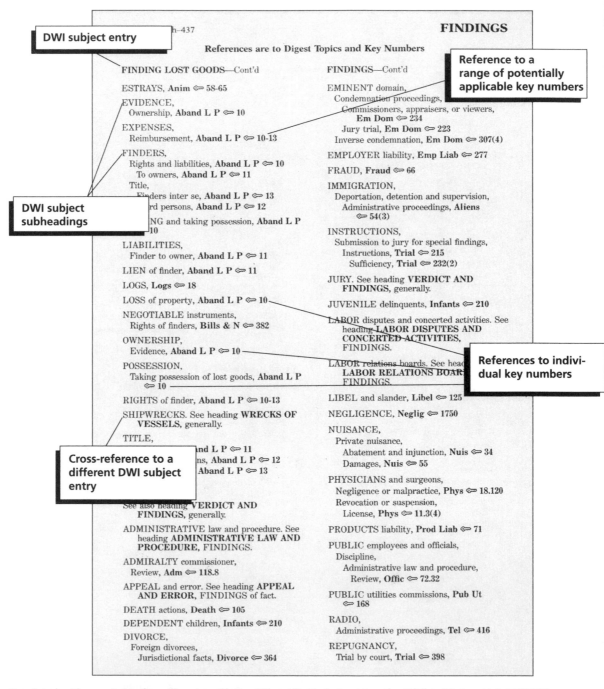

Reprinted with permission from Thomson Reuters/West, *West's Federal Practice Digest*, 4th Ser., Vol. 98 (2002), p. 437. © 2002 Thomson Reuters/West.

The index, as a hardcover volume, is updated with a pocket part. The pocket part entry under "Finding Lost Goods" provides an additional topic and key number reference that may be relevant.

FIGURE 4.18   DESCRIPTIVE-WORD INDEX, POCKET PART

```
98 F P D 4th-151                                                    FINES

                 References are to Digest Topics and Key Numbers
                                                            ┌─────────────────────┐
                                                            │ One new relevant    │
FIDUCIARY AND OTHER          FINANCIAL PRIVACY ACT          │ entry is listed.    │
CONFIDENTIAL RELATIONS—Cont'd                               └─────────────────────┘
                               Generally, Banks ☞ 151
HEALTH care professionals, Health ☞ 578
                             FINDING LOST GOODS
INDIANS,
   Fiduciary duty of officials, agencies, and agents,   MISLAID property, Aband L P ☞ 10
      Indians ☞ 117
   Government's fiduciary duty, Indians ☞ 105           FINDINGS

PROPERTY taxes,                                         ARBITRATION and award, Alt Disp Res ☞ 307
   Domicile or residence, Tax ☞ 2202
   Ownership or possession of property, Tax ☞ 2191      ASYLUMS, actions and proceedings, Asylums ☞ 48

TORTIOUS inducement of breach of fiduciary duty,        HEALTH care professionals, disciplinary
   Torts ☞ 204                                             proceedings, Health ☞ 221

TORTIOUS interference in general, Torts ☞ 204           IMMIGRATION. See heading IMMIGRATION,
                                                           FINDINGS.
UNFAIR trade practices, Antitrust ☞ 253
                                                        MEDICAL malpractice, Health ☞ 835
UNITED STATES,
   Indians,                                             MEDICARE, administrative proceedings, Health
      Fiduciary duty of government in general,             ☞ 551
         Indians ☞ 105
      Fiduciary duty of officials, agencies, and agents, NEGLIGENCE,
         Indians ☞ 117                                     Health care professionals, Health ☞ 835


FIFTEENTH AMENDMENT                                     FINES AND PENALTIES

POLITICAL activities, Const Law ☞ 1482                  ADMINISTRATIVE law and procedure in general,
                                                           Ex post facto, Const Law ☞ 2790
STANDING to raise Fifteenth Amendment issues in
   general, Const Law ☞ 729                             AIR pollution, Environ Law ☞ 296

                                                        ANTITRUST, Antitrust ☞ 1005
FIFTH AMENDMENT
                                                        ATTORNEY and client,
DUE process,                                               Discipline, Atty & C ☞ 59.11
   Generally. See heading DUE PROCESS,
      generally.                                        CIVIL rights violations, Civil R ☞ 1807
   Incorporation of other constitutional provisions,
      Const Law ☞ 3855                                  CONSTITUTIONAL law,
   Relationship to similar provisions, Const Law           Due process. See heading DUE PROCESS,
      ☞ 3855                                                  FINES and penalties.
                                                           Equal protection, Const Law ☞ 3758
                                                           Ex post facto,
FIGHTING                                                      Administrative law and procedure in general,
                                                                Const Law ☞ 2790
ANIMALS, regulation of, Anim ☞ 3.5(7)                         Civil penalties as criminal penalties in disguise,
                                                                Const Law ☞ 2789
COCKFIGHTING, Anim ☞ 3.5(7)                                 Impairment of obligation of contract, Const Law
                                                              ☞ 2763
CRUELTY to animals, Anim ☞ 3.5(7)                          Vested rights, Const Law ☞ 2647

DOGFIGHTING, Anim ☞ 3.5(7)                              CREDIT,
                                                           Imprisonment, Fines ☞ 12
WORDS,
   Speech, freedom of, Const Law ☞ 1562                 CRUELTY to animals, Anim ☞ 3.5(10)


FILED RATE OR TARIFF                                    DRUGS and controlled substances, Controlled Subs
                                                           ☞ 12
ANTITRUST,
   Filed rate doctrine,                                 DUE process. See heading DUE PROCESS, FINES
      Regulated industries,                                and penalties.
         Exemptions, Antitrust ☞ 906
                                                        EMPLOYEE pension and benefit plans. See heading
                                                           EMPLOYEE PENSION AND BENEFIT
FILING                                                     PLANS, FINES and penalties.

TAX sales,                                              EMPLOYMENT taxes, Tax ☞ 3296
   Delinquent list, Tax ☞ 2916
```

The next step is looking up the topic "Abandoned and Lost Property" in the subject volumes. The outline at the beginning of the topic identifies a range of key numbers that may be relevant.

FIGURE 4.19   KEY NUMBER OUTLINE, "ABANDONED AND LOST PROPERTY" TOPIC

ABANDONED AND LOST PROPERTY

SUBJECTS INCLUDED

General nature of relinquishment of property or other rights of any kind by abandonment, as distinguished from dedication, surrender, waiver, etc.

Effect of abandonment by way of extinguishment of the title or right

Finding and taking of possession of lost goods of another, whereby the finder may acquire title thereto

Nature, requisites and incidents of such finding and possession

Rights, duties and liabilities of finders of lost goods as to the owners or losers and as to others in general

SUBJECTS EXCLUDED AND COVERED BY OTHER TOPICS

Estrays, see ANIMALS

Lost instruments in writing, establishment of and action on, see LOST INSTRUMENTS

Negotiable paper, rights of finders, see BILLS AND NOTES

Particular persons or personal relations, abandonment of, see specific topics

Particular species of property, rights, remedies, or proceedings, abandonment of, see specific topics

Reversion of property to the state, see ESCHEAT

Rewards for recovery of lost goods, etc., see REWARDS

Sales of lost goods, see SALES

Wrecks and vessels and goods derelict at sea, see SHIPPING

For detailed references to other topics, see Descriptive-Word Index

_____

Analysis

_____

I. ABANDONMENT, ☞1–9.

II. FINDING LOST GOODS, ☞10–13.

_____

I. ABANDONMENT.
       ☞1. Nature and elements.
         1.1. —— In general.
         2. —— Intent.
         3. —— Acts and omissions.
         4. Evidence and questions for jury.
         5. Operation and effect.

II. FINDING LOST GOODS.
       ☞10. In general; loss of property.
         11. Rights and liabilities of finder as to owner.

Relevant key number

FIGURE 4.19   KEY NUMBER OUTLINE, "ABANDONED AND LOST PROPERTY" TOPIC *(Continued)*

ABANDONED & LOST PROPERTY   1 F P D 4th—2

II. FINDING LOST GOODS.—Continued.

Relevant key numbers

    12. Title and rights of finder as to third persons.

    13. Title and rights of finders inter se.

For detailed references to other topics, see Descriptive-Word Index

---

The case summaries under key number 10 include several potentially relevant cases from the federal district courts in Florida.

FIGURE 4.20   CASE SUMMARIES UNDER "ABANDONED AND LOST PROPERTY" TOPIC

1 F P D 4th—11   **ABANDONED & LOST PROPERTY**   ☞10

For references to other topics, see Descriptive-Word Index

matters were property of the estate, failed to prove that the state had abandoned its property rights with respect to the documents; although state apparently ceased looking for the documents after 1866 and 138 years went by before state asserted a claim, debtor did not clearly establish state's intent to relinquish its rights to the documents, and state presented evidence that efforts had been made to recover public records such as these following the Civil War but that records of the executive department had not been turned over.

In re Willcox, 329 B.R. 554.

Cl.Ct. 1990. Evidence did not support finding that assignee of working interest in oil and gas lease on property that was to be condemned abandoned its equipment after condemnation proceeding.

Paul v. U.S., 21 Cl.Ct. 415, affirmed 937 F.2d 623.

☞**5. Operation and effect.**

Library references

C.J.S. Abandonment § 12.

W.D.Mo. 2000. Under Missouri law, those who abandon property lose title.

In re Seizure of $82,000 More or Less, 119 F.Supp.2d 1013.

Currency which was hidden in forfeited vehicle's gas tank was owned by no one after it was abandoned by its original owners, but rather it went back into state of nature analogous to wild animals.

In re Seizure of $82,000 More or Less, 119 F.Supp.2d 1013.

D.N.J. 1994. When landowner or other bailee possesses property abandoned by another person, bailee may lawfully remove property from premises under New Jersey law, or may himself leave premises, without being liable for any subsequent loss.

Sgro v. Getty Petroleum Corp., 854 F.Supp. 1164, affirmed 96 F.3d 1434.

E.D.Va. 1995. Under the law of finds, abandoned personalty ceases to be the property of any person unless and until it is reduced to possession with intent to acquire title to, or ownership of, it, and thus it may be appropriated by anyone, if it has not been reclaimed by the former owner, by appropriating and reducing it to possession with intent to become the owner, provided the taking is fair, and the first person to reduce the property to possession, either actual or constructive, becomes its owner, but the required possession is a high degree of control over the property.

Bemis v. RMS Lusitania, 884 F.Supp. 1042, affirmed 99 F.3d 1129, certiorari denied 118 S.Ct. 1558, 523 U.S. 1093, 140 L.Ed.2d 791.

II. FINDING LOST GOODS.

☞**10. In general; loss of property.** ——— **Key number 10**

Library references

C.J.S. Finding Lost Goods §§ 1, 2.

C.A.5 (La.) 2000. A find differs from salvage in that the property has either been abandoned or never owned by any person, and the property belongs to the finder.

Adams v. Unione Mediterranea Di Sicurta, 220 F.3d 659, rehearing denied, certiorari denied 121 S.Ct. 1191, 531 U.S. 1192, 149 L.Ed.2d 107, on remand 2001 WL 986867, subsequent determination 234 F.Supp.2d 614, affirmed 364 F.3d 646, rehearing denied, certiorari denied UMS Generali Marine S.p.A. v. Adams, 125 S.Ct. 478, 160 L.Ed.2d 356, on remand 234 F.Supp.2d 614, affirmed 364 F.3d 646, rehearing denied, and rehearing denied, certiorari denied 125 S.Ct. 478, 160 L.Ed.2d 356.

Summaries of federal circuit court cases are listed first.

C.A.2 (N.Y.) 1998. Although the law of finds has been held to apply in some admiralty proceedings, finds law also exists independently in New York State law.

Dluhos v. Floating and Abandoned Vessel, Known as New York, 162 F.3d 63.

C.A.5 (Tex.) 1996. Archaeological Resources Protection Act (ARPA) did not vest collector with ownership of tokens that he had excavated from national forest, based on collector's contention that, because tokens were between 50 and 100 years old and thus were not "archaeological resources" for purposes of ARPA, ARPA thereby conveyed ownership to him as private collector of coins; ARPA did not authorize private individuals to remove coins less than 100 years old from public land and to retain ownership, nor did statute divest United States of ownership, but, rather, ARPA simply did not regulate private collection of such nonarchaeological resources. Archaeological Resources Protection Act of 1979, §§ 12, 12(b), 16 U.S.C.A. §§ 470kk, 470kk(b).

U.S. v. Shivers, 96 F.3d 120.

Even assuming that Archaeological Resources Protection Act (ARPA) regulated private collection of nonarchaeological resources, statute did not transfer or vest ownership of such nonarchaeological resources in collectors who find them, by providing that private collectors need not obtain permit for collection of certain artifacts; by allowing for private collection of nonarchaeological resources, statute did not thereby entitles collectors to retain or own what they had collected. Archaeological Resources Protection Act of 1979, § 12(b), 16 U.S.C.A. § 470kk(b).

U.S. v. Shivers, 96 F.3d 120.

† This Case was not selected for publication in the National Reporter System
For cited U.S.C.A. sections and legislative history, see United States Code Annotated

FIGURE 4.20   CASE SUMMARIES UNDER "ABANDONED AND LOST PROPERTY" TOPIC *(Continued)*

⚷10   **ABANDONED & LOST PROPERTY**   1 F P D 4th—12

For later cases, see same Topic and Key Number in Pocket Part

"Arrowhead exception" to Archaeological Resources Protection Act (ARPA) did not support collector's contention that, by inference, he was entitled to return of tokens which he had excavated from national forest, and which had been seized from him by federal government; arrowhead exception was not intended to encourage removal of arrowheads from public lands, but rather to exempt such removal from ARPA's civil and criminal penalty provisions, arrowhead exception was limited to those found on surface of public lands, unlike tokens excavated by collector, and ARPA expressly provided that removal of arrowheads could be penalized under other regulations or statutes.   Archaeological Resources Protection Act of 1979, § 7(a)(3), 16 U.S.C.A. § 470ff(a)(3); 36 C.F.R. § 296.3(a)(3)(iii).
    U.S. v. Shivers, 96 F.3d 120.

Under federal common law of finds, United States, not collector, was owner of tokens which collector had removed from site located within national forest, since tokens excavated by collector were buried in soil belonging to United States, and, under common law of finds, United States also owned tokens embedded in that soil.
    U.S. v. Shivers, 96 F.3d 120.

Federal common law of finds generally assigns ownership of abandoned property without regard to where property is found, subject to two exceptions, such that, when abandoned property is embedded in soil, it belongs to owner of the soil, and, when owner of land where the property is found, whether on or embedded in soil, has constructive possession of property, that property is not "lost" and belongs to owner of land.
    U.S. v. Shivers, 96 F.3d 120.

Archaeological Resources Protection Act (ARPA) does not confer to private collectors ownership of nonarchaeological resources that they discover on public lands; instead, federal common law of finds still applies.   Archaeological Resources Protection Act of 1979, § 12(b), 16 U.S.C.A. § 470kk(b).
    ...F.3d 120.

Under finds law, title to ...sts in person who re... his or her possession, is made, however, pre...requisites for divesting title must be satisfied.
    R.M.S. Titanic, Inc. v. Wrecked and Abandoned Vessel, 286 F.3d 194, certiorari denied 123 S.Ct. 118, 537 U.S. 885, 154 L.Ed.2d 144.

D.Del. 1986. Demonstration of possession and control of abandoned property is prerequisite to award of title under law of finds.
    Indian River Recovery Co. v. The China, 645 F.Supp. 141.

Law does not require one who discovers abandoned property actually to ha... but rather, law protects rights of ... discover abandoned property, and ... tually engaged in reducing it to ... complete this project without inter...
    Indian River Recovery Co. v. The China, 645 F.Supp. 141.

M.D.Fla. 1993. Under law of finds, title vests in person who reduces property to his or her possession unless abandoned property is embedded in soil, in which case it belongs to soil's owner, or if owner of land has constructive possession of property.
    Lathrop v. Unidentified, Wrecked & Abandoned Vessel, 817 F.Supp. 953.

Under maritime law, "find" assumes that property is abandoned and has returned to state of nature so that ownership is assigned to first person to reduce property to either actual or constructive possession.
    Lathrop v. Unidentified, Wrecked & Abandoned Vessel, 817 F.Supp. 953.

S.D.Fla. 1998. Under the law of finds, a finder acquires title to lost or abandoned property by occupancy, i.e. by taking possession of the property and exercising dominion and control over it.
    Sea Services of the Keys, Inc. v. Abandoned 29' Midnight Exp. Vessel, 16 F.Supp.2d 1369.

Law of finds, a common law doctrine, dictates that the finder of abandoned property must continuously possess or be in the process of reducing to possession the property which he has found.
    Sea Services of the Keys, Inc. v. Abandoned 29' Midnight Exp. Vessel, 16 F.Supp.2d 1369.

Common law of finds generally assigns ownership of the abandoned property without regard to where the property is found.
    Sea Services of the Keys, Inc. v. Abandoned 29' Midnight Exp. Vessel, 16 F.Supp.2d 1369.

When the owner of the land where the property is found has constructive possession of the property such that the property is not lost, it belongs to the owner of the land.
    Sea Services of the Keys, Inc. v. Abandoned 29' Midnight Exp. Vessel, 16 F.Supp.2d 1369.

S.D.Fla. 1986. Law of finds, a common-law doctrine, dictates that finder of abandoned property must continuously possess or be in

† **This Case was not selected for publication in the National Reporter System**
For cited U.S.C.A. sections and legislative history, see United States Code Annotated

The next step is checking the pocket part for this volume. The entry under key number 10 in the pocket part lists two cases from the federal courts in Virginia.

FIGURE 4.21   DIGEST VOLUME, POCKET PART

---

1 F P D 4th—1

ABANDONED AND LOST PROPERTY

I. ABANDONMENT.

Library references
C.J.S. Abandonment § 2 et seq.

⟜1. **Nature and elements.**
See ⟜1.1.

⟜1.1. —— **In general.**
E.D.Va. 1990. Columbus-America Discovery Group, Inc. v. Unidentified, Wrecked and Abandoned Sailing Vessel, 742 F.Supp. 1327, reversed Columbus-America Discovery Group v. Atlantic Mut. Ins. Co., 974 F.2d 450, certiorari denied 113 S.Ct. 1625, 507 U.S. 1000, 123 L.Ed.2d 183, on remand 1993 WL 580900, rescinded 56 F.3d 556, certiorari denied 116 S.Ct. 352, 516 U.S. 938, 133 L.Ed.2d 248, certiorari denied Grimm v. Columbus-America Discovery Group, Inc., 116 S.Ct. 521, 516 U.S. 990, 133 L.Ed.2d 429.
Bkrtcy.S.D.Ohio 2006. Under Ohio law, "abandoned property" is property over which the owner has relinquished all right, title, claim, and possession with the intention of not reclaiming it or resuming its ownership, possession, or enjoyment.—In re Panel Town of Dayton, Inc., 338 B.R. 764.
Under Ohio law, abandonment of property requires affirmative proof of intent to abandon, coupled with acts or omissions implementing the intent.—Id.

⟜2. —— **Intent.**
E.D.Va. 1990. Columbus-America Discovery Group, Inc. v. Unidentified, Wrecked and Abandoned Sailing Vessel, 742 F.Supp. 1327, reversed Columbus-America Discovery Group v. Atlantic Mut. Ins. Co., 974 F.2d 450, certiorari denied 113 S.Ct. 1625, 507 U.S. 1000, 123 L.Ed.2d 183, on remand 1993 WL 580900, rescinded 56 F.3d 556, certiorari denied 116 S.Ct. 352, 516 U.S. 938, 133 L.Ed.2d 248, certiorari denied Grimm v. Columbus-America Discovery Group, Inc., 116 S.Ct. 521, 516 U.S. 990, 133 L.Ed.2d 429.
Bkrtcy.S.D.Ohio 2006. Under Ohio law, the intent to abandon property must be shown by unequivocal and decisive acts indicative of abandonment.—In re Panel Town of Dayton, Inc., 338 B.R. 764.
Under Ohio law, a debtor's delay in attempting to retrieve already converted property does not show intent to abandon that property.—Id.

⟜3. —— **Acts and omissions.**
D.S.C. 2006. Under South Carolina law, to abandon a right, there must be some clear and unmistakable affirmative act or series of acts indicating a purpose to repudiate ownership.—Willcox v. Stroup, 358 B.R. 824, stay granted 358 B.R. 835, affirmed 467 F.3d 409, stay denied 127 S.Ct. 851, 166 L.Ed.2d 658, certiorari denied 127 S.Ct. 2105.
E.D.Va. 1990. Columbus-America Discovery Group, Inc. v. Unidentified, Wrecked and Abandoned Sailing Vessel, 742 F.Supp. 1327, reversed Columbus-America Discovery Group v. Atlantic Mut. Ins. Co., 974 F.2d 450, certiorari denied 113 S.Ct. 1625, 507 U.S. 1000, 123 L.Ed.2d 183, on remand 1993 WL 580900, rescinded 56 F.3d 556, certiorari denied 116 S.Ct. 352, 516 U.S. 938, 133 L.Ed.2d 248, certiorari denied Grimm v. Columbus-America Discovery Group, Inc., 116 S.Ct. 521, 516 U.S. 990, 133 L.Ed.2d 429.

ABATEMENT & REVIVAL

⟜4. **Evidence and questions for jury.**
C.A.4 (Va.) 1992. Columbus-America Discovery Group v. Atlantic Mut. Ins. Co., 974 F.2d 450, certiorari denied 113 S.Ct. 1625, 507 U.S. 1000, 123 L.Ed.2d 183, on remand 1993 WL 580900, rescinded 56 F.3d 556, certiorari denied 116 S.Ct. 352, 516 U.S. 938, 133 L.Ed.2d 248, certiorari denied Grimm v. Columbus-America Discovery Group, Inc., 116 S.Ct. 521, 516 U.S. 990, 133 L.Ed.2d 429.
Bkrtcy.S.D.Ohio 2006. Under Ohio law, judgment debtor's owner did not abandon its equipment and inventory, which had been located in two buildings sold to judgment creditor at a foreclosure sale, where there was no evidence that owner intended to abandon the property but, instead, the opposite was true, as owner repeatedly attempted to collect the property before being locked out of the premises by judgment creditor, and though following judgment creditor's blatant conversion, owner delayed for a few months before again demanding the property, such delay did not indicate an abandonment, but merely that owner was unsure up until that time how best to regain control of the property.—In re Panel Town of Dayton, Inc., 338 B.R. 764.
Legal standard for abandonment i̶n̶ ̶O̶h̶i̶o̶ quires evidence of the intent to aband̶o̶n̶ to be direct, affirmative, or reasonab̶l̶e̶ exclusive inference of throwing away.̶

> Pocket part entry for key number 10

II. FINDING LOST GOODS.

Library references
C.J.S. Finding Lost Goods § 1 et seq.

⟜10. **In general; loss of property.**
C.A.4 (Va.) 2006. To establish a claim under the law of finds, a finder must show (1) intent to reduce property to possession, (2) actual or constructive possession of the property, and (3) that the property is either unowned or abandoned.—R.M.S. Titanic, Incorporated v. The Wrecked and Abandoned Vessel, 435 F.3d 521.
E.D.Va. 1990. Columbus-America Discovery Group, Inc. v. Unidentified, Wrecked and Abandoned Sailing Vessel, 742 F.Supp. 1327, reversed Columbus-America Discovery Group v. Atlantic Mut. Ins. Co., 974 F.2d 450, certiorari denied 113 S.Ct. 1625, 507 U.S. 1000, 123 L.Ed.2d 183, on remand 1993 WL 580900, rescinded 56 F.3d 556, certiorari denied 116 S.Ct. 352, 516 U.S. 938, 133 L.Ed.2d 248, certiorari denied Grimm v. Columbus-America Discovery Group, Inc., 116 S.Ct. 521, 516 U.S. 990, 133 L.Ed.2d 429.

⟜12. **Title and rights of finder as to third persons.**
E.D.Va. 1990. Columbus-America Discovery Group, Inc. v. Unidentified, Wrecked and Abandoned Sailing Vessel, 742 F.Supp. 1327, reversed Columbus-America Discovery Group v. Atlantic Mut. Ins. Co., 974 F.2d 450, certiorari denied 113 S.Ct. 1625, 507 U.S. 1000, 123 L.Ed.2d 183, on remand 1993 WL 580900, rescinded 56 F.3d 556, certiorari denied 116 S.Ct. 352, 516 U.S. 938, 133 L.Ed.2d 248, certiorari denied Grimm v. Columbus-America Discovery Group, Inc., 116 S.Ct. 521, 516 U.S. 990, 133 L.Ed.2d 429.

ABATEMENT AND REVIVAL

II. ANOTHER ACTION PENDING.

Library references
C.J.S. Abatement and Revival § 16 et seq.

† This Case was not selected for publication in the National Reporter System

---

Reprinted with permission from Thomson Reuters/West, *West's Federal Practice Digest*, 4th Ser., Pocket Part, Vol. 1 (2007), p. 1. © 2007 Thomson Reuters/West.

At the end of *West's Federal Practice Digest*, Fourth Series, are a series of noncumulative interim pamphlets with cases decided after the pocket part was published. Under the topic "Abandoned and Lost Property" in this example, no new cases are summarized under key number 10.

FIGURE 4.22   NONCUMULATIVE INTERIM PAMPHLET

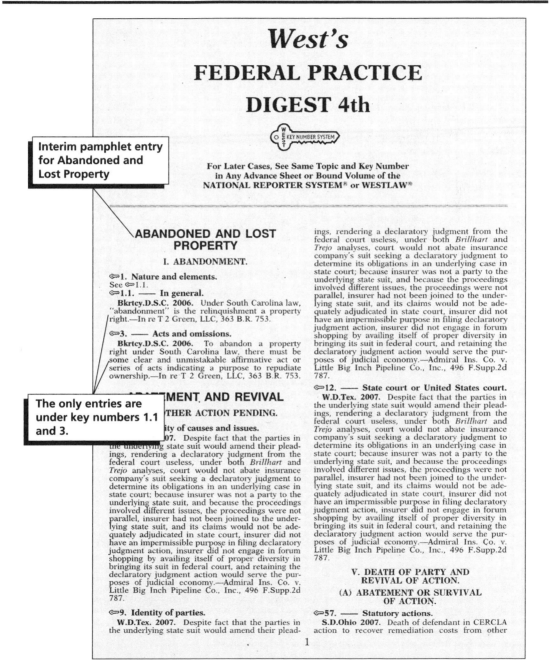

Interim pamphlet entry for Abandoned and Lost Property

The only entries are under key numbers 1.1 and 3.

West's
FEDERAL PRACTICE
DIGEST 4th

For Later Cases, See Same Topic and Key Number
in Any Advance Sheet or Bound Volume of the
NATIONAL REPORTER SYSTEM® or WESTLAW®

ABANDONED AND LOST PROPERTY

I. ABANDONMENT.

1. Nature and elements.
See 1.1.
1.1. —— In general.
  Bkrtcy.D.S.C. 2006. Under South Carolina law, "abandonment" is the relinquishment a property right.—In re T 2 Green, LLC, 363 B.R. 753.

3. —— Acts and omissions.
  Bkrtcy.D.S.C. 2006. To abandon a property right under South Carolina law, there must be some clear and unmistakable affirmative act or series of acts indicating a purpose to repudiate ownership.—In re T 2 Green, LLC, 363 B.R. 753.

....MENT AND REVIVAL

...THER ACTION PENDING.

...ity of causes and issues.
  ....07. Despite fact that the parties in the underlying state suit would amend their pleadings, rendering a declaratory judgment from the federal court useless, under both *Brillhart* and *Trejo* analyses, court would not abate insurance company's suit seeking a declaratory judgment to determine its obligations in an underlying case in state court; because insurer was not a party to the underlying state suit, and because the proceedings involved different issues, the proceedings were not parallel, insurer had not been joined to the underlying state suit, and its claims would not be adequately adjudicated in state court, insurer did not have an impermissible purpose in filing declaratory judgment action, insurer did not engage in forum shopping by availing itself of proper diversity in bringing its suit in federal court, and retaining the declaratory judgment action would serve the purposes of judicial economy.—Admiral Ins. Co. v. Little Big Inch Pipeline Co., Inc., 496 F.Supp.2d 787.

9. Identity of parties.
  W.D.Tex. 2007. Despite fact that the parties in the underlying state suit would amend their plead-

ings, rendering a declaratory judgment from the federal court useless, under both *Brillhart* and *Trejo* analyses, court would not abate insurance company's suit seeking a declaratory judgment to determine its obligations in an underlying case in state court; because insurer was not a party to the underlying state suit, and because the proceedings involved different issues, the proceedings were not parallel, insurer had not been joined to the underlying state suit, and its claims would not be adequately adjudicated in state court, insurer did not have an impermissible purpose in filing declaratory judgment action, insurer did not engage in forum shopping by availing itself of proper diversity in bringing its suit in federal court, and retaining the declaratory judgment action would serve the purposes of judicial economy.—Admiral Ins. Co. v. Little Big Inch Pipeline Co., Inc., 496 F.Supp.2d 787.

12. —— State court or United States court.
  W.D.Tex. 2007. Despite fact that the parties in the underlying state suit would amend their pleadings, rendering a declaratory judgment from the federal court useless, under both *Brillhart* and *Trejo* analyses, court would not abate insurance company's suit seeking a declaratory judgment to determine its obligations in an underlying case in state court; because insurer was not a party to the underlying state suit, and because the proceedings involved different issues, the proceedings were not parallel, insurer had not been joined to the underlying state suit, and its claims would not be adequately adjudicated in state court, insurer did not have an impermissible purpose in filing declaratory judgment action, insurer did not engage in forum shopping by availing itself of proper diversity in bringing its suit in federal court, and retaining the declaratory judgment action would serve the purposes of judicial economy.—Admiral Ins. Co. v. Little Big Inch Pipeline Co., Inc., 496 F.Supp.2d 787.

V. DEATH OF PARTY AND REVIVAL OF ACTION.

(A) ABATEMENT OR SURVIVAL OF ACTION.

57. —— Statutory actions.
  S.D.Ohio 2007. Death of defendant in CERCLA action to recover remediation costs from other

1

Reprinted with permission from Thomson Reuters/West, *West's Federal Practice Digest*, 4th Ser., October 2007 Pamphlet (2007), p. 1. © 2007 Thomson Reuters/West.

On the inside front cover of the interim pamphlet is the closing table indicating the last volumes of the reporters with cases summarized in this pamphlet. The *Federal Supplement*, Second Series, closes with volume 496.

FIGURE 4.23   NONCUMULATIVE INTERIM PAMPHLET, CLOSING TABLE

Closing with Cases Reported in

Supreme Court Reporter .... 127 S.Ct.
Federal Reporter, Third Series 494 F.3d 1026
Federal Appendix .... 231 Fed.Appx.
Federal Supplement, Second Series 496 F.Supp.2d
Federal Rules Decisions .... 242 F.R.D. 661
Bankruptcy Reporter .... 371 B.R. 570
Federal Claims Reporter .... 77 Fed.Cl. 709
Military Justice Reporter — U.S.Armed Forces .... 65 M.J. 248
Military Justice Reporter — A.F.Ct.Crim.App. .... 65 M.J. 745
Veterans Appeals Reporter .... 21 Vet.App. 359

COPYRIGHT © 2007 Thomson/West

To find cases decided after the interim pamphlet closed, the next step is checking the mini-digest in the back of each individual volume of F. Supp. 2d after volume 496. Most of them do not include any entries under "Abandoned and Lost Property." The example below comes from 502 F. Supp. 2d, which lists one case under key number 10.

FIGURE 4.24 502 F. Supp. 2d, MINI-DIGEST

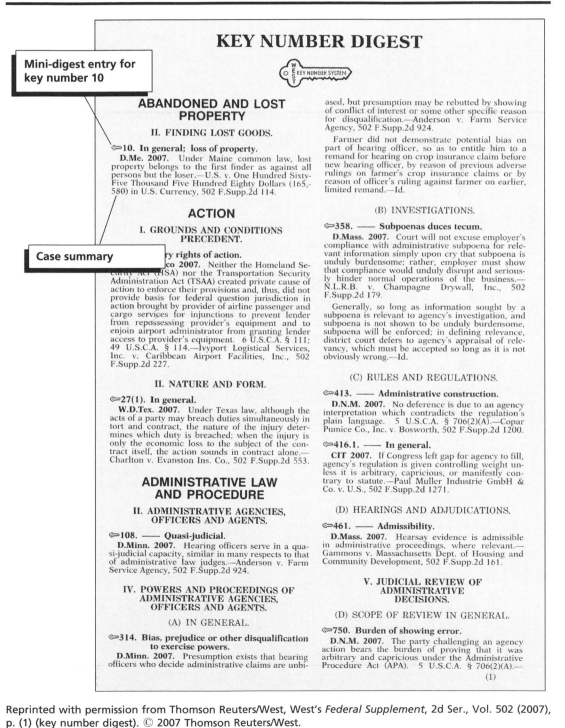

KEY NUMBER DIGEST

Mini-digest entry for key number 10

ABANDONED AND LOST PROPERTY

II. FINDING LOST GOODS.

⌾10. **In general; loss of property.**
D.Me. 2007. Under Maine common law, lost property belongs to the first finder as against all persons but the loser.—U.S. v. One Hundred Sixty-Five Thousand Five Hundred Eighty Dollars (165,-580) in U.S. Currency, 502 F.Supp.2d 114.

ACTION

I. GROUNDS AND CONDITIONS PRECEDENT.

Case summary

...ry rights of action.
...co 2007. Neither the Homeland Security Act (HSA) nor the Transportation Security Administration Act (TSAA) created private cause of action to enforce their provisions and, thus, did not provide basis for federal question jurisdiction in action brought by provider of airline passenger and cargo services for injunctions to prevent lender from repossessing provider's equipment and to enjoin airport administrator from granting lender access to provider's equipment. 6 U.S.C.A. § 111; 49 U.S.C.A. § 114.—Ivyport Logistical Services, Inc. v. Caribbean Airport Facilities, Inc., 502 F.Supp.2d 227.

II. NATURE AND FORM.

⌾27(1). **In general.**
W.D.Tex. 2007. Under Texas law, although the acts of a party may breach duties simultaneously in tort and contract, the nature of the injury determines which duty is breached; when the injury is only the economic loss to the subject of the contract itself, the action sounds in contract alone.— Charlton v. Evanston Ins. Co., 502 F.Supp.2d 553.

ADMINISTRATIVE LAW AND PROCEDURE

II. ADMINISTRATIVE AGENCIES, OFFICERS AND AGENTS.

⌾108. —— **Quasi-judicial.**
D.Minn. 2007. Hearing officers serve in a quasi-judicial capacity, similar in many respects to that of administrative law judges.—Anderson v. Farm Service Agency, 502 F.Supp.2d 924.

IV. POWERS AND PROCEEDINGS OF ADMINISTRATIVE AGENCIES, OFFICERS AND AGENTS.

(A) IN GENERAL.

⌾314. **Bias, prejudice or other disqualification to exercise powers.**
D.Minn. 2007. Presumption exists that hearing officers who decide administrative claims are unbi-

ased, but presumption may be rebutted by showing of conflict of interest or some other specific reason for disqualification.—Anderson v. Farm Service Agency, 502 F.Supp.2d 924.

Farmer did not demonstrate potential bias on part of hearing officer, so as to entitle him to a remand for hearing on crop insurance claim before new hearing officer, by reason of previous adverse rulings on farmer's crop insurance claims or by reason of officer's ruling against farmer on earlier, limited remand.—Id.

(B) INVESTIGATIONS.

⌾358. —— **Subpoenas duces tecum.**
D.Mass. 2007. Court will not excuse employer's compliance with administrative subpoena for relevant information simply upon cry that subpoena is unduly burdensome; rather, employer must show that compliance would unduly disrupt and seriously hinder normal operations of the business.— N.L.R.B. v. Champagne Drywall, Inc., 502 F.Supp.2d 179.

Generally, so long as information sought by a subpoena is relevant to agency's investigation, and subpoena is not shown to be unduly burdensome, subpoena will be enforced; in defining relevance, district court defers to agency's appraisal of relevancy, which must be accepted so long as it is not obviously wrong.—Id.

(C) RULES AND REGULATIONS.

⌾413. —— **Administrative construction.**
D.N.M. 2007. No deference is due to an agency interpretation which contradicts the regulation's plain language. 5 U.S.C.A. § 706(2)(A).—Copar Pumice Co., Inc. v. Bosworth, 502 F.Supp.2d 1200.

⌾416.1. —— **In general.**
CIT 2007. If Congress left gap for agency to fill, agency's regulation is given controlling weight unless it is arbitrary, capricious, or manifestly contrary to statute.—Paul Muller Industrie GmbH & Co. v. U.S., 502 F.Supp.2d 1271.

(D) HEARINGS AND ADJUDICATIONS.

⌾461. —— **Admissibility.**
D.Mass. 2007. Hearsay evidence is admissible in administrative proceedings, where relevant.— Gammons v. Massachusetts Dept. of Housing and Community Development, 502 F.Supp.2d 161.

V. JUDICIAL REVIEW OF ADMINISTRATIVE DECISIONS.

(D) SCOPE OF REVIEW IN GENERAL.

⌾750. **Burden of showing error.**
D.N.M. 2007. The party challenging an agency action bears the burden of proving that it was arbitrary and capricious under the Administrative Procedure Act (APA). 5 U.S.C.A. § 706(2)(A).—

(1)

This is the opinion in *Sea Services of the Keys, Inc. v. The Abandoned 29' Midnight Express Vessel*, a case summarized in the main subject volume of the digest. You would want to review this case, as well as others summarized in the digest, in conducting your research.

FIGURE 4.25 *SEA SERVICES OF THE KEYS, INC. v. THE ABANDONED 29' MIDNIGHT EXPRESS VESSEL*, 16 F. Supp. 2d 1369 (S.D. Fla. 1998)

SEA SERVICES OF KEYS v. 29' MIDNIGHT EXPRESS VESSEL   **1369**
Cite as 16 F.Supp.2d 1369 (S.D.Fla. 1998)

"specifically provide[ ]" otherwise, prevailing defendants can recover attorney's fees from the government pursuant to the EAJA. *See Clay Printing*, 13 F.3d at 818 ("Until another statute 'specifically provide[s]' that ADEA defendants cannot get such fees from the United States, the plain language of the EAJA will continue to control.").

Another distinction between Title VII and the ADEA is that Title VII specifically provides for attorney's fees from the United States whereas the ADEA is silent as to the United States. Thus, were this Court to hold that the EAJA did not apply to actions involving the government under the ADEA, it is unclear whether a prevailing defendant could recover attorney's fees from the government at all. The EAJA's purpose is to create a statutory basis for attorney's fees from the United States where there was none before. *See generally* H.R.Rep. No. 1418, 96th Cong., 2d. Sess., 1980 U.S.C.C.A.N. 4984. The "substantially justified" standard was meant to offset "[t]he deterrent effect created by [a private party's] inability to recover fees against the government" and prevent "precedent ... established on the basis of an uncontested order rather than the thoughtful presentation and consideration of opposing views." *Id.* There is simply no indication that the EAJA meant to exempt prevailing ADEA defendants from its broad application.[3]

Conclusion

The Court has found that (1) the EEOC was not substantially justified in initiating and continuing to litigate this case and (2) the EAJA's substantially justified standard governs this case. The Court will remand the case to the Magistrate for a determination of (1) whether Defendants meet the technical requirements of 28 U.S.C. § 2412(d)(2)(B) and (2) if so, the specific amount of attorney's fees to be awarded to Defendants.

3. While the Court concludes that the EAJA, including the provision containing the "substantially justified" standard, is generally applicable to ADEA cases, in order for the "substantially justified" standard to be used in the instant case, Defendants must meet certain technical requirements: at the time the EEOC filed the instant

Accordingly, after a careful review of the record, and the Court being otherwise fully advised, it is

ORDERED and ADJUDGED that the March 12, 1998 Report and Recommendation of the Honorable William C. Turnoff, U.S. Magistrate–Judge, be and the same is hereby, REVERSED in its entirety. It is further

ORDERED and ADJUDGED that the above-styled case be, and the same is hereby, REMANDED to the Honorable William C. Turnoff, U.S. Magistrate–Judge, for a determination of (1) whether Defendants meet the technical requirements of 28 U.S.C. § 2412(d)(2)(B) and (2) if so, the specific amount of attorney's fees to be awarded to Defendants.

**SEA SERVICES OF THE KEYS, INC.,
a Florida Corporation, d/b/a Sea
Tow Islamorada, Plaintiff,**

v.

**THE ABANDONED 29' MIDNIGHT EX-
PRESS VESSEL, and Two (2) 200HP
Mercury Offshore Outboard Motors, No.
OD213890 and No. OD222754, and all
tackle and appurtenances salvaged from
the vessel, in rem, Defendant.**

No. 96–10119–CIV.

United States District Court,
S.D. Florida.

May 18, 1998.

Suit was brought to determine ownership rights to defendant vessel. Upon plain-

action, CDI's and Wellpoints' net worth could not exceed $7,000,000 (individually) and each company had to have less than 500 employees. 28 U.S.C. § 2412(d)(2)(B). Accordingly, the Court will remand to the Magistrate for a determination of whether Defendants meet these technical requirements.

FIGURE 4.25 *SEA SERVICES OF THE KEYS, INC. v. THE ABANDONED 29' MIDNIGHT EXPRESS VESSEL*, 16 F. Supp. 2d 1369 (S.D. Fla. 1998) *(Continued)*

1370   16 FEDERAL SUPPLEMENT, 2d SERIES

tiff's motion for summary judgment, the District Court, James Lawrence King, J., held that plaintiff acquired title to abandoned vessel under common law of finds.

Motion granted.

1. Abandoned and Lost Property ⚖10

Under the law of finds, a finder acquires title to lost or abandoned property by occupancy, i.e. by taking possession of the property and exercising dominion and control over it.

2. Abandoned and Lost Property ⚖1.1

Under the law of finds, dereliction or renunciation of property requires both the intention to abandon and external action; there must be a voluntary intention to abandon, or evidence from which such intention may be presumed.

3. Shipping ⚖213

Plaintiff which retrieved vessel acquired title to vessel under common law of finds; original owner of vessel intended to abandon the boat, which was tied to a stranger's lobster trap and left alone in rough seas with its identification numbers and identifying papers removed.

4. Abandoned and Lost Property ⚖10

Law of finds, a common law doctrine, dictates that the finder of abandoned property must continuously possess or be in the process of reducing to possession the property which he has found.

5. Shipping ⚖213

In the absence of an intent to possess the vessel, which owner discovered tied to his lobster trap and left alone in rough seas with its identification numbers and identifying papers removed, owner of lobster trap did not divest vessel of its abandoned status.

6. Abandoned and Lost Property ⚖10

Common law of finds generally assigns ownership of the abandoned property without regard to where the property is found.

7. Abandoned and Lost Property ⚖10

When the owner of the land where the property is found has constructive possession of the property such that the property is not lost, it belongs to the owner of the land.

8. Shipping ⚖213

Owner of lobster trap, who discovered vessel left alone in rough seas with its identification numbers and identifying papers removed, did not constructively possess vessel because it was tied to his lobster trap.

David Paul Horan, Key West, FL, for Plaintiff.

Paulette R. Taylor, Assistant Attorney General, Miami, FL, for Defendant.

ORDER GRANTING SUMMARY FINAL JUDGMENT FOR PLAINTIFF

JAMES LAWRENCE KING, District Judge.

THIS CAUSE comes before the Court upon Plaintiff's Motion for Summary Judgment, filed April 28, 1998. The State of Florida Department of Environmental Protection ("Department") filed a response on May 11, 1998.

Factual Background

This case arises from a dispute over ownership rights to the Defendant vessel. Plaintiff claims ownership of the vessel under the law of finds and, alternatively, the law of salvage, asserting that it took possession of an abandoned vessel or salvaged the vessel when it was in a condition of marine peril. The Department contends that the vessel was neither abandoned nor in marine peril and that it is the rightful owner of the vessel due to the vessel's status as contraband.

The evidence before the Court consists of Plaintiff's Verified Complaint, Affidavits of Gene Mincey ("Mincey") and Steven Rieke ("Rieke") (attached to Dep't's Mot. for Summ. J.), and an Affidavit of Lt. George Steinmetz ("Steinmetz") (attached to Dep't's Mot. to Dismiss). Plaintiff states the following in its Verified Complaint: On October 7, 1996, at approximately 9:30 a.m., Plaintiff set out to retrieve the Defendant vessel after having received a call over VHF radio reporting an abandoned vessel. Before leaving

FIGURE 4.25 *SEA SERVICES OF THE KEYS, INC. v. THE ABANDONED 29' MIDNIGHT EXPRESS VESSEL*, 16 F. Supp. 2d 1369 (S.D. Fla. 1998) *(Continued)*

SEA SERVICES OF KEYS v. 29' MIDNIGHT EXPRESS VESSEL   **1371**
Cite as 16 F.Supp.2d 1369 (S.D.Fla. 1998)

port to locate the vessel, Plaintiff's captain informed the Florida Marine Patrol of the vessel's existence. After the Patrol responded that it did not have boats available to salvage the Defendant vessel, Plaintiff's captain stated that he would respond to the vessel. When Plaintiff's captain contacted the Coast Guard, it informed him that it had turned the matter over to the Florida Marine Patrol. According to Plaintiff, the marine conditions were "dangerous," consisting of five to seven foot seas and winds 15–20 MPH, with gusts of 25 MPH. When Plaintiff located the Defendant vessel, it was tied to a lobster trap and taking waves across its bow. The bow was down and the engines were rising out of the water with each successive wave. The boat had taken at least one foot of water, and the amount increased with every wave. Plaintiff's captain estimated that the vessel would sink within minutes. Plaintiff, at great personal risk, managed to tow the vessel to shore, purging the water out over the transom as it moved the vessel forward. One of Plaintiff's captains was injured in the process. During the tow, Plaintiff's captain noticed that the vessel's bilge switches were in the "off" position. Plaintiff summarizes that at its own risk, in perilous conditions, it saved the Defendant vessel from total loss.

The affidavits of Mincey and Rieke state the following: On October 7, 1996, at approximately 7:30 a.m., Mincey and Rieke were checking their lobster traps when they discovered the Defendant vessel tied to one of Mincey's traps. At that time, the boat was secured to the lobster buoy, with its bow toward the waves and engines out of the water. The bilge pumps were on, and there was no water in the boat. The boat did not appear to Mincey to have any physical damage. Mincey did notice, however, that there were no Florida registration numbers on the boat. Mincey and Rieke observed that the weather conditions were "rough," and that the seas were up to five feet. The men observed the boat for approximately one hour and then called the Florida Marine Patrol. Mincey could have towed the boat, but chose not to do so "because, in [his] experience, the circumstances under which [he] found the boat indicated to [him] that it

could have been involved in some type of illegal activity."

Finally, there is Steinmetz's affidavit, which was originally presented to the Court in conjunction with the Department's Motion to Dismiss but is now being relied upon by Plaintiff. Plaintiff asserts that Steinmetz's affidavit confirms that the weather conditions were adverse. Steinmetz does state that there were "adverse weather conditions" and "dangers of boarding a vessel of this type." He further states, "Due to the weather conditions I felt that it would be prudent for U.S.C.G. to respond in there [sic] 41 foot vessel."

Legal Standard

Summary judgment is appropriate only where it is shown that no genuine dispute as to any material fact exists and that the moving party is entitled to judgment as a matter of law. Fed.R.Civ.P. 56; *Celotex Corp. v. Catrett,* 477 U.S. 317, 322, 106 S.Ct. 2548, 91 L.Ed.2d 265 (1986). In ruling on the moving party's motion, the court must view the evidence in the light most favorable to the non-moving party. *Anderson v. Liberty Lobby, Inc.,* 477 U.S. 242, 255, 106 S.Ct. 2505, 91 L.Ed.2d 202 (1986). The court "should 'resolve all reasonable doubts about the facts in favor of the non-movant' and draw 'all justifiable inferences ... in his favor.'" *United States v. Four Parcels of Real Property,* 941 F.2d 1428, 1437 (11th Cir.1991)(alteration in original) (citation omitted).

Initially, the moving party bears the burden of pointing to that part of the record which shows the absence of a genuine issue of material fact. If the movant meets its burden, the burden then shifts to the non-moving party to establish that a genuine dispute of material fact exists. *Hairston v. Gainesville Sun Pub. Co.,* 9 F.3d 913, 918 (11th Cir.1993). To meet this burden, the non-moving party must go beyond the pleadings and "come forward with significant, probative evidence demonstrating the existence of a triable issue of fact." *Chanel, Inc. v. Italian Activewear of Florida, Inc.,* 931 F.2d 1472, 1477 (11th Cir.1991). If the evidence relied on is such that a reasonable jury could

FIGURE 4.25 *SEA SERVICES OF THE KEYS, INC. v. THE ABANDONED 29' MIDNIGHT EXPRESS VESSEL*, 16 F. Supp. 2d 1369 (S.D. Fla. 1998) *(Continued)*

1372   16 FEDERAL SUPPLEMENT, 2d SERIES

return a verdict in favor of the non-moving party, then the court should refuse to grant summary judgment. *Hairston*, 9 F.3d at 919. However, a mere scintilla of evidence in support of the non-moving party's position is insufficient to defeat a motion for summary judgment. *Anderson*, 477 U.S. at 252, 106 S.Ct. 2505.

Discussion

[1–3] Because the Court finds that Plaintiff has acquired title to the Defendant vessel under the common law of finds, the Court need not address whether there are any disputed issues of material fact as to the existence of marine peril. "[U]nder the law of finds, a finder acquires title to lost or abandoned property by 'occupancy,' i.e. by taking possession of the property and exercising dominion and control over it." *Treasure Salvors, Inc. v. Unidentified Wrecked & Abandoned Sailing Vessel*, 640 F.2d 560, 571 (5th Cir.1981). Thus, in order for a party to be entitled to ownership under the law of finds, the vessel must have been "abandoned" by its previous owner. "Dereliction or renunciation of property requires both the intention to abandon and external action.... There must be a voluntary intention to abandon, or evidence from which such intention may be presumed." *The No. 105*, 97 F.2d 425, 426 (5th Cir.1938). Clearly, the original owner of the Defendant vessel intended to abandon the boat. The boat was tied to a stranger's lobster trap and left alone in rough seas. There were no identifying papers on the boat. The abandoning party made no effort to reclaim the boat and had even gone so far as to scratch off the Florida registration numbers. Even the Department observed that "the vessel was 'abandoned' because the true owner cannot be located. All of the identification numbers were removed from the vessel. Consequently, the true identity of the vessel cannot be determined." (Dep't's Mem. in Opp'n to Pl.'s Mot. for Summ. J., at 6).

[4, 5] The Department contends, however, that even though the original owner abandoned the vessel, the vessel was taken into possession by Mincey and thus was not abandoned when Plaintiff towed it to shore. This Court finds, however, that Mincey did not actually or constructively possess the Defendant vessel so as to destroy its abandoned status. First, Mincey did not actually possess the vessel. "The law of finds, a common law doctrine, dictates that the finder of abandoned property must continuously possess or be in the process of reducing to possession the property which he has found." *MDM Salvage, Inc. v. Unidentified Wrecked & Abandoned Sailing Vessel*, 631 F.Supp. 308, 311 (S.D.Fla.1986). "It is well established that a finder does not acquire title merely on the strength of his discovery of lost or abandoned property." *Treasure Salvors*, 640 F.2d at 571. Rather, title accrues only if "a first finder maintains appropriate possession and control." *MDM Salvage, Inc.*, 631 F.Supp. at 311. The affidavits of Mincey and Rieke clearly show that Mincey has not acquired to title of the vessel. Mincey undertook no efforts to tow the vessel to shore. Mincey did not in any way attempt to possess the vessel. In fact, Mincey states in his affidavit that he intended to leave the vessel alone because he thought it might have been involved in illegal activity. In the absence of an intent to possess the vessel, Mincey cannot be held to divest the vessel of its abandoned status. *See The No. 105*, 97 F.2d at 426 (finding award of title inappropriate where "[t]here was no evidence before the court indicating [the] intention [to possess]."). A finding that under these circumstances Mincey possessed the Defendant vessel would contravene the policies behind the common law of finds. As the former Fifth Circuit has explained:

Although cases involving the principles of the law of finds are few and far between, we think that a basic principle emerges with some clarity from the cases which have considered problems similar to the one presented here. Persons who actually reduce lost or abandoned objects to possession and persons who are actively and ably engaged in efforts to do so are legally protected against interference from others whereas persons who simply discover or locate such property, but do not undertake to reduce it to possession are not. This principle reflects a very simple policy to afford protection to persons who actually

FIGURE 4.25   *SEA SERVICES OF THE KEYS, INC. v. THE ABANDONED 29' MIDNIGHT EXPRESS VESSEL*, **16 F. Supp. 2d 1369 (S.D. Fla. 1998) (Continued)**

SEA SERVICES OF KEYS v. 29' MIDNIGHT EXPRESS VESSEL   **1373**
Cite as 16 F.Supp.2d 1369 (S.D.Fla. 1998)

endeavor to return lost or abandoned goods to society as an incentive to undertake such expensive and risky ventures; the law does not clothe mere discovery with an exclusive right to the discovered property because such a rule would provide little encouragement to the discoverer to pursue the often strenuous task of actually retrieving the property and returning it to a socially useful purpose and yet would bar others from attempting to do so. *Treasure Salvors,* 640 F.2d at 572.

[6–8] The Department argues that, despite the fact that Mincey did nothing to return the Defendant vessel to society, Mincey constructively possessed the vessel because it was tied to his lobster trap. However, "[t]he common law of finds generally assigns ownership of the abandoned property without regard to where the property is found." *Klein v. Unidentified Wrecked and Abandoned Sailing Vessel,* 758 F.2d 1511, 1514 (11th Cir.1985). There is an exception to this general rule that occurs "when the owner of the land where the property is found (whether on or embedded in the soil) has constructive possession of the property such that the property is not 'lost,' it belongs to the owner of the land." *Id.* Constructive possession of a land owner is not established from the mere fact that a vessel is affixed to his land. Rather, constructive possession is establish only when the land owner has the power to possesses the vessel and the *intention* to exercise control over it. *See* 1 Am. Jur.2d *Abandoned, Lost, and Unclaimed Property* § 18 (1994) ("Constructive possession, for this purpose, is generally defined as knowingly having both the power and intention, at a given time, to exercise dominion or control over the property."). The Department relies on *Klein* to support the proposition that Mincey had constructive possession of the Defendant vessel. In *Klein,* however, the Eleventh Circuit found that the United

States had clearly displayed an intent to possess a shipwreck embedded in its soil. 758 F.2d at 1514. It observed:

> Since 1975 the United States has had constructive possession of the wreck by virtue of a Preliminary Archeological Assessment of Biscayne National Monument prepared for Park Service. This assessment noted the presence of an 18th century shipwreck in the area of the [defendant] wreck. Furthermore, the United States has had the power and the intention to exercise dominion and control over the shipwreck. Thus the United States has never legally lost the subject shipwreck and, as the owner of the land on and/or in which the shipwreck is located, it owns the shipwreck.

Id. The case at bar is completely distinguishable from *Klein.* First, there are the obvious, but perhaps technical, factual differences. Whereas in *Klein,* the vessel was embedded in the United States' land, in the instant case the vessel was merely tied to a lobster trap owned by Mincey. Furthermore, in *Klein* the defendant vessel had been embedded in the United States' land for hundreds of years. In the instant case, the vessel had been recently tied to the lobster buoy when Mincey discovered it. The more important distinction is that Mincey did not possess the requisite intention to exercise dominion over the Defendant vessel. As observed above, Mincey's affidavit clearly shows an intention not to possess the vessel in fear that it was involved in illegal activity. A property owner who discovers a vessel affixed to his property and then himself abandons the vessel cannot be said to have, by virtue of owning the property, constructively possessed that vessel. Because the Court concludes that the vessel was abandoned and subsequently possessed by Plaintiff, it need not address the issue of whether or not marine peril existed so as to justify a salvage award.[1]

---

1. The Court notes that Plaintiff would most likely be entitled to summary judgment under the law of salvage. The parties do not dispute that the conditions were dangerous and that Plaintiff, at its own peril, undertook to rescue the Defendant vessel. The Department presents evidence that the boat was not in danger of sinking at 8:30 a.m. because its bow was in the wind and rising and falling with the waves. The Department

does not, however, present any evidence to contradict Plaintiff's evidence that the vessel was in peril of sinking at 10:00 a.m. Given the "rough" conditions, a boat's condition can easily change from safe to disastrous in a matter of minutes, depending on the force and direction of the wind, waves, and tide. Furthermore, as Plaintiff points out, any prolonged exposure of the outboard motors to sea water will lead to corrosion

FIGURE 4.25 *SEA SERVICES OF THE KEYS, INC. v. THE ABANDONED 29' MIDNIGHT EXPRESS VESSEL*, 16 F. Supp. 2d 1369 (S.D. Fla. 1998) (Continued)

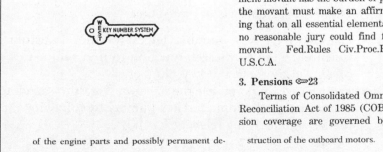

1374   16 FEDERAL SUPPLEMENT, 2d SERIES

Conclusion

The State of Florida, for over a year and a half and at taxpayer expense, has fought to retain possession of this twenty-nine foot vessel, which it never undertook efforts to salvage, tow, or restore. Plaintiff, at its own personal risk, battled the elements to return the Defendant vessel to a condition useful to society, only to later find itself having to wage another battle with the state to retain the fruits of its labor:

> As grave as the perils of sea are and were, the gravest perils to the treasure itself came not from the sea, but from two unlikely sources. Agents of two governments, Florida and the United States, who have the highest responsibility to protect the rights and property of citizens, claimed the treasure as belonging to the United States and Florida.... It would amaze and surprise most citizens of this country, when their dream, at the greatest of costs, was realized, that agents of their respective governments would, on the most flimsy of grounds, lay claim to the treasure.

Treasure Salvors, Inc. v. Unidentified, Wrecked and Abandoned Sailing Vessel, 459 F.Supp. 507, 511 (S.D.Fla.1978).

Accordingly, after a careful review of the record, and the Court being otherwise fully advised, it is

ORDERED and ADJUDGED that Plaintiff's Motion for Summary Judgment be, and the same is hereby, GRANTED. Final Judgment be, and the same is hereby, ENTERED in favor of Plaintiff.

Timothy S. BOWERS, Plaintiff,

v.

BLUE CROSS BLUE SHIELD OF GEORGIA, Defendant.

No. Civ.A. 1:97–CV–2980–RWS.

United States District Court, N.D. Georgia, Atlanta Division.

Aug. 28, 1998.

Former employee brought suit for equitable relief against health insurer of Employee Retirement Income Security Act (ERISA) after health insurer first issued and then cancelled Consolidated Omnibus Budget Reconciliation Act of 1985 (COBRA) conversion policy and then cancelled it because employee was Medicare recipient. On cross-motions for summary judgment, the District Court, Story, J., held that material issues of fact precluded summary judgment on claims that insurer waived right to deny coverage to Medicare recipient and that insurer was equitably estopped from denying coverage.

Motions denied.

1. Federal Civil Procedure ⟷2544

When the nonmovant has the burden of proof at trial, the movant may carry its burden at summary judgment by demonstrating the absence of an essential element of the nonmovant's claim. Fed.Rules Civ.Proc.Rule 56, 28 U.S.C.A.

2. Federal Civil Procedure ⟷2544

For issues on which the summary judgment movant has the burden of proof at trial, the movant must make an affirmative showing that on all essential elements of the case no reasonable jury could find for the nonmovant. Fed.Rules Civ.Proc.Rule 56, 28 U.S.C.A.

3. Pensions ⟷23

Terms of Consolidated Omnibus Budget Reconciliation Act of 1985 (COBRA) conversion coverage are governed by Employee

of the engine parts and possibly permanent de-   struction of the outboard motors.

F. CHECKLIST FOR CASE RESEARCH

1. SELECT A PRINT DIGEST

- ❏ Use *West's Federal Practice Digest* to locate all federal cases.
- ❏ Use a state digest to locate state and federal cases from an individual state.
- ❏ Use a regional digest to locate state cases only within the region.
- ❏ Use a combined digest to locate state and federal cases from all United States jurisdictions.

2. LOCATE TOPICS AND KEY NUMBERS IN A PRINT DIGEST

- ❏ From a case on point, use the headnotes at the beginning of the decision to identify relevant topics and key numbers.
- ❏ From the Descriptive-Word Index, look up relevant subjects, check the pocket part for new index headings, and look up the topics and key numbers in the subject volumes.
- ❏ From a topic entry, review subjects included and excluded and the outline of key numbers.

3. READ THE CASE SUMMARIES IN THE PRINT DIGEST

- ❏ Use the court and date abbreviations to target appropriate cases.

4. UPDATE PRINT DIGEST RESEARCH

- ❏ Check the pocket part for the subject volume.
- ❏ Check any cumulative or noncumulative interim pamphlets at the end of the digest set.
- ❏ Check the closing table on the inside front cover of the most recent interim pamphlet (if there is no interim pamphlet, check the closing table on the inside front cover of the pocket part).
- ❏ If necessary, check the mini-digests in the back of each reporter volume published after the latest volume listed in the closing table.

5. ELECTRONIC CASE RESEARCH

- ❏ In Westlaw, search for cases by subject.
  - Use the West Key Number Digest Outline (Custom Digest) function or the KeySearch function to find summaries of cases organized by topic and key number.
  - From a case on point, use the Custom Digest to search for cases under a particular topic and key number by following the link to the key number in a relevant headnote.

❑ In LexisNexis, search for cases by subject

- Use the Topic or Headnote search function to find citations to cases organized by topic and headnote subject.
- From a case on point, use the "More like this headnote" option to search for cases under the same headnote subject.

❑ In Westlaw and LexisNexis, execute word searches for cases using federal, state, or combined databases.

❑ Selected cases may be available on the Internet.

CHAPTER 5

RESEARCH WITH CITATORS

A. Introduction to citators

B. Using Shepard's in LexisNexis for case research

C. Using KeyCite in Westlaw for case research

D. Using Shepard's Citations in print for case research

E. Sample pages for case research with Shepard's and KeyCite

F. Checklist for case research with citators

A. INTRODUCTION TO CITATORS

1. THE PURPOSE OF A CITATOR

Virtually all cases contain citations to legal authorities, including other cases, secondary sources, statutes, and regulations. These decisions can affect the continued validity of the authorities they cite. For example, earlier cases can be reversed or overruled, or statutes can be held unconstitutional. Even if an authority remains valid, the discussion of the authority in later cases can be helpful in your research. As a consequence, when you find an authority that helps you answer a research question, you will often want to know whether the authority has been cited elsewhere, and if so, what has been said about it.

The tool that helps you do this is called a citator. Citators catalog cases, secondary sources, and other authorities, analyzing what they say about the sources they cite. Some citators also track the status of statutes and regulations, indicating, for example, whether a statute has been amended or repealed. Citators will help you determine whether an authority is still "good law," meaning it has not been changed or invalidated since it was published. They will also help you locate additional authorities that pertain to your research question.

The most well-known print citator is Shepard's Citations. Because Shepard's was, for many years, the only citator most lawyers ever used, checking citations came to be known as "Shepardizing." Generations of law students learned how to interpret print Shepard's entries, which are filled with symbols and abbreviations. (You can see a sample print entry in **Figure 5.13** in Section D, below.) Today, however, few legal researchers use Shepard's in print. Many libraries no longer carry Shepard's in print. Instead, virtually all legal researchers use electronic citators. Shepard's is still a well-respected citator. It is available in LexisNexis. Westlaw also has its own citator called KeyCite, and other electronic service providers offer their own citators.

Because print citators are becoming unavailable, this chapter focuses on electronic citators. Sections B and C explain how to use Shepard's in LexisNexis and KeyCite in Westlaw for case research. Section D provides a brief discussion of Shepard's in print. Citators can be used in researching many types of authority, including cases, statutes, regulations, and some secondary sources. The process of using a citator, however, is the same for almost any type of authority. Accordingly, for purposes of introducing you to this process, this chapter focuses on the use of citators in case research. Later chapters in this book discuss the use of Shepard's and KeyCite in researching other types of authority.

2. When to Use a Citator in Case Research

You must check every case on which you rely to answer a legal question to make sure it is still good law. In general, you will want to use Shepard's or KeyCite early in your research, after you have identified what appear to be a few key cases, to make sure you do not build your analysis on authority that is no longer valid. Using a citator at this stage will help direct you to other relevant authorities as well. You should also check every case you cite before handing in your work to make sure each one continues to be authoritative. Citing bad authority is every attorney's nightmare, and failing to check your citations can constitute professional malpractice. As a consequence, now is the time to get in the habit of updating your case research carefully.

3. Choosing Among Citators

Because Shepard's and KeyCite are the most widely used citators, they are the focus of this chapter, but they are not the only citators. Other electronic service providers have their own citators. For example, the Loislaw service's citator is called GlobalCite. The VersusLaw service's citator is called V.Cite. (The Internet addresses for these services appear in Appendix A.) And although Shepard's and KeyCite provide largely the same information, they are not identical. As a result, you must decide which citator(s) to use for your research.

The decision will depend on several factors. Shepard's and KeyCite are the most accepted citators in legal research, and you should use them whenever you have access to them. Certainly, while you are in law school, you should use both services enough to become comfortable with them. When you are out of school, you may continue to have access to one or both services. As of this writing, Shepard's and KeyCite are fairly economical to use, costing subscribers only a few dollars per citation, and many law libraries that have discontinued subscriptions to Shepard's in print provide free public access to these services. If you do not have access to Shepard's or KeyCite but do have access to another citator, you should use it, understanding that the coverage of the citator may be limited to holdings within that service's database.

Using either Shepard's or KeyCite should be sufficient to verify the continued validity of a case as long as you interpret the information they provide carefully. Shepard's and KeyCite do not simply list sources that have cited a case; they also analyze how later sources have interpreted the case. Characterizing the treatment of a case requires the exercise of editorial judgment. From time to time, Shepard's and KeyCite will characterize the status of a case differently. And while both Shepard's and KeyCite are generally reliable, both occasionally contain errors. Therefore, if a case is especially important to your analysis, you would do well to check it in more than one citator.

If you are looking for research references, you may also want to use more than one citator. Any citator should provide references to later cases that you can use for research, but not all include references to secondary sources. Shepard's and KeyCite include references to secondary sources, but they do not index all the same secondary sources. Thus, you may get slightly different research results in each service. Of course, there is more than one way to find almost any source, so a single citator—even one that does not include references to secondary sources—may be sufficient for your research when used in combination with other research tools. If you are having trouble finding relevant information, however, consider using a different citator to see if it identifies additional research references.

4. TERMS AND PROCEDURAL CONCEPTS USED IN CITATOR RESEARCH

Before you begin learning how to use citators, it is important to understand the terminology and procedural concepts used in the process. A case citator contains entries for decided cases that list the later authorities (cases, secondary sources, and other forms of authority) that have cited the case. This chapter uses the term "original case" to describe the case that is the subject of the citator entry. The terms "citing case" and "citing source" refer to the later authorities that cite the original case. Thus, for example, if you located the case of *Bennett v. Stanley*, 748 N.E.2d 41 (Ohio 2001), and wanted to use a citator to verify its continued validity, *Bennett* would be referred to as the original case. The later authorities that cite *Bennett* would be referred to as citing cases (for cases) or citing sources (for all other types of authority).

Two procedural concepts you need to understand are direct and indirect case history. Direct history refers to the all of the opinions issued in conjunction with a single piece of litigation. One piece of litigation may generate multiple opinions. A case may be appealed to a higher court, resulting in opinions from both an intermediate appellate court and the court of last resort. A higher court may remand a case, that is, send a case back to a lower court, for reconsideration, again resulting in opinions issued by both courts. Or a court might issue separate opinions to resolve individual matters arising in a case. All of these opinions, whether issued before or after the original case, constitute direct history. Opinions issued before the original case may be called prior history; those issued after may be called subsequent history or subsequent appellate history, as appropriate. Indirect history refers to an opinion generated from a different piece of litigation than the original case. Every unrelated case that cites the original case is part of the indirect history of the original case.

Both direct and indirect case history can be positive, negative, or neutral. Thus, if the original case is affirmed by a higher court, it has positive direct history, but if the original case is reversed, it has negative direct history. A related opinion in the same litigation on a different issue could be neutral; the opinion resolving the second issue could have no effect on the continued validity of the opinion resolving the first issue. Similarly, if the original case is relied upon by a court deciding a later, unrelated case, the original case has positive indirect history, but if the original case is overruled, it has negative indirect history. A citing case could discuss the original case in a way that does not include any positive or negative analysis. In that situation, the indirect history would be considered neutral.

B. USING SHEPARD'S IN LEXISNEXIS FOR CASE RESEARCH

To use Shepard's in LexisNexis effectively, you need to know how to access the service, interpret the entries, and customize the display and other options to target the information you want.

1. ACCESSING SHEPARD'S

One way to access Shepard's is by selecting the Shepard's tab from the top of the LexisNexis screen and entering the citation you want to Shepardize. Shepard's offers two options for retrieving entries. You can select Shepard's for Research or for Validation. The research entry will be the most complete; it will list all citing cases and sources for the original case. The validation entry is more limited. If you are not sure which option you need, choose Shepard's for Research. If it contains more information than you need, you can limit the display after you retrieve the entry.

Another way to access Shepard's is from a case. If you are viewing a case, you can choose the *Shepardize* option at the top of the display to Shepardize the case without having to enter the citation.

2. INTERPRETING SHEPARD'S ENTRIES

Once you have retrieved the entry for the original case, you must evaluate the information you find. **Figure 5.1** shows part of a Shepard's entry. One of the first things you will notice in a Shepard's entry is a symbol such as a red stop sign or a yellow triangle. These symbols are called Shepard's Signals, and they indicate the type of treatment the original case has received from the citing cases. If you retrieve the full text of a case before Shepardizing it, you will also see a Shepard's Signal at the beginning of the case. A list of Shepard's signals with their definitions appears in **Figure 5.2**.

FIGURE 5.1   SHEPARD'S® ENTRY EXCERPT FOR 748 N.E.2d 41

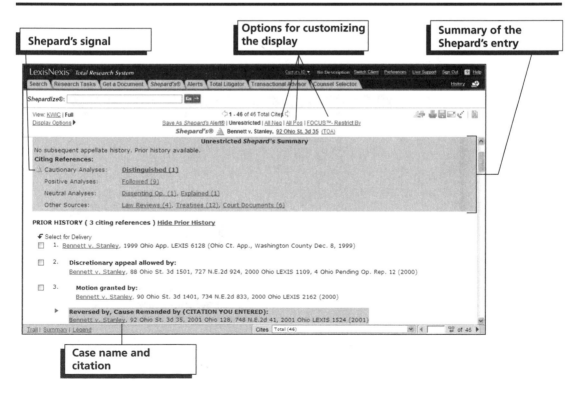

FIGURE 5.1   SHEPARD'S® ENTRY EXCERPT FOR 748 N.E.2d 41 *(Continued)*

> **Citing cases from the same state as the original case are listed after direct history.**

> **Treatment of the original case**

> **Federal cases organized by circuit are listed after cases from the original case's state.**

> **State cases from other states follow federal cases.**

> **Secondary sources follow citing cases.**

Reprinted with permission of LexisNexis. SHEPARD's entry for 748 N.E.2d 41.

FIGURE 5.2   SHEPARD'S® SIGNALS

SIGNAL	MEANS
Red stop sign	Warning: Negative treatment is indicated. This signal is used when the case has been reversed, overruled, or has other strong negative treatment.
Orange square surrounding the letter Q	Questioned: Validity questioned by citing references. This signal is used when the authoritative value of the case has been questioned, but the case has not expressly been reversed or overruled.
Yellow triangle	Caution: Possible negative treatment. This signal is used when the case has received treatment that could be negative, such as being distinguished or criticized.
Green diamond surrounding a plus sign	Positive treatment is indicated. This signal is used when the case has received positive treatment, such as being affirmed or followed.
Blue circle surrounding the letter A	Citing references with neutral analysis available. This signal is used when the case has received treatment that is neither positive nor negative, such as being explained.
Blue circle surrounding the letter I	Citation information available. This signal is used when the case has been cited, but no history or treatment codes have been assigned to the citing sources.

It is often difficult to reduce the status of a case to a single notation. Determining the continued validity of an original case often requires study of the citing cases. For example, an original case with a negative Shepard's Signal such as a red stop sign may no longer be good law for one of its points, but it may continue to be authoritative on other points. If you were to rely on the red stop sign without further inquiry, you might miss a case that is important for the issue you are researching. As a consequence, although Shepard's Signals can be helpful research tools, you should not rely on them in deciding whether the original case is valid. Always research the Shepard's entry and review the citing cases carefully to satisfy yourself about the status of the original case.

Along with the Shepard's Signal, you will see a summary of the entry. This summary highlights certain parts of the entry. For example, if the direct history of the case is negative, the summary will indicate negative subsequent appellate history. If appropriate, it will identify the nature of the treatment (followed, distinguished, overruled, etc.) that citing cases have given the original case. It will also indicate the number and type of citing sources, and can be customized to display the headnotes in the original case containing concepts discussed in the citing cases.

Following the summary, you will find details on the direct history of the case. Prior and subsequent opinions arising from the same litigation will be listed along with notations indicating the effect of any subsequent appellate history on the validity of the original case. The citation for the original case will be highlighted so you can identify it easily within the history. To retrieve any citing case in the direct history, use the link to the case name.

After the direct history, a listing of all citing cases in the indirect history of the original case will appear. When you Shepardize a federal case, the list will begin with federal cases divided according to circuit. For each circuit, appellate cases will appear first, followed by federal district court cases. After all of the federal cases, state cases will be listed alphabetically by state, again with cases from higher courts first, followed by those from subordinate courts. When you Shepardize a state case, the list of citing cases will begin with cases from the same state as the original case. Then you will see federal cases by circuit and cases from other states.

Shepard's provides information about each citing case in the entry. Along with the full name and citation to the citing case, the entry will note the treatment the citing case has given the original case. Often, the citing case will simply have "cited" the original case without significant analysis. If, however, the citing case has given the original case treatment that could affect its continued validity (e.g., following, explaining, criticizing, or distinguishing it), Shepard's will note that. You can view a citing case from the beginning by following the link to the case name. Below the full citation, however, Shepard's will give you the pinpoint citation to the page or pages on which the original case is cited. If the citing case is published in more than one reporter, pinpoint citations for each reporter can be displayed. By following the link to the pinpoint citation, you can go directly to the portion of the citing case that discusses the original case.

Another feature in a Shepard's entry is the headnote references. You may recall from Chapter 4, on case research, that headnotes are summary paragraphs added by case editors identifying the key points in the case. If a citing case cites the original case for a point that is summarized in a headnote at the beginning of the original case, the headnote will be referenced in the Shepard's entry. In the example citation, *Bennett* discusses a point of law that is summarized in headnote 11. A citing case, *Kiracofe v. Ketcham*, has cited *Bennett* for the same proposition of law summarized in headnote 11. Thus, the Shepard's entry includes the reference to headnote 11. The illustrations in **Figures 5.3** through **5.5** trace a headnote from an original case to a Shepard's entry to a citing case. You may again recall from Chapter 4 that West publishes many

FIGURE 5.3   HEADNOTE 11 FROM THE ORIGINAL CASE, *BENNETT v. STANLEY*

Reprinted with permission of LexisNexis, from LexisNexis 748 N.E.2d 41.

FIGURE 5.4   SHEPARD'S® ENTRY EXCERPT FOR *BENNETT v. STANLEY*

Reprinted with permission of LexisNexis. SHEPARD's entry for 748 N.E.2d 41.

FIGURE 5.5   *KIRACOFE v. KETCHAM*, CITING *BENNETT v. STANLEY*

Headnote 11 of *Bennett*

LexisNexis® Total Research System   Custom ID ▾ · No Description   Switch Client | Preferences | Live Support | Sign Out   ❔ Help

Search | Research Tasks | Get a Document | Shepard's® | Alerts | Total Litigator | Transactional Advisor | Counsel Selector   History 🔍

FOCUS™ Terms [   ]   Search Within Original Results (1 - 1) ▾ Go ➜ Advanced...

View: Case Brief | **Full** | Custom   ⟲ 1 of 1 ⟳   📄 📑 💾 ☑ 📋
                                            More Like This | More Like Selected Text | *Shepardize®* | TOA
                                            Kiracofe v. Ketcham, 2005 Ohio 5271 (Copy w/ Cite)   Pages: 7

[*P14] ᴴᴺ³✛The attractive-nuisance doctrine is a form of tort liability recognized by the Ohio Supreme Court in *Bennett v. Stanley* (2001), 92 Ohio St.3d 35, 42, 2001 Ohio 128, 748 N.E.2d 41. Under this doctrine, a possessor of land may be subject to civil liability for physical harm sustained by a child trespasser under certain circumstances where the landowner is aware of an artificial condition on the property that poses an unreasonable risk of death or serious bodily harm to children and the owner is aware that children frequent the area where the condition exists. Id.; see also Restatement of the Law 2d, Torts (1965), Section 339.

[*P15] In the instant case, the Kiracofes have failed to present any evidence to demonstrate that the mere presence of a semi-tractor and trailer on a residential lot poses an unreasonable risk of death or serious bodily injury. The Kiracofes merely claim that some unfortunate event could occur if the neighborhood children were to play on the truck. However, the mere allegation that an injury could happen because of some artificial [**10] condition does not amount to evidence that the condition poses an unreasonable risk of harm. Put simply, there is no indication that this truck, when parked on residential property, poses any more risk of harm than the average motor vehicle. Therefore, appellants have failed to fulfill their burden of demonstrating that a genuine issue of material fact exists concerning whether the presence of the truck creates a nuisance in violation of the deed restriction. Accordingly, the third assignment of error is overruled.

[*P16] Appellants next claim that Richard Ketcham violated the deed restrictions by using the property for business purposes. They argue that the sole use of the truck is to facilitate Ketcham's employment with Gladieux Trading & Marketing Co. According to their argument, by taking the truck directly from the residence to his pick-up location and returning directly to the residence from his drop-off location Ketcham is using the residence to enable his business activity. Appellants point to the Michigan Supreme Court decision in Borsvold v. United Dairies (1957), 347 Mich. 672, 81 N.W.2d 378, for the proposition that continual parking of a commercial [**11] vehicle on residential property, plus daily operation of that vehicle from that location, violated a deed restriction prohibiting business use of the property.

[*P17] Appellants' reliance on *Borsvold* is misplaced. The factual circumstances in that case are distinguishable from the case sub judice. The primary fact influencing that court's decision was that the property was being used solely as an extension of the garage operation being

▲ Outline   Page Select a Reporter ▾ [   ] 🔢 ◀ Doc [   ] 🔢 of 1   ▶ ◀ Term [   ] 🔢 of ___ ▶

Reprinted with permission of LexisNexis, from LexisNexis 2005 Ohio 5271.

state and federal reporters and adds headnotes to those cases. LexisNexis headnotes are different from West headnotes, and the two sets of headnotes do not correspond to each other. The LexisNexis headnotes are the ones that are automatically displayed in the Shepard's entry.

After the list of citing cases, you will find other citing sources. Statutory annotations appear next to let you know whether the original case has been summarized in the research references in an annotated code. (Annotated codes are discussed in Chapter 6, on statutory research.) Secondary sources follow, divided by type of authority (law review articles, treatises, etc.). Shepard's entries do not include references to A.L.R. Annotations (a type of secondary source described in Chapter 3); because A.L.R. is published by West, references to that publication appear only in KeyCite. The last item in the entry is court documents. These are filings submitted by parties in other cases that have cited the original case, not documents issued by a court.

All of these references will help you determine whether the original case remains valid. They will also help you find additional research sources. You will often want to view the full Shepard's entry to get the most complete information about the original case.

3. CUSTOMIZING THE OPTIONS

Although the full Shepard's entry provides the most complete information about the original case, you may want to view a more limited entry depending on your research task. Shepard's offers several options for customizing the display to focus on the information most relevant to you.

As an initial matter, you can choose Shepard's for Validation (KWIC) when you enter the citation to view a restricted Shepard's entry limited to citing cases that have given the original case significant treatment. You can switch between the validation (KWIC) and research (FULL) views using the links in the top left corner of the screen. From the full Shepard's entry, you also have several options for customizing the display. Using the links in the center at the top of the screen and the "display options" function at the top left, you can limit the display as indicated (e.g., all positive cases; all negative cases).

The FOCUS™-Restrict By option allows the greatest degree of customization. From this screen, you can limit the display by type of analysis, jurisdiction of citing cases and sources, headnote, date, or terms you specify. In the headnote restrictions, you may have the option to choose whether to display LexisNexis, West, or official reporter headnotes, although that will not be true for all cases. You can combine the choices to restrict the entry according to multiple criteria. **Figure 5.6** shows the FOCUS™-Restrict By options.

One additional option you will notice at the top of the Shepard's entry allows you to Save as Shepard's Alert®. This option does not limit the display you see on the screen. It allows you to customize

FIGURE 5.6 SHEPARD'S® FOCUS™-RESTRICT BY OPTIONS

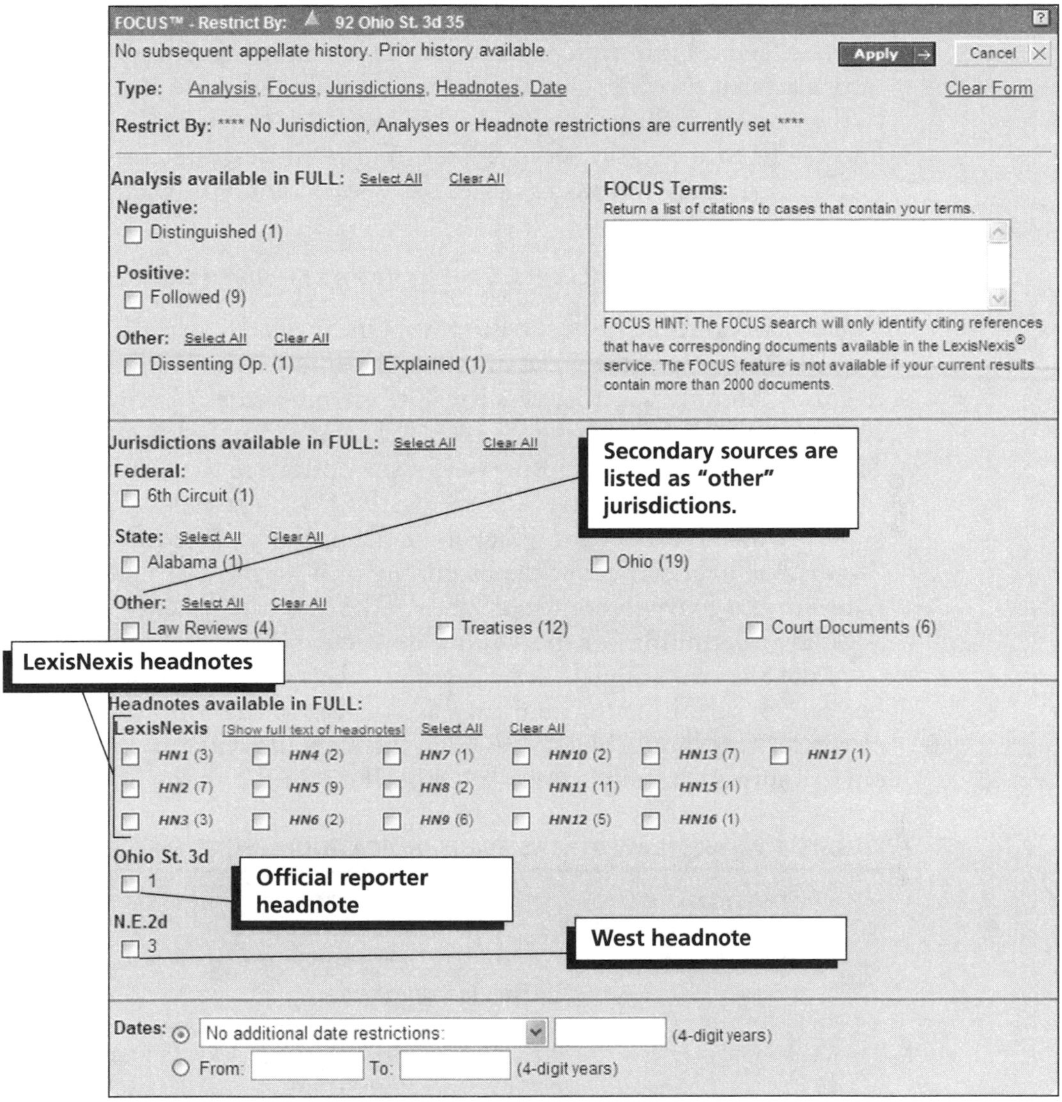

Reproduced by permission of LexisNexis. LexisNexis, Shepard's® Focus™-Restrict By Options.

your research in a different way. If you find a case that is especially useful, you may want to monitor it over time to make sure it remains valid and to review any new citing cases or sources added to the Shepard's entry. This will be especially useful when you are working on a project over a long period of time. Shepard's Alert® automatically Shepardizes the authorities you select and delivers periodic reports to you. To set up a Shepard's Alert®, choose the Save as Shepard's Alert® option or the Alerts tab at the top of the screen and follow the instructions to specify the content, delivery format, and frequency of the report.

C. USING KEYCITE IN WESTLAW FOR CASE RESEARCH

Westlaw provides a citator called KeyCite. KeyCite is available for cases, statutes, and administrative materials. It is similar to Shepard's in the information it provides, and the process of using KeyCite is very similar to the process of Shepardizing. To use KeyCite effectively, you need to know how to access the service, interpret the entries, and customize the display and other options to target the information you want.

1. ACCESSING KEYCITE AND INTERPRETING THE ENTRIES

You can access KeyCite in several ways. One way is by selecting the Key-Cite link at the top of the Westlaw screen and entering the citation you want to check. Another way to access KeyCite is from a case. When you view a case, a KeyCite box appears under the "links for" tab at the left margin. You can access KeyCite by choosing one of the options in the KeyCite box.

KeyCite is linked with cases in Westlaw's databases with a notation system similar to Shepard's Signals in LexisNexis. A symbol called a "status flag" will appear at the beginning of both the case and the Key-Cite entry to give you some indication of the case's treatment in KeyCite. Westlaw's definitions of the status flags are explained in **Figure 5.7**.

Like Shepard's Signals, KeyCite status flags are useful research tools, but cannot substitute for your own assessment of the continued validity of a case. You should always research the KeyCite entry and review the citing sources carefully to satisfy yourself about the status of a case.

FIGURE 5.7   WESTLAW STATUS FLAGS INDICATING KEYCITE HISTORY

NOTATION	MEANS
Red flag	The case is no longer good law for at least one of the points it contains.
Yellow flag	The case has some negative history, but has not been reversed or overruled.
Blue H	The case has direct history that is not known to be negative.
Green C	The case has citing references, but no direct history or negative citing references.

Once you have retrieved the entry for the original case, you must evaluate the information you find. One of the first things you will notice about KeyCite is that the entry for the original case is divided into three parts: full history, direct history, and citing references. **Figure 5.8** shows

FIGURE 5.8 KEYCITE FULL HISTORY ENTRY FOR 748 N.E.2d 41

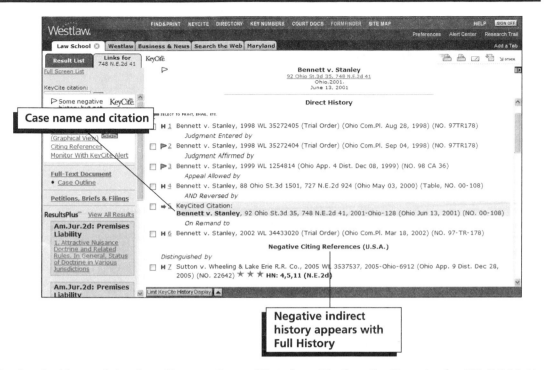

Reprinted with permission from Thomson Reuters/West, from Westlaw, KeyCite entry for 748 N.E.2d 41. © 2008 Thomson Reuters/West.

the full history of a case in KeyCite. The full history includes the direct history of the original case, as well as any negative indirect history that could affect the validity of the original case. Procedural phrases (e.g., affirmed, reversed) and other notations (e.g., distinguished, disagreed with, overruled) will indicate the effects of these cases on the validity of the original case. The citation for the original case will be highlighted so you can identify it easily within the history. If the direct history of the original case includes any separate but related cases, those will be listed after any negative indirect history. You can retrieve any case listed in the entry by using the link to the number next to the citation.

The direct history option shows the history of the case in chart form; it is sometimes called Graphical KeyCite. **Figure 5.9** shows a Graphical KeyCite display. Graphical KeyCite is useful when you are checking the validity of a case with complex history because it allows you to see a snapshot of any prior or subsequent history. Graphical KeyCite uses bands of color to identify the level of the court that issued each decision in a case's history, working from lowest to highest level. The original case is marked to make it easily identifiable on the screen. You can view the entire history of the original case in thumbnail view on a single screen, or you can

FIGURE 5.9   GRAPHICAL KEYCITE DISPLAY FOR 748 N.E.2d 41

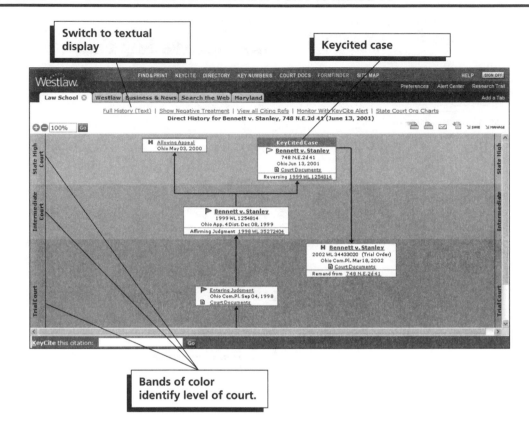

Reprinted with permission from Thomson Reuters/West, from Westlaw, KeyCite entry for 748 N.E.2d 41.
© 2008 Thomson Reuters/West.

use the zoom in and out feature to focus on specific aspects of the original
case's history. If you are viewing the entire case history in thumbnail view,
you can enlarge a chart box by rolling the cursor over the block. Graphical
KeyCite shows only direct history. Therefore, you need to switch back to
the textual format to view any indirect history or citing sources.

The citing references portion of the entry shows the complete
indirect history of the original case along with other citing sources.
Figure 5.10 shows a citing references entry in KeyCite. KeyCite organizes citing cases by type and depth of treatment, not by jurisdiction the
way Shepard's does. The KeyCite entry is divided into sections for
negative cases, positive cases, secondary sources (including A.L.R. Annotations), and court documents. The negative cases section lists any
negative indirect history; the list here will include notations to tell you
what negative treatment the original case received (e.g., distinguished,
overruled, etc.). It then lists citing cases that give the original case positive
treatment. The positive citing cases are organized by depth of treatment
and then by jurisdiction within the depth of treatment category.

FIGURE 5.10   KEYCITE CITING REFERENCES ENTRY FOR 748 N.E.2d 41

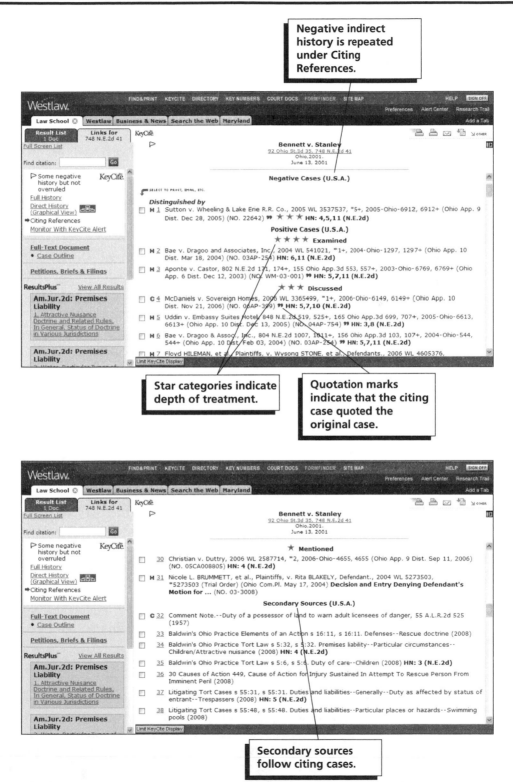

Negative indirect history is repeated under Citing References.

Star categories indicate depth of treatment.

Quotation marks indicate that the citing case quoted the original case.

Secondary sources follow citing cases.

FIGURE 5.11   DEFINITIONS OF KEYCITE STAR CATEGORIES

NUMBER OF STARS	MEANING	DEFINED
Four stars	Examined	Contains an extended discussion of the original case, usually more than a printed page of text
Three stars	Discussed	Contains a substantial discussion of the original case, usually more than a paragraph but less than a printed page
Two stars	Cited	Contains some discussion of the original case, usually less than a paragraph
One star	Mentioned	Contains a brief reference to the original case, usually in a string citation

KeyCite uses a system of star categories to indicate depth of treatment. The star categories indicate how much discussion of the original case you will find in the citing case. There are four star categories: (a) examined (four stars); (b) discussed (three stars); (c) cited (two stars); and (d) mentioned (one star). **Figure 5.11** delineates how West defines these terms.

You can retrieve any citing case or source by using the link to the number next to the citation. The citing case or source will appear in a new window, and Westlaw automatically displays the portion of the citing case or source that cites the original case. If a citing case quotes the original case, quotation marks will appear after the citation to the citing case in the KeyCite entry.

Headnote references also follow the citations to citing cases and sources. The headnote references in KeyCite work the same way as those in Shepard's. If a citing case cites the original case for a proposition of law summarized in a headnote at the beginning of the original case, the headnote reference will appear in the KeyCite entry. The headnote references in KeyCite correspond only to West headnotes, not LexisNexis headnotes or headnotes in an official reporter.

2. CUSTOMIZING THE OPTIONS

Although the full KeyCite entry provides the most complete information about the original case, you may want to view a more limited entry depending on your research task. KeyCite offers several options for customizing the display to focus on the information most relevant to you.

To limit the display, select the "Limit KeyCite Display" option at the bottom of the screen. From the full history of the case, choosing this

FIGURE 5.12   KEYCITE LIMITED DISPLAY OPTIONS

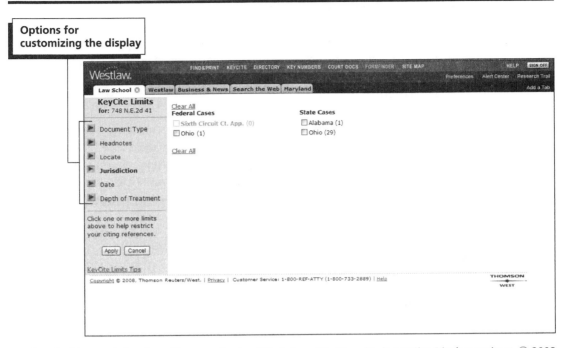

Reprinted with permission from Thomson Reuters/West, from Westlaw, Limit KeyCite Display options. © 2008 Thomson Reuters/West.

option will allow you to show negative treatment only. From the list of citing references, you will have a menu of options, as shown in **Figure 5.12**. You can limit the display by document type, headnote, terms you specify (using the Locate function), jurisdiction, date, or depth of treatment. Although each option appears on a different screen, you can combine options to limit the entry according to multiple criteria. As noted above, KeyCite displays only West headnotes; you cannot customize the display to show LexisNexis or official reporter headnotes.

KeyCite also allows you to customize your research with an alert. Like Shepard's Alert®, KeyCite Alert automatically checks the authorities you select and delivers periodic reports to you. To set up a KeyCite Alert, choose the option to "Monitor with KeyCite Alert" and follow the instructions to specify the content, delivery format, and frequency of the report.

D. USING SHEPARD'S CITATIONS IN PRINT FOR CASE RESEARCH

As noted earlier, many libraries no longer carry Shepard's in print. Nevertheless, it is possible that you will need to know how to use the print version of Shpeard's. To summarize the process briefly, Shepardizing cases in print requires four steps:

- locating the correct set of Shepard's books to check the citation
- locating the correct volumes within the set of Shepard's
- locating the entry for the case within each volume
- interpreting the entries.

Shepard's publishes multiple sets of books that correspond roughly to the publications they cover. Thus, to Shepardize a federal case, you would use *Shepard's Federal Citations*, and to Shepardize an Indiana case you would use either *Shepard's Indiana Citations* or *Shepard's North Eastern Citations*, assuming that the case appears in both the Indiana official and West regional reporters.

Shepard's volumes are not cumulative; each one covers a specific period of time. Therefore, once you locate the correct set of Shepard's, you must collect all of the hardcover volumes that contain entries for the citation you are Shepardizing, as well as any softcover supplements. On the front cover of the most recent supplement, you will see a section entitled "What Your Library Should Contain." Use this section to determine which Shepard's volumes you need to use.

Once you have compiled the volumes and supplements you need to check, you must look up the citation in each one to see if an entry appears. The entries will be organized numerically by volume and page number. Be aware, however, that some Shepard's volumes cover more than one reporter, so you must take care to look in the correct section of the book.

If the original case has a Shepard's entry, the entry will list citing cases and sources in the same order in which they would appear in Shepard's in LexisNexis. **Figure 5.13** contains an example of a print Shepard's entry. The citations to citing cases may be accompanied by letter notations. These are history and treatment codes that tell you the relationship between the original case and the citing cases. For example, if the original case has been reversed, you will find the letter "r" next to the citation to the case that reversed the original case. If the original case has been followed by later decisions, you will find the letter "f" next to the citations to cases that followed the original case. You may also find superscript numbers in some of the citations. These are headnote references. They serve the same purpose as headnote references in the electronic citators, indicating the proposition for which the citing source cited the original case. You can use the tables at the beginning of each print volume to identify the symbols and abbreviations in the entry. If you do not find an entry for the case, it has not been cited during the period covered by the Shepard's volume.

FIGURE 5.13   SHEPARD'S® ENTRY FOR *KENNEY v. SCIENTIFIC, INC.*

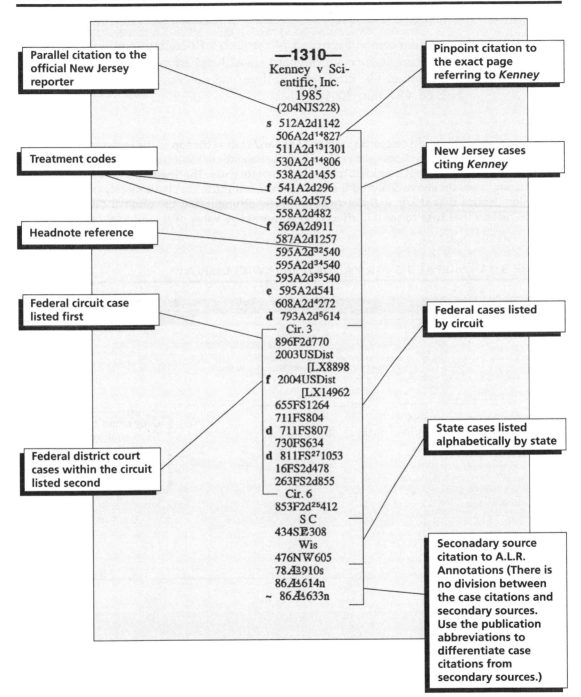

E. SAMPLE PAGES FOR CASE RESEARCH WITH SHEPARD'S AND KEYCITE

Beginning below, **Figures 5.14** through **5.19** contain sample screen shots illustrating features of Shepard's and KeyCite not illustrated earlier in this chapter. The citing case in these examples is *Bennett v. Stanley*, 748 N.E.2d 41 (Ohio 2001).

To Shepardize a case, access Shepard's from the Shepard's tab at the top of the LexisNexis screen and enter the citation. You can choose either Shepard's for Validation (KWIC), which limits the display, or Shepard's for Research (FULL), which displays the complete entry. The Shepard's for Validation entry shows citing cases that have analyzed the original case, not those that have merely cited it without discussion. Notice that *Uddin v. Embassy Suites Hotel* distinguished the original case. You might want to review that case to see if it affects the authoritative value of the original case.

FIGURE 5.14   SHEPARD'S FOR VALIDATION (KWIC) DISPLAY

FIGURE 5.14   SHEPARD'S FOR VALIDATION (KWIC) DISPLAY *(Continued)*

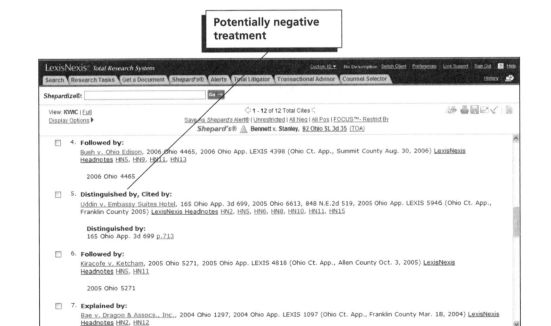

Reproduced by permission of LexisNexis. From LexisNexis, Shepard's entry for 748 N.E.2d 41.

Following the link to *Uddin v. Embassy Suites Hotel* retrieves the case. References to the original case are highlighted.

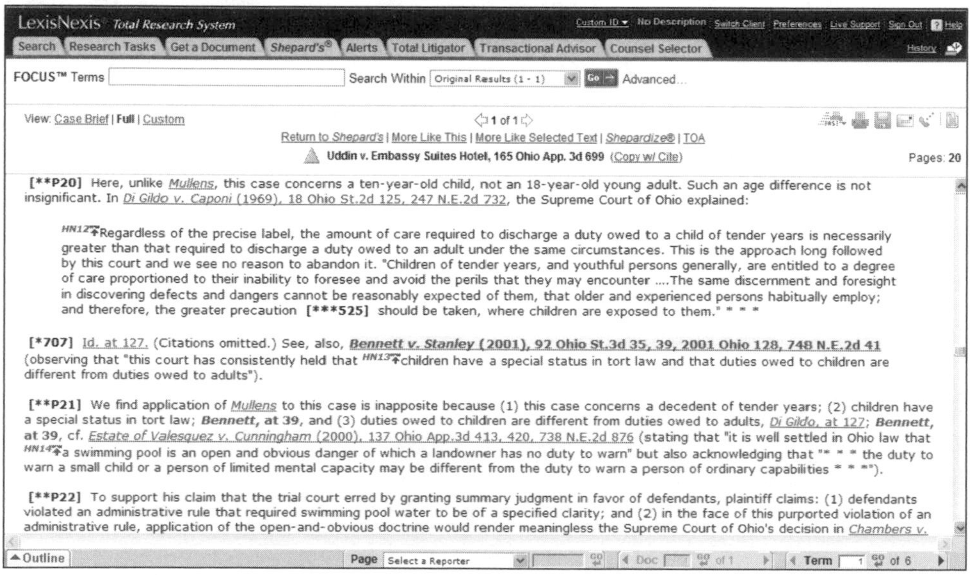

FIGURE 5.15   SHEPARD'S CITING CASE

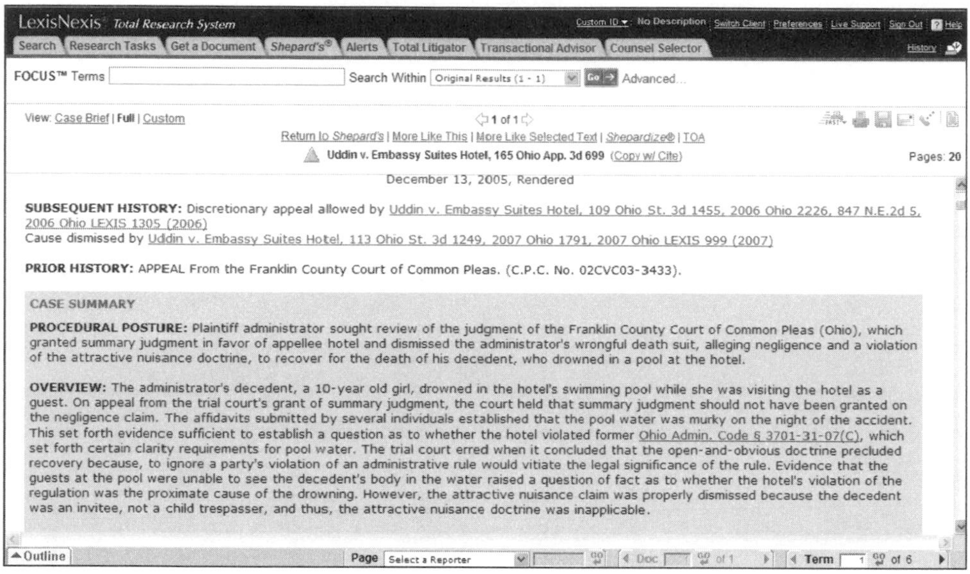

Reproduced by permission of LexisNexis. From LexisNexis, 165 Ohio App. 699.

When you view the Full History of a case in KeyCite, you can limit the display using the button at the bottom of the screen. Notice the difference between KeyCite's analysis of the citing cases and Shepard's. KeyCite does not characterize *Uddin* as distinguishing the original case. KeyCite does, however, characterize a different case, *Sutton v. Wheeling & Lake Erie R.R. Co.*, as distinguishing the original case. Shepard's did not list this case in the KWIC view because it characterizes *Sutton* as merely citing the original case. Neither entry has an error; this is simply an example of differences in editorial judgment regarding the citing cases' analysis of the original case.

FIGURE 5.16   KEYCITE FULL HISTORY ENTRY FOR 748 N.E.2d 41

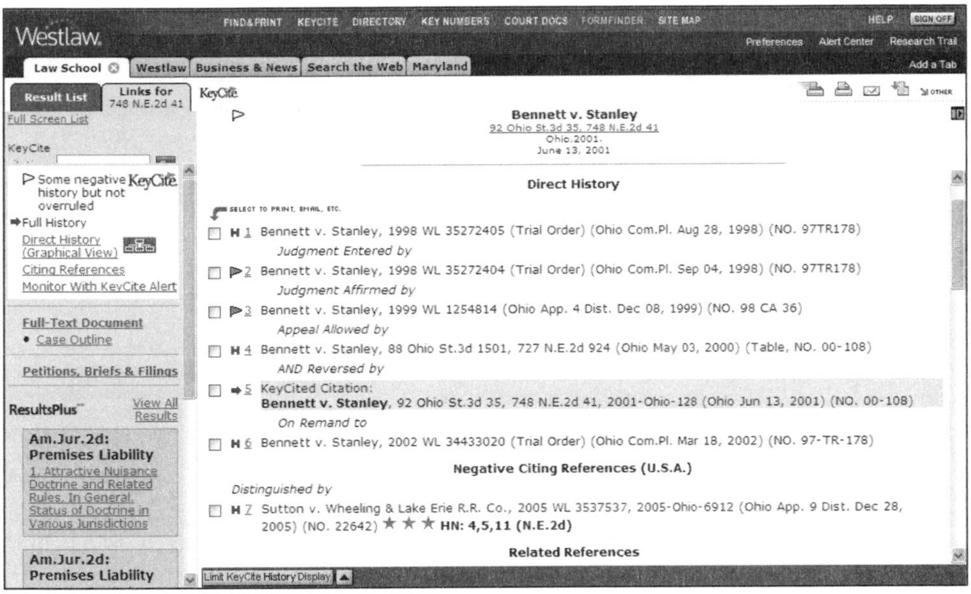

Reprinted with permission from Thomson Reuters/West, from Westlaw, KeyCite entry for 748 N.E.2d 41. © 2008 Thomson Reuters/West.

From the Citing References screen, the Limit KeyCite Display button retrieves a menu with additional options for limiting the KeyCite display. This example shows the option to limit the display to cases that cite the original case for the proposition summarized in headnote 1. Notice that the text of the headnotes appears below the list of headnotes. The Shepard's FOCUS™-Restrict By option will also display the full text of LexisNexis headnotes.

FIGURE 5.17   KEYCITE LIMITED DISPLAY OPTIONS

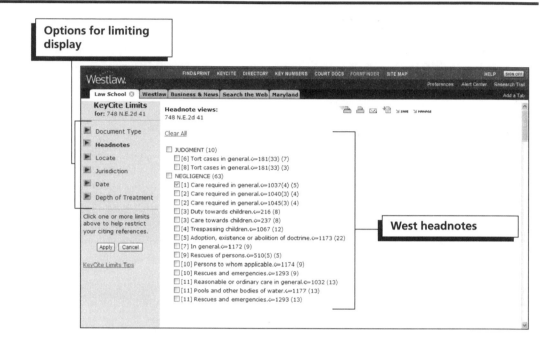

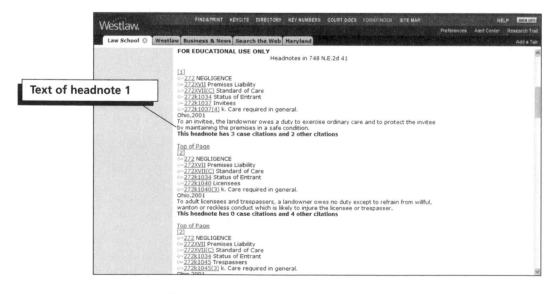

Reprinted with permission from Thomson Reuters/West, from Westlaw, Limit KeyCite Display options. © 2008 Thomson Reuters/West.

The limited KeyCite entry shows only cases that cite the original case for the proposition of law summarized in headnote 1. KeyCite only provides references to West headnotes, not LexisNexis or official reporter headnotes.

FIGURE 5.18   KEYCITE LIMITED CITING REFERENCES ENTRY FOR 748 N.E.2d 41

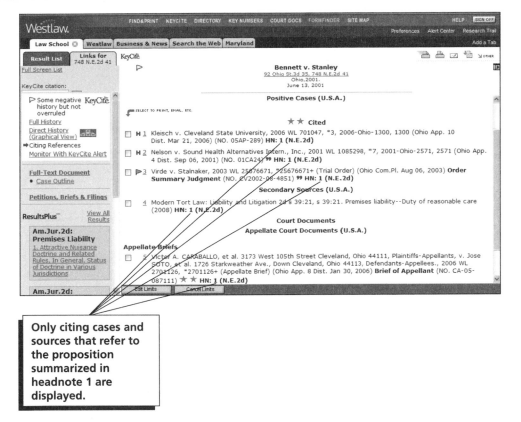

Only citing cases and sources that refer to the proposition summarized in headnote 1 are displayed.

Reprinted with permission from Thomson Reuters/West, from Westlaw, KeyCite entry for 748 N.E.2d 41. © 2008 Thomson Reuters/West.

Selecting a case from the list opens a window showing the citing case's citations to the original case.

FIGURE 5.19   KEYCITE CITING CASE DISPLAY

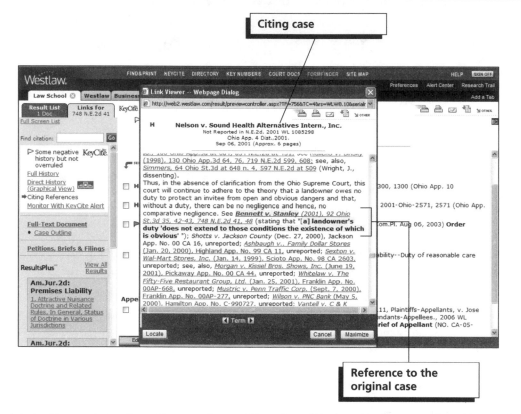

Reprinted with permission from Thomson Reuters/West, from Westlaw, KeyCite entry for 748 N.E.2d 41. © 2008 Thomson Reuters/West.

F. CHECKLIST FOR CASE RESEARCH WITH CITATORS

∎

1. USE SHEPARD'S IN LEXISNEXIS

❐ Access Shepard's from the Shepard's tab or from a relevant case.
❐ Interpret the entry.

- A summary of the entry with a Shepard's Signal appears first; use the Shepard's Signal as a qualified indicator of case status, not a definitive determination.
- The full entry begins with direct history, followed by citing cases (divided by jurisdiction) and other citing sources.
- Use the descriptions of the history (e.g., affirmed, reversed) and treatment (e.g., followed, distinguished, overruled) to identify citing cases that may affect the validity of the original case.
- Use headnote references to identify citing cases that discuss propositions most relevant to your research.

❐ Customize the options.

- Use Shepard's for Validation to retrieve an abbreviated entry.
- Use the display options and All Neg and All Pos restrictions to limit the display.
- Use FOCUS™-Restrict By to limit the display by type of analysis, jurisdiction, headnote, date, or terms you specify.
- Create a Shepard's Alert® for automatic updates to the Shepard's entry for the original case.

2. USE KEYCITE IN WESTLAW

❐ Access KeyCite from the KeyCite link or from a relevant case.
❐ Interpret the entry.

- Use the KeyCite status flag as a qualified indicator of case status, not a definitive determination.
- View the Full History of the original case to see direct history and negative indirect history.
- View the Direct History (Graphical View) to see the history of the original case in chart form.
- View the Citing References to see indirect history and citing sources; negative cases appear first, followed by positive cases (divided by depth of treatment and then by jurisdiction) and citing sources.
- Use the descriptions of the history (e.g., affirmed, reversed) and treatment (e.g., distinguished, disagreed with, overruled) to identify citing cases that may affect the validity of the original case.

- Use headnote references to identify citing cases that discuss propositions most relevant to your research.
- Use quotation marks to identify citing cases that quote the original case.

☐ Customize the options.

- In the Full History view, use the Limit KeyCite Display option to show negative treatment only.
- In the Citing References view, use the Limit KeyCite Display option to limit the display by headnote, specific terms using Locate, jurisdiction, date, document type, or depth of treatment.
- Create a KeyCite Alert for automatic updates to the KeyCite entry for the original case.

STATUTORY RESEARCH

A. Introduction to statutory law

B. Researching statutes in print

C. Researching statutes electronically

D. Citing statutes

E. Sample pages for print statutory research

F. Checklist for statutory research

A. INTRODUCTION TO STATUTORY LAW

1. THE PUBLICATION OF STATUTORY LAW

Statutes enacted by a legislature are organized by subject matter into what is called a "code." Codes are published by jurisdiction; each jurisdiction that enacts statutes collects them in its own code. Thus, the federal government publishes the federal code, which contains all federal statutes. Statutes for each state are published in individual state codes. Most codes contain too many statutes to be included in a single volume. Instead, a code usually consists of a multivolume set of books containing all of the statutes passed within a jurisdiction. The federal code also includes the text of the United States Constitution. Most state codes contain the text of the state constitution, and many include the text of the United States Constitution as well.

When a federal law is enacted, it is published in three steps: (1) it is published as a separate document; (2) it is included in a chronological listing of all statutes passed within a session of Congress; and (3) it is reorganized by subject matter and placed within the code. In the first step of the process, every law passed by Congress is assigned a public law number. The public law number indicates the session of Congress in which the law was passed and the order in which it was passed. Thus, Public Law 103-416 was the 416th law passed during the 103d session of Congress. Each public law is published in a separate booklet or pamphlet containing the full text of the law as it was passed by Congress. This booklet is known as a slip law and is identified by its public law number.

In the second step of the process, slip laws for a session of Congress are compiled together in chronological order. Laws organized within this chronological compilation are called session laws because they are organized according to the session of Congress during which they were enacted. Session laws are compiled in a publication called *United States Statutes at Large.* A citation to *Statutes at Large* will tell you the volume of *Statutes at Large* containing the law and the page number on which the text of the law begins. Thus, a citation to 108 Stat. 4305 tells you that this law can be located in volume 108 of *Statutes at Large*, beginning on page 4305. Both the slip law and session law versions of a statute should be identical. The only difference is the form of publication.

The third step in the process is the codification of the law. When Congress enacts a law, it enacts a block of legislation that may cover a wide range of topics. A single bill can contain provisions applicable to many different parts of the government. For example, a drug abuse prevention law could contain provisions applicable to subject areas such as food and drugs, crimes, and public health. If federal laws remained organized chronologically by the date of passage, it would be virtually impossible to research the law by subject. Laws relating to individual subjects could have been passed at so many different times that it would be extremely difficult to find all of the relevant provisions.

In the third step of the process, therefore, the pieces of the bill are reorganized according to the different subjects they cover, and they are placed by subject, or codified, within the federal code. Once legislation is codified, it is much easier to locate because it can be indexed by subject much the way cases are indexed by subject in a digest.

Figure 6.1 illustrates the publication process.

Figure 6.2 contains an example of a statute that has been codified within the federal code.

2. TITLE AND SUBJECT-MATTER ORGANIZATION OF CODES

Although all codes are organized by subject, not all codes are numbered the same way. The federal code is organized into what are called "Titles." There are fifty Titles in the federal code, and each Title covers a different subject area. Title 18, for instance, contains the laws pertaining to federal crimes, and Title 35 contains the laws pertaining to patents. Each Title is subdivided into chapters, and each chapter is further subdivided into sections. To locate a provision of the federal code from its citation, you would need to know the Title and the section number assigned to it.

FIGURE 6.1   PUBLICATION PROCESS FOR A FEDERAL STATUTE

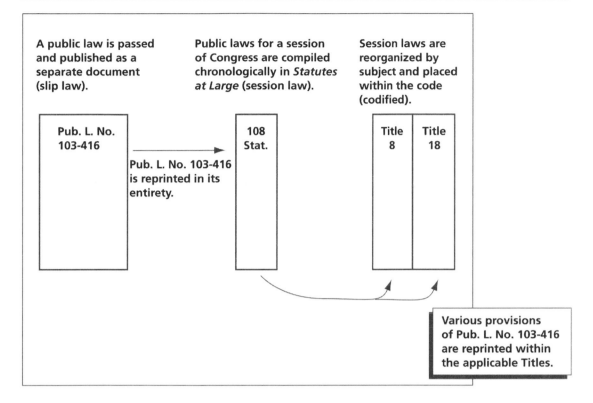

For example, the provision of the federal code prohibiting bank robbery is located in Title 18, section 2113.

Not all codes are organized this way. Some states organize their codes by subject name, rather than Title number. Within each subject name, the code is then usually subdivided into chapters and sections. To find a provision of the code from its citation, you would need to know the subject area and the section number assigned to that provision. For example, the provision of New York law that prohibits issuing a bad check is located in the subject volume of the New York code containing the Penal Law, section 190.05.

3. OFFICIAL VS. UNOFFICIAL CODES AND ANNOTATED VS. UNANNOTATED CODES

Although there is only one "code" for each jurisdiction, in the sense that each jurisdiction has only one set of statutes in force, the text of the laws may be published in more than one set of books or electronic database. Sometimes a government arranges for the publication of its laws; this is

FIGURE 6.2   10 U.S.C.A. § 816

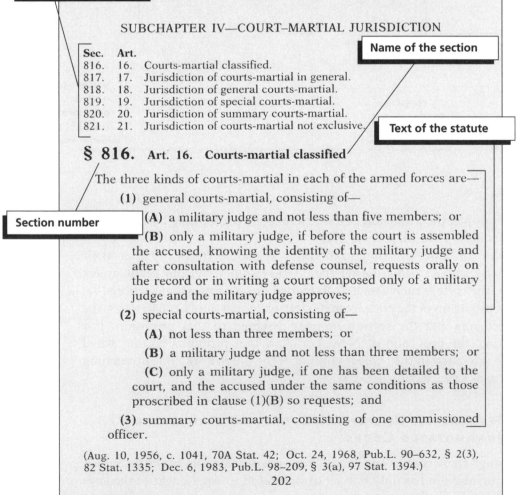

10 § 815
Note 113

cial punishment rendered that document inadmissible. U. S. v. Stewart, CMA 1981, 12 M.J. 143.

Where military personnel records jacket copy of record of nonjudicial punishment showed that appeal was, as required, considered by a judge advocate, his failure to sign form did not affect its admissibility and, similarly, where copy disclosed that attachments were made, presumably to the original, failure to list them in form did not render record inadmissible. U. S. v. Berry, ACMR 1977, 2

g course of rehearing, tri-ed into evidence four rec-

ARMED FORCES   Subt. A

ords of nonjudicial punishment, one record of vacation of suspended punishment, and one record of conviction by summary court-martial and where, although record of accused's trial by summary court-martial did not on its face meet requirements for admissibility established by Booker decision, military judge elicited from trial defense counsel that latter was aware of case law concerning admissibility of summary court-martial record, had resolved issue of exhibit's admissibility, and did not object to offer, military judge was not required to take further action prior to admitting exhibit in evidence. U. S. v. Alford, ACMR 1979, 6 M.J. 907.

> **Outline of sections within this subchapter of the code**

> **Name of the section**

> **Text of the statute**

> **Section number**

SUBCHAPTER IV—COURT–MARTIAL JURISDICTION

Sec.	Art.	
816.	16.	Courts-martial classified.
817.	17.	Jurisdiction of courts-martial in general.
818.	18.	Jurisdiction of general courts-martial.
819.	19.	Jurisdiction of special courts-martial.
820.	20.	Jurisdiction of summary courts-martial.
821.	21.	Jurisdiction of courts-martial not exclusive.

§ 816.   Art. 16.   Courts-martial classified

The three kinds of courts-martial in each of the armed forces are—

(1) general courts-martial, consisting of—

(A) a military judge and not less than five members; or

(B) only a military judge, if before the court is assembled the accused, knowing the identity of the military judge and after consultation with defense counsel, requests orally on the record or in writing a court composed only of a military judge and the military judge approves;

(2) special courts-martial, consisting of—

(A) not less than three members; or

(B) a military judge and not less than three members; or

(C) only a military judge, if one has been detailed to the court, and the accused under the same conditions as those proscribed in clause (1)(B) so requests; and

(3) summary courts-martial, consisting of one commissioned officer.

(Aug. 10, 1956, c. 1041, 70A Stat. 42; Oct. 24, 1968, Pub.L. 90–632, § 2(3), 82 Stat. 1335; Dec. 6, 1983, Pub.L. 98–209, § 3(a), 97 Stat. 1394.)

202

FIGURE 6.3 CHARACTERISTICS OF OFFICIAL AND UNOFFICIAL CODES

OFFICIAL CODES	UNOFFICIAL CODES
Published under government authority (e.g., U.S.C.)	Published by a commercial publisher without government authorization (e.g., U.S.C.A. and U.S.C.S.)
Many or may not contain research references (annotations). U.S.C. is not an annotated code.	Usually contain research references (annotations). Both U.S.C.A. and U.S.C.S. are annotated codes.

known as an "official" code.[1] Sometimes a commercial publisher will publish the laws for a jurisdiction without government authorization; this is known as an "unofficial" code. Some jurisdictions have both official and unofficial codes, but in other jurisdictions, only one or the other type of code will be available. If both official and unofficial codes are published for a jurisdiction, they will usually be organized and numbered identically (e.g., all sets will be organized by subject or by Title). For federal laws, the government publishes an official code, *United States Code* or U.S.C. Two other sets of the federal code are also available through commercial publishers, *United States Code Annotated* (U.S.C.A.) and *United States Code Service* (U.S.C.S.).

In addition, a published code can come in one of two formats: annotated or unannotated. An annotated code contains the text of the law, as well as different types of research references. The research references may include summaries of cases or citations to secondary sources discussing a statute. An unannotated code contains only the text of the law. It may have a few references to the statutes' original public law numbers, but other than that, it will not contain research references. Most unofficial codes are annotated codes. Official codes may or may not be annotated. As you might imagine, an annotated code is much more useful as a research tool than an unannotated code.

In the federal code, U.S.C. (the official code) is an unannotated code. The two unofficial codes, U.S.C.A. and U.S.C.S., are annotated codes. See **Figure 6.3** for a summary of the characteristics of official and unofficial codes.

---

[1]The government may publish the code itself, or it may arrange for a commercial publisher to publish the code. As long as the government arranges for the publication, the code is an official code, even if it is physically produced by a commercial publisher.

4. METHODS OF LOCATING STATUTES

You can locate statutes in many ways. Four common techniques are searching by citation, by subject, by words in the document, or by the name of an act. If you have the citation to a statute that you have obtained from another source, such as a secondary source, you can easily locate the statute in a print code or retrieve it from an electronic database.

Researching by subject is often a useful way to locate statutes. The index to a code will be organized by subject, and using an index is one of the most common subject searching techniques for statutory research. All print codes have subject indices. If you are searching electronically, you may or may not have access to the index. Every code also has a table of contents, which you can view in print or electronically. Reviewing the table of contents can be a difficult way to begin your research unless you know the subject area of the statute you are trying to find. Once you find a relevant provision of the code, however, viewing the table of contents can help you find related code sections, as described more fully below.

Word searching is another way to locate statutes electronically. Because legislatures often use technical terms in statutes, however, word searching can be more difficult than subject searching if you are not already familiar with the statutory terminology.

An additional search option is locating a statute by name. Many statutes are known by their popular names, such as the Americans with Disabilities Act. In print, you can use a directory listing statutes according to their popular names. In an electronic service, you can use a statute's name as a word search; many services also have popular name search options.

Regardless of the search method you use initially to locate a relevant section of a code, you should plan to expand your search to consider the entire statutory scheme. Rarely will an individual code section viewed in isolation resolve your research question. More often you will need to research interrelated code provisions. For example, assume you retrieved a code provision applicable to your research issue but failed to retrieve a nearby section containing definitions of terms used in the applicable provision. If you relied only on the one section your initial search revealed, your research would not be accurate. Because electronic sources often retrieve individual code sections as separate documents, it is especially easy to lose sight of the need to research multiple sections when you are working online. Whether you use print or electronic sources for statutory research, however, be sure to research the entire statutory scheme to ensure that you consider all potentially applicable code sections.

Once you have located a relevant code section, the easiest way to research a statutory scheme is to use the statutory outline or table of contents to identify related code provisions. In print, you will often find a chapter or subchapter outline of sections, as **Figure 6.2** shows.

And of course, all you have to do is turn the pages to see preceding and subsequent code sections. Electronic sources often either display or provide links to statutory outlines or tables of contents, and many have functions that allow you to browse preceding and subsequent code sections.

Sections B and C, below, explain how to research statutes in print and electronically.

B. RESEARCHING STATUTES IN PRINT

The process of researching statutes is fairly uniform for state and federal codes. This section illustrates the process of researching federal statutes in detail using U.S.C.A. You should be able to adapt this process to almost any kind of statutory research. After the detailed discussion of U.S.C.A., this section discusses two additional sources for federal statutory research, U.S.C. and U.S.C.S., as well as state statutes, rules of procedure, and uniform codes and model acts. This section concludes with a discussion of statutory citators.

1. RESEARCHING FEDERAL STATUTES

a. Researching Federal Statutes in *United States Code Annotated*

You can research federal statutes in U.S.C.A. in several ways. The most common way to locate statutes is to search by subject using the General Index. You can also use tables accompanying the code to search by the popular name of the law or public law number.

(1) Researching in U.S.C.A. by subject

Researching federal statutes by subject in U.S.C.A. is a four-step process:

i.   Look up the topics you want to research in the General Index.
ii. Locate the relevant code section(s) in the main volumes of U.S.C.A. and evaluate the material in the accompanying annotations.
iii. Update your research using the pocket part.
iv. Update your research using the supplementary pamphlets at the end of the code.

Because U.S.C.A. contains the United States Constitution, you can locate federal constitutional provisions by subject the same way you would locate any federal statute.

(i) Using the general index

The General Index to U.S.C.A. is an ordinary subject index that consists of a series of softcover books. It is published annually, so be sure to check the most recent set of index books.

Using the General Index is just like using any other subject index. Topics are listed alphabetically. Next to each topic are references to the Title and section number(s) of the statutory provisions relevant to that topic. The abbreviation "et seq." means that the index is referring to a series of sections beginning with the section listed; often, this will be a reference to an entire chapter within the Title. The index also contains cross-references to other subjects relevant to the topic. An example of an index page appears in **Figure 6.4**.

(ii) Locating statutes and reading the annotations

Once you have located relevant Title and section numbers in the General Index, the next step is finding the statute within the books. The books are organized numerically by Title, although some Titles span more than one volume. Using the Title number, you should be able to locate the correct volume. The sections within the Title will be listed in numerical order within the volume.[2] As noted earlier, an outline of the statute will appear at the beginning of each chapter or subchapter.

Following the text of the code section, you may find a series of annotations with additional information about the statute. **Figure 6.5** describes some of the types of information you can find in the annotations in U.S.C.A.

Not all statutes have annotations. Those that do may not contain all of the information in **Figure 6.5** or may have additional information. The information provided depends on the research references that are appropriate for that statute. If a statute has any annotations, they will always follow after the text of the code section. **Figure 6.6** shows the annotations accompanying 10 U.S.C.A. § 816.

(iii) Updating statutory research using pocket parts

Like other hardcover books used in legal research, U.S.C.A. volumes are updated with pocket parts. If the pocket part gets too big to fit in the back of the book, you should find a separate softcover pamphlet on the shelf next to the hardcover volume.

The pocket part is organized in the same way as the main volume. Therefore, to update your research, you need only look up the section numbers you located in the main volume. The pocket part will show any revisions to the statute, as well as additional annotations if, for example, new cases interpreting the section have been decided. If the pocket part shows new statutory language, the text in the pocket part supersedes the

---

[2]If the statute was enacted after the main volume was published, you will not find it in the hardcover book. More recent statutes will appear in the pocket part or noncumulative supplements, which are explained in the next section.

FIGURE 6.4 EXCERPT FROM THE U.S.C.A. GENERAL INDEX

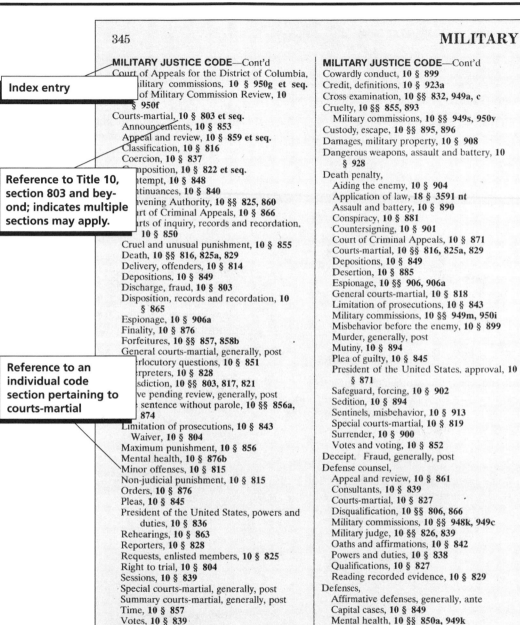

345

MILITARY

Index entry

Reference to Title 10, section 803 and beyond; indicates multiple sections may apply.

Reference to an individual code section pertaining to courts-martial

MILITARY JUSTICE CODE—Cont'd
Court of Appeals for the District of Columbia, military commissions, 10 § 950g et seq.
of Military Commission Review, 10 § 950f
Courts-martial, 10 § 803 et seq.
  Announcements, 10 § 853
  Appeal and review, 10 § 859 et seq.
  Classification, 10 § 816
  Coercion, 10 § 837
  Composition, 10 § 822 et seq.
  Contempt, 10 § 848
  Continuances, 10 § 840
  Convening Authority, 10 §§ 825, 860
  Court of Criminal Appeals, 10 § 866
  Courts of inquiry, records and recordation, 10 § 850
  Cruel and unusual punishment, 10 § 855
  Death, 10 §§ 816, 825a, 829
  Delivery, offenders, 10 § 814
  Depositions, 10 § 849
  Discharge, fraud, 10 § 803
  Disposition, records and recordation, 10 § 865
  Espionage, 10 § 906a
  Finality, 10 § 876
  Forfeitures, 10 §§ 857, 858b
  General courts-martial, generally, post
  Interlocutory questions, 10 § 851
  Interpreters, 10 § 828
  Jurisdiction, 10 §§ 803, 817, 821
  Leave pending review, generally, post
  Life sentence without parole, 10 §§ 856a, 874
  Limitation of prosecutions, 10 § 843
    Waiver, 10 § 804
  Maximum punishment, 10 § 856
  Mental health, 10 § 876b
  Minor offenses, 10 § 815
  Non-judicial punishment, 10 § 815
  Orders, 10 § 876
  Pleas, 10 § 845
  President of the United States, powers and duties, 10 § 836
  Rehearings, 10 § 863
  Reporters, 10 § 828
  Requests, enlisted members, 10 § 825
  Right to trial, 10 § 804
  Sessions, 10 § 839
  Special courts-martial, generally, post
  Summary courts-martial, generally, post
  Time, 10 § 857
  Votes, 10 § 839
  Without military judge, 10 § 840 et seq.
  Witnesses, 10 § 847
Courts of Criminal Appeals, generally, this index
Courts of inquiry, 10 § 935
  Competency, 18 § 3481
  Interpreters, 10 § 828
  Judge Advocate General, 10 § 3037
  President of the United States, powers and duties, 10 § 836
  Records and recordation, 10 § 850
  Reporters, 10 § 828
  Witnesses, 10 § 847; 18 § 3481

MILITARY JUSTICE CODE—Cont'd
Cowardly conduct, 10 § 899
Credit, definitions, 10 § 923a
Cross examination, 10 §§ 832, 949a, c
Cruelty, 10 §§ 855, 893
  Military commissions, 10 §§ 949s, 950v
Custody, escape, 10 §§ 895, 896
Damages, military property, 10 § 908
Dangerous weapons, assault and battery, 10 § 928
Death penalty,
  Aiding the enemy, 10 § 904
  Application of law, 18 § 3591 nt
  Assault and battery, 10 § 890
  Conspiracy, 10 § 881
  Countersigning, 10 § 901
  Court of Criminal Appeals, 10 § 871
  Courts-martial, 10 §§ 816, 825a, 829
  Depositions, 10 § 849
  Desertion, 10 § 885
  Espionage, 10 §§ 906, 906a
  General courts-martial, 10 § 818
  Limitation of prosecutions, 10 § 843
  Military commissions, 10 §§ 949m, 950i
  Misbehavior before the enemy, 10 § 899
  Murder, generally, post
  Mutiny, 10 § 894
  Plea of guilty, 10 § 845
  President of the United States, approval, 10 § 871
  Safeguard, forcing, 10 § 902
  Sedition, 10 § 894
  Sentinels, misbehavior, 10 § 913
  Special courts-martial, 10 § 819
  Surrender, 10 § 900
  Votes and voting, 10 § 852
Deceipt. Fraud, generally, post
Defense counsel,
  Appeal and review, 10 § 861
  Consultants, 10 § 839
  Courts-martial, 10 § 827
  Disqualification, 10 §§ 806, 866
  Military commissions, 10 §§ 948k, 949c
  Military judge, 10 §§ 826, 839
  Oaths and affirmations, 10 § 842
  Powers and duties, 10 § 838
  Qualifications, 10 § 827
  Reading recorded evidence, 10 § 829
Defenses,
  Affirmative defenses, generally, ante
  Capital cases, 10 § 849
  Mental health, 10 §§ 850a, 949k
  Motions, 10 § 839
  Sex offenses, 10 § 920
Deferment, sentence and punishment, 10 § 857a
Definitions, 10 § 801
  Correctional custody, 10 § 815
  Credit, 10 § 923a
  Drunken driving, 10 § 911
  Marriage, 10 § 920
  Military commissions, post
  Sex offenses, 10 § 920
  Stalking, 10 § 920a
  Unborn children, 10 § 919a

FIGURE 6.5   INFORMATION CONTAINED IN U.S.C.A. ANNOTATIONS

CATEGORIES OF INFORMATION IN ANNOTATIONS	CONTENTS
Historical Note Sometimes this section is called Historical and Statutory Notes.	Contains the history of the section, including summaries of amendments and the public law numbers and *Statutes at Large* citations for the laws containing the revisions. This section can also refer to the legislative history of the statute (for more discussion of legislative history, see Chapter 7).
Cross-References	Contains cross-references to related provisions of the code.
Library References Sometimes this section is subdivided into categories for Administrative Law, American Digest System, Encyclopedias, Law Reviews, Texts and Treatises, and Forms.	Contains references to related topics and key numbers in the West digest system, as well as references to legal encyclopedia sections with information on the subject (see Chapter 4 for more discussion of the digest system and Chapter 3 for more discussion of legal encyclopedias).
Code of Federal Regulations Sometimes this appears as a separate section, and sometimes it is included with Library References, under the Administrative Law category.	Contains references to administrative agency regulations implementing the statute (for more discussion of administrative regulations, see Chapter 8).
Law Review Articles Sometimes this appears as a separate section, and sometimes it is included with Library References, under the Law Reviews category.	Contains references to relevant law review articles (for more discussion of law reviews and other legal periodicals, see Chapter 3).
Notes of Decisions	Contains summaries of cases interpreting the statute. If the statute has been discussed in a large number of cases, the Notes of Decisions will be divided into subject categories, and each category will be assigned a number. Cases on each subject will be listed under the appropriate number. *Note that these subject and number categories do not correspond to the topics and key numbers within the West digest system.*

FIGURE 6.6   ANNOTATIONS ACCOMPANYING 10 U.S.C.A. § 816

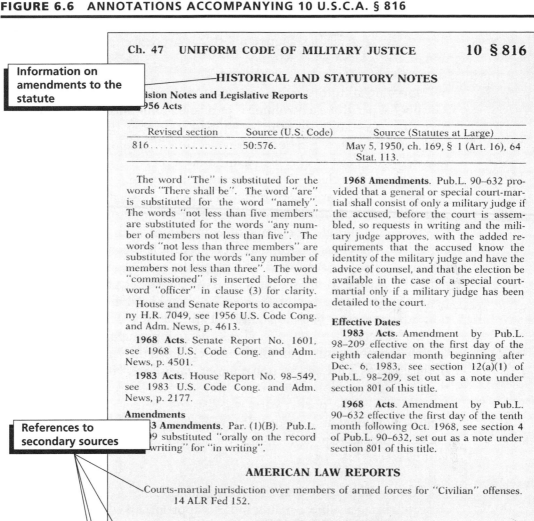

Information on amendments to the statute

Ch. 47   UNIFORM CODE OF MILITARY JUSTICE   **10 § 816**

HISTORICAL AND STATUTORY NOTES

ision Notes and Legislative Reports
956 Acts

Revised section	Source (U.S. Code)	Source (Statutes at Large)
816	50:576.	May 5, 1950, ch. 169, § 1 (Art. 16), 64 Stat. 113.

The word "The" is substituted for the words "There shall be". The word "are" is substituted for the word "namely". The words "not less than five members" are substituted for the words "any number of members not less than five". The words "not less than three members" are substituted for the words "any number of members not less than three". The word "commissioned" is inserted before the word "officer" in clause (3) for clarity.

House and Senate Reports to accompany H.R. 7049, see 1956 U.S. Code Cong. and Adm. News, p. 4613.

1968 Acts. Senate Report No. 1601, see 1968 U.S. Code Cong. and Adm. News, p. 4501.

1983 Acts. House Report No. 98–549, see 1983 U.S. Code Cong. and Adm. News, p. 2177.

Amendments

3 **Amendments**. Par. (1)(B). Pub.L.
9 substituted "orally on the record
writing" for "in writing".

1968 Amendments. Pub.L. 90–632 provided that a general or special court-martial shall consist of only a military judge if the accused, before the court is assembled, so requests in writing and the military judge approves, with the added requirements that the accused know the identity of the military judge and have the advice of counsel, and that the election be available in the case of a special court-martial only if a military judge has been detailed to the court.

Effective Dates

1983 Acts. Amendment by Pub.L. 98–209 effective on the first day of the eighth calendar month beginning after Dec. 6, 1983, see section 12(a)(1) of Pub.L. 98–209, set out as a note under section 801 of this title.

1968 Acts. Amendment by Pub.L. 90–632 effective the first day of the tenth month following Oct. 1968, see section 4 of Pub.L. 90–632, set out as a note under section 801 of this title.

AMERICAN LAW REPORTS

Courts-martial jurisdiction over members of armed forces for "Civilian" offenses. 14 ALR Fed 152.

LIBRARY REFERENCES

References to secondary sources

Administrative Law
General courts-martial, see West's Federal Practice Manual § 6292.
Nature, types and composition of courts-martial, see West's Federal Practice Manual § 6290.
Special courts-martial, see West's Federal Practice Manual § 6293.

American Digest System
Armed Services ⟐43.
Military Justice ⟐870.

West digest topics and key numbers

Encyclopedias
C.J.S. Military Justice §§ 138, 139, 143, 145, 147, 153.
54 Am Jur 2d, Military, and Civil Defense § 216.

Forms
3 Fed Procedural Forms L Ed, Armed Forces, Civil Disturbances, and National Defense § 5:71.

203

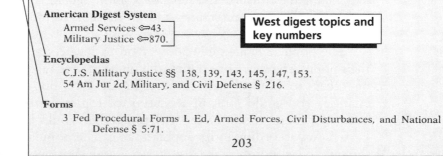

text in the main volume. If no reference to the section appears in the pocket part, the statute has not been amended, and no new research references are available. **Figure 6.7** shows a portion of the pocket part update to 10 U.S.C.A. § 816.

(iv) Updating statutory research using supplementary pamphlets

The pocket part for each volume is published only once a year. Congress may change a statute after the pocket part is printed, however, and cases interpreting a statute can be issued at any time. Therefore, to update your research, you need to check an additional source.

At the end of the U.S.C.A. set, you should find a series of softcover pamphlets. These are supplements that are published after the pocket part. They are noncumulative, meaning that each pamphlet covers a specific time period. The dates of coverage of each pamphlet should appear on the cover. To update your research thoroughly, you must look for your code section in each pamphlet published since the pocket part. If a change to the statute appears in an earlier pamphlet, the later pamphlets will refer back to the earlier pamphlet. Later pamphlets will not, however, refer back to additional annotations. Therefore, to locate all new annotations, you must check each supplementary pamphlet.

The noncumulative pamphlets are organized the same way as the rest of the code: by Title and section number. Therefore, you need to look up the Title and section number of the statute you are researching. The pamphlet, like the pocket part, will list any changes to the statute, as well as additional annotations. If no reference to the section appears in the noncumulative pamphlet, then there is no additional information for you to research.

(2) *The popular name and conversion tables*

Research using a subject-matter index is appropriate when you know the subject you want to research but do not know the exact statute you need to find. Sometimes, however, you will know which statute you need to find. In that situation, the easiest way to find the citation may be through the popular name table or the conversion tables. In U.S.C.A., the popular name table is published as a separate volume accompanying the General Index. The conversion tables appear in separate softcover "Tables" volumes.

The popular name table allows you to locate statutes according to their popular names. For example, if you wanted to research the Freedom of Access to Clinic Entrances Act (FACE Act) but did not know its citation, you could look up a variety of topics in the General Index until you found it. An easier way to do this would be to look up the FACE Act according to its popular name. The popular name table lists the public law number, the *Statutes at Large* citation, and the Title and section numbers where the act is codified within U.S.C.A. Remember

FIGURE 6.7 POCKET PART UPDATE FOR 10 U.S.C.A. § 816

10 § 815
Note 106

ARMED FORCES

106. —— Appeal

Claims of service member attacking Article 15 non-judicial punishment proceeding were justici-[able based on] claims attacked the procedure em-[ployed in the] [invest]igation phase of proceeding, and [the merits] of punishment decision relating to [diso]beying a direct order. Jefferson [v. U.S., ...].2004, 60 Fed.Cl. 433. Armed

> **New statutory language supersedes the language in the main volume.**

[109. —— M]iscellaneous nonjudicial punishments admissible

U.S. v. Simmons, 44 M.J. 819 (A.F. Ct. Crim. App. 1996), review granted in part 46 M.J. 396, [main volume] affirmed 48 M.J. 193.

110. —— Miscellaneous nonjudicial punishments inadmissible

Accused convicted of willful disobedience of a superior commissioned officer's order that he inoculated with anthrax vaccine was not entitled to sentencing credit for prior nonjudicial punishment he received for refusal to get the vaccination, where the offense for which the accused was tried was a separate incident from the one for which he received nonjudicial punishment. U.S. v. Washington, 54 M.J. 936 (A.F. Ct. Crim. App. 2001), review granted 56 M.J. 245, set aside 57 M.J. 394, on remand 2003 WL 59775. Military Justice ☞ 1324

SUBCHAPTER IV—COURT–MARTIAL JURISDICTION

§ 816. Art. 16. Courts-martial classified

The three kinds of courts-martial in each of the armed forces are—

(1) general courts-martial, consisting of—

(A) a military judge and not less than five members or, in a case in which the accused may be sentenced to a penalty of death, the number of members determined under section 825a of this title (article 25a); or

[See main volume for text of (B); (2) and (3)]

(Aug. 10, 1956, c. 1041, 70A Stat. 42; Oct. 24, 1968, Pub.L. 90–632, § 2(3), 82 Stat. 1335; Dec. 6, 1983, Pub.L. 98–209, § 3(a), 97 Stat. 1394; Dec. 28, 2001, Pub.L. 107–107, Div. A, Title V, § 582(a), 115 Stat. 1124.)

HISTORICAL AND STATUTORY NOTES

> **New annotations follow the text of the statute.**

Revision Notes and Legislative Reports

2001 Acts. House Conference Report No. 107–333 and Statement by President, see 2001 U.S. Code Cong. and Adm. News, p. 1021.

Amendments

2001 Amendments. Par. (1)(A). Pub.L. 107–107, § 582(a), struck out "five members; or" and inserted "five members or, in a case in which the accused may be sentenced to a penal-[ty of death, the number of members] under section 825a of this title (article 25a); or".

Effective and Applicability Provisions

2001 Acts. Pub.L. 107–107, Div. A, Title V, § 582(d), Dec. 28, 2001, 115 Stat. 1125, provided that: "The amendments made by this section [enacting section 825a of this title and amending this section and section 829 of this title] shall apply with respect to offenses committed after December 31, 2002."

LIBRARY REFERENCES

American Digest System

Armed Services ☞43.
Military Justice ☞870.

Corpus Juris Secundum

CJS Military Justice § 139, Classification and Composition.

CJS Military Justice § 141, Trial by Military Judge Alone.

Research References

ALR Library

14 ALR, Fed. 152, Comment Note.--Courts-Martial Jurisdiction Over Members of Armed Forces for "Civilian" Offenses.

11 ALR 5th 218, Use of Prior Military Conviction to Establish Repeat Offender Status.

Encyclopedias

45 Am. Jur. Trials 351, Court-Martial Defense by the Nonmilitary Lawyer.

Am. Jur. 2d Military and Civil Defense § 227, Numeric Composition of Court-Martial.

Forms

Federal Procedural Forms § 5:32, Introduction; Constitutional Authority.

Treatises and Practice Aids

Federal Procedure, Lawyers Edition § 5:77, Generally; Constitutional Authority for Courts-Martial.

Federal Procedure, Lawyers Edition § 5:99, General Court-Martial.

Federal Procedure, Lawyers Edition § 5:106, Generally; Number of Members.

Federal Procedure, Lawyers Edition § 5:117, Trial by Military Judge Alone.

28

FIGURE 6.8   FACE ACT ENTRY, POPULAR NAME TABLE

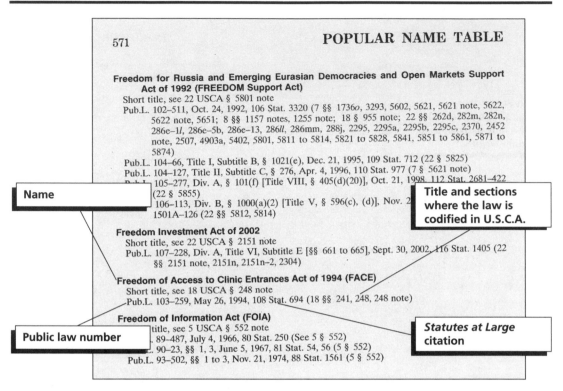

Reprinted with permission from Thomson Reuters/West, *United States Code Annotated*, 2008 Popular Name Table, p. 571. © 2008 Thomson Reuters/West.

that when a law is passed by a legislature, it may affect many different areas of the law and, therefore, may be codified in many different places within the code. Thus, the popular name table may refer you to a number of different Titles and sections. For many well-known statutes, however, the popular name table is an efficient way to locate the law within the code. **Figure 6.8** shows the popular name table entry for the FACE Act.

Another way to locate a statute in U.S.C.A. is through the conversion tables. If you know the public law number for a statute, you can use the tables to find the *Statutes at Large* citation and the Titles and sections where the law has been codified. Once you know the Title and section numbers, you can locate the statute by citation. **Figure 6.9** is an example from the conversion table showing where the FACE Act is codified.

Because the popular name and conversion tables are published annually, there is no pocket part update for the tables. At the end of each noncumulative supplement, however, you will find updates to the tables. Therefore, if you are unable to find the material you want in the General

FIGURE 6.9   CONVERSION TABLE ENTRY FOR PUB. L. NO. 103-259, THE FACE ACT

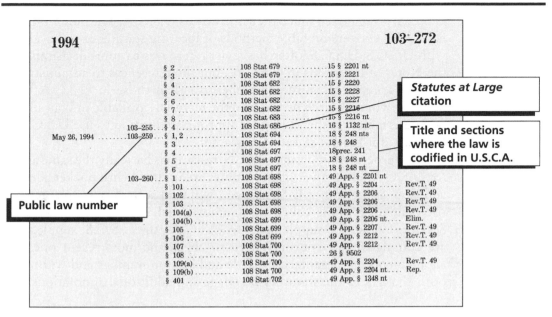

Reprinted with permission from Thomson Reuters/West, Tables Vol. II, *United States Code Annotated*, 2008, p. 655. © 2008 Thomson Reuters/West.

Index or Tables, check for more recent material in the noncumulative supplements.

b. Researching Federal Statutes in *United States Code*

The index, popular name, and conversion table methods of locating statutes are all available with U.S.C. The main difference in researching U.S.C. concerns updating. The index and main volumes of the code are published every six years. In the intervening years, U.S.C. is not updated with pocket parts. Instead, it is updated with hardcover cumulative supplements. A new supplement is issued each year until the next publication of the main set.

In theory, using the supplements should be sufficient to update your research. In practice, however, the system presents some difficulties. Laws can be changed more frequently than the supplements are published, and the government is often two or three years behind in publishing the supplements. To update completely, you would need to research session and slip laws published since the latest supplement. Therefore, U.S.C. is not usually an appropriate source for locating the most current version of a statute, and because it lacks the research references contained in the annotated federal codes, it is not the most useful statutory research tool.

c. Researching Federal Statutes in *United States Code Service*

U.S.C.S. is organized much the same way as U.S.C.A. The index, popular name, and conversion table methods of locating statutes are all available with U.S.C.S. U.S.C.S. often has fewer references to court decisions than the Notes of Decisions in U.S.C.A., but the references to administrative materials are often more comprehensive than those in U.S.C.A.[3] The nature of your research project and the materials available in your library will determine whether it is more appropriate for you to use U.S.C.S. or U.S.C.A. for federal statutory research.

The process of updating U.S.C.S. research is basically the same as that for U.S.C.A. Hardcover main volumes are updated with pocket parts. In addition, at the end of U.S.C.S., you will find softcover supplements to the code as a whole called the Cumulative Later Case and Statutory Service. Unlike the supplements to U.S.C.A., the U.S.C.S. supplements are cumulative, so you only need to check the most recent one. The supplements are organized by Title and section number and will reflect both changes to the statutory language and additional annotations.

2. RESEARCHING STATE CODES, RULES OF PROCEDURE, AND UNIFORM LAWS AND MODEL ACTS

a. State Codes

State codes have many of the same features of U.S.C.A. All have subject indices that can be used to locate statutes. Some also have popular name tables. Most do not, however, have the equivalent of the conversion tables. In addition, the updating process for state statutory research can vary. Virtually all state codes are updated with pocket parts, but some have different or additional updating tools. You may want to check with a reference librarian if you have questions about updating statutory research for a particular state. Sample pages illustrating the process of state statutory research appear in Section E of this chapter.

b. Rules of Procedure

You are probably learning about rules of procedure governing cases filed in court in your Civil Procedure class. Whenever you are preparing to file a document or take some action that a court requires or permits, the court's rules of procedure will tell you how to accomplish your task. The rules of procedure for most courts are published as part of the code for the jurisdiction where the court is located. For example, the Federal Rules of Civil Procedure appear with Title 28 in the federal

---

[3]Chapter 8 explains administrative materials and administrative law research.

code. In many states, court procedural rules are published in a separate Rules volume.

If you want to locate procedural rules, therefore, one way to find them is through the applicable code. In print, you can locate them using the subject index, or you can go directly to the rules themselves if they are published in a separate volume. Many procedural rules have been interpreted in court opinions, and you need to research those opinions to understand the rules' requirements fully. If you locate rules in an annotated code, summaries of the decisions will follow the rules, just as they do any other provision of the code. You can update your research with the pocket part and any cumulative or noncumulative supplements accompanying the code.

A couple of caveats about locating rules of procedure are in order. First, understanding the rules can be challenging. As with any other type of research, you may want to locate secondary sources for commentary on the rules and citations to cases interpreting the rules to make sure you understand them. For the Federal Rules of Civil Procedure, two helpful treatises are *Moore's Federal Practice* and Wright & Miller's *Federal Practice and Procedure*. For state procedural rules, a state "deskbook," or handbook containing practical information for lawyers practicing in the jurisdiction, may contain both the text of the rules and helpful commentary on them. If you locate the rules through a secondary source, however, be sure to update your research because the rules can be amended at any time.

Second, virtually all jurisdictions have multiple types and levels of courts, and each of these courts may have its own procedural rules. Therefore, be sure you locate the rules for the appropriate court. Determining which court is the appropriate one may require separate research into the jurisdiction of the courts.

Third, many individual districts, circuits, or divisions of courts have local rules with which you must comply. Local rules cannot conflict with the rules of procedure published with the code, but they may add requirements that do not appear in the rules of procedure. Local rules usually are not published with the code, but you can obtain them from a number of sources, including the court itself, a secondary source such as a practice "deskbook," or a web site or online database. To be sure that your work complies with the court's rules, do not neglect any local rules that may add to the requirements spelled out in the rules of procedure.

c. Uniform Laws and Model Acts

Uniform laws and model acts, as explained in Chapter 3, are proposed statutes that can be adopted by legislatures. Technically, they are secondary sources; their provisions do not take on the force of law unless they are adopted by a legislature. If your research project involves a statute based on a uniform law or model act, however, you may want to research these sources.

Many uniform laws and model acts are published in a multivolume set of books entitled *Uniform Laws Annotated, Master Edition* (ULA). The ULA set is organized like an annotated code. It contains the text of the uniform law or model act and annotations summarizing cases from jurisdictions that have adopted the statute. It also provides commentary that can help you interpret the statute. Chapter 3, on secondary sources, provides a more detailed explanation of how to use the ULA set.

3. USING A CITATOR FOR STATUTORY RESEARCH

Chapter 5 discusses citators and how to use them in conducting case research. Citators are also available as research and updating tools for state and federal statutes. Statutory citator entries typically include information about the history of a statute (i.e., whether it has been amended or repealed), as well as lists of citing cases and sources. As noted in Chapter 5, many law libraries no longer carry Shepard's in print. Therefore, specific information about statutory citators appears in the next section on electronic research. As explained in more detail below, Shepard's for statutes is available in LexisNexis, and KeyCite for statutes is available in Westlaw.

Using a citator in statutory research is useful in two situations. First, citators can provide you with the most complete research references for statutory research. Some print sources (as well as many free Internet databases) provide access only to unannotated versions of codes. If you do not have access to an annotated code, a citator is a useful tool for locating cases interpreting a statute. Even if you are using an annotated code, the statutory annotations often do not list every citing case or source that has cited the statute. If the annotations are too sparse to give you the information you need about a statute, you may find more complete information in a citator.

Second, citators are updated more frequently than print (and some electronic) sources. Therefore, a citator may provide you with the most recent information about the history of the statute (such as any amendments), as well as the most recent research references. Just as you would not want to cite a case that is no longer good law, you would not want to cite a statute that has been repealed or declared unconstitutional. Using a citator, therefore, is the better practice in statutory research.

C. RESEARCHING STATUTES ELECTRONICALLY

Much statutory material is available electronically. This section discusses search options for researching statutes using Westlaw, LexisNexis, and

Internet sources. As noted above, the features of the electronic statutory citators (Shepard's in LexisNexis and KeyCite in Westlaw) are also explained in this section.

1. WESTLAW

Westlaw contains annotated versions of many codes, including the federal code, all fifty state codes, and the District of Columbia code. The annotated version of the federal code in Westlaw is derived from U.S.C.A., although U.S.C. is also available. For most jurisdictions, you will find court rules of procedure included with the code, and for some you will find local court rules as well.

a. Viewing an Individual Code Section

The display for an individual code section begins with a heading containing, among other things, the citation for the section. The text of the statute then appears, followed by annotations like those in a print code. A notation at the end of each section will tell you the date through which it is updated.

When you retrieve an individual code section, you have several options for viewing the complete statutory outline. You can view the table of contents for the statutory chapter and the entire code using the Table of Contents link in the left hand menu. By following the links in the table of contents display, you can view the surrounding statutory material. You can also use the "Previous Section" and "Next Section" links in the heading to browse preceding or subsequent code sections. **Figure 6.10** shows how a federal statute appears in Westlaw.

b. Searching for Statutes

Westlaw offers several search options for statutory research. The first step is selecting the statutory database you want to search. You can select a database in several ways. You can use the Directory link at the top of the screen or enter a database name in the "Search these databases" box in the Shortcuts section on the left side of the screen. Under the Law School tab, the Resources section also lists databases you can search. The search screen varies somewhat depending on which option you select. Westlaw provides up to six statutory research options: Search, which allows you to execute a word search; Find by Citation; Table of Contents; Statutes Index; Popular Name Table; and 50 State Surveys. If you do not see the search option you want listed across the top of the search screen, try accessing the database a different way. If you select the database from the Directory or view the statutory table of contents, the search screen

FIGURE 6.10   EXCERPT FROM 10 U.S.C.A. § 816 IN WESTLAW

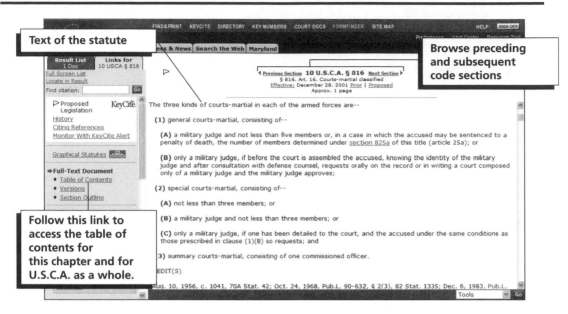

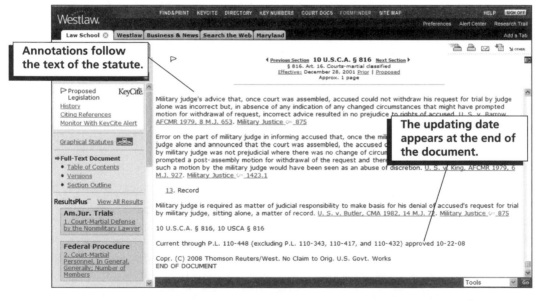

Reprinted with permission from Thomson Reuters/West, from Westlaw, 10 U.S.C.A. § 816. © 2008 Thomson Reuters/West.

will show all available search options. **Figure 6.11** shows the Westlaw Table of Contents search screen and the search options available for researching U.S.C.A.

As noted above, the Search option allows you to execute a word search. Note that a word search in a database containing an annotated code will search both the statutory language and the annotations. Thus, it

FIGURE 6.11 WESTLAW U.S.C.A. TABLE OF CONTENTS SEARCH SCREEN

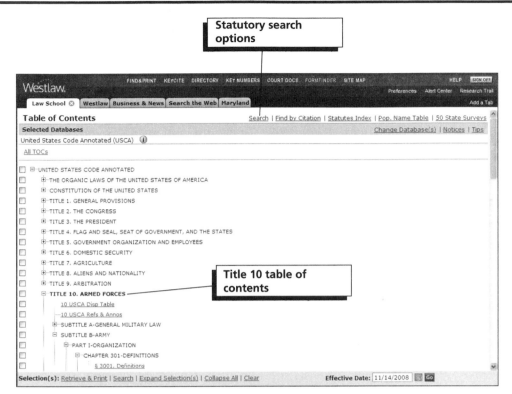

Reprinted with permission from Thomson Reuters/West, from Westlaw, U.S.C.A. Table of Contents search screen. © 2008 Thomson Reuters/West.

will retrieve documents when the search terms appear in the annotations, such as in a case summary, even if they do not appear in the statutory language unless you specifically limit your search to words in the statute itself. (Word searching in general and techniques for limiting a search are discussed in Chapter 10, on electronic legal research.) Word searching is useful when you are searching for unique terms that are not likely to be included in the statutory index or table of contents.

The second option, Find by Citation, involves retrieving a code section when you know its citation. Selecting this option brings up a list of templates you can use to retrieve statutory citations. You do not have to choose a statutory database to retrieve a statute from its citation. You can use the Find by Citation box in the Shortcuts section or use the Find & Print link at the top of the screen.

The Table of Contents option allows you to browse a code's table of contents. The table of contents will be organized by Title or subject. You can drill down from the main Title or subject headings to chapters and individual code sections. You can also execute a word search within selected portions of the code by checking the box in the table of contents next to each item you want to search. Table of Contents searching is a good option when you are familiar enough with the code to know which subject areas are likely to contain relevant statutes but do not have specific statutory citations. It is also an excellent feature for viewing an entire statutory scheme.

The Statutes Index allows you to search the code's subject index just as you would if you were researching in print. Westlaw's statutory indices are identical to West print indices, although West reports that the electronic versions are updated more frequently than the print versions are. The index entries will refer you to statutory provisions the same way a print index would. This is a good research option when you want to search by subject because the index is organized around concepts instead of individual terms in a document and contains cross-references to related terms and concepts. Word searches, by contrast, will search only for the precise terms you specify.

The Popular Name Table lists laws by their popular names. It is the electronic version of the print popular name table. Choosing the Popular Name Table option displays an alphabetical list of acts by their popular names. The link to an act's popular name will retrieve an entry listing the Title(s) and section(s) where the act is codified. When you know the popular name of a statute but do not have its citation, this is a good research option.

The option for 50 State Surveys accesses a database that West describes as containing "a variety of topical surveys providing references to applicable state laws." It consists mostly of secondary material describing state law on a variety of topics and providing citations to state statutory provisions. It may be useful when you are researching the law of multiple jurisdictions.

c. Using KeyCite in Statutory Research

Even though the statutes in Westlaw's databases are usually up to date, you may still want to use KeyCite in your research. As noted above, using a statutory citator ensures that your research is fully updated. In addition, a citator will provide the most complete research references because it will list every case that has cited the statute and may be more up to date than the statutory annotations.

The process of using KeyCite for statutes is virtually identical to the process of using it for cases. You can enter a citation or access the service from a statute you are viewing. The KeyCite entry is divided into sections for history and citing references. The history section will list amendments and other legislative action affecting the statute, along with legislative history documents if they are available. (Federal legislative history is discussed in Chapter 7.) The citing references list citing cases and

FIGURE 6.12   KEYCITE HISTORY ENTRY FOR 10 U.S.C.A. § 816

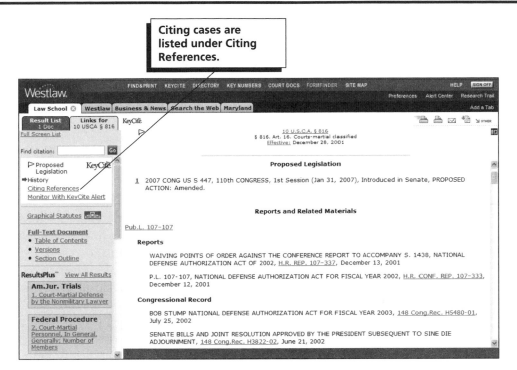

Reprinted with permission from Thomson Reuters/West, KeyCite entry for 10 U.S.C.A. § 816 © 2008 Thomson Reuters/West.

secondary sources. You can customize the display using the "Limit Key-Cite Display" option, and you can monitor a KeyCite statutory entry with KeyCite Alert. An example KeyCite statutory entry appears in **Figure 6.12.**

2. LEXISNEXIS

LexisNexis also contains annotated versions of many codes, including the federal code, all fifty state codes, and the District of Columbia code. The annotated version of the federal code in LexisNexis is derived from U.S.C.S. For most jurisdictions, you will find court rules of procedure included with the code, and for some you will find local court rules as well.

a. Viewing an Individual Code Section

The display for an individual code section begins with a heading containing, among other things, the citation for the section and a notation with the date through which it is updated. The text of the statute then appears, followed by annotations like those in a print code. When you retrieve an individual code section, you have several options for viewing the complete statutory outline. You can view the table of contents for the statutory chapter and the entire code from the TOC link in the top left corner of the screen. You can also browse preceding or subsequent code sections using the Book Browse function. **Figure 6.13** shows how a federal statute appears in LexisNexis.

b. Searching for Statutes

LexisNexis offers several statutory research options, including citation, word, table of contents, and popular name searching. You can retrieve a statute from its citation using the Get A Document function. This is the easiest way to locate a statute when you know its citation.

For word or table of contents searches, the first step is selecting a database, which LexisNexis calls a Source, in which to search. A list of Sources appears under the Search tab, Sources option. You can select one of the sources listed or choose a general category of authority to view additional source options. Once you have selected a statutory source, the search screen will give you the option of executing a word search or browsing the table of contents. If you execute a word search in an annotated code, LexisNexis will look for your search terms in both the statutory language and in any annotations unless you specifically limit your search to words in the statute itself. (Word searching in general and techniques for limiting a search are discussed in Chapter 10, on electronic legal research.)

To browse the table of contents, you can drill down through the main Title or subject headings to individual code sections. You can also restrict your word search to individual Titles, chapters, or sections of the code by checking the box next to each part of the code you want to search. Again, word searching is useful if you are searching for specific statutory terms, and browsing the table of contents is useful for viewing an entire statutory scheme. The table of contents also provides a mechanism for searching statutory subject categories because LexisNexis does not offer index searching as of this writing. **Figure 6.14** shows the search screen for searching U.S.C.S.

You can also search the U.S.C.S. Popular Name Table to locate federal statutes by name. As of this writing, you can access the popular name table by following this path: Federal Legal—U.S., United States Code Service (USCS) Materials, USCS—Popular Name Table. Once you select this Source, you can execute a word search for the name of an act or browse the alphabetical list. Follow the link to an act's popular name to retrieve an entry listing the Title(s) and section(s) where the act is codified. LexisNexis does not allow you to browse state statutes by popular name. If you need to find a state statute by name, you can use the popular name as a word search to locate the act.

FIGURE 6.13 EXCERPT FROM 10 U.S.C.S. § 816 IN LEXISNEXIS

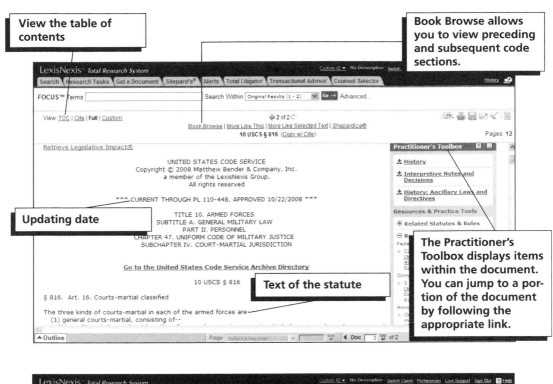

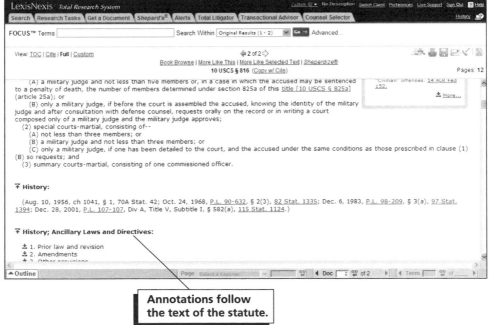

Reprinted with permission of LexisNexis. From LexisNexis, 10 U.S.C.S. § 816.

FIGURE 6.14   LEXISNEXIS U.S.C.S. SEARCH SCREEN

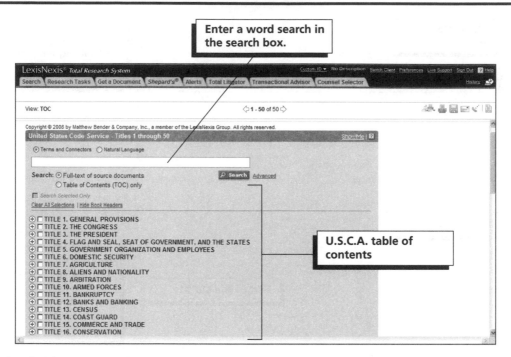

Reprinted with permission of LexisNexis. From LexisNexis, U.S.C.S. search screen.

c. Using Shepard's for Statutory Research

Even though the statutes in LexisNexis's databases are usually up to date, you may still want to use Shepard's in your research. As noted above, using a statutory citator ensures that your research is fully updated. In addition, a citator will provide the most complete research references because it will list every case that has cited the statute and may be more up to date than the statutory annotations.

The process of using Shepard's for statutes is virtually identical to the process of using it for cases. You can enter a citation or access the service from a statute you are viewing. A Shepard's entry shows the history of the statute first, indicating, for example, whether the statute has been amended. After the legislation's history, the entry lists citing cases and sources. You can customize the display to focus on the information most relevant to your research, and you can monitor a statutory Shepard's entry with Shepard's Alert®. An example of a Shepard's statutory entry appears in **Figure 6.15**.

3. INTERNET SOURCES

The federal code, all fifty state codes, and the District of Columbia code are available on the Internet. You can locate them through government

FIGURE 6.15   SHEPARD'S ENTRY FOR 10 U.S.C.S. § 816

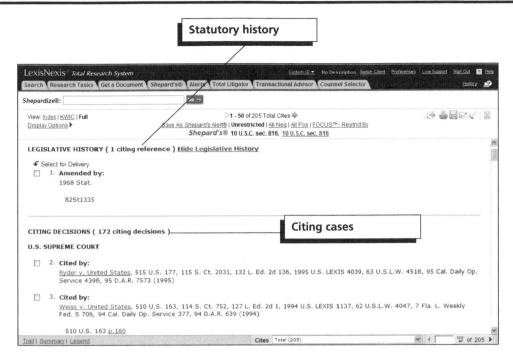

Reprinted with permission of LexisNexis. From LexisNexis, Shepard's entry for 10 U.S.C.S. § 816.

web sites, such as the web site for the House of Representatives, or general legal research web sites. Often these sites have search functions that will allow you to retrieve statutes using word, subject, or table of contents searches. As of this writing, index searching is available for only a few states, and Cornell Law School's Legal Information Institute site offers a popular name table for the United States Code. Appendix A lists the Internet addresses for web sites that may be useful for statutory research. In addition, court rules of procedure, including local court rules, are often available on court web sites. If the code or rules of procedure you need to research are available and up to date on the Internet, this can be an economical alternative to LexisNexis and Westlaw research.

Two caveats, however, are important to mention. First, the codes available on the Internet are usually unannotated codes, so you will only find the statutory text, not any additional research references. Second, it is important to check the date of any statutory material you use. Statutory compilations available on the Internet may be updated only as frequently as official print sources. If the material is not up to date, you will need to update your research. Therefore, if you use an Internet source for statutory research, it is especially important to use a citator to obtain research references and update your research.

D. CITING STATUTES

The citation format for statutes is the same using either the *ALWD Manual* or the *Bluebook*. The general rules for citing statutes can be found in Rule 14 in the *ALWD Manual* and Bluepages B6 in the *Bluebook*.

Citations to statutes can be broken into two components: (a) information identifying the code and code section; and (b) parenthetical information containing the date of the code and any relevant supplements; this section may also include a reference to the publisher of the code. To find out the exact requirements for a citation to a particular code, you must look at Appendix 1 in the *ALWD Manual* or Table T.1 in the *Bluebook*, both of which tell you how to cite codes from every jurisdiction in the United States. Appendix 1 and Table T.1 include information on which code to cite if more than one is published, how to abbreviate the name of the code, and whether the name of the publisher must be included with the date in the parenthetical.

In a citation to a Title code, you will ordinarily give the Title number, the abbreviated name of the code, the section symbol, the section number, and a parenthetical containing the date the book was published and, if necessary, the publisher.

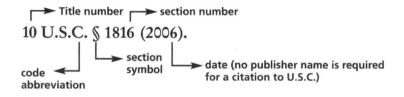

In a citation to a subject-matter code, you will ordinarily list the abbreviated name of the code, the section symbol, the section number, and a parenthetical containing the date the book was published and, if necessary, the publisher.

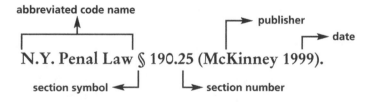

In this example, Appendix 1 and Table T.1 provide that citations to McKinney's *Consolidated Laws of New York Annotated* must include the name of the publisher in the parenthetical, which is why you see the reference to McKinney in this citation. In both examples, note that there is a space between the section symbol (§) and the section number.

Sometimes determining which date or dates to include in the parenthetical can be confusing. The answer is always a function of where a reader would have to look to find the full and up-to-date language of the statute in the print code. If the full statute is contained in the main volume of the code, the date in the parenthetical should refer only to the main volume. If the full statute is contained only in the pocket part, the date should refer only to the pocket part. If the reader must refer both to the main volume and to the pocket part, the parenthetical should list both dates. In making this determination, you should consider *only* the language of the statute itself, not the annotations. If the full text of the statute itself is in the main volume, you do not need to cite the pocket part even if it contains additional annotations. Once you have determined which date to place in the parenthetical, you should then refer to Appendix 1 or Table T.1 to determine whether the publisher must also be included. The following are examples of citations with different date information included in the parenthetical.

N.Y. Penal Law § 190.05 (McKinney 2004).

In this example, Appendix 1 and Table T.1 require the name of the publisher, and the full text of the statute can be found in the main volume.

N.Y. Penal Law § 190.05 (McKinney Supp. 2009).

In this example, Appendix 1 and Table T.1 require the name of the publisher, and the full text of the statute can be found in the pocket part.

N.Y. Penal Law § 190.05 (McKinney 2004 & Supp. 2009).

In this example, Appendix 1 and Table T.1 require the name of the publisher, and the reader must refer both to the main volume and to the pocket part to find the full text of the statute.

In citations to a code for which no publisher is required, the only difference would be the omission of the publisher's name, as in the example below.

Haw. Rev. Stat. § 328-1 (1993).

When you look at the entries in Table T.1 of the *Bluebook*, you will notice that the names of the codes are in large and small capital letters, e.g., N.Y. PENAL LAW § 190.05 (McKinney 1999). Remember that this is the type style for law review footnotes, not for briefs and memoranda. According to Bluepages B13, large and small capitals are never used in briefs and memoranda. Therefore, in briefs and memoranda, you should use regular type when citing statutes. You should not use all capital letters, nor should you use large and small capital letters.

E. SAMPLE PAGES FOR PRINT STATUTORY RESEARCH

Beginning on the next page, **Figures 6.16** through **6.19** contain sample pages from U.S.C.A. Members of the military are subject to a special set of federal criminal laws called the Uniform Code of Military Justice (UCMJ). The U.S.C.A. sample pages show the research process you would follow if you were researching the composition and jurisdiction of courts-martial under the UCMJ. **Figures 6.20** through **6.23** contain sample pages from Vernon's *Texas Statutes and Codes Annotated* showing the process for researching Texas products liability statutes concerning inherently dangerous products.

The first step in U.S.C.A. research is using the most recent General Index to locate relevant code sections. This example shows what you would find if you looked under "Military Justice Code."

FIGURE 6.16   EXCERPT FROM U.S.C.A. GENERAL INDEX

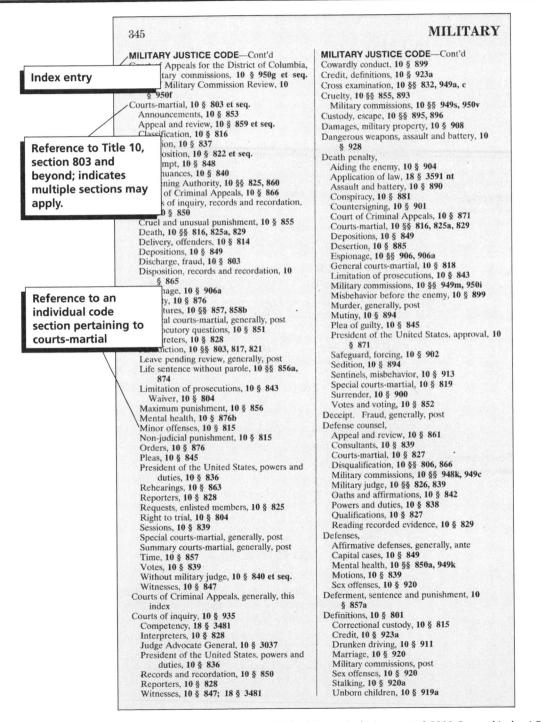

345   **MILITARY**

Callout boxes:
- Index entry
- Reference to Title 10, section 803 and beyond; indicates multiple sections may apply.
- Reference to an individual code section pertaining to courts-martial

MILITARY JUSTICE CODE—Cont'd
Court of Appeals for the District of Columbia, military commissions, 10 § 950g et seq.
Military Commission Review, 10 § 950f
Courts-martial, 10 § 803 et seq.
  Announcements, 10 § 853
  Appeal and review, 10 § 859 et seq.
  Classification, 10 § 816
  Composition, 10 § 837
  Composition, 10 § 822 et seq.
  Contempt, 10 § 848
  Continuances, 10 § 840
  Convening Authority, 10 §§ 825, 860
  Court of Criminal Appeals, 10 § 866
  Courts of inquiry, records and recordation, 10 § 850
  Cruel and unusual punishment, 10 § 855
  Death, 10 §§ 816, 825a, 829
  Delivery, offenders, 10 § 814
  Depositions, 10 § 849
  Discharge, fraud, 10 § 803
  Disposition, records and recordation, 10 § 865
  Espionage, 10 § 906a
  Felony, 10 § 876
  Forfeitures, 10 §§ 857, 858b
  General courts-martial, generally, post
  Interlocutory questions, 10 § 851
  Interpreters, 10 § 828
  Jurisdiction, 10 §§ 803, 817, 821
  Leave pending review, generally, post
  Life sentence without parole, 10 §§ 856a, 874
  Limitation of prosecutions, 10 § 843
    Waiver, 10 § 804
  Maximum punishment, 10 § 856
  Mental health, 10 § 876b
  Minor offenses, 10 § 815
  Non-judicial punishment, 10 § 815
  Orders, 10 § 876
  Pleas, 10 § 845
  President of the United States, powers and duties, 10 § 836
  Rehearings, 10 § 863
  Reporters, 10 § 828
  Requests, enlisted members, 10 § 825
  Right to trial, 10 § 804
  Sessions, 10 § 839
  Special courts-martial, generally, post
  Summary courts-martial, generally, post
  Time, 10 § 857
  Votes, 10 § 839
  Without military judge, 10 § 840 et seq.
  Witnesses, 10 § 847
Courts of Criminal Appeals, generally, this index
Courts of inquiry, 10 § 935
  Competency, 18 § 3481
  Interpreters, 10 § 828
  Judge Advocate General, 10 § 3037
  President of the United States, powers and duties, 10 § 836
  Records and recordation, 10 § 850
  Reporters, 10 § 828
  Witnesses, 10 § 847; 18 § 3481

MILITARY JUSTICE CODE—Cont'd
Cowardly conduct, 10 § 899
Credit, definitions, 10 § 923a
Cross examination, 10 §§ 832, 949a, c
Cruelty, 10 §§ 855, 893
  Military commissions, 10 §§ 949s, 950v
Custody, escape, 10 §§ 895, 896
Damages, military property, 10 § 908
Dangerous weapons, assault and battery, 10 § 928
Death penalty,
  Aiding the enemy, 10 § 904
  Application of law, 18 § 3591 nt
  Assault and battery, 10 § 890
  Conspiracy, 10 § 881
  Countersigning, 10 § 901
  Court of Criminal Appeals, 10 § 871
  Courts-martial, 10 §§ 816, 825a, 829
  Depositions, 10 § 849
  Desertion, 10 § 885
  Espionage, 10 §§ 906, 906a
  General courts-martial, 10 § 818
  Limitation of prosecutions, 10 § 843
  Military commissions, 10 §§ 949m, 950i
  Misbehavior before the enemy, 10 § 899
  Murder, generally, post
  Mutiny, 10 § 894
  Plea of guilty, 10 § 845
  President of the United States, approval, 10 § 871
  Safeguard, forcing, 10 § 902
  Sedition, 10 § 894
  Sentinels, misbehavior, 10 § 913
  Special courts-martial, 10 § 819
  Surrender, 10 § 900
  Votes and voting, 10 § 852
Deceipt. Fraud, generally, post
Defense counsel,
  Appeal and review, 10 § 861
  Consultants, 10 § 839
  Courts-martial, 10 § 827
  Disqualification, 10 §§ 806, 866
  Military commissions, 10 §§ 948k, 949c
  Military judge, 10 §§ 826, 839
  Oaths and affirmations, 10 § 842
  Powers and duties, 10 § 838
  Qualifications, 10 § 827
  Reading recorded evidence, 10 § 829
Defenses,
  Affirmative defenses, generally, ante
  Capital cases, 10 § 849
  Mental health, 10 §§ 850a, 949k
  Motions, 10 § 839
  Sex offenses, 10 § 920
Deferment, sentence and punishment, 10 § 857a
Definitions, 10 § 801
  Correctional custody, 10 § 815
  Credit, 10 § 923a
  Drunken driving, 10 § 911
  Marriage, 10 § 920
  Military commissions, post
  Sex offenses, 10 § 920
  Stalking, 10 § 920a
  Unborn children, 10 § 919a

188

CHAPTER 6: STATUTORY RESEARCH

The next step is looking up the statute in the main volume. Because the index indicates that several code provisions may be applicable, you might want to review the subchapter outline. The individual code section sets out the classifications of courts-martial.

FIGURE 6.17 10 U.S.C.A. § 816

---

10 § 815
Note 113

ARMED FORCES   Subt. A

cial punishment rendered that document inadmissible. U. S. v. Stewart, CMA 1981, 12 M.J. 143.

Where military personnel records jacket copy of record of nonjudicial punishment showed that appeal was, as required, considered by a judge advocate, his failure to sign form did not affect its admissibility and, similarly, where copy ~~d that attachments were made,~~ ~~ably to the original, failure to list~~ ~~form did not render record inad-~~ . U. S. v. Berry, ACMR 1977, 2 .

114. Rehearing
Where, during course of rehearing, trial counsel offered into evidence four rec-

ords of nonjudicial punishment, one record of vacation of suspended punishment, and one record of conviction by summary court-martial and where, although record of accused's trial by summary court-martial did not on its face meet requirements for admissibility established by Booker decision, military judge elicited from trial defense counsel that latter was aware of case law concerning admissibility of summary court-martial record, had resolved issue of exhibit's admissibility, and did not object to offer, military judge was not required to take further action prior to admitting exhibit in evidence. U. S. v. Alford, ACMR 1979, 6 M.J. 907.

SUBCHAPTER IV—COURT–MARTIAL JURISDICTION

Sec.	Art.	
816.	16.	Courts-martial classified.
817.	17.	Jurisdiction of courts-martial in general.
818.	18.	Jurisdiction of general courts-martial.
819.	19.	Jurisdiction of special courts-martial.
820.	20.	Jurisdiction of summary courts-martial.
821.	21.	Jurisdiction of courts-martial not exclusive.

§ 816.   Art. 16.   Courts-martial classified

The three kinds of courts-martial in each of the armed forces are—

(1) general courts-martial, consisting of—

(A) a military judge and not less than five members; or

(B) only a military judge, if before the court is assembled the accused, knowing the identity of the military judge and after consultation with defense counsel, requests orally on the record or in writing a court composed only of a military judge and the military judge approves;

(2) special courts-martial, consisting of—

(A) not less than three members; or

(B) a military judge and not less than three members; or

(C) only a military judge, if one has been detailed to the court, and the accused under the same conditions as those proscribed in clause (1)(B) so requests; and

(3) summary courts-martial, consisting of one commissioned officer.

(Aug. 10, 1956, c. 1041, 70A Stat. 42; Oct. 24, 1968, Pub.L. 90–632, § 2(3), 82 Stat. 1335; Dec. 6, 1983, Pub.L. 98–209, § 3(a), 97 Stat. 1394.)

202

Outline of sections within this subchapter of the code

Name of the section

Text of the statute

Section number

Reprinted with permission from Thomson Reuters/West, *United States Code Annotated*, Title 10 (1998), p. 202. © 1998 Thomson Reuters/West.

The annotations list a variety of research references.

FIGURE 6.18   ANNOTATIONS ACCOMPANYING 10 U.S.C.A. § 816

Ch. 47   UNIFORM CODE OF MILITARY JUSTICE   **10 § 816**

HISTORICAL AND STATUTORY NOTES

Information on amendments to the statute

...tes and Legislative Reports

Revised section	Source (U.S. Code)	Source (Statutes at Large)
816................	50:576.	May 5, 1950, ch. 169, § 1 (Art. 16), 64 Stat. 113.

The word "The" is substituted for the words "There shall be". The word "are" is substituted for the word "namely". The words "not less than five members" are substituted for the words "any number of members not less than five". The words "not less than three members" are substituted for the words "any number of members not less than three". The word "commissioned" is inserted before the word "officer" in clause (3) for clarity.

House and Senate Reports to accompany H.R. 7049, see 1956 U.S. Code Cong. and Adm. News, p. 4613.

1968 Acts. Senate Report No. 1601, see 1968 U.S. Code Cong. and Adm. News, p. 4501.

1983 Acts. House Report No. 98–549, see 1983 U.S. Code Cong. and Adm. News, p. 2177.

Amendments
1983 Amendments. Par. (1)(B). Pub.L. 98–209 substituted "orally on the record ..." for "in writing".

1968 Amendments. Pub.L. 90–632 provided that a general or special court-martial shall consist of only a military judge if the accused, before the court is assembled, so requests in writing and the military judge approves, with the added requirements that the accused know the identity of the military judge and have the advice of counsel, and that the election be available in the case of a special court-martial only if a military judge has been detailed to the court.

Effective Dates
1983 Acts. Amendment by Pub.L. 98–209 effective on the first day of the eighth calendar month beginning after Dec. 6, 1983, see section 12(a)(1) of Pub.L. 98–209, set out as a note under section 801 of this title.

1968 Acts. Amendment by Pub.L. 90–632 effective the first day of the tenth month following Oct. 1968, see section 4 of Pub.L. 90–632, set out as a note under section 801 of this title.

References to secondary sources

AMERICAN LAW REPORTS

Courts-martial jurisdiction over members of armed forces for "Civilian" offenses. 14 ALR Fed 152.

LIBRARY REFERENCES

Administrative Law
General courts-martial, see West's Federal Practice Manual § 6292.
Nature, types and composition of courts-martial, see West's Federal Practice Manual § 6290.
Special courts-martial, see West's Federal Practice Manual § 6293.

American Digest System
Armed Services ⟨⟩43.
Military Justice ⟨⟩870.

West digest topics and key numbers

Encyclopedias
C.J.S. Military Justice §§ 138, 139, 143, 145, 147, 153.
54 Am Jur 2d, Military, and Civil Defense § 216.

Forms
3 Fed Procedural Forms L Ed, Armed Forces, Civil Disturbances, and National Defense § 5:71.

203

FIGURE 6.18   ANNOTATIONS ACCOMPANYING 10 U.S.C.A. § 816 *(Continued)*

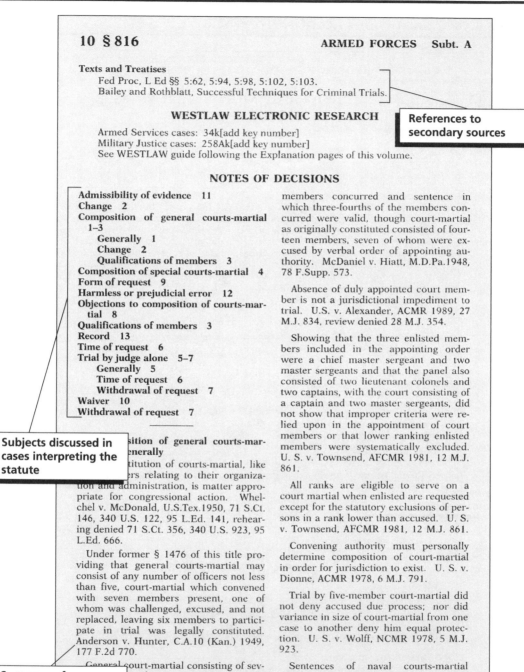

The next step is checking the pocket part. The pocket part shows new statutory language that supersedes the language in the main volume. It also shows additional research references. After checking the pocket part, be sure to check any noncumulative supplements. Because the supplements are noncumulative, all supplements published after the pocket part must be checked for amendments to the statute or new annotations.

FIGURE 6.19   POCKET PART ENTRY FOR 10 U.S.C.A. § 816

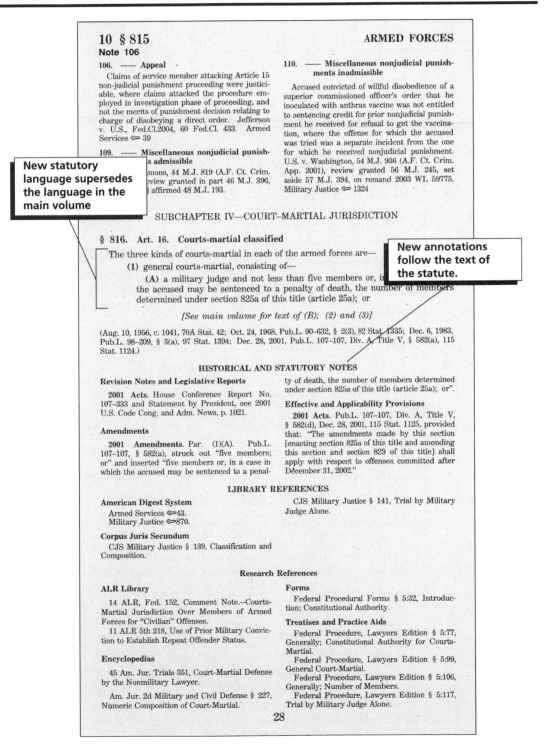

10 § 815
Note 106

ARMED FORCES

106. —— **Appeal**

Claims of service member attacking Article 15 non-judicial punishment proceeding were justiciable, where claims attacked the procedure employed in investigation phase of proceeding, and not the merits of punishment decision relating to charge of disobeying a direct order.   Jefferson v. U.S., Fed.Cl.2004, 60 Fed.Cl. 433.   Armed Services ⟆ 39

109. —— **Miscellaneous nonjudicial punish-ments admissible**

mons, 44 M.J. 819 (A.F. Ct. Crim. eview granted in part 46 M.J. 396, I affirmed 48 M.J. 193.

110. —— **Miscellaneous nonjudicial punish-ments inadmissible**

Accused convicted of willful disobedience of a superior commissioned officer's order that he inoculated with anthrax vaccine was not entitled to sentencing credit for prior nonjudicial punishment he received for refusal to get the vaccination, where the offense for which the accused was tried was a separate incident from the one for which he received nonjudicial punishment. U.S. v. Washington, 54 M.J. 936 (A.F. Ct. Crim. App. 2001), review granted 56 M.J. 245, set aside 57 M.J. 394, on remand 2003 WL 59775. Military Justice ⟆ 1324

> New statutory language supersedes the language in the main volume

SUBCHAPTER IV—COURT–MARTIAL JURISDICTION

§ 816.   Art. 16.   Courts-martial classified

The three kinds of courts-martial in each of the armed forces are—

(1) general courts-martial, consisting of—

(A) a military judge and not less than five members or, i the accused may be sentenced to a penalty of death, the number of members determined under section 825a of this title (article 25a); or

> New annotations follow the text of the statute.

[See main volume for text of (B); (2) and (3)]

(Aug. 10, 1956, c. 1041, 70A Stat. 42; Oct. 24, 1968, Pub.L. 90–632, § 2(3), 82 Stat. 1335; Dec. 6, 1983, Pub.L. 98–209, § 3(a), 97 Stat. 1394; Dec. 28, 2001, Pub.L. 107–107, Div. A, Title V, § 582(a), 115 Stat. 1124.)

HISTORICAL AND STATUTORY NOTES

Revision Notes and Legislative Reports

2001 **Acts.** House Conference Report No. 107–333 and Statement by President, see 2001 U.S. Code Cong. and Adm. News, p. 1021.

Amendments

2001 **Amendments.** Par. (1)(A). Pub.L. 107–107, § 582(a), struck out "five members; or" and inserted "five members or, in a case in which the accused may be sentenced to a penal-

ty of death, the number of members determined under section 825a of this title (article 25a); or".

Effective and Applicability Provisions

2001 **Acts.** Pub.L. 107–107, Div. A, Title V, § 582(d), Dec. 28, 2001, 115 Stat. 1125, provided that: "The amendments made by this section [enacting section 825a of this title and amending this section and section 829 of this title] shall apply with respect to offenses committed after December 31, 2002."

LIBRARY REFERENCES

American Digest System

Armed Services ⟆43.
Military Justice ⟆870.

Corpus Juris Secundum

CJS Military Justice § 139, Classification and Composition.

CJS Military Justice § 141, Trial by Military Judge Alone.

Research References

ALR Library

14 ALR, Fed. 152, Comment Note.--Courts-Martial Jurisdiction Over Members of Armed Forces for "Civilian" Offenses.

11 ALR 5th 218, Use of Prior Military Conviction to Establish Repeat Offender Status.

Encyclopedias

45 Am. Jur. Trials 351, Court-Martial Defense by the Nonmilitary Lawyer.

Am. Jur. 2d Military and Civil Defense § 227, Numeric Composition of Court-Martial.

Forms

Federal Procedural Forms § 5:32, Introduction; Constitutional Authority.

Treatises and Practice Aids

Federal Procedure, Lawyers Edition § 5:77, Generally; Constitutional Authority for Courts-Martial.

Federal Procedure, Lawyers Edition § 5:99, General Court-Martial.

Federal Procedure, Lawyers Edition § 5:106, Generally; Number of Members.

Federal Procedure, Lawyers Edition § 5:117, Trial by Military Judge Alone.

28

FIGURE 6.19   POCKET PART ENTRY FOR 10 U.S.C.A. § 816 (Continued)

ARMED FORCES   10 § 819

Federal Procedure, Lawyers Edition § 5:352, Prohibition Upon Double Punishment; Other [restr]ictions Upon Nonjudicial Punishment.

[We]st's Federal Administrative Practice [§ 6]474, Overview of How the Military Justice [Syst]em Works.

[We]st's Federal Administrative Practice [§ 64]82, Courts-Martial -- Nature, Types and Composition.

West's Federal Administrative Practice § 6484, Jurisdiction of Courts-Martial -- General Courts-Martial.

West's Federal Administrative Practice § 6485, Jurisdiction of Courts-Martial -- Special Courts-Martial.

Newer cases interpreting the statute

NOTES OF DECISIONS

5. Trial by judge alone—Generally

U.S. v. Turner, 45 M.J. 531 (N.M.Ct.Crim. App. 1996), set aside 47 M.J. 348, [main volume] reconsideration denied 48 M.J. 392, certiorari denied 119 S.Ct. 1578, 526 U.S. 1099, 143 L.Ed.2d 673, review denied 50 M.J. 332.

While an accused has the absolute right to request trial by military judge alone, there is no concomitant absolute right to have it approved, and the ultimate decision to grant or deny such a request is within the sound discretion of the military judge. U.S. v. Dodge, 59 M.J. 821 (A.F. Ct. Crim. App. 2004), affirmed in part, reversed in part 60 M.J. 368, on remand 60 M.J. 873, review granted 60 M.J. 369. Military Justice ⫗ 874.1

6. —— Time of request

Requirement of UCMJ article that accused's request for a court composed only of a military judge be made before court is assembled is a matter of procedure, and not jurisdictional; thus, a military judge-alone request made after assembly can be approved by the trial judge, if

justified by the circumstances. U.S. v. Jungbluth, 48 M.J. 953 (N.M.Ct.Crim.App. 1998), review denied 52 M.J. 294. Military Justice ⫗ 875

12. Harmless or prejudicial error

U.S. v. Turner, 45 M.J. 531 (N.M.Ct.Crim. App. 1996), [main volume] set aside 47 M.J. 348, reconsideration denied 48 M.J. 392, certiorari denied 119 S.Ct. 1578, 526 U.S. 1099, 143 L.Ed.2d 673, review denied 50 M.J. 332.

There was no substantial compliance with Article 16 procedures for choice of forum, where accused was never advised of his forum rights, and never expressly elected trial by military judge alone on the record, either personally or through counsel; moreover, the error was not harmless, where accused received the jurisdictional maximum punishment on sentencing, and the record of trial did not otherwise establish that the forum selection was the accused's choice. U.S. v. Goodwin, 60 M.J. 849 (N.M.Ct. Crim.App. 2005). Military Justice ⫗ 874.1; Military Justice ⫗ 1423.1

§ 817.   Art. 17.   Jurisdiction of courts-martial in general

NOTES OF DECISIONS

I. GENERALLY

20. Expiration of term of enlistment—Generally

Air Force had authority to retain jurisdiction over member of Air Force after his term of service expired, where court-martial charges were pending against member at end of his enlistment period. Williams v. U.S., Fed.Cl. 2006, 71 Fed.Cl. 194. Military Justice ⫗ 515

Where the appellate courts are invoked by an accused following his court-martial conviction and a sentence rehearing is authorized on appeal, an intervening administrative discharge does not serve to terminate jurisdiction over the person of the accused for purposes of that rehearing. U.S. v. Davis, U.S. Armed Forces

2006, 63 M.J. 171. Military Justice ⫗ 521; Military Justice ⫗ 1434

22. —— Formal discharge

Military prisoner's claim for damages against federal officials, for alleged constitutional violations that arose from injuries soldier sustained after he received complete punitive discharge from service, were barred, on basis that alleged activity was incident to his service to military, since soldier was incarcerated at military prison and he was still subject to Uniform Code of Military Justice (UCMJ). Ricks v. Nickels, C.A.10 (Kan.) 2002, 295 F.3d 1124, certiorari denied 123 S.Ct. 630, 537 U.S. 1056, 154 L.Ed.2d 536. United States ⫗ 50.10(5)

§ 819.   Art. 19.   Jurisdiction of special courts-martial

Subject to section 817 of this title (article 17), special courts-martial have jurisdiction to try persons subject to this chapter for any noncapital offense made punishable by this chapter and, under such regulations as the President may prescribe, for capital offenses. Special courts-martial may, under such limitations as the President may prescribe, adjudge any punishment not forbidden by this chapter except death, dishonorable discharge, dismissal, confinement for more than one year, hard labor without confinement for more than three months, forfeiture of pay exceeding two-thirds pay per month, or forfeiture of pay for more than one year. A bad-conduct discharge, confinement for more than six months, or forfeiture of pay for more than six months may not be adjudged unless a complete record of the proceedings and testimony has been made, counsel having the qualifications prescribed under section 827(b) of this title (article

29

In state statutory research, the first step is using the subject index to locate relevant code sections. This example shows what you would find if you looked under "Products Liability" in the General Index to Vernon's *Texas Statutes and Codes Annotated*.

FIGURE 6.20 VERNON'S *TEXAS STATUTES AND CODES ANNOTATED* GENERAL INDEX

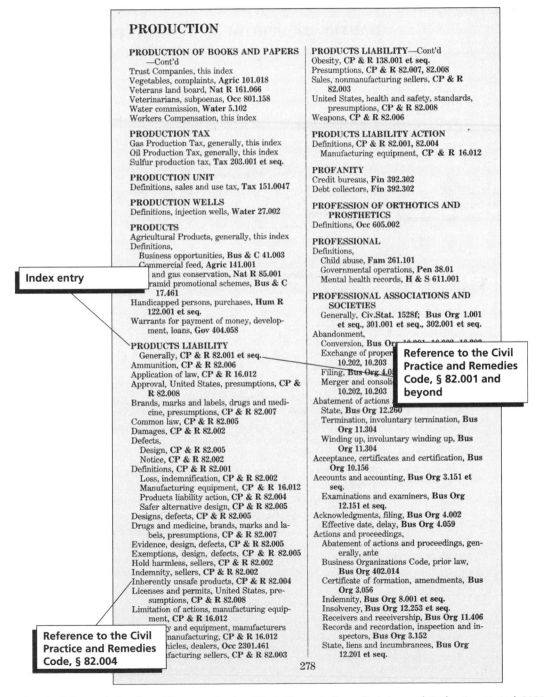

PRODUCTION

PRODUCTION OF BOOKS AND PAPERS
—Cont'd
Trust Companies, this index
Vegetables, complaints, **Agric 101.018**
Veterans land board, **Nat R 161.066**
Veterinarians, subpoenas, **Occ 801.158**
Water commission, **Water 5.102**
Workers Compensation, this index

PRODUCTION TAX
Gas Production Tax, generally, this index
Oil Production Tax, generally, this index
Sulfur production tax, **Tax 203.001 et seq.**

PRODUCTION UNIT
Definitions, sales and use tax, **Tax 151.0047**

PRODUCTION WELLS
Definitions, injection wells, **Water 27.002**

PRODUCTS
Agricultural Products, generally, this index
Definitions,
    Business opportunities, **Bus & C 41.003**
    Commercial feed, **Agric 141.001**
    [Oil] and gas conservation, **Nat R 85.001**
    [Py]ramid promotional schemes, **Bus & C**
        17.461
Handicapped persons, purchases, **Hum R**
    122.001 et seq.
Warrants for payment of money, develop-
    ment, loans, **Gov 404.058**

PRODUCTS LIABILITY
Generally, **CP & R 82.001 et seq.**
Ammunition, **CP & R 82.006**
Application of law, **CP & R 16.012**
Approval, United States, presumptions, **CP &**
    R 82.008
Brands, marks and labels, drugs and medi-
    cine, presumptions, **CP & R 82.007**
Common law, **CP & R 82.005**
Damages, **CP & R 82.002**
Defects,
    Design, **CP & R 82.005**
    Notice, **CP & R 82.002**
Definitions, **CP & R 82.001**
    Loss, indemnification, **CP & R 82.002**
    Manufacturing equipment, **CP & R 16.012**
    Products liability action, **CP & R 82.004**
    Safer alternative design, **CP & R 82.005**
Designs, defects, **CP & R 82.005**
Drugs and medicine, brands, marks and la-
    bels, presumptions, **CP & R 82.007**
Evidence, design, defects, **CP & R 82.005**
Exemptions, design, defects, **CP & R 82.005**
Hold harmless, sellers, **CP & R 82.002**
Indemnity, sellers, **CP & R 82.002**
Inherently unsafe products, **CP & R 82.004**
Licenses and permits, United States, pre-
    sumptions, **CP & R 82.008**
Limitation of actions, manufacturing equip-
    ment, **CP & R 16.012**
[Machiner]y and equipment, manufacturers
    [and] manufacturing, **CP & R 16.012**
[Ve]hicles, dealers, **Occ 2301.461**
[Manu]facturing sellers, **CP & R 82.003**

PRODUCTS LIABILITY—Cont'd
Obesity, **CP & R 138.001 et seq.**
Presumptions, **CP & R 82.007, 82.008**
Sales, nonmanufacturing sellers, **CP & R**
    82.003
United States, health and safety, standards,
    presumptions, **CP & R 82.008**
Weapons, **CP & R 82.006**

PRODUCTS LIABILITY ACTION
Definitions, **CP & R 82.001, 82.004**
    Manufacturing equipment, **CP & R 16.012**

PROFANITY
Credit bureaus, **Fin 392.302**
Debt collectors, **Fin 392.302**

PROFESSION OF ORTHOTICS AND
    PROSTHETICS
Definitions, **Occ 605.002**

PROFESSIONAL
Definitions,
    Child abuse, **Fam 261.101**
    Governmental operations, **Pen 38.01**
    Mental health records, **H & S 611.001**

PROFESSIONAL ASSOCIATIONS AND
    SOCIETIES
Generally, **Civ.Stat. 1528f; Bus Org 1.001**
    et seq., 301.001 et seq., 302.001 et seq.
Abandonment,
    Conversion, **Bus Org** [10.001, 10.002, 10.003]
    Exchange of proper[ty]
        10.202, 10.203
    Filing, **Bus Org 4.05**[1]
    Merger and consoli[dation]
        10.202, 10.203
Abatement of actions [and proceedings,]
    State, **Bus Org 12.260**
    Termination, involuntary termination, **Bus**
        Org 11.304
    Winding up, involuntary winding up, **Bus**
        Org 11.304
Acceptance, certificates and certification, **Bus**
    Org 10.156
Accounts and accounting, **Bus Org 3.151 et**
    seq.
    Examinations and examiners, **Bus Org**
        12.151 et seq.
Acknowledgments, filing, **Bus Org 4.002**
    Effective date, delay, **Bus Org 4.059**
Actions and proceedings,
    Abatement of actions and proceedings, gen-
        erally, ante
    Business Organizations Code, prior law,
        Bus Org 402.014
    Certificate of formation, amendments, **Bus**
        Org 3.056
Indemnity, **Bus Org 8.001 et seq.**
Insolvency, **Bus Org 12.253 et seq.**
Receivers and receivership, **Bus Org 11.406**
Records and recordation, inspection and in-
    spectors, **Bus Org 3.152**
State, liens and incumbrances, **Bus Org**
    12.201 et seq.

278

Index entry

Reference to the Civil Practice and Remedies Code, § 82.001 and beyond

Reference to the Civil Practice and Remedies Code, § 82.004

The next step is looking up the statute in the main volume. Because the index indicates that a range of sections may be relevant to products liability issues, you should review the chapter outline.

FIGURE 6.21   TEXAS CIVIL PRACTICE AND REMEDIES CODE CHAPTER 82

CHAPTER 82.   PRODUCTS LIABILITY

Section
82.001.   Definitions.
82.002.   Manufacturer's Duty to Indemnify.
82.003.   Liability of Nonmanufacturing Sellers.
82.004.   Inherently Unsafe Products.
82.005.   Design Defects.
82.006.   Firearms and Ammunition.
82.007.   Medicines.
82.008.   Compliance With Government Standards.

Chapter outline

Cross References

Limitation of actions, products liability, see V.T.C.A., Civil Practice & Remedies Code § 16.012.

Law Review and Journal Commentaries

The Products Liability Act of 1993: How it Changes Texas Law. William D. Farrar, 45 Baylor L.Rev. 633 (1993).

Westlaw Electronic Research

See Westlaw Electronic Research Guide following the Preface.

§ 82.001.   Definitions

In this chapter:

(1) "Claimant" means a party seeking relief, including a plaintiff, counter-claimant, or cross-claimant.

(2) "Products liability action" means any action against a manufacturer or seller for recovery of damages arising out of personal injury, death, or property damage allegedly caused by a defective product whether the action is based in strict tort liability, strict products liability, negligence, misrepresentation, breach of express or implied warranty, or any other theory or combination of theories.

(3) "Seller" means a person who is engaged in the business of distributing or otherwise placing, for any commercial purpose, in the stream of commerce for use or consumption a product or any component part thereof.

(4) "Manufacturer" means a person who is a designer, formulator, constructor, rebuilder, fabricator, producer, compounder, processor, or assembler of any product or any component part thereof and who places the product or any component part thereof in the stream of commerce.

Added by Acts 1993, 73rd Leg., ch. 5, § 1, eff. Sept. 1, 1993.

Research References

ALR Library
79 ALR 4th 278, Products Liability: Seller's Right to Indemnity from Manufacturer.
96 ALR 3rd 22, Products Liability: Modern Cases Determining Whether Product is Defectively Designed.

Encyclopedias
TX Jur. 3d Government Tort Liability § 13, Generally; Waiver of Sovereign Immunity.
TX Jur. 3d Products Liability § 1, Generally.
TX Jur. 3d Products Liability § 6, Indemnification, Generally.

249

The code section on inherently unsafe products sets out limits on liability for manufacturers and sellers of those products.

FIGURE 6.22   TEXAS CIVIL PRACTICE AND REMEDIES CODE § 82.004

---

§ 82.003   LIABILITY IN TORT
                                                                    Title 4

Historical and Statutory Notes

Section 23.02(c), (d) of Acts 2003, 78th Leg., ch. 204 provides:

"(c) Articles 4, 5, and 8 of this Act apply to an action filed on or after July 1, 2003. An action filed before July 1, 2003, is governed by the law in effect immediately before the change in law made by Articles 4, 5, and 8, and that law is continued in effect for that purpose.

"(d) Except as otherwise provided in this section or by a specific provision in an article, this

Act applies only to an action filed on or after the effective date [Sept. 1, 2003] of this Act. An action filed before the effective date of this Act, including an action filed before that date in which a party is joined or designated after that date, is governed by the law in effect immediately before the change in law made by this Act, and that law is continued in effect for that purpose."

Law Review and Journal Commentaries

Texas tort law—2003; It was a very____year. Michael D. Morrison, 56 Baylor L.Rev. 423 (2004).

Library References

Products Liability ⚖25.
Westlaw Topic No. 313A.
C.J.S. Products Liability § 40.

> **Name of the section**

Research References

Encyclopedias
TX Jur. 3d Products Liability § 20, Generally.
TX Jur. 3d Products Liability § 30, Generally.
TX Jur. 3d Products Liability § 82, Generally.

Forms
[...]ence Pleading & Practice
[...] 202:69, Introductory Comments.

> **Section number**

Treatises and Practice Aids
TX Practice Guide, Personal Injury 2d Ch. 4.I, I. Determining Theory to Sue Upon.
TX Practice Guide, Personal Injury 2d Ch. 3.III, III. Special Considerations With Product Liability Investigations.
Texas Practice Guide Torts CH 4.D, Strict Product Liability.

> **Text of the statute**

§ 82.004.   Inherently Unsafe Products

(a) In a products liability action, a manufacturer or seller shall not be liable if:

(1) the product is inherently unsafe and the product is known to be unsafe by the ordinary consumer who consumes the product with the ordinary knowledge common to the community; and

(2) the product is a common consumer product intended for personal consumption, such as sugar, castor oil, alcohol, tobacco, and butter, as identified in Comment i to Section 402A of the Restatement (Second) of Torts.

(b) For purposes of this section, the term "products liability action" does not include an action based on manufacturing defect or breach of an express warranty.

Added by Acts 1993, 73rd Leg., ch. 5, § 1, eff. Sept. 1, 1993.

258

FIGURE 6.22   TEXAS CIVIL PRACTICE AND REMEDIES CODE § 82.004 (Continued)

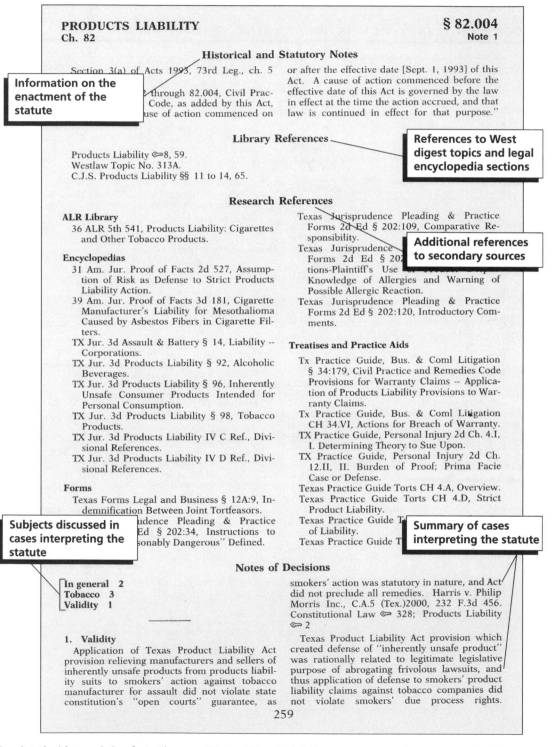

PRODUCTS LIABILITY   § 82.004
Ch. 82   Note 1

Historical and Statutory Notes

Information on the enactment of the statute

Section 3(a) of Acts 1993, 73rd Leg., ch. 5 ... through 82.004, Civil Practice Code, as added by this Act, ...use of action commenced on

or after the effective date [Sept. 1, 1993] of this Act. A cause of action commenced before the effective date of this Act is governed by the law in effect at the time the action accrued, and that law is continued in effect for that purpose."

Library References

References to West digest topics and legal encyclopedia sections

Products Liability ⊙8, 59.
Westlaw Topic No. 313A.
C.J.S. Products Liability §§ 11 to 14, 65.

Research References

ALR Library
   36 ALR 5th 541, Products Liability: Cigarettes and Other Tobacco Products.

Encyclopedias
   31 Am. Jur. Proof of Facts 2d 527, Assumption of Risk as Defense to Strict Products Liability Action.
   39 Am. Jur. Proof of Facts 3d 181, Cigarette Manufacturer's Liability for Mesothalioma Caused by Asbestos Fibers in Cigarette Filters.
   TX Jur. 3d Assault & Battery § 14, Liability -- Corporations.
   TX Jur. 3d Products Liability § 92, Alcoholic Beverages.
   TX Jur. 3d Products Liability § 96, Inherently Unsafe Consumer Products Intended for Personal Consumption.
   TX Jur. 3d Products Liability § 98, Tobacco Products.
   TX Jur. 3d Products Liability IV C Ref., Divisional References.
   TX Jur. 3d Products Liability IV D Ref., Divisional References.

Forms
   Texas Forms Legal and Business § 12A:9, Indemnification Between Joint Tortfeasors.

Subjects discussed in cases interpreting the statute

...udence Pleading & Practice ...Ed § 202:34, Instructions to ...sonably Dangerous" Defined.

Texas Jurisprudence Pleading & Practice Forms 2d Ed § 202:109, Comparative Responsibility.
Texas Jurisprudence ... Forms 2d Ed § 20? ...tions-Plaintiff's Use ... Knowledge of Allergies and Warning of Possible Allergic Reaction.
Texas Jurisprudence Pleading & Practice Forms 2d Ed § 202:120, Introductory Comments.

Additional references to secondary sources

Treatises and Practice Aids

   Tx Practice Guide, Bus. & Coml Litigation § 34:179, Civil Practice and Remedies Code Provisions for Warranty Claims -- Application of Products Liability Provisions to Warranty Claims.
   Tx Practice Guide, Bus. & Coml Litigation CH 34.VI, Actions for Breach of Warranty.
   TX Practice Guide, Personal Injury 2d Ch. 4.I, I. Determining Theory to Sue Upon.
   TX Practice Guide, Personal Injury 2d Ch. 12.II, II. Burden of Proof; Prima Facie Case or Defense.
   Texas Practice Guide Torts CH 4.A, Overview.
   Texas Practice Guide Torts CH 4.D, Strict Product Liability.
   Texas Practice Guide T? of Liability.
   Texas Practice Guide T?

Notes of Decisions

In general   2
Tobacco   3
Validity   1

1. Validity
   Application of Texas Product Liability Act provision relieving manufacturers and sellers of inherently unsafe products from products liability suits to smokers' action against tobacco manufacturer for assault did not violate state constitution's "open courts" guarantee, as

smokers' action was statutory in nature, and Act did not preclude all remedies. Harris v. Philip Morris Inc., C.A.5 (Tex.)2000, 232 F.3d 456. Constitutional Law ⊙ 328; Products Liability ⊙ 2

   Texas Product Liability Act provision which created defense of "inherently unsafe product" was rationally related to legitimate legislative purpose of abrogating frivolous lawsuits, and thus application of defense to smokers' product liability claims against tobacco companies did not violate smokers' due process rights.

Summary of cases interpreting the statute

259

The next step is checking the pocket part. The pocket part shows new statutory language that supersedes the language in the main volume, as well as new research references. The state code may include cumulative or noncumulative supplements in addition to the pocket part. If so, you need to check those supplements to further update your research.

FIGURE 6.23   POCKET PART ENTRY FOR TEXAS CIVIL PRACTICE AND REMEDIES CODE § 82.004

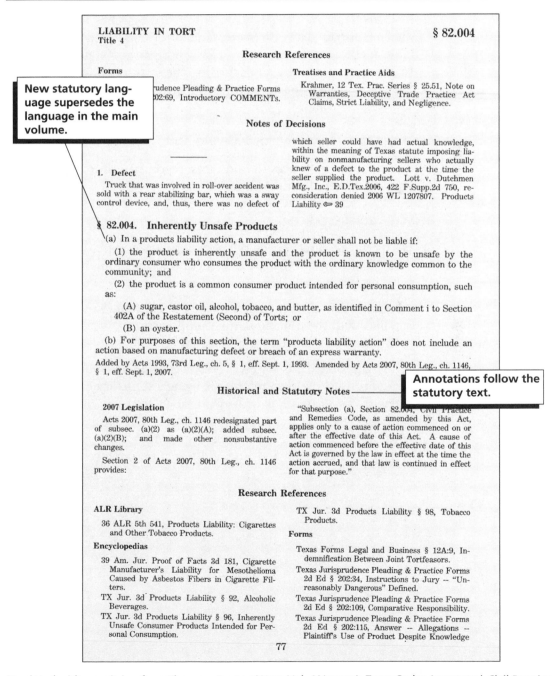

Reprinted with permission from Thomson Reuters/West, Vol. 4 Vernon's *Texas Codes Annotated*, Civil Practice and Remedies Code, Cumulative Annual Pocket Part, p. 77 (2007). © 2007 Thomson Reuters/West.

F. CHECKLIST FOR STATUTORY RESEARCH

1. LOCATE A STATUTE

❒ Use an index to search by subject.

❒ Use the popular name table to locate a statute from its popular name.

❒ For federal statutes, use the conversion tables to locate a statute using its public law number.

❒ In LexisNexis and Westlaw, execute word searches for statutes in the appropriate database (state, federal, or combined), browse the table of contents for the code, or search for an act by popular name. In Westlaw, search by subject using the statutory index.

❒ On the Internet, locate statutes on government or general legal research web sites.

2. READ THE STATUTE AND ACCOMPANYING ANNOTATIONS

❒ Use research references to find cases, secondary sources, and other research materials interpreting the statute.

3. UPDATE YOUR RESEARCH

❒ With print research, check the pocket part accompanying the main volume and any cumulative or noncumulative supplements accompanying the code.

  ▪ In U.S.C.A., update entries to the popular name and conversion tables with the noncumulative supplements.

  ▪ In state codes, check for additional updating tools.

❒ With state or federal statutory research, update your research or find additional research references using a statutory citator such as Shepard's in LexisNexis or KeyCite in Westlaw.

❒ With Internet research, check the date of the statute and update your research accordingly; consider using a statutory citator to update your research and find additional research references.

FEDERAL LEGISLATIVE HISTORY RESEARCH

- A. Introduction to federal legislative history
- B. Researching federal legislative history in print
- C. Researching federal legislative history electronically
- D. Citing federal legislative history
- E. Sample pages for federal legislative history research
- F. Checklist for federal legislative history research

A. INTRODUCTION TO FEDERAL LEGISLATIVE HISTORY

When a legislature passes a statute, it does so with a goal in mind, such as prohibiting or regulating certain types of conduct. Despite their best efforts, however, legislators do not always draft statutes that express their intentions clearly, and it is almost impossible to draft a statute that contemplates every possible situation that may arise under it. Accordingly, lawyers and judges are often called upon to determine the meaning of an ambiguous statute. Lawyers must provide guidance about what the statute permits or requires their clients to do. In deciding cases, judges must determine what the legislature intended when it passed the statute.

If you are asked to analyze an ambiguous statute, you have a number of tools available to help with the task. If the courts have already resolved the ambiguity, secondary sources, statutory annotations, citators, or other research resources can lead you to cases that explain the meaning of the statute.

If the ambiguity has not yet been resolved, however, you face a bigger challenge. You could research similar statutes to see if they shed light on the provision you are interpreting. You could also look to the language of the statute itself for guidance. You may have studied what are called "canons of construction" in some of your other classes. These canons are principles used to determine the meaning of a statute. For example, one canon provides that statutory terms are to be construed according to their ordinary and plain meaning. Another states that remedial statutes are to be broadly construed, while criminal statutes are to be narrowly construed.[1] Although these tools can be helpful in interpreting statutes, they rarely provide the complete answer to determining the legislature's intent.

One of the best ways to determine legislative intent is to research the paper trail of documents that legislators create during the legislative process. These documents are known as the legislative history of the statute. This chapter discusses various types of documents that make up a statute's legislative history and explains how to locate and use them. At the state level, the types of legislative history documents produced and their ease of accessibility vary widely; therefore, this chapter discusses only federal legislative history.

1. THE PROCESS OF ENACTING A LAW

"Legislative history" is a generic term used to refer to a variety of documents produced during the legislative process; it does not refer to a single document or research tool. Courts consider some legislative history documents more important than others, depending on the type of information in the document and the point in the legislative process when the document was created. Understanding what legislative history consists of, as well as the value of different legislative history documents, requires an understanding of the legislative process. **Figure 7.1** illustrates this process.

The legislative process begins when a bill is introduced into the House of Representatives or the Senate by a member of Congress. After the bill is introduced, it is usually referred to a committee. The committee can hold hearings on the bill to obtain the views of experts and interested parties, or it can refer the bill to a subcommittee to hold hearings. If the committee is not in favor of the bill, it usually takes no action. This ordinarily causes the bill to expire in the committee, although the sponsor is free to reintroduce the bill in a later session of Congress. If the committee is in favor of the bill, it will recommend passage to the full chamber of the House or Senate. The recommendation is presented

---

[1]*See generally* Abner J. Mikva & Eric Lane, AN INTRODUCTION TO STATUTORY INTERPRETATION AND THE LEGISLATIVE PROCESS 114-119 (Aspen Publishers 2d ed. 2002).

FIGURE 7.1   HOW A BILL BECOMES A LAW

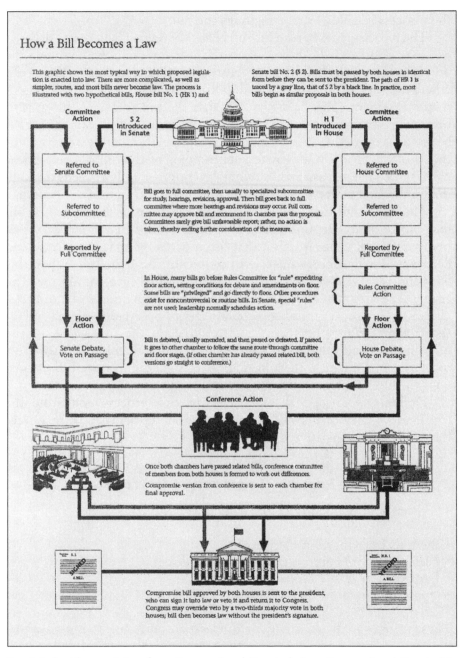

Reprinted with permission from Congressional Quarterly Inc., *Congressional Quarterly's Guide to Congress*, CQ Press, 5th Ed. (2000), p. 1093. Copyright © 2000 CQ Press, a division of SAGE Publications, Inc.

in a committee report that contains the full text of the bill and an analysis of each provision. Because the committee presents its views in a report, this process is called "reporting out" the bill.

The bill then goes before the full House or Senate, where it is debated and may be amended. The members of the House or Senate vote on the bill. If it is passed, the bill goes before the other chamber of Congress, where the same process is repeated. If both chambers pass the bill, it goes to the President. The President can sign the bill into law, allow it to become law without a signature, or veto it. If the bill is vetoed, it goes back to Congress. Congress can override the President's veto if two-thirds of the House and Senate vote in favor of the bill. Once a bill is passed into law, it is assigned a public law number and proceeds through the publication process described in Chapter 6, on statutory research.

This is a simplified explanation of how legislation is enacted. A bill may make many detours along this path before becoming a law or being defeated. One situation that often occurs is that the House and Senate will pass slightly different versions of the same bill. When this happens, the bill is sent to what is called a conference committee. The conference committee consists of members of both houses of Congress, and its job is to attempt to reconcile the two versions of the bill. If the committee members are able to agree on the provisions of the bill, the compromise version is sent back to both chambers of Congress to be reapproved. If both houses approve the compromise bill, it then goes to the President.

Documents created at each stage of this process constitute the legislative history of a law. The next section describes the major sources that make up a legislative history.

2. SOURCES OF FEDERAL LEGISLATIVE HISTORY

There are four major sources of federal legislative history:

- the bills introduced in Congress
- hearings before committees or subcommittees
- floor debates in the House and Senate
- committee reports.

These sources are listed in order from least authoritative to most authoritative. Although some of these sources are generally considered to have more weight than others, none should be viewed in isolation. Each item contributes to the documentation of the legislature's intent. In fact, you may find that the documents contain information that is either contradictory or equally as ambiguous as the underlying statute. It is rare when an inquiry into legislative history will give you a definitive answer to a question of statutory interpretation. What is more likely is that the documents will equip you with information you can use to support your arguments for the proper interpretation of the statute.

a. Bills

The bill introduced into Congress, and any later versions of the bill, can be helpful in determining Congressional intent. Changes in language and addition or deletion of specific provisions may shed light on the goal the legislature was attempting to accomplish with the bill. Analysis of changes to a bill, however, requires speculation about the reasons behind the changes. Consequently, this is often considered an insufficient indication of legislative intent unless it is combined with other materials indicating intent to achieve a particular objective.

b. Hearings

Hearings before committees and subcommittees consist of the testimony of experts and interested parties called to give their views on the bill. These documents may contain transcripts of testimony, documents, reports, studies, or any other information requested by or submitted to the hearing committee. Unlike interpretation of different versions of a bill, interpretation of hearings does not require speculation. The individuals or groups providing information usually give detailed explanations and justifications for their positions.

Congress uses hearings to gather information. As a consequence, individuals or groups with opposing views are often represented, and their goal is to persuade Congress to act in a particular way. This results in the inclusion of information both for and against the legislation in the hearing documents. Sometimes it is possible to ascertain whether material from a particular source motivated Congress to act in a particular way, but this is not always the case. Therefore, hearing documents must be used carefully in determining Congressional intent.

c. Floor Debates

Floor debates are another source of legislative history. They are published in a daily record of Congressional proceedings called the *Congressional Record*. Unlike hearings, which include commentary that may or may not have been persuasive to the committee, floor debates consist of statements by the legislators themselves. Thus, the debates can be a good source of information about Congress's intent in passing a bill. Debates may consist of transcripts of comments or exchanges taking place on the floor of Congress. In addition, members of Congress are permitted to submit prepared statements setting forth their views. Statements by a bill's sponsors may be especially useful in determining legislative intent.

Different members of Congress may give different reasons for supporting legislation, however, and they are permitted to amend or supplement their statements after the fact. As a consequence, floor debates are not a definitive source for determining legislative intent.

d. Committee Reports

Committee reports are generally considered to be the most authoritative legislative history documents. They usually contain the committee's reasons for recommending the bill, a section-by-section analysis of the bill, and the views of any committee members who dissent from the committee's conclusions. If a bill is sent to a conference committee to work out compromise language, the conference committee usually prepares a report. This report discusses only the provisions that differed before the House and Senate. It usually contains the agreed-upon language of the bill and an explanation of the compromise.

3. METHODS OF LOCATING FEDERAL LEGISLATIVE HISTORY DOCUMENTS

You can locate federal legislative history documents the same ways you locate most other forms of legal authority: by citation; by subject; and, for documents available electronically, by words in the document. Although federal legislative history documents have their own citations, those created in conjunction with legislation that is enacted into law are often organized by the public law number, *Statutes at Large* citation, or bill numbers associated with the legislation. Not all federal legislative history documents, however, are associated with legislation enacted into law. As a consequence, the methods you choose to research federal legislative history will depend on the type of material you need. If you are researching the history of an individual statute, your approach will be different than if you are looking for legislative activity on a particular subject, without regard for whether a statute was passed on the topic.

If you are researching the history of an individual statute, it is important to remember that not all legislation is accompanied by all of the documents described above. A committee might elect not to hold hearings. Or the bill could be amended during floor debate, in which case the amendment would not have any history to be documented elsewhere. In addition, you may not always need to look at all of these documents to resolve your research question. If you are trying to determine Congress's intent in enacting a specific provision within a statute, and a committee report sets out the goals Congress was attempting to accomplish with that provision, you might not need to go any further in your research.

Often, however, the committee reports will not discuss the provision you need to interpret. In that case, you may need to delve further into the legislative history, reviewing floor debates or hearings to see if the provision was discussed in either of those sources. In other instances, you may need to compile a complete legislative history.

Your research path will depend largely on the scope of your assignment. You will almost always begin with the statute itself. From there, you should be able to use the bill number, public law number, or *Statutes at Large* citation to locate documents relating to the statute. In most cases, you will probably want to begin by reviewing committee reports. If the committee reports do not address your question, you will then need to assess which other sources of legislative history are likely to assist you and which research tools provide the most efficient means of accessing those documents. If your research takes you beyond readily accessible committee reports, you may want to consult with a reference librarian for assistance in compiling the relevant documents. Remember also that a statute may be amended after its original enactment. Legislative history documents relevant to any amendments will be associated with the bill numbers, public law numbers, or *Statutes at Large* citations of the amending legislation.

If you are trying to find out about legislative activity on a specific topic, rather than the history of an individual statute, you will need to conduct subject or word searches. Because most bills are not passed into law, you may find documents relating to bills that have expired. In addition, you may locate documents unrelated to a bill. For example, committees can hold hearings on any subject within their jurisdiction, even if no legislation on the subject has been introduced.

Some research tools lend themselves more easily than others to subject and word searching, and some are more comprehensive in their coverage than others. Therefore, you will need to determine how much information you need, such as whether you need information on bills that have expired as well as existing legislation, and how far back in time you want to search. Again, you would be well advised to consult with a reference librarian for assistance in developing your research plan for this type of research.

The remainder of this chapter discusses methods for locating legislative history documents. The next section discusses print research tools that are accessible at many law libraries. Unlike some other sources of authority, however, legislative history is often easiest to access through electronic means. In particular, Internet research sites made available by the government and commercial providers may be the most economical and user-friendly ways to locate federal legislative history.

A description of print and electronic research tools follows.

B. RESEARCHING FEDERAL LEGISLATIVE HISTORY IN PRINT

Four print sources of legislative history are available in many law libraries:

1. compiled legislative histories containing all of the legislative history documents on a statute
2. *United States Code Congressional and Administrative News*, or U.S.C.C.A.N., which contains selected committee reports on bills passed into law
3. Congressional Information Service (CIS) materials containing committee reports and hearings on microfiche, as well as citations to floor debates in the *Congressional Record*
4. the *Congressional Record*, which contains floor debates on legislation.

You would not necessarily research each of these sources in order. Some documents may be accessible through more than one of these research tools. Therefore, you should assess the scope of your research project to determine which source is most likely to provide the information you need.

1. COMPILED LEGISLATIVE HISTORIES

Legislative histories for major pieces of legislation are sometimes compiled and published as separate volumes. In this situation, an author or publisher collects all of the legislative history documents on the legislation and publishes them in a single place. If a legislative history on the statute you are researching has already been compiled, your work has been done for you. Therefore, if you are researching a major piece of legislation, you should begin by looking for a compiled legislative history.

There are two ways to locate a compiled legislative history. The first is to look in the online catalog in your library. Compiled legislative histories can be published as individual books that are assigned call numbers and placed on the shelves. The second is to look for the statute in a reference source listing compiled legislative histories. One example of this type of reference book is *Sources of Compiled Legislative Histories: A Bibliography of Government Documents, Periodical Articles, and Books*, by Nancy P. Johnson. This book will refer you to books, government documents, and periodical articles that either reprint the legislative history for the statute or, at a minimum, contain citations to and discussion of the legislative history. This book is organized by public law number, so you would need to know the public law number of the statute to get started. You should be able to find the public law number following code sections in U.S.C. or an annotated code. HeinOnline, an electronic subscription service discussed more fully below, has an online directory of compiled legislative histories derived from Professor Johnson's book. Another good reference for compiled legislative histories is *Federal Legislative Histories: An Annotated Bibliography and Index to Officially Published Sources*, by Bernard D. Reams, Jr.

2. UNITED STATES CODE CONGRESSIONAL AND ADMINISTRATIVE NEWS

United States Code Congressional and Administrative News, or U.S.C.C.A.N., is a readily available source of committee reports on bills passed into law. For each session of Congress, U.S.C.C.A.N. publishes a series of volumes containing, among other things, the text of laws passed by Congress (organized by *Statutes at Large* citation) and selected committee reports. References to reports in U.S.C.C.A.N. usually include the year the book was published and the starting page of the document. Thus, to find a report cited as 1996 U.S.C.C.A.N. 2166,[2] you would need to locate the 1996 edition of U.S.C.C.A.N., find the volumes labeled "Legislative History," and turn to page 2166. U.S.C.C.A.N. does not reprint all committee reports for all legislation. Nevertheless, U.S.C.C.A.N. is often a good starting place for research into committee reports because it is available at many law libraries and is fairly easy to use.

U.S.C.C.A.N. is a West publication; therefore, you can find cross-references to it in the annotations in U.S.C.A. The cross-references are usually listed in the Historical and Statutory Notes section of the annotations. If the statute has been amended, the Historical and Statutory Notes section will explain the major changes resulting from later enactments, and the legislative history section of the Historical and Statutory Notes will refer you to the year and page number of any committee reports reprinted in U.S.C.C.A.N. **Figure 7.2** shows U.S.C.C.A.N. references in U.S.C.A., and **Figure 7.3** shows the starting page of a committee report in U.S.C.C.A.N.

3. CONGRESSIONAL INFORMATION SERVICE

Congressional Information Service (CIS) is another commercial publisher of legislative history documents, but its materials are more comprehensive than those available through U.S.C.C.A.N. CIS compiles, among other documents, committee reports and hearings on microfiche.[3]

---

[2]This is not a complete citation. Refer to Section D below for citation rules for U.S.C.C.A.N.
[3]CIS also makes this material available electronically through an Internet service called LexisNexis Congressional. Refer to Section C below for a discussion of electronic research sources.

FIGURE 7.2   EXCERPT FROM ANNOTATIONS ACCOMPANYING 18 U.S.C.A. § 2441

HISTORICAL AND STATUTORY NOTES

Revision Notes and Legislative Reports

1996 Acts. House Report No. 104–698, see 1996 U.S. Code Cong. and Adm. News, p. 2166.

House Report No. 104–788, see 1996 U.S. Code Cong. and Adm. News, p. 4021.

1997 Acts. House Conference Report No. 105–401, see 1997 U.S. Code Cong. and Adm. News, p. 2896.

U.S.C.C.A.N. references

References in Text

Section 101 of the Immigration and Nationality Act, referred to in subsec. (b), is section 101 of Act June 27, 1952, c. 477, Title I, 66 Stat. 166, which is classified to section 1101 of Title 8, Aliens and Nationality.

Codifications

Section 584 of Pub.L. 105–118, which directed that section 2401 of title 18 be amended, was executed to section 2441 of Title 18, despite parenthetical refer-

ence to "section 2401 of Title 18", as the probable intent of Congress.

Amendments

1997 Amendments. Subsec. (a). Pub.L. 105–118, § 583(1), substituted "war crime" for "grave breach of the Geneva Conventions".

Subsec. (b). Pub.L. 105–118, § 583(2), substituted "war crime" for "breach" each place it appeared.

Subsec. (c). Pub.L. 105–118, § 583(3), rewrote subsec. (c). Prior to amendment, subsec. (c) read as follows: "(c) Definitions.—As used in this section, the term 'grave breach of the Geneva Conventions' means conduct defined as a grave breach in any of the international conventions relating to the laws of warfare signed at Geneva 12 August 1949 or any protocol to any such convention, to which the United States is a party."

14

Reprinted with permission from Thomson Reuters/West, *United States Code Annotated*, Vol. 18 (2000) p. 14. © 2000 Thomson Reuters/West.

In addition, CIS provides citations to floor debates published in the *Congressional Record*. CIS is a good resource for finding the complete legislative history of a statute, as well as for searching by subject.

Although CIS compiles legislative history documents on microfiche, the tools for locating these materials are published in books. The CIS finding tools consist of the Index volumes, the Abstracts volumes, and the Legislative Histories volumes. CIS publishes a new set of Index, Abstracts, and Legislative Histories[4] volumes for each calendar year. Monthly softcover booklets containing the Index and Abstracts are published for the current year. For each four-year period from 1970 through 1998, the annual indices have been combined into cumulative indices, e.g., the *1995–1998 Four-Year Cumulative Index*.

The easiest way to locate the complete legislative history of a bill enacted into law is to use the Legislative Histories volumes. These volumes are organized by public law number. If you know the year the law was

---

[4]CIS began publishing a separate Legislative Histories volume in 1984. For legislation passed before 1984, the listings of legislative histories appear at the end of the Abstracts volume for each year.

FIGURE 7.3 STARTING PAGE, HOUSE JUDICIARY COMMITTEE REPORT ON THE WAR CRIMES ACT OF 1996

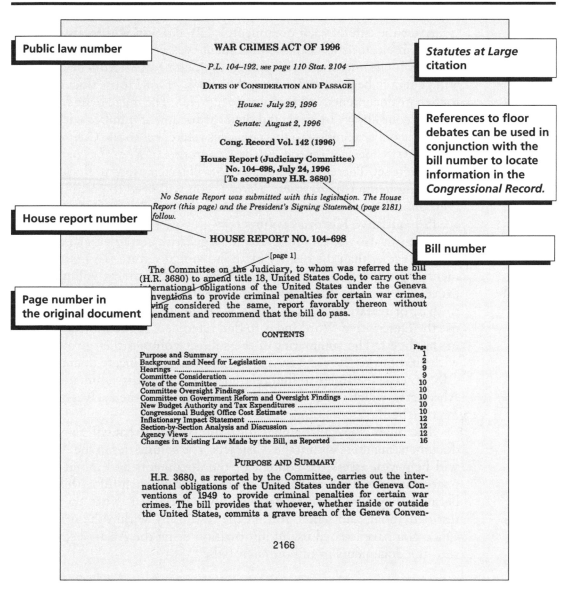

Reprinted with permission from Thomson Reuters/West, *United States Code Congressional and Administrative News*, 104th Congress-Second Session 1996, Vol. 5 (1997), p. 2166. © 1997 Thomson Reuters/West.

passed and the public law number, you can look it up in the appropriate volume of CIS Legislative Histories. CIS will list all of the documents in the legislative history, as well as a very brief summary of each document.

After the title of each document, a CIS citation will be listed. This citation indicates the year the document was created and the number assigned to the microfiche containing the document. Microfiche numbers will generally begin with PL for public laws, H for House documents, S for Senate documents, or J for joint documents. The microfiche should be filed in your library by year, and then by document number within each year. The only exception to this concerns references to the *Congressional Record*. CIS does not reproduce the *Congressional Record* as part of this microfiche set. Therefore, although CIS will list citations to floor debates appearing in the *Congressional Record*, you will need to go to the *Congressional Record* itself to read the debates. **Figure 7.4** shows a page from a CIS Legislative Histories volume.

You can also use CIS to search for legislative activity on a particular subject, rather than the history of an individual statute. To locate documents by subject, you can use the Index and Abstracts volumes. The process of locating documents using the Index and Abstracts is similar to that for researching cases with a West digest. In digest research, you use the Descriptive-Word Index to find references to the subject volumes in the digest. The summaries in the subject volumes then provide you with citations to the cases themselves. Similarly, to locate documents in CIS, you use the Index to find references to document summaries in the Abstracts, which then lead to the documents themselves on CIS microfiche.

The Index is a regular alphabetical subject index that will refer you to document numbers within the Abstracts. The summaries in the Abstracts will help you assess the content of the documents and target specific pages with useful information. They are especially helpful with hearings because they allow you to determine who testified, what the witness testified about, and where to find the testimony within the document. Once you have located useful information using the Abstracts, you can read the documents in full on microfiche.

4. CONGRESSIONAL RECORD

The *Congressional Record* is the record of all activity on the floor of the House and Senate. Therefore, it is the source you will use to find floor debates on a bill, regardless of whether the bill was passed into law. There are several ways to locate information in the *Congressional Record*, which are discussed below. First, however, it is important to understand how the *Congressional Record* is organized.

A new volume of the *Congressional Record* is published for each session of Congress. While Congress is in session, the current volume

FIGURE 7.4 CIS LEGISLATIVE HISTORIES ENTRY FOR PUB. L. NO. 104-192

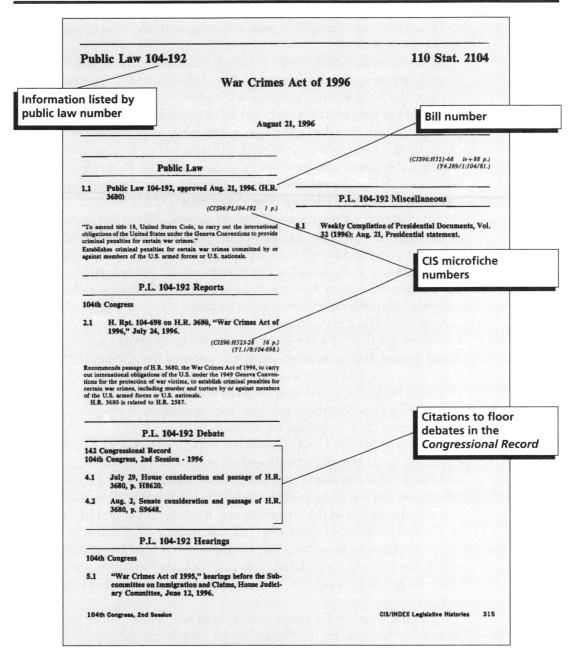

Reprinted from *CIS/Annual* with permission of LexisNexis. Copyright 1997 LexisNexis Academic and Library Solutions, a division of Reed Elsevier Inc. All Rights Reserved. *CIS/Annual 1996*, Legislative Histories of U.S. Public Laws (1997), p. 315.

of the *Congressional Record* is published daily as a softcover pamphlet; this is called the daily edition. At the end of each session of Congress, the daily editions are compiled into a hardbound set; this is called the permanent edition.

The material in these two editions should be identical, but the pages in each are numbered differently. The daily edition is separated into different sections, including sections for House (H) and Senate (S) materials, and the pages within each section are numbered separately. In the permanent edition, all of the pages are numbered consecutively. References to the *Congressional Record* will vary, therefore, depending on whether they are to the permanent or daily edition. References to both editions will give the volume and page number, but the page numbering will differ for each edition. Thus, 142 Cong. Rec. H8620[5] refers to volume 142 of the *Congressional Record*, page 8,620 of the House section of the daily edition. The "H" before the page number alerts you that the reference is to the daily edition. By contrast, a citation to 142 Cong. Rec. 11,352 refers to volume 142 of the *Congressional Record*, page 11,352 of the permanent edition. Because the page number contains no letter designation, the reference is to the permanent edition. **Figure 7.5** is an excerpt from the daily edition.

There are several ways to find citations to material in the *Congressional Record*. If you are looking for debates on a specific statute, you will find *Congressional Record* citations in the CIS Legislative Histories volumes. In the listing summarizing the statute's legislative history documents, CIS provides the dates and page numbers of references to the legislation in the *Congressional Record*.

You can also use U.S.C.C.A.N. to find *Congressional Record* references. At the beginning of each report published in U.S.C.C.A.N., you will find a list of the dates when the House and Senate considered the bill, which you can use in conjunction with the bill number to locate material in the daily edition of the *Congressional Record*. At the end of each issue of the daily edition of the *Congressional Record*, you will find a Daily Digest of Congressional activity for that day. If you know the date on which the bill was considered, you can look up the bill number in the Daily Digest to find references to the legislation within that issue of the *Congressional Record*.

The index to the *Congressional Record* will allow you to find information on a piece of legislation or to search by subject. If you are researching the permanent edition of the *Congressional Record*, the index will be published in a separate volume. During the current session of Congress, softcover interim indices for the daily edition are published

---

[5]The citations here are not complete. Refer to Section D below for citation rules for the *Congressional Record*.

FIGURE 7.5   CONGRESSIONAL RECORD, DAILY EDITION

Comments on the War Crimes Act in the House of Representatives

H8620   CONGRESSIONAL RECORD—HOUSE   *July 29, 1996*

Mr. Speaker, H.R. 740, introduced by [the] gentleman from New Mexico [Mr. ___ F] and the gentleman from New [Mexi]co [Mr. SKEEN] would permit the [Puebl]o of Isleta Indian Tribe to file a [claim] in the U.S. Court of Federal [Claim]s for certain aboriginal lands ac[quire]d from the tribe by the United [State]s. The tribe was erroneously advised [by the Bureau of] Indian Affairs in [regar]d to this claim, and as a result [Isleta] filed a claim for aboriginal lands before the expiration of the statute of limitations.

The court's jurisdiction would apply only to claims accruing on or before August 13, 1946, as provided in the Indian Claims Commission Act.

The Pueblo of Isleta Tribe seeks the opportunity to present the merits of its aboriginal land claims, which otherwise would be barred as untimely. The tribe cites numerous precedents for conferring jurisdiction under similar circumstances, such as the case of the Zuni Indian Tribe in 1978.

An identical bill passed the Senate in the 103d Congress, but was not considered by the House. In the 102d Congress, H.R. 1206, amended to the current language, passed the House, but was not considered by the Senate before adjournment. On June 11, 1996, the Judiciary Committee favorably reported this bill by unanimous voice vote.

Mr. Speaker, I reserve the balance of my time.

Mr. SCOTT. Mr. Speaker, I yield myself such time as I may consume.

Mr. Speaker, I think the bill has been explained that was introduced by the gentleman from New Mexico [Mr. SKEEN] and the gentleman from New Mexico [Mr. SCHIFF]. It is a fair bill, and I would just urge colleagues to support it at this time.

Mr. Speaker, I yield back the balance of my time.

Mr. RICHARDSON. Mr. Speaker, I wish to extend my strong support for H.R. 740 which deals with the Pueblo of Isleta Indian land claims. H.R. 740 comes before Congress for a vote which will correct a 45-year-old injustice. In 1951, the Pueblo of Isleta was given erroneous advice by employees of the Bureau of Indian Affairs regarding the nature of the claim the Pueblo could mount under the Indian Claims Commission Act of 1946. This is documented and supported by testimony. The Pueblo was not made aware of the fact that a land claim could be made based upon aboriginal use and occupancy. As a result, it lost the opportunity to make such a claim.

The Pueblo of Isleta was a victim of circumstances beyond its control, and this bill is an opportunity for us to correct this wrong. No expenditure or appropriations of funds are provided for in this bill; only the opportunity for the Pueblo to make a claim for aboriginal lands which the Isletas believe to be rightfully theirs. This bill may be the last chance for the United States to correct an injustice which occurred many years ago because of misinformation from the BIA.

Therefore, I urge my colleagues to support H.R. 740.

Mr. SMITH of Texas. Mr. Speaker, I have no further requests for time, and I yield back the balance of my time.

The SPEAKER pro tempore. The question is on the motion offered by the gentleman from Texas [Mr. SMITH] that the House suspend the rules and pass the bill, H.R. 740.

The question was taken; and (two-thirds having voted in favor thereof) the rules were suspended and the bill was passed.

A motion to reconsider was laid on the table.

WAR CRIMES ACT OF 1996

Mr. SMITH of Texas. Mr. Speaker, I move to suspend the rules and pass the bill (H.R. 3680) to amend title 18, United States Code, to carry out the international obligations of the United States under the Geneva Conventions to provide criminal penalties for certain war crimes.

The Clerk read as follows:

H.R. 3680

Be it enacted by the Senate and House of Representatives of the United States of America in Congress assembled,

SECTION 1. SHORT TITLE.

This Act may be cited as the "War Crimes Act of 1996".

SEC. 2. CRIMINAL PENALTIES FOR CERTAIN WAR CRIMES.

(a) IN GENERAL.—Title 18, United States Code, is amended by inserting after chapter 117 the following:

"CHAPTER 118—WAR CRIMES

"Sec.
"2401. War crimes.

"§2401. War crimes

"(a) OFFENSE.—Whoever, whether inside or outside the United States, commits a grave breach of the Geneva Conventions, in any of the circumstances described in subsection (b), shall be fined under this title or imprisoned for life or any term of years, or both, and if death results to the victim, shall also be subject to the penalty of death.

"(b) CIRCUMSTANCES.—The circumstances referred to in subsection (a) are that the person committing such breach or the victim of such breach is a member of the armed forces of the United States or a national of the United States (as defined in section 101 of the Immigration and Nationality Act).

"(c) DEFINITIONS.—As used in this section, the term 'grave breach of the Geneva Conventions' means conduct defined as a grave breach in any of the international conventions relating to the laws of warfare signed at Geneva 12 August 1949 or any protocol to any such convention, to which the United States is a party."

(b) CLERICAL AMENDMENT.—The table of chapters for part I of title 18, United States Code, is amended by inserting after the item relating to chapter 117 the following new item:

"118. War crimes .... 2401".

The SPEAKER pro tempore. Pursuant to the rule, the gentleman from Texas [Mr. SMITH] and the gentleman from Virginia [Mr. SCOTT] each will control 20 minutes.

The Chair recognizes the gentleman from Texas [Mr. SMITH].

GENERAL LEAVE

Mr. SMITH of Texas. Mr. Speaker, I ask unanimous consent that all Members may have 5 legislative days to revise and extend their remarks on the bill under consideration.

The SPEAKER pro tempore. Is there objection to the request of the gentleman from Texas?

There was no objection.

Mr. SMITH of Texas. Mr. Speaker, I yield myself such time as I may consume.

Mr. Speaker, H.R. 3680 is designed to implement the Geneva conventions for the protection of victims of war. Our colleague, the gentleman from North Carolina, WALTER JONES, should be commended for introducing this bill and for his dedication to such a worthy goal.

□ 1445

Mr. Speaker, the Geneva Conventions of 1949 codified rules of conduct for military forces to which we have long adhered. In 1955 Deputy Under Secretary of State Robert Murphy testified to the Senate that—

The Geneva Conventions are another long step forward towards mitigating the severity of war on its helpless victims. They reflect enlightened practices as carried out by the United States and other civilized countries, and they represent largely what the United States would do, whether or not a party to the Conventions. Our own conduct has served to establish higher standards and we can only benefit by having them incorporated in a stronger body of wartime law.

Mr. Speaker, the United States ratified the Conventions in 1955. However, Congress has never passed implementing legislation.

The Conventions state that signatory countries are to enact penal legislation punishing what are called grave breaches, actions such as the deliberate killing of prisoners of war, the subjecting of prisoners to biological experiments, the willful infliction of great suffering or serious injury on civilians in occupied territory.

While offenses covering grave breaches can in certain instances be prosecutable under present Federal law, even if they occur overseas, there are a great number of instances in which no prosecution is possible. Such nonprosecutable crimes might include situations where American prisoners of war are killed, or forced to serve in the Army of their captors, or American doctors on missions of mercy in foreign war zones are kidnapped or murdered. War crimes are not a thing of the past, and Americans can all too easily fall victim to them.

H.R. 3680 was introduced in order to implement the Geneva Conventions. It prescribes severe criminal penalties for anyone convicted of committing, whether inside or outside the United States, a grave breach of the Geneva Conventions, where the victim or the perpetrator is a member of our Armed Forces. In future conflicts H.R. 3680 may very well deter acts against Americans that violate the laws of war.

Mr. Speaker, I urge my colleagues to support this legislation, and I reserve the balance of my time.

Mr. SCOTT. Mr. Speaker, I yield myself such time as I may consume.

Mr. Speaker, as the gentleman from Texas has fully explained, H.R. 3680 implements this country's international roughly every two weeks. The interim indices are not cumulative; thus, you would need to check each one to find out if activity on the bill or subject you are researching has taken place.

The index is divided into two sections, one with a subject index, and the other containing the history of bills and resolutions. Either section will refer you to pages with relevant material. In using the section with the history of bills and resolutions, a couple of caveats are in order. First, you will need to know the House and Senate bill numbers of the legislation, not the public law number. A bill cannot be assigned a public law number until it is passed into law, and floor debates, by definition, take place before the passage of a bill. The CIS Legislative Histories volumes and the committee reports in U.S.C.C.A.N. will provide the bill numbers. Second, be sure to check both the House and Senate listings for activity on the bill; either chamber of Congress could act at any time on a piece of pending legislation.

C. RESEARCHING FEDERAL LEGISLATIVE HISTORY ELECTRONICALLY

As noted earlier in this chapter, electronic sources are often easier to use in locating legislative history than print sources. In particular, Internet sources can be extremely useful in legislative history research. No matter which electronic source you use, your research strategy will still largely be governed by whether you are looking for information on an individual statute or searching by subject.

As with print research, electronic research into the legislative history of an individual statute is easiest if you have a citation identifying the legislation. Most electronic services will allow you to search using a public law number, bill number, or *Statutes at Large* citation. Conducting a word search using the popular name of the act is also an effective strategy. Searching simply by topic or with general keywords is the least efficient means of researching for material on an individual statute. It is possible that you could miss important documents if you do not have the correct terms in the search; in addition, you are likely to retrieve material on other pieces of legislation unrelated to your research. By contrast, topic or keyword searching is most effective when you want to find out about legislative activity on a particular subject.

One exception to these general approaches concerns electronic research in the *Congressional Record*. Conducting *Congressional Record* research online is easiest if you have the House and Senate bill numbers or the dates and page numbers of *Congressional Record* references to the bill. You can locate this information using the print sources described above or some of the electronic sources described below. You can also conduct a word search using the popular name of the act or general key-words, and in some sources, you can use the *Congressional Record* index.

Another thing to be aware of when you conduct electronic legislative history research concerns hearings. Some electronic services provide access to testimony provided at hearings, which consists of transcripts of testimony and prepared statements of witnesses, but not to reports, studies, or other documents submitted to the committee. Therefore, if you need the complete content of a congressional hearing, you must choose your research source carefully and may need to obtain the document in print or microfiche.

1. LexisNexis and Westlaw

Both LexisNexis and Westlaw provide access to many legislative history documents. Both services have databases containing the full text of bills introduced in Congress, selected committee reports, floor debates in the *Congressional Record*, and congressional testimony, although not complete hearing documents. Additionally, both have databases containing compiled legislative histories for certain major pieces of legislation. LexisNexis provides electronic access to the CIS microfiche set, although it is usually available only to law firms and other commercial subscribers. Most academic subscriptions to LexisNexis do not allow access to this material, so you may not be able to access it with a student password. You may, however, have access to the same information through LexisNexis Congressional, which is described in the next section.

In Westlaw, you can retrieve a legislative history document from its citation as long as the document is included in Westlaw's database. If you are searching for the history of an individual statute, the U.S.C.A. annotations will contain links to any congressional reports reproduced in U.S.C.C.A.N., including those issued in connection with amendments to the statute. (U.S.C.C.A.N. is discussed in Section B, above.) The Key-Cite entry for the statute will also list references to legislative history documents. In the databases for individual types of legislative documents or compiled legislative histories, you can conduct word searches. The difficulty with word searching in a compiled legislative history is that it will retrieve documents containing the specified words, but will not produce a complete list of legislative history documents for the statute. Therefore, it is a search technique you will ordinarily use when you are looking for particular information in a statute's legislative history, not when you need the full history of a statute.

In LexisNexis, you can also retrieve a legislative history document from its citation as long as the document is included in the LexisNexis database. The U.S.C.S. annotations will not link to legislative history documents, however, even if those documents are contained in the LexisNexis database, nor will the Shepard's entry list legislative history beyond *Statutes at Large* citations to later enactments affecting the statute. In the databases for individual types of legislative documents, you can conduct word searches, which, as noted above, will be most useful when you are looking for information by subject. The databases containing compiled legislative histories permit word searches. Some also allow you to view a list of all of the documents in the statute's history, along with other information about the statute. These histories are especially useful when you need to locate the full history of a major piece of legislation.

2. INTERNET SOURCES

The federal government provides free Internet access to many legislative history documents through Thomas, a web site maintained by the Library of Congress, and GPO Access, a web site maintained by the Government Printing Office (GPO). The Internet addresses for both of these sites are listed in Appendix A. The introductory screens for the Thomas and GPO Access sites appear in **Figures 7.6**, and **7.7**, respectively.

Thomas will provide you with the text of bills introduced, House and Senate roll call votes, public laws, the text of the *Congressional Record*, committee reports, and other information on the legislative process, although not to congressional hearings or testimony. Thomas will also allow you to search in several ways. You can browse or search by public law number, report number, or committee name. Word searching is also available. You can search for documents issued during a particular session of Congress, or you can search multiple sessions simultaneously. To access the *Congressional Record*, you can browse the contents of individual issues or search by subject using the *Congressional Record* index.

An effective way to locate the history of an individual piece of legislation in Thomas is with the public law or bill number. You can browse public laws by number for a particular session of Congress or use the bill number to retrieve a Bill Summary and Status report. This report will provide links to the text of the statute and to all of the legislative history documents in Thomas's database, including congressional reports and floor debates in the *Congressional Record*.

GPO Access also makes some legislative history documents available. Here, you will find the text of bills introduced into Congress, selected reports and hearings, and the *Congressional Record*. You can browse most documents by session of Congress. You can also conduct word searches for documents issued during a particular session, or you can search multiple sessions simultaneously. If you know the bill number, you can enter it as your word search to locate documents related to a specific piece of legislation.

FIGURE 7.6   INTRODUCTORY SCREEN FOR THOMAS

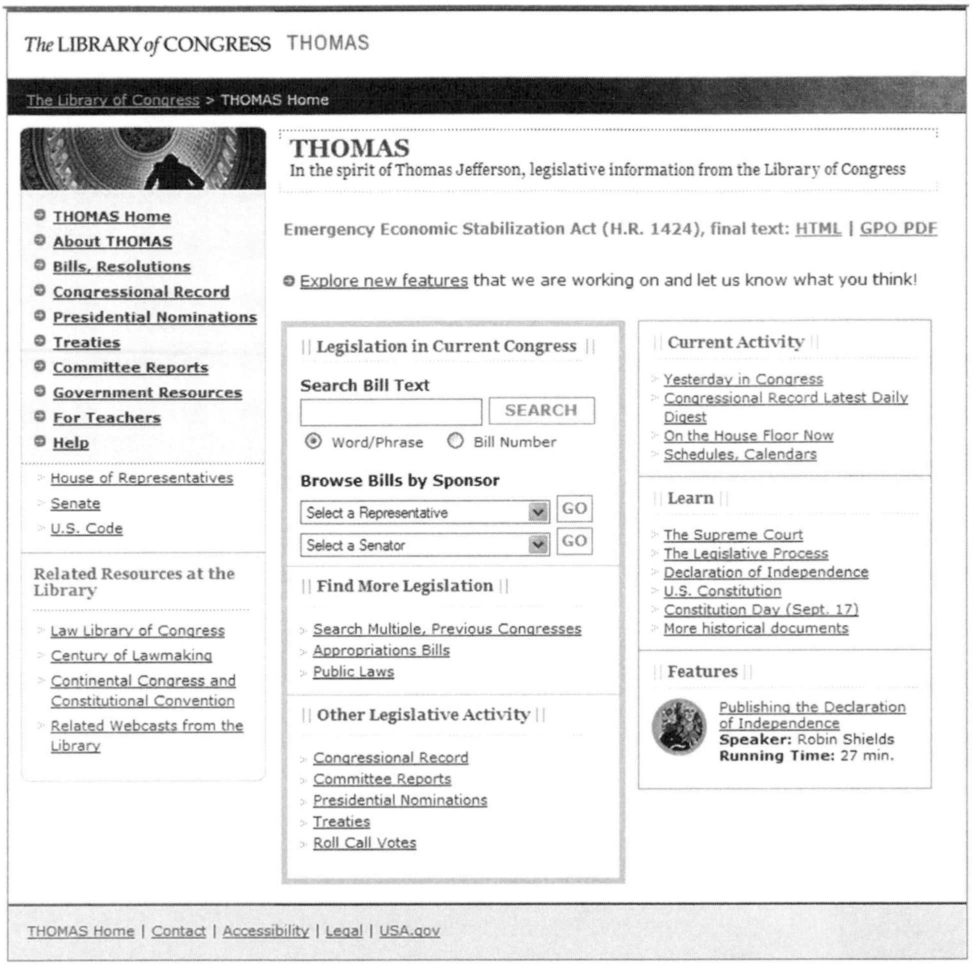

The LIBRARY *of* CONGRESS   THOMAS

The Library of Congress > THOMAS Home

THOMAS
In the spirit of Thomas Jefferson, legislative information from the Library of Congress

○ THOMAS Home
○ About THOMAS
○ Bills, Resolutions
○ Congressional Record
○ Presidential Nominations
○ Treaties
○ Committee Reports
○ Government Resources
○ For Teachers
○ Help
▷ House of Representatives
▷ Senate
▷ U.S. Code

Related Resources at the Library

▷ Law Library of Congress
▷ Century of Lawmaking
▷ Continental Congress and Constitutional Convention
▷ Related Webcasts from the Library

Emergency Economic Stabilization Act (H.R. 1424), final text: HTML | GPO PDF

○ Explore new features that we are working on and let us know what you think!

|| Legislation in Current Congress ||

Search Bill Text

[   ] [SEARCH]

⦿ Word/Phrase   ○ Bill Number

Browse Bills by Sponsor

[Select a Representative ▾] [GO]
[Select a Senator ▾] [GO]

|| Find More Legislation ||

▷ Search Multiple, Previous Congresses
▷ Appropriations Bills
▷ Public Laws

|| Other Legislative Activity ||

▷ Congressional Record
▷ Committee Reports
▷ Presidential Nominations
▷ Treaties
▷ Roll Call Votes

|| Current Activity ||

▷ Yesterday in Congress
▷ Congressional Record Latest Daily Digest
▷ On the House Floor Now
▷ Schedules, Calendars

|| Learn ||

▷ The Supreme Court
▷ The Legislative Process
▷ Declaration of Independence
▷ U.S. Constitution
▷ Constitution Day (Sept. 17)
▷ More historical documents

|| Features ||

Publishing the Declaration of Independence
Speaker: Robin Shields
Running Time: 27 min.

THOMAS Home | Contact | Accessibility | Legal | USA.gov

FIGURE 7.7   INTRODUCTORY SCREENS FOR GPO ACCESS, LEGISLATIVE INFORMATION

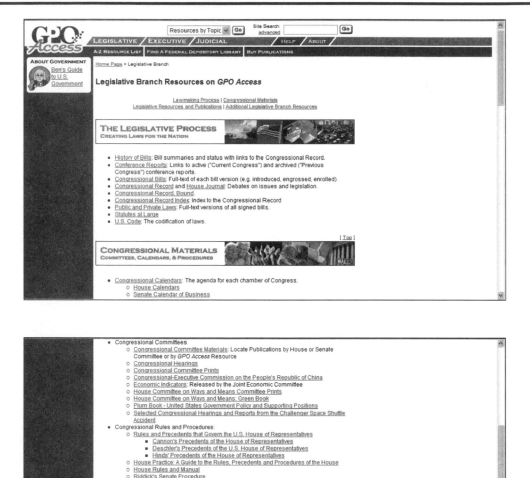

To access the *Congressional Record* through GPO Access, you can search in several ways: by citation, by subject using the *Congressional Record* index, by word, or by browsing the contents of individual issues. GPO Access contains the daily edition of the *Congressional Record* from 1994 forward and limited access to the permanent edition from 1999 forward, both in .pdf format.

GPO Access does not aggregate legislative information on a bill or public law the way Thomas does. To find complete information about a piece of legislation, you would need to search the database for each type of document you want to research. Therefore, GPO Access may be most useful to you when you are searching for a specific document or when you are searching by subject. Many hearings accessible through GPO Access are .pdf versions of the print documents. Thus, unlike most other electronic sources, GPO Access provides the complete hearing content, including attachments and other documents, not just testimony.

Both Thomas and GPO Access add documents to their databases regularly, but neither provides complete historical access to legislative documents. For some types of information, coverage extends to the early 1970s, but for others, only to the early 1990s. If you are researching fairly recent legislative documents, however, Thomas and GPO Access are excellent tools to use.

3. SUBSCRIPTION SERVICES

HeinOnline and LexisNexis Congressional are two subscription services available at many law libraries that you can use for federal legislative history research. HeinOnline is best known for its comprehensive database of legal periodicals, but it also contains many other types of information, including legislative documents. As noted above, HeinOnline has a database of compiled legislative histories derived from Nancy P. Johnson's reference book, *Sources of Compiled Legislative Histories: A Bibliography of Government Documents, Periodical Articles, and Books*. This database provides citations to many compiled legislative histories and full text access to some. **Figure 7.8** shows an entry from this directory. HeinOnline also has its own collection of compiled legislative histories, the U.S. Federal Legislative History Title Collection. This is a database containing full-text legislative histories on major pieces of legislation. Many of these compiled legislative histories contain complete .pdf versions of the legislative documents, including hearings.

LexisNexis Congressional (formerly known as Congressional Universe) is a commercial research service that provides electronic access to

FIGURE 7.8 HEINONLINE *SOURCES OF COMPILED LEGISLATIVE HISTORIES* ENTRY

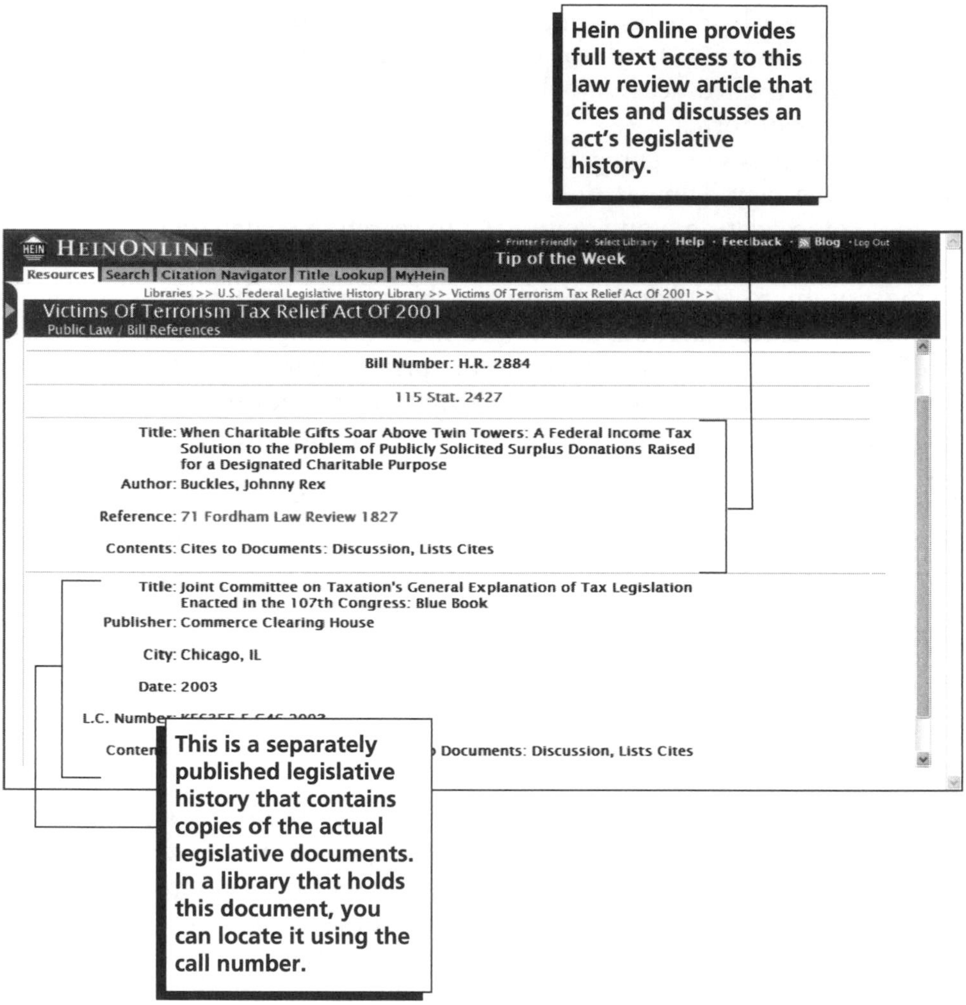

Hein Online provides full text access to this law review article that cites and discusses an act's legislative history.

HEINONLINE

· Printer Friendly · Select Library · **Help** · Feedback · 🔊 Blog · Log Out

Tip of the Week

Resources | Search | Citation Navigator | Title Lookup | MyHein

Libraries >> U.S. Federal Legislative History Library >> Victims Of Terrorism Tax Relief Act Of 2001 >>

Victims Of Terrorism Tax Relief Act Of 2001
Public Law / Bill References

Bill Number: H.R. 2884

115 Stat. 2427

Title: When Charitable Gifts Soar Above Twin Towers: A Federal Income Tax Solution to the Problem of Publicly Solicited Surplus Donations Raised for a Designated Charitable Purpose
Author: Buckles, Johnny Rex

Reference: 71 Fordham Law Review 1827

Contents: Cites to Documents: Discussion, Lists Cites

Title: Joint Committee on Taxation's General Explanation of Tax Legislation Enacted in the 107th Congress: Blue Book
Publisher: Commerce Clearing House

City: Chicago, IL

Date: 2003

L.C. Number: KF6255 E C46 2003

Contents: Cites to Documents: Discussion, Lists Cites

This is a separately published legislative history that contains copies of the actual legislative documents. In a library that holds this document, you can locate it using the call number.

Reproduced with permission of HeinOnline. © 2008 HeinOnline.

FIGURE 7.9   SEARCH OPTIONS FOR CONGRESSIONAL PUBLICATIONS IN LEXISNEXIS CONGRESSIONAL

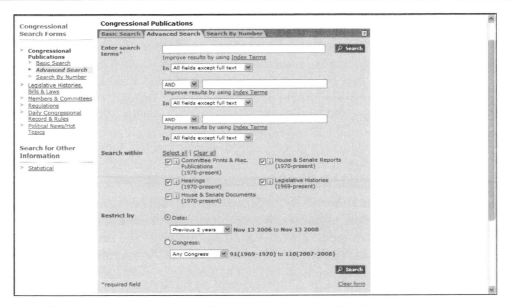

Reprinted with permission of LexisNexis, LexisNexis Congressional search options.

the CIS legislative histories microfiche set, as well as other legislative resources. Its database includes committee reports, hearing testimony (but not complete hearing documents), bills, and the *Congressional Record*. Within LexisNexis Congressional, you can search the full text of the documents in its database, or you can search by number. The easiest way to locate all of the available documents on a piece of legislation is to search by number using the bill number, public law number, or *Statutes at Large* citation. Searching this way retrieves an entry that lists the legislative history documents associated with the statute. The links in the document will retrieve abstracts (summaries) of the documents available. From the abstract, you can retrieve the full text of a document by following the appropriate link.[6] Full-text searching is also an option. You can search for multiple types of documents, such as reports or hearings, simultaneously, although floor debates are in a separate database containing the *Congressional Record*. **Figure 7.9** shows some of the search options for congressional documents.

---

[6]Sometimes LexisNexis Congressional will provide a reference to a document that is not contained within its database. If that happens, you can use the citation provided by LexisNexis Congressional to locate the document in the CIS microfiche set.

D. CITING FEDERAL LEGISLATIVE HISTORY

Citations to legislative history documents are covered in *ALWD Manual* Rule 15 and *Bluebook* Bluepages B6.1.6 and Rule 13. This chapter discusses citations to committee reports and floor debates because those are the sources you are most likely to cite in a brief or memorandum.

In the *Bluebook*, the examples contained in Rule 13 show some of the congressional document abbreviations in large and small capital letters. According to Bluepages B13, however, legislative documents in briefs and memoranda should appear in ordinary type.

1. COMMITTEE REPORTS

Using either the *ALWD Manual* or the *Bluebook*, a citation to a committee report consists of four elements: (1) the abbreviation for the type of document; (2) the report number; (3) the pinpoint reference to the cited material; and (4) a parenthetical containing the date of the report.

Although citations to reports in both formats contain the same elements, the document abbreviations, report number, and date differ in their presentation, as illustrated in the following examples. Here is an example of a citation to a report issued by the House of Representatives in *ALWD Manual* format:

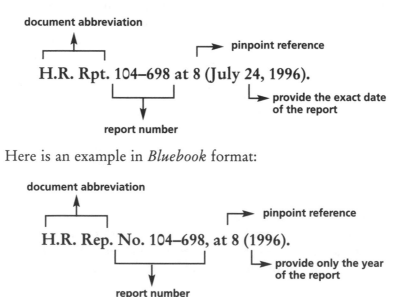

Here is an example in *Bluebook* format:

Both the *ALWD Manual* and the *Bluebook* require a parallel citation to U.S.C.C.A.N. if the report is reprinted there. A citation to a report reprinted in U.S.C.C.A.N. consists of six elements: (1) the report citation, as discussed above; (2) a notation that the citation is to a reprint of the document; (3) the year of the U.S.C.C.A.N. volume; (4) the publication name (U.S.C.C.A.N.); (5) the starting page of the report in U.S.C.C.A.N.; and (6) the pinpoint reference to the page in U.S.C.C.A.N. containing the cited material.

Although the elements of a U.S.C.C.A.N. citation in either *ALWD Manual* or *Bluebook* format are the same, the presentation of the citation varies slightly depending on which format you use. Here is an example in *ALWD Manual* format:

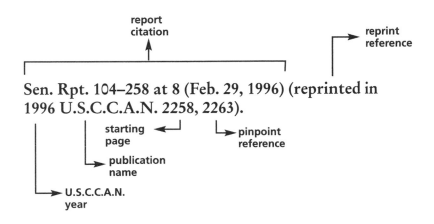

Here is an example in *Bluebook* format:

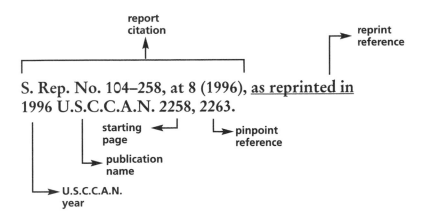

If you locate a report in U.S.C.C.A.N., you can still find the page numbers for the original document. Throughout the report, U.S.C.C.A.N. provides the page numbers of the original document in brackets.

2. FLOOR DEBATES

Floor debates are published in the *Congressional Record*. As explained earlier in this chapter, two versions of the *Congressional Record* are published. The daily edition is published during the current session of Congress, and the permanent edition is published at the close of the session. Both the *ALWD Manual* and the *Bluebook* require citation to the permanent edition if possible. A citation to the permanent edition using either the *ALWD Manual* or the *Bluebook* consists of four elements: (1) the volume number of the *Congressional Record*; (2) the abbreviation Cong. Rec.; (3) the page number with the information cited; and (4) a parenthetical containing the year.

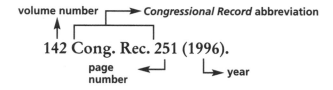

A citation to the daily edition contains the same elements, except that the parenthetical must indicate that the citation is to the daily edition and provide the exact date of the daily edition.

```
                              ┌──► page numbering for the daily edition
142 Cong. Rec. H8620 (daily ed. July 29, 1996).
    parenthetical identifying   ◄──┘              └──► exact date
    the citation as one to the                         of the daily edition
    daily edition
```

E. SAMPLE PAGES FOR FEDERAL LEGISLATIVE HISTORY RESEARCH

Beginning on the next page, **Figures 7.10** through **7.16** contain sample pages illustrating what you would find if you researched legislative history documents associated with the War Crimes Act of 1996 in print using U.S.C.C.A.N. and electronically using Thomas and LexisNexis Congressional.

The first step is locating the statute to find the public law number. U.S.C. or any annotated code will provide the public law number. If you locate the statute in U.S.C.A., the annotations will also provide citations to U.S.C.C.A.N.

FIGURE 7.10 18 U.S.C.A. § 2441 AND ACCOMPANYING ANNOTATIONS

Ch. 118   WAR CRIMES

18 § 2441

Pub.L. 90–321, Title II, § 202(b), May 29, 1968, 82 Stat. 162, added item "42. Extortionate credit transactions".

Pub.L. 90–284, Title I, § 104(b), Title X, § 1002(b), Apr. 11, 1968, 82 Stat. 77, 92, added items "102. Riots" and "12. Civil disorders", respectively.

1965 Amendments. Pub.L. 89–141, § 3, Aug. 28, 1965, 79 Stat. 581, added item "84. Presidential assassination, kidnaping, and assault".

1956 Amendments. Aug. 1, 1956, c. 825, § 2(a), 70 Stat. 798, substituted

"Chapter 3, Animals, birds, fish, and plants" for "Chapter 3, Animals, birds, and fish".

Act July 18, 1956, c. 629, § 202, 70 Stat. 575, added item "68. Narcotics".

Act July 14, 1956, c. 595, § 2, 70 Stat. 540, added item "2. Aircraft and Motor Vehicles".

1949 Amendments. Act May 24, 1949, c. 139, § 1, 63 Stat. 89, struck out the words "constituting crimes" from heading for chapter 21, and inserted "Chapter 50, Gambling—1081".

CHAPTER 118—WAR CRIMES

Sec.
2441.   War crimes.

HISTORICAL AND STATUTORY NOTES

Amendments
1996 Amendments. Pub.L. 104–294, Title VI, § 605(p)(2), Oct. 11, 1996, 110

Stat. 3510, redesignated former item 2401 as 2441.

WESTLAW COMPUTER ASSISTED LEGAL RESEARCH

WESTLAW supplements your legal research in many ways. WESTLAW allows you to

• update your research with the most current information

• expand your library with additional resources

• retrieve current, comprehensive history citing references to a case with KeyCite

For more information on using WESTLAW to supplement your research, see the WESTLAW Electronic Research Guide, which follows the Explanation.

§ 2441. War crimes

(a) **Offense.**—Whoever, whether inside or outside the United States, commits a war crime, in any of the circumstances described in subsection (b), shall be fined under this title or imprisoned for life or any term of years, or both, and if death results to the victim, shall also be subject to the penalty of death.

(b) **Circumstances.**—The circumstances referred to in subsection (a) are that the person committing such war crime or the victim of such war crime is a member of the Armed Forces of the United

Statutory provision

13

FIGURE 7.10   18 U.S.C.A. § 2441 AND ACCOMPANYING ANNOTATIONS (*Continued*)

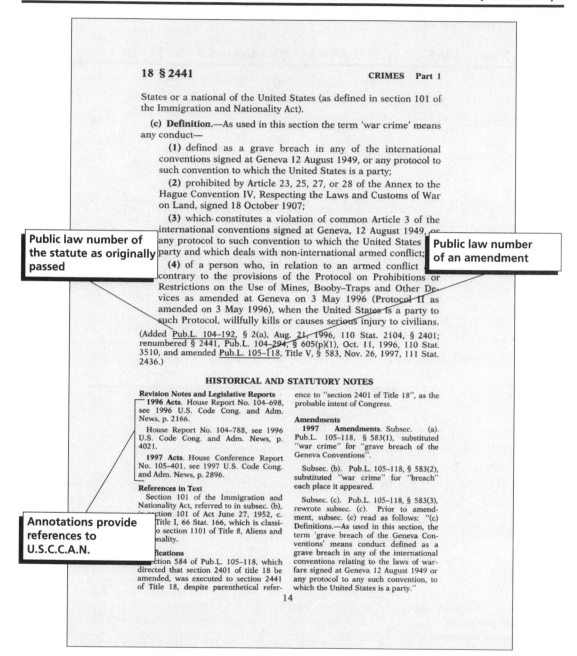

18 § 2441   CRIMES   Part 1

States or a national of the United States (as defined in section 101 of the Immigration and Nationality Act).

(c) **Definition.**—As used in this section the term 'war crime' means any conduct—

(1) defined as a grave breach in any of the international conventions signed at Geneva 12 August 1949, or any protocol to such convention to which the United States is a party;

(2) prohibited by Article 23, 25, 27, or 28 of the Annex to the Hague Convention IV, Respecting the Laws and Customs of War on Land, signed 18 October 1907;

(3) which constitutes a violation of common Article 3 of the international conventions signed at Geneva, 12 August 1949, or any protocol to such convention to which the United States is a party and which deals with non-international armed conflict;

(4) of a person who, in relation to an armed conflict contrary to the provisions of the Protocol on Prohibitions or Restrictions on the Use of Mines, Booby-Traps and Other Devices as amended at Geneva on 3 May 1996 (Protocol II as amended on 3 May 1996), when the United States is a party to such Protocol, willfully kills or causes serious injury to civilians.

(Added Pub.L. 104–192, § 2(a), Aug. 21, 1996, 110 Stat. 2104, § 2401; renumbered § 2441, Pub.L. 104–294, § 605(p)(1), Oct. 11, 1996, 110 Stat. 3510, and amended Pub.L. 105–118, Title V, § 583, Nov. 26, 1997, 111 Stat. 2436.)

Public law number of the statute as originally passed

Public law number of an amendment

HISTORICAL AND STATUTORY NOTES

Revision Notes and Legislative Reports
1996 Acts. House Report No. 104–698, see 1996 U.S. Code Cong. and Adm. News, p. 2166.

House Report No. 104–788, see 1996 U.S. Code Cong. and Adm. News, p. 4021.

1997 Acts. House Conference Report No. 105–401, see 1997 U.S. Code Cong. and Adm. News, p. 2896.

References in Text
Section 101 of the Immigration and Nationality Act, referred to in subsec. (b), is section 101 of Act June 27, 1952, c. [ ], Title I, 66 Stat. 166, which is classified to section 1101 of Title 8, Aliens and [Natio]nality.

[Codi]fications
[Se]ction 584 of Pub.L. 105–118, which directed that section 2401 of title 18 be amended, was executed to section 2441 of Title 18, despite parenthetical refer-

ence to "section 2401 of Title 18", as the probable intent of Congress.

Amendments
1997 Amendments. Subsec. (a). Pub.L. 105–118, § 583(1), substituted "war crime" for "grave breach of the Geneva Conventions".

Subsec. (b). Pub.L. 105–118, § 583(2), substituted "war crime" for "breach" each place it appeared.

Subsec. (c). Pub.L. 105–118, § 583(3), rewrote subsec. (c). Prior to amendment, subsec. (c) read as follows: "(c) Definitions.—As used in this section, the term 'grave breach of the Geneva Conventions' means conduct defined as a grave breach in any of the international conventions relating to the laws of warfare signed at Geneva 12 August 1949 or any protocol to any such convention, to which the United States is a party."

Annotations provide references to U.S.C.C.A.N.

14

To locate a report in U.S.C.C.A.N., locate the edition of U.S.C.C.A.N. for the appropriate year, locate the volumes labeled "Legislative History," and turn to the page number provided in the annotations. In this case, the committee report is in 1996 U.S.C.C.A.N. beginning on page 2166.

FIGURE 7.11 HOUSE JUDICIARY COMMITTEE REPORT REPRINTED IN U.S.C.C.A.N.

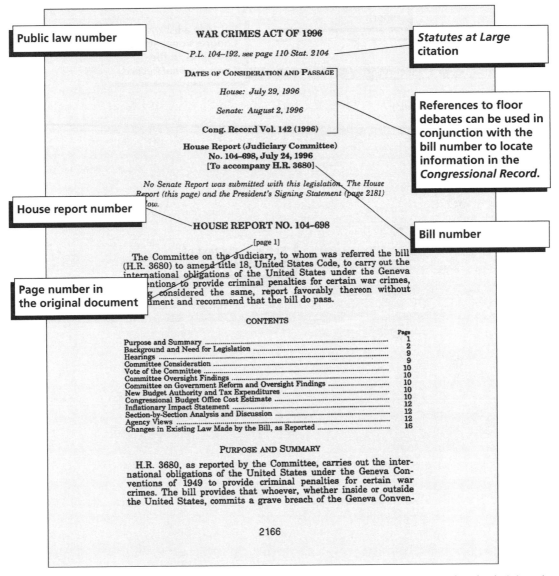

Reprinted with permission from Thomson Reuters/West, *United States Code Congressional and Administrative News*, 104th Congress-Second Session 1996, Vol. 5 (1997), p. 2166. © 1997 Thomson Reuters/West.

Reports on this Act are also available through Thomas. Browsing by public law number retrieves the Bill Summary and Status report.

FIGURE 7.12   BILL SUMMARY AND STATUS REPORT IN THOMAS

Following the link to House Report 104-698 retrieves the same House Judiciary Committee report reprinted in U.S.C.C.A.N.

FIGURE 7.13 HOUSE JUDICIARY COMMITTEE REPORT IN THOMAS

104TH CONGRESS

Report

HOUSE OF REPRESENTATIVES

2d Session

104-698
WAR CRIMES ACT OF 1996

JULY 24, 1996- Committed to the Committee of the Whole House on the State of the Union and ordered to be printed

Mr. SMITH of Texas, from the Committee on the Judiciary, submitted the following

REPORT

[To accompany H.R. 3680]

[Including cost estimate of the Congressional Budget Office]

The Committee on the Judiciary, to whom was referred the bill (H.R. 3680) to amend title 18, United States Code, to carry out the international obligations of the United States under the Geneva Conventions to provide criminal penalties for certain war crimes, having considered the same, report favorably thereon without amendment and recommend that the bill do pass.

CONTENTS	Page
Purpose and Summary	1
Background and Need for Legislation	2
Hearings	9
Committee Consideration	9
Vote of the Committee	10
Committee Oversight Findings	10

[+]
FEEDBACK

PURPOSE AND SUMMARY

H.R. 3680, as reported by the Committee, carries out the international obligations of the United States under the Geneva Conventions of 1949 to provide criminal penalties for certain war crimes. The bill provides that whoever, whether inside or outside the United States, commits a grave breach of the Geneva Conventions (where the perpetrator or the victim is a member of the armed forces of the United States or a national of the United States) shall be fined or imprisoned for life or any terms of years, or both, and if death results to the victim, shall also be subject to the penalty of death.

BACKGROUND AND NEED FOR LEGISLATION

I. THE GENEVA CONVENTIONS

Four Geneva Conventions for the Protection of Victims of War, dated August 12, 1949, were ratified by the United States on July 14, 1955:

Convention for the Amelioration of the Condition of the Wounded and Sick in Armed Forces in the Field (`Convention I');

Convention for the Amelioration of the Condition of Wounded, Sick and Shipwrecked Members of Armed Forces at Sea (`Convention II');

Convention Relative to the Treatment of Prisoners of War (`Convention III'); and

Convention Relative to the Protection of Civilian Persons in Time of War (`Convention IV').

Deputy Under Secretary of State Robert Murphy testified in 1955 as to the purpose of the conventions:

The Geneva conventions are another long step forward toward mitigating the severities of war on its helpless victims. They reflect enlightened practices as carried out by the United States and other civilized countries and they represent largely what the United States would do whether or not a party to the conventions. Our own conduct has served to establish higher standards and we can only benefit by having them incorporated in a stronger body of conventional wartime law. * * *

[–]
FEEDBACK

To locate legislative documents in LexisNexis Congressional, access the LexisNexis Congressional web site from your library's network. You can search in several ways. One option is to search by public law number under "Legislative Histories, Bills & Laws."

FIGURE 7.14   SEARCH OPTIONS, LEXISNEXIS CONGRESSIONAL

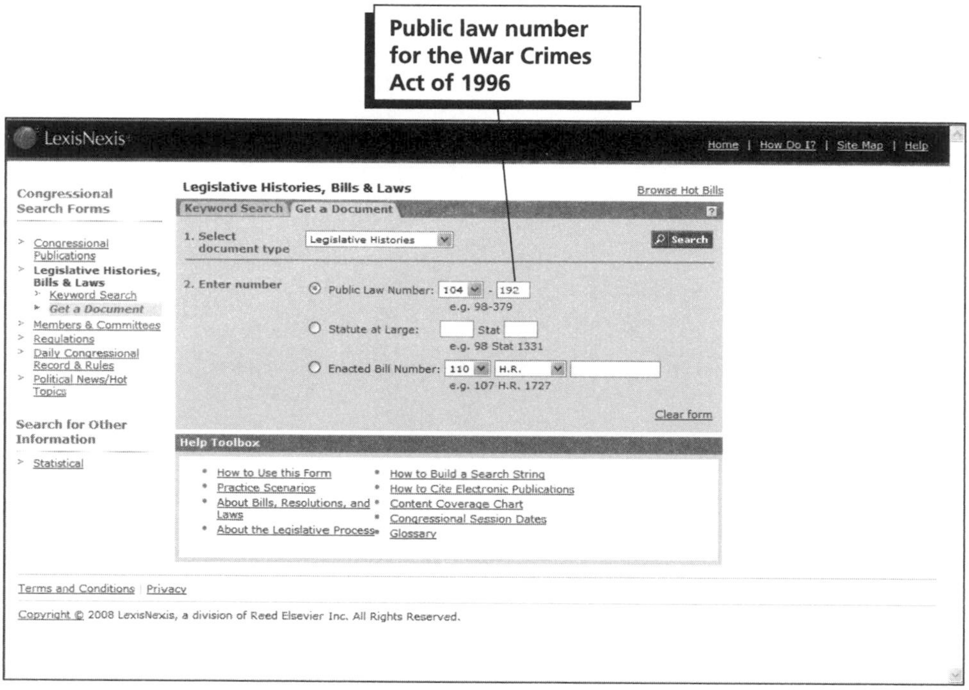

Reprinted with permission of LexisNexis, LexisNexis Congressional search screen.

This search retrieved a list of legislative history documents for the War Crimes Act of 1996. Follow these links to access abstracts (summaries) and the full text of the individual legislative history documents.

FIGURE 7.15 SEARCH RESULTS, LEXISNEXIS CONGRESSIONAL

Retrieve the text of the public law.

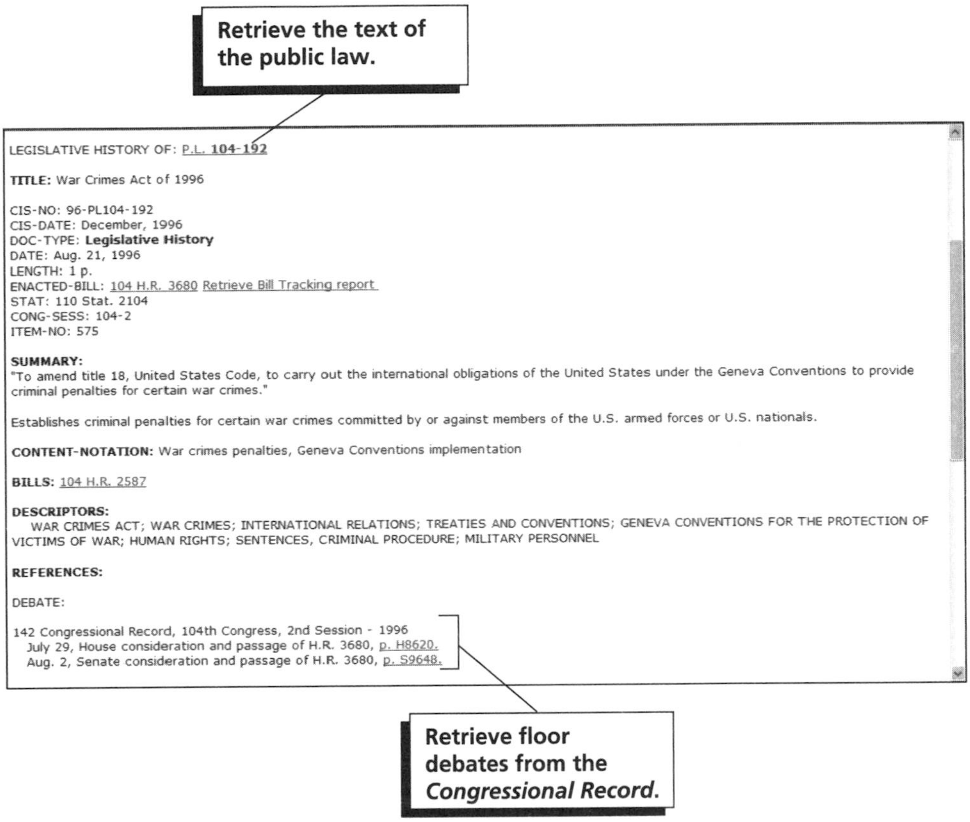

LEGISLATIVE HISTORY OF: P.L. 104-192

TITLE: War Crimes Act of 1996

CIS-NO: 96-PL104-192
CIS-DATE: December, 1996
DOC-TYPE: **Legislative History**
DATE: Aug. 21, 1996
LENGTH: 1 p.
ENACTED-BILL: 104 H.R. 3680 Retrieve Bill Tracking report
STAT: 110 Stat. 2104
CONG-SESS: 104-2
ITEM-NO: 575

SUMMARY:
"To amend title 18, United States Code, to carry out the international obligations of the United States under the Geneva Conventions to provide criminal penalties for certain war crimes."

Establishes criminal penalties for certain war crimes committed by or against members of the U.S. armed forces or U.S. nationals.

CONTENT-NOTATION: War crimes penalties, Geneva Conventions implementation

BILLS: 104 H.R. 2587

DESCRIPTORS:
  WAR CRIMES ACT; WAR CRIMES; INTERNATIONAL RELATIONS; TREATIES AND CONVENTIONS; GENEVA CONVENTIONS FOR THE PROTECTION OF VICTIMS OF WAR; HUMAN RIGHTS; SENTENCES, CRIMINAL PROCEDURE; MILITARY PERSONNEL

REFERENCES:

DEBATE:

142 Congressional Record, 104th Congress, 2nd Session - 1996
  July 29, House consideration and passage of H.R. 3680, p. H8620.
  Aug. 2, Senate consideration and passage of H.R. 3680, p. S9648.

Retrieve floor debates from the *Congressional Record*.

Reprinted with permission of LexisNexis, LexisNexis Congressional search results.

To view floor debates on the bill, use the links to the _Congressional Record_. This example shows part of the debate in the House of Representatives.

FIGURE 7.16   _CONGRESSIONAL RECORD_ EXCERPT FROM LEXISNEXIS CONGRESSIONAL

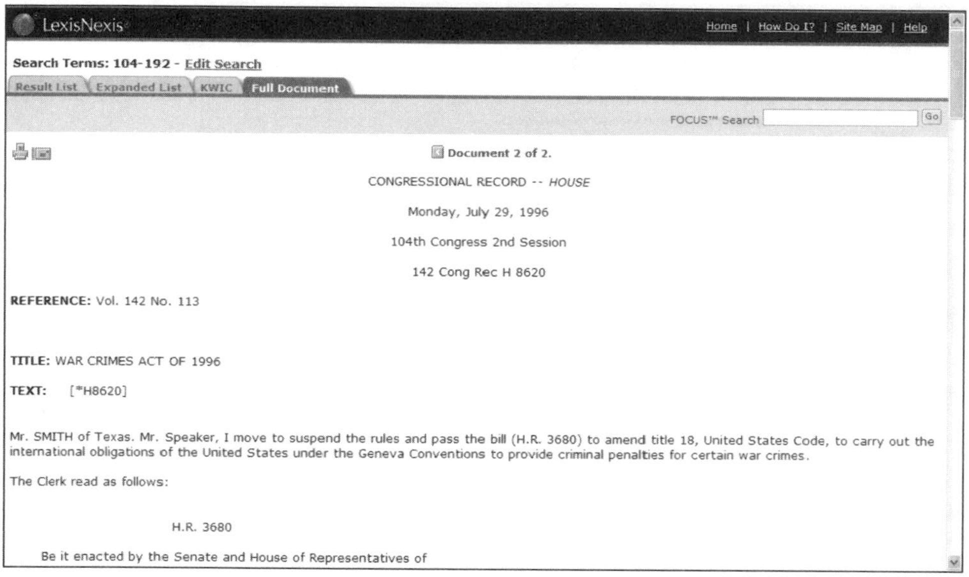

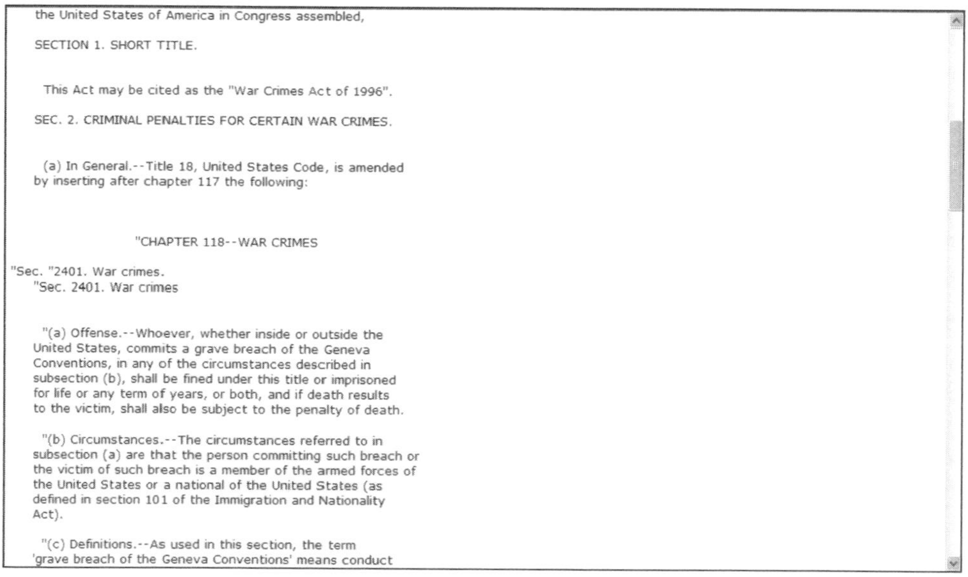

Reprinted with permission of LexisNexis, LexisNexis Congressional abstract entries.

F. CHECKLIST FOR FEDERAL LEGISLATIVE HISTORY RESEARCH

Because the same legislative documents can be accessed through a variety of print and electronic resources, this section provides both a research checklist and a summary chart in **Figure 7.17** setting out where you can locate legislative history documents.

1. IDENTIFY THE SCOPE OF YOUR RESEARCH

❐ Determine whether you need the history of an individual statute or material on a general subject.

❐ To research the history of an individual statute, begin by locating the statute.

■ The public law number should follow the statute in U.S.C. or an annotated code.

■ To determine congressional intent, start with committee reports; use U.S.C.C.A.N., a compiled legislative history, the CIS microfiche set, or an electronic source to locate committee reports.

■ For more comprehensive legislative history research, locate floor debates, hearings, and prior versions of the bill in addition to committee reports; use a compiled legislative history, the CIS microfiche set (in conjunction with the *Congressional Record*), or an electronic source to locate a statute's complete legislative history.

❐ To research material on a general subject, use the CIS microfiche set or an electronic source.

❐ If necessary, consult a reference librarian for assistance in determining the appropriate scope of your research and locating necessary documents.

2. LOCATE A COMPILED LEGISLATIVE HISTORY

❐ Search the library's online catalog for separately published legislative histories.

❐ Use Johnson, *Sources of Compiled Legislative Histories*, or Reams, *Federal Legislative Histories*.

3. LOCATE COMMITTEE REPORTS IN U.S.C.C.A.N.

❐ Use annotations in U.S.C.A. to locate cross-references to committee reports reprinted in U.S.C.C.A.N.

4. LOCATE COMPLETE LEGISLATIVE HISTORIES IN THE CIS MICROFICHE SET

❐ Look up the public law number in the Legislative Histories volumes (after 1984) to locate listings of all legislative history documents for an individual statute.

❐ Use the Index and Abstracts volumes if you do not have the public law number or need to locate information by subject.

5. LOCATE FLOOR DEBATES IN THE *CONGRESSIONAL RECORD* USING PRINT RESOURCES

❐ Locate references to floor debates using the CIS Legislative Histories volumes or reports reprinted in U.S.C.C.A.N.

❐ Use the *Congressional Record* index to locate information by subject or bill number.

6. SEARCH FOR LEGISLATIVE HISTORY ELECTRONICALLY

❐ Search by public law number, *Statutes at Large* citation, or bill number to locate the legislative history of an individual piece of legislation.

❐ Use subject or word searches to locate information by subject.

❐ Use Westlaw and LexisNexis to locate legislative documents using compiled legislative histories or databases containing individual types of legislative documents.

❐ Use Thomas or GPO Access for free Internet access to legislative documents.

- Use Thomas's Bill Summary and Status report to locate documents related to an individual piece of legislation.
- Use GPO Access to locate *Congressional Record* entries by citation and for .pdf versions of the *Congressional Record* and selected hearings.

❐ Use HeinOnline for electronic access to Johnson, *Sources of Compiled Legislative Histories,* or full-text legislative histories in the U.S. Federal Legislative History Title Collection.

❐ Use LexisNexis Congressional if your library subscribes to this service for electronic access to the CIS microfiche set.

FIGURE 7.17 RESEARCH SUMMARY FOR FEDERAL LEGISLATIVE HISTORY

TO LOCATE THIS TYPE OF DOCUMENT	USE THIS PRINT RESOURCE	OR THIS ELECTRONIC RESOURCE
Bills	Compiled legislative histories, CIS microfiche	Thomas, GPO Access, LexisNexis Congressional, LexisNexis, Westlaw, selected compiled legislative histories available through HeinOnline
Hearings	Compiled legislative histories, CIS microfiche	Complete hearing documents: GPO Access, selected compiled legislative histories available through HeinOnline
		Congressional testimony: LexisNexis Congressional, LexisNexis, Westlaw
Floor debates	Compiled legislative histories, *Congressional Record*	*Congressional Record* accessed through Thomas, GPO Access, LexisNexis Congressional, LexisNexis, Westlaw, selected compiled legislative histories available through HeinOnline
Committee reports	Compiled legislative histories, U.S.C.C.A.N., CIS microfiche	Thomas, GPO Access, LexisNexis Congressional, LexisNexis, Westlaw, selected compiled legislative histories available through HeinOnline

CHAPTER 8

FEDERAL ADMINISTRATIVE LAW RESEARCH

A. Introduction to federal administrative law

B. Researching federal regulations in print

C. Researching federal regulations electronically

D. Citing federal regulations

E. Sample pages for federal administrative law research

F. Checklist for federal administrative law research

A. INTRODUCTION TO FEDERAL ADMINISTRATIVE LAW

1. ADMINISTRATIVE AGENCIES AND REGULATIONS

Administrative agencies exist at all levels of government. Examples of federal administrative agencies include the Food and Drug Administration (FDA), the Environmental Protection Agency (EPA), and the Federal Communications Commission (FCC). Agencies are created by statute, but they are part of the executive branch because they "enforce" or implement a legislatively created scheme. In creating an agency, a legislature will pass what is known as "enabling" legislation. Enabling legislation defines the scope of the agency's mission and "enables" it to perform its functions, which may include promulgating regulations and adjudicating controversies, among other functions. If an agency is empowered to create regulations, those regulations cannot exceed the authority granted by the legislature. Thus, for example, while the FCC may be able to establish regulations concerning television licenses, it would not be able to promulgate regulations concerning the labeling of drugs because that would exceed the authority granted to it by Congress in its enabling legislation.

Federal agencies often create regulations to implement statutes passed by Congress. Sometimes Congress cannot legislate with the level of detail necessary to implement a complex legislative scheme. In those circumstances, Congress charges an agency with enforcing the statute, and the agency will develop procedures for implementing more general legislative mandates. In the Family and Medical Leave Act, for instance, Congress mandated that an employer allow an employee with a "serious health condition" to take unpaid medical leave. Pursuant to the statute, the Department of Labor has promulgated more specific regulations defining what "serious health condition" means.

In format, a regulation looks like a statute. It is, in essence, a rule created by a government entity, and many times administrative regulations are called "rules." In operation, they are indistinguishable from statutes, although the methods used to create, modify, and repeal them are different from those applicable to statutes. Federal administrative agencies are required to conform to the procedures set out in the Administrative Procedure Act (APA) in promulgating regulations. State agencies may be required to comply with similar statutes at the state level. Without going into too much detail, the APA frequently requires agencies to undertake the following steps: (1) notify the public when they plan to promulgate new regulations or change existing ones; (2) publish proposed regulations and solicit comments on them before the regulations become final; and (3) publish final regulations before they go into effect to notify the public of the new requirements.

At the federal level, regulations and proposed regulations are published in the *Federal Register*. The *Federal Register* is a daily publication reporting the activities of the executive branch of government. A new volume is published each year. It begins on the first business day of the new year with page one and is consecutively paginated from that point on until the last business day of the year.

After final regulations are published in the *Federal Register*, they are codified in the *Code of Federal Regulations* (C.F.R.). Like U.S.C., the C.F.R. is divided into fifty "Titles." The C.F.R. Titles are subdivided into chapters, which are usually named for the agencies issuing the regulations. Chapters are subdivided into Parts covering specific regulatory areas, and Parts are further subdivided into sections. To find a regulation, you would need to know its Title, Part, and section number. Thus, a citation to 16 C.F.R. § 1211.14 tells you that the regulation is published in Title 16 of the C.F.R. in Part 1211, section number 1211.14. **Figure 8.1** illustrates what federal regulations look like.

The C.F.R. is updated once a year in four separate installments. Titles 1 through 16 are updated on January 1 of each year, Titles 17 through 27 on April 1, Titles 28 through 41 on July 1, and Titles 42 through 50 on October 1. Because a new set of C.F.R. volumes is published annually, the C.F.R. is not updated with pocket parts. Instead, new or amended regulations are published in the *Federal Register*. They are not codified within the C.F.R. until a new set is published.

FIGURE 8.1   REGULATIONS IN 16 C.F.R. PART 1211

§ 1210.18

CPSA, 15 U.S.C. 2055(a)(2), the Freedom of Information Act as amended, 5 U.S.C. 552, and the Commission's regulations under that act, 16 CFR part 1015.

§ 1210.18   Refusal of Importation.

(a) *For noncompliance with reporting and recordkeeping requirements.* The Commission has determined that compliance with the recordkeeping and reporting requirements of this subpart is necessary to ensure that lighters comply with this part 1210. Therefore, pursuant to section 17(g) of the CPSA, 15 U.S.C. 2066(g), the Commission may refuse to permit importation of any lighters with respect to which the manufacturer or importer has not complied with the recordkeeping and reporting requirements of this subpart. Since the records are required to demonstrate that production lighters comply with the specifications for the surrogate, the Commission may refuse importation of lighters if production lighters do not comply with the specifications required by this subpart or if any other recordkeeping or reporting requirement in this part is violated.

(b) *For noncompliance with this standard and for lack of a certification certificate.* As provided in section 17(a) of the CPSA, 15 U.S.C. 2066(a), products subject to this standard shall be refused admission into the customs territory of the United States if, among other reasons, the product fails to comply with this standard or is not accompanied by the certificate required by this standard.

Subpart C—Stockpiling

AUTHORITY: 15 U.S.C. 2058(g)(2), 2079(d).

§ 1210.20   Stockpiling.

(a) *Definition. Stockpiling* means to manufacture or import a product that is subject to a consumer product safety rule between the date of issuance of the rule and its effective date at a rate which is significantly greater than the rate at which the product was produced during a base period. Statutory authority for promulgating the regulations poses of this rule the option of the manufacturer or importer, any 1-

16 CFR Ch. II (1–1–07 Edition)

year period during the 5-year period prior to July 12, 1993.

(c) *Prohibited act.* Manufacturers and importers of disposable and novelty cigarette lighters shall Outline of the Part ture or import lighters comply with the require part between July 12, 1993 and July 12, 1994, at a rate that is greater than the rate of production or importation during the base period plus 20 per cent of that rate.

PART 1211—SAFETY STANDARD FOR AUTOMATIC RESIDENTIAL GARAGE DOOR OPERATORS

Subpart A—The Standard

Sec.
1211.1   Effective date.
1211.2   Definition.
1211.3   Units of measurement.
1211.4   General requirements for protection against risk of injury.
1211.5   General testing parameters.
1211.6   General entrapment protection requirements.
1211.7   Inherent entrapment protection requirements.
1211.8   Secondary entrapment protection requirements.
1211.9   Additional entrapment protection requirements.
1211.10 Requirements for all entrapment protection devices.
1211.11 Requirements for photoelectric sensors.
1211.12 Requirements for edge sensors.
1211.13 Inherent force activated secondary door sensors.
1211.14 Instruction manual.
1211.15 Field-installed labels.
1211.16 UL marking requirement.
1211.17 Statutory labeling requirement.

Subpart B—Certification

1211.20 Purpose, scope, and application.
1211.21 Effective date.
1211.22 Definitions.
1211.23 Certification testing.
1211.24 Product certification and labeling by manufacturers.
1211.25 Product certification and labeling by importers.

Subpart C—Recordkeeping

1211.30 Effective date.
1211.31 Recordkeeping requirements.

AUTHORITY: Sec. 203 of Pub. L. 101–608, 104 Stat. 3110; 15 U.S.C. 2063 and 2065.

FIGURE 8.1   REGULATIONS IN 16 C.F.R. PART 1211 *(Continued)*

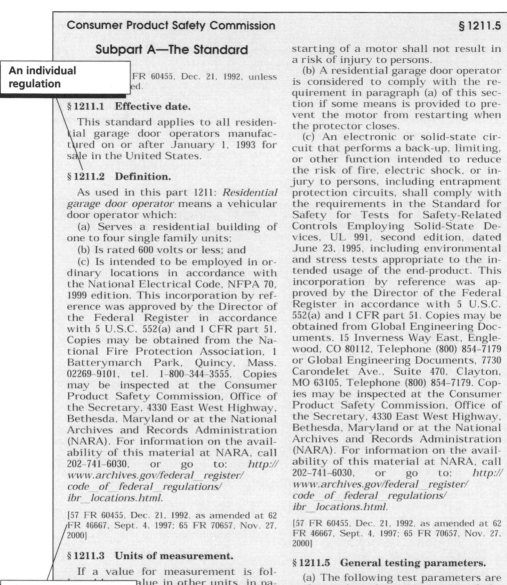

Consumer Product Safety Commission   § 1211.5

Subpart A—The Standard

An individual regulation

[57 FR 60455, Dec. 21, 1992, unless otherwise noted.]

§ 1211.1   Effective date.

This standard applies to all residential garage door operators manufactured on or after January 1, 1993 for sale in the United States.

§ 1211.2   Definition.

As used in this part 1211: *Residential garage door operator* means a vehicular door operator which:

(a) Serves a residential building of one to four single family units;

(b) Is rated 600 volts or less; and

(c) Is intended to be employed in ordinary locations in accordance with the National Electrical Code, NFPA 70, 1999 edition. This incorporation by reference was approved by the Director of the Federal Register in accordance with 5 U.S.C. 552(a) and 1 CFR part 51. Copies may be obtained from the National Fire Protection Association, 1 Batterymarch Park, Quincy, Mass. 02269-9101, tel. 1-800-344-3555. Copies may be inspected at the Consumer Product Safety Commission, Office of the Secretary, 4330 East West Highway, Bethesda, Maryland or at the National Archives and Records Administration (NARA). For information on the availability of this material at NARA, call 202-741-6030, or go to: *http:// www.archives.gov/federal_register/ code_of_federal_regulations/ ibr_locations.html.*

[57 FR 60455, Dec. 21, 1992, as amended at 62 FR 46667, Sept. 4, 1997; 65 FR 70657, Nov. 27, 2000]

§ 1211.3   Units of measurement.

Citations to the *Federal Register* where the regulations were originally published

If a value for measurement is followed by a value in other units, in parentheses, the second value may be approximate. The first stated requirement.

[57 FR 60455, Dec. 21, 1992, as amended at 65 FR 70657, Nov. 27, 2000]

§ 1211.4   General requirements for protection against risk of injury.

(a) If an automatically reset protective device is employed, automatic re-

starting of a motor shall not result in a risk of injury to persons.

(b) A residential garage door operator is considered to comply with the requirement in paragraph (a) of this section if some means is provided to prevent the motor from restarting when the protector closes.

(c) An electronic or solid-state circuit that performs a back-up, limiting, or other function intended to reduce the risk of fire, electric shock, or injury to persons, including entrapment protection circuits, shall comply with the requirements in the Standard for Safety for Tests for Safety-Related Controls Employing Solid-State Devices, UL 991, second edition, dated June 23, 1995, including environmental and stress tests appropriate to the intended usage of the end-product. This incorporation by reference was approved by the Director of the Federal Register in accordance with 5 U.S.C. 552(a) and 1 CFR part 51. Copies may be obtained from Global Engineering Documents, 15 Inverness Way East, Englewood, CO 80112, Telephone (800) 854-7179 or Global Engineering Documents, 7730 Carondelet Ave., Suite 470, Clayton, MO 63105, Telephone (800) 854-7179. Copies may be inspected at the Consumer Product Safety Commission, Office of the Secretary, 4330 East West Highway, Bethesda, Maryland or at the National Archives and Records Administration (NARA). For information on the availability of this material at NARA, call 202-741-6030, or go to: *http:// www.archives.gov/federal_register/ code_of_federal_regulations/ ibr_locations.html.*

[57 FR 60455, Dec. 21, 1992, as amended at 62 FR 46667, Sept. 4, 1997; 65 FR 70657, Nov. 27, 2000]

§ 1211.5   General testing parameters.

(a) The following test parameters are to be used in the investigation of the circuit covered by § 1211.4(c) for compliance with the Standard for Safety for Tests for Safety-Related Controls Employing Solid-State Devices, UL 991, second edition, dated June 23, 1995, as incorporated by reference in paragraph (b)(3) of this section:

(1) With regard to electrical supervision of critical components, an operator being inoperative with respect to

323

2. METHODS OF LOCATING REGULATIONS

You can locate federal regulations in several ways. Three common techniques are searching by citation, by subject, or by words in the document. Once you know the Title and Part or section number of a regulation, you can locate it in the C.F.R. in print or electronically. An easy way to find citations to relevant regulations is through an annotated code. Because regulations implement statutory schemes, you will often begin regulatory research by consulting the enabling statute, and the statute's annotations may include citations to regulations. The annotations will not ordinarily direct you to a specific regulation; instead, they will direct you to the Title and Part of the C.F.R. with regulations applicable to the area of law you are researching.

Researching by subject is another useful way to locate regulations. You can search by subject in print using the index to the C.F.R. If you are searching electronically, you may or may not have access to the index. Each Title and Part of the C.F.R. has a table of contents, which you can view in print or electronically to browse by subject. Reviewing the table of contents can be a difficult way to begin your research unless you know which agency promulgated the regulations you are trying to find. Once you find a relevant regulation, however, viewing the table of contents can help you find related regulations, as described more fully below.

Word searching is another way to locate regulations electronically. Because regulators often use technical terms in regulations, however, word searching can be more difficult than subject searching if you are not already familiar with the regulatory terminology.

Two additional avenues for regulatory research are the telephone and e-mail. Agency staff can be an invaluable resource for understanding the agency's operations, as well as for staying up to date on the agency's activities. If you practice in an area of law subject to agency regulation, do not hesitate to contact agency staff for information. Regulatory notices published in the *Federal Register* typically provide the name and contact information of an agency staff member who can provide additional information about the regulations.

Regulatory research is similar to statutory research in that you will often need to research interrelated regulations, not individual sections of the C.F.R., to answer your research question. Therefore, regardless of the search method you use initially to locate a relevant regulation, you should plan to expand your search to consider the entire regulatory scheme. Because electronic sources often retrieve individual regulations as separate documents, it is especially easy to lose sight of the need to research multiple sections when you are working online. Whether you use print or electronic sources, you can view the detailed outline of sections at the beginning of the Part, as illustrated in **Figure 8.1**, and browse preceding and subsequent sections of the C.F.R. to ensure that you consider all potentially applicable regulations.

Sections B and C, below, explain how to research regulations in print and electronically. Because the federal government has made much regulatory material available on the Internet, most researchers conduct C.F.R. research electronically. The electronic versions of official government sources, however, are updated on the same schedule as the print versions, and the process of updating regulations with official government sources, whether print or electronic, is the same. Therefore, information on updating regulatory research with official government sources appears in Section C on electronic research. If you are updating federal regulations in print, you can follow the same steps using the print versions of the updating tools.

B. RESEARCHING FEDERAL REGULATIONS IN PRINT

1. LOCATING AND UPDATING REGULATIONS IN PRINT

Researching federal regulations entails two steps:

a. locating regulations
b. updating your research.

This section describes how to complete these steps using print research resources.

a. Locating Regulations

The C.F.R. is published as a set of softcover books. Once you locate the C.F.R. set, the next question is how to find regulations relevant to your research issue. There are two ways to accomplish this. One way is to use the cross-references to the C.F.R. in U.S.C.S. or U.S.C.A. The other is to go directly to the C.F.R. itself, using a subject index to refer you to relevant C.F.R. provisions.[1]

Because regulations are often used to implement statutory schemes, U.S.C.S. and U.S.C.A. frequently contain cross-references to applicable regulations. Thus, if your research leads you to statutes, the annotations are a useful tool to guide you toward regulations that bear on the area of law you are researching. You may recall from Chapter 6 that U.S.C.S.

---

[1]Subject-matter services used for researching specific subject areas of the law may also contain the text of regulations. Researching with subject-matter services is covered in Chapter 9.

FIGURE 8.2 ANNOTATIONS TO 15 U.S.C.S. § 2063

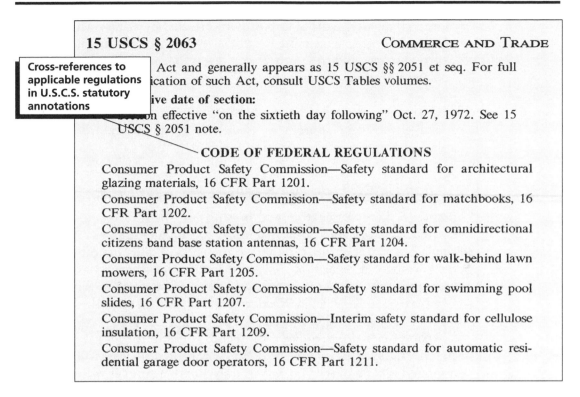

15 USCS § 2063   COMMERCE AND TRADE

Cross-references to applicable regulations in U.S.C.S. statutory annotations

... Act and generally appears as 15 USCS §§ 2051 et seq. For full ...ication of such Act, consult USCS Tables volumes.

...ive date of section:

...on effective "on the sixtieth day following" Oct. 27, 1972. See 15 USCS § 2051 note.

CODE OF FEDERAL REGULATIONS

Consumer Product Safety Commission—Safety standard for architectural glazing materials, 16 CFR Part 1201.

Consumer Product Safety Commission—Safety standard for matchbooks, 16 CFR Part 1202.

Consumer Product Safety Commission—Safety standard for omnidirectional citizens band base station antennas, 16 CFR Part 1204.

Consumer Product Safety Commission—Safety standard for walk-behind lawn mowers, 16 CFR Part 1205.

Consumer Product Safety Commission—Safety standard for swimming pool slides, 16 CFR Part 1207.

Consumer Product Safety Commission—Interim safety standard for cellulose insulation, 16 CFR Part 1209.

Consumer Product Safety Commission—Safety standard for automatic residential garage door operators, 16 CFR Part 1211.

Reprinted from *United States Code Service, Lawyer's Edition* with permission of LexisNexis. Copyright 1996 by Lawyer's Cooperative Publishing. *United States Code Service*, Title 15 Commerce and Trade §§ 1701-2800 (1996), p. 104.

contains more extensive regulatory annotations than U.S.C.A. does. **Figure 8.2** shows C.F.R. cross-references in U.S.C.S. annotations.

Another way to locate regulations is to use the CFR Index and Finding Aids. This is a subject index within the C.F.R. set itself. Like all other C.F.R. volumes, it is a softcover book, and it is published annually.

b. Updating Regulations

As noted above, the C.F.R. is published once a year in four separate installments and is updated through the *Federal Register*, not with pocket parts. Updating C.F.R. research with the *Federal Register* is a two-step process:

- Use a monthly publication called the List of CFR Sections Affected (LSA) to find any *Federal Register* notices indicating that the regulation has been affected by agency action. Each monthly issue of the LSA is cumulative. Therefore, the current month's LSA will contain updates from the date of the latest C.F.R. volume through the end of the previous month.

- Use a cumulative table of C.F.R. Parts affected by agency action in the *Federal Register*. This table is published daily. It lists updates for the current month and will update your research from the last day covered by the LSA until the present.

These are the same steps you would follow to update your research using official government sources in electronic form. Therefore, they are explained in more detail in Section C, below.

2. USING A CITATOR FOR REGULATORY RESEARCH

Chapter 5 discusses citators and how to use them in conducting case research. Citators are also available for researching federal regulations. Regulatory citator entries typically contain lists of cases and other sources that have cited a regulation. As noted in Chapter 5, many law libraries no longer carry Shepard's in print. The electronic citators (Shepard's in LexisNexis, and KeyCite in Westlaw) are available for federal regulations, and they are explained in more detail in Section C, below.

Using a citator in regulatory research is useful for locating research references. As of this writing, only Westlaw provides access to a complete annotated version of the C.F.R. Virtually all other sources, whether print or electronic, provide access only to unannotated regulations.[2] Therefore, a citator is a useful tool for locating cases interpreting a regulation. Even if you are using an annotated version of the C.F.R., the regulatory annotations often do not list every citing case or source that has cited the regulation. If the annotations are too sparse to give you the information you need about a regulation, you may find more complete information in a citator.

C. RESEARCHING FEDERAL REGULATIONS ELECTRONICALLY

LexisNexis, Westlaw, and government web sites are all useful sources for regulatory research. This section discusses search options in all three of these sources. It also discusses use of electronic citators for regulatory research.

---

[2]Some administrative regulations are reproduced as part of the U.S.C.S. and U.S.C.A. sets and may have limited annotations; however, the coverage is very limited.

1. LEXISNEXIS AND WESTLAW

The C.F.R. is available in LexisNexis and Westlaw. LexisNexis and Westlaw incorporate changes to regulations as they appear in the *Federal Register* so that the version of the C.F.R. you see in these services is ordinarily up to date. You can check the date through which the regulation is updated by checking the updating date at the beginning or end of the document. The *Federal Register* is also available in both services, although LexisNexis's and Westlaw's continuous updating of the C.F.R. make it unnecessary to use the *Federal Register* for updating regulations. The continuous updates also mean, however, that the versions of the C.F.R. in the LexisNexis and Westlaw databases are not official sources for regulations. If you need the official source, you must use a print or electronic government source for the C.F.R. and *Federal Register*.

In LexisNexis, you can retrieve administrative regulations and *Federal Register* entries from their citations. The U.S.C.S. annotations in LexisNexis also provide links to regulations. To search by subject, you must first select the C.F.R. database from the source directory. The search screen automatically displays the table of contents. You can drill down through the table of contents to search by subject, or you can execute a word search. Once you locate a relevant regulation, you can view the table of contents for the Part from the TOC link in the top left corner of the screen. To Shepardize a regulation, you can enter the citation or access the service from a regulation you are viewing. The Shepard's entry will list cases and other sources that have cited the regulation.

In Westlaw, you can also retrieve administrative regulations and *Federal Register* entries from their citations. As noted above, Westlaw provides access to an annotated version of the C.F.R. through its RegulationsPlus feature. Once you access a regulation, the directory on the left side of the screen will indicate whether any "notes of decisions," like those in West statutory annotations, are available. In addition, the U.S.C.A. annotations in Westlaw also provide some links to regulations, although the references are not as complete as those in U.S.C.S. To search by subject, you can access the C.F.R. table of contents or RegulationsPlus Index from the Site Map. Another way to access these search features is by selecting the C.F.R. database and following the appropriate links in the top right corner of the screen. You can also execute a word search from the search screen. Once you locate a relevant regulation, you can view the table of contents for the Part from the Table of Contents link on the left hand menu. To use KeyCite, you can enter the citation or access the service from a regulation you are viewing. The KeyCite entry will be divided into sections showing the history of the regulation and citing references listing cases and other sources that have cited the regulation.

2. GOVERNMENT SOURCES

Because the C.F.R. and *Federal Register* are government publications, they are widely available on the Internet free of charge. The Government Printing Office's GPO Access service is one of the best places to research federal regulations, especially because it provides the official version of the C.F.R. in .pdf format. Sites for individual agencies can also be good sources for federal regulations. Internet addresses for several useful sites for federal regulatory research are listed in Appendix A. **Figure 8.3** shows the main C.F.R. research page in GPO Access.

If you use the Internet to locate C.F.R. provisions, you should pay careful attention to the date of the material you are using. Internet sources of regulations usually are no more up to date than the print version of the C.F.R. In GPO Access, for example, the official C.F.R. database is only updated four times per year as the new print editions of the C.F.R. become available, although the *Federal Register* database is updated daily.

GPO Access offers an unofficial version of the C.F.R. called the *Electronic Code of Federal Regulations* (e-CFR). The e-CFR is updated

FIGURE 8.3   GPO ACCESS C.F.R. SEARCH OPTIONS

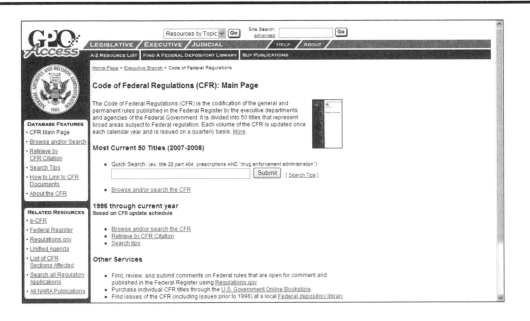

daily to incorporate changes to regulations as they are published in the *Federal Register*, in the same way that LexisNexis and Westlaw continually update their C.F.R. databases. Although the e-CFR is not an official source for regulations, it is a useful research tool. By comparing the official C.F.R. text with the e-CFR version, you can determine quickly and easily whether a regulation has been changed since the latest official edition of the C.F.R. was published. If you need an official source and citation for the change, you can then retrieve the *Federal Register* page containing the change in the GPO Access *Federal Register* database.

Although no reason exists to doubt the accuracy of the e-CFR, there may be times when, out of an abundance of caution, you want to double check your research by updating it with official government sources. An alternative method of updating in GPO Access requires you to research two sources:

- Use a monthly publication called the List of CFR Sections Affected (LSA) to find any *Federal Register* notices indicating that the regulation has been affected by agency action.
- Use the Current List of CFR Parts Affected to update from the date of the LSA until the present.

The official updating sources available online are the same as those available in print. Therefore, these are also the steps you must follow to update print research.

The LSA lists each C.F.R. section affected by agency action. It is a cumulative publication. The current month's LSA will contain updates from the date of the latest C.F.R. volume through the end of the previous month. For example, if the latest C.F.R. volume had been published on January 2 and today's date were October 15, the current LSA would be dated September, and it would contain updates from January 2 through September 30.

To locate references to a regulation in the LSA, you can search for the regulation's citation in the LSA database. You can also browse the .pdf version of the LSA, which is organized numerically by Title number, and within each Title, numerically by Part and section number. If you do not find the Part or section listed in the LSA, there have been no changes to the regulation. If you do find the Part or section listed, the LSA will refer you to the page or pages of the *Federal Register* containing information on the agency's action. **Figure 8.4** shows the LSA search options, and **Figure 8.5** is an example of a page from the .pdf version of the September 2007 LSA. It indicates changes to several regulations in 16 C.F.R. Part 1211.

FIGURE 8.4   GPO ACCESS LSA SEARCH OPTIONS

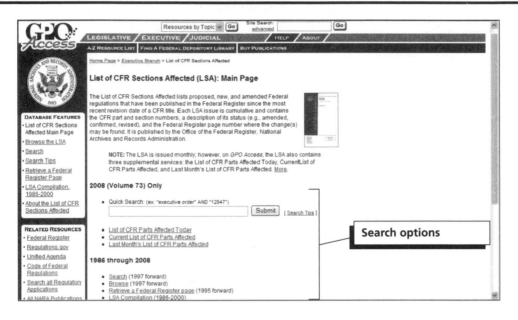

You can retrieve the *Federal Register* page by citation in the GPO Access *Federal Register* database (or in print[3]) and read about the change. **Figure 8.6** shows the page from the *Federal Register* with the change to 16 C.F.R. § 1211.14.

The second updating step requires you to use the Current List of CFR Parts Affected, which is listed as one of the LSA search options (see **Figure 8.4**). This table lists all of the C.F.R. Parts affected by notices published in the *Federal Register* during the current month and will update your research from the last day covered by the LSA until the present. Thus, if today's date were October 15, the Current List of CFR Parts Affected would contain updates since the September LSA, covering the period from October 1 through October 15. (In print, this information appears in a table called CFR Parts Affected that appears in the Reader's Aids section in back of each issue of the *Federal Register*. The print table is also cumulative for the current month.)

The table lists only the Parts affected by agency action, not individual sections. Therefore, if the table contains a reference to the C.F.R. Part you are researching, you need to retrieve the relevant page from the *Federal Register* to determine the section or sections within the C.F.R. Part affected by agency action. If the table does not list the Part you are

---

[3]Because the *Federal Register* is consecutively paginated throughout the year, locating an individual page number in print can be difficult. The LSA has a table in the back listing the range of page numbers contained in each daily issue. You can use this table to identify the precise day on which the change was reported in the *Federal Register*.

FIGURE 8.5   SEPTEMBER 2007 LIST OF CFR SECTIONS AFFECTED

CHANGES JANUARY 3, 2007 THROUGH SEPTEMBER 28, 2007

> The listing for Title 16 begins here.

osed Rules:

.....................................3083	
700—799 (Ch. VII) 50912	
740...8315	
744...31005	
772...31005	
806 ....52316, 53970	
922...40775	

TITLE 16—COMMERCIAL PRACTICES

Chapter I—Federal Trade Commission (Parts 0—999)

0.9 Revised 9434
0.20 Added 9434
4.10 (d) and (e) revised 28853
4.11 (j) added.................................28853
18.1 (c)(9) revised 902
305.2 Revised; eff. 2-29-08.............49965
305.3 (a)(1), (d) and (r) revised;
  eff. 2-29-08 49966
305.4 (a)(1), (b)(5) and (c) revised;
  eff. 2-29-08 49966
305.5 (a) revised; eff. 2-29-08.........49967
305.7 (a) and (b) revised; eff. 2-29-
  08 49967
305.8 (a)(1) revised; eff. 2-29-08........49967
305.9 Removed; eff. 2-29-08..............49967
305.10 Revised; eff. 2-29-08 49967
305.11 Revised; eff. 2-29-08 49967
305.12 Revised; eff. 2-29-08 49969
305.13 Redesignated as 305.19; eff.
  2-29-08 49971
305.14 Redesignated as 305.20;
  new 305.14 added; eff. 2-29-08
  49971
305.15 Redesignated as 305.21;
  new 305.15 added; eff. 2-29-08
  49971
305.16 Redesignated as 305.22; eff.
  2-29-08..................................49971
  Added; eff. 2-29-08 49973
305.17 Redesignated as 305.23; eff.
  2-29-08..................................49971
305.18 Redesignated as 305.24; eff.
  2-29-08..................................49971
305.19 Redesignated as 305.25; eff.
  2-29-08..................................49971
  (a)(1) revised; eff. 2-29-08.............49974
305.20 Redesignated from 305.14;
  eff. 2-29-09 49971
  Heading and (a) revised; (b),
  (c)(1)(i), (ii) introductory

text and (d) amended; eff. 2-
  29-08..49974
305.21 Redesignated from 305.15;
  eff. 2-29-08 49971
305.22 Redesignated from 305.16;
  eff. 2-29-08 49971
  Amended; eff. 2-29-08....................49974
305.23 Redesignated from 305.17;
  eff. 2-29-08 49971
305.24 Redesignated from 305.18;
  eff. 2-29-08 49971
305.25 Redesignated from 305.19;
  eff. 2-29-08 49971
  Removed; eff. 2-29-08....................49974
305 Appendix A1 revised; eff. 2-29-
  08 49974
  Appendices A2, A3 and A4 re-
  vised; eff. 2-29-08 49975
  Appendices A5 and A6 revised;
  eff. 2-29-08 49976
  Appendices A7, A8, and B1 re-
  vised; eff. 2-29-08 49977
  Appendices B2 and B3 revised;
  eff. 2-29-08 49978
  Appendices C1, C2 and D1
  through D5 revised; eff. 2-29-
  08..49979
  Appendices E, F1 and F2 re-
  vised; eff. 2-29-08 49981
  Appendices G1 through G8 re-
  vised; eff. 2-29-08 49982
  Appendices H, I, J1 and J2 re-
  vised; eff. 2-29-08 49983
  Appendix K revised
  L amended; eff. 2-
311.4 Revised..............
436 Revised ....
437 Added..................

> *Federal Register* pages with changes to regulations in Part 1211

Chapter II—Consumer Product Safety Commission (Parts 1000—1799)

1211.7 (a), (b), (f) and (g) revised;
  eff. 2–21–08 54817
1211.10 (a)(1) revised; (a)(6) added;
  eff. 2–21–08 54817
1211.13 (c) added; eff. 2–21–08 54817
1211.14 (b)(2) revised......................54818
1407 Added...................................1450
  Figures 1, 2 and 3 corrected 2184
1615.1 (c)(3) and Diagram 1 correctly amended........................13689
1615.4 (b)(1) and (d)(3)(i)(A) correctly amended........................13689

FIGURE 8.6 *FEDERAL REGISTER*, **SEPTEMBER 27, 2007**

Federal Register / Vol. 72, No. 187 / Thursday, September 27, 2007 / Rules and Regulations   **54817**

Pursuant to section 605(b) of the Regulatory Flexibility Act, 5 U.S.C. 605(b), in the NPR the Commission certified that this rule will not have a significant impact on a substantial number of small entities. The Commission also certified in the NPR that this rule will have no environmental impact.

Public Law 101–608 contains a preemption provision. It states: "those provisions of laws of States or political subdivisions which relate to the labeling of automatic residential garage door openers and those provisions which do not provide at least the equivalent degree of protection from the risk of [injury associated with automatic] openers as the [rule" are] [ ]der 15 U.S.C. [ ], section

The *Federal Register* entry contains the amendments to the regulations.

R Part 1211

Consumer protection, Imports, Labeling, Reporting and recordkeeping requirements.

■ Accordingly, 16 CFR part 1211 is amended as follows:

PART 1211—SAFETY STANDARDS FOR AUTOMATIC RESIDENTIAL GARAGE DOOR OPERATORS

■ 1. The authority citation for part 1211 continues to read as follows:

Authority: Sec. 203 of Pub. L. 101–608, 104 Stat. 3110; 15 U.S.C. 2063 and 2065.

■ 2. Section 1211.7 is amended by revising paragraphs (a), (b), (f) and (g) to read as follows:

§ 1211.7   Inherent entrapment protection requirements.

(a)(1) Other than for the first 1 foot (305mm) of door travel from the full upmost position both with and without any external entrapment protection device functional, the operator of a downward moving residential garage door shall initiate reversal of the door within 2 seconds of contact with the obstruction as specified in paragraph (b) of this section. After reversing the door, the operator shall return the door to, and stop at, the full upmost position. Compliance shall be determined in accordance with paragraphs (b) through (i) of this section.

(2) The door operator is not required to return the door to, and stop the door at, the full upmost position when the operator senses a second obstruction during the upward travel.

(3) The door operator is not required to return the door to, and stop the door at, the full upmost position when a control is actuated to stop the door

during the upward travel—but the door can not be moved downward until the operator reverses the door a minimum of 2 inches (50.8 mm).

(b)(1) A solid object is to be placed on the floor of the test installation and at various heights under the edge of the door and located in line with the driving point of the operator. When tested on the floor, the object shall be 1 inch (25.4 mm) high. In the test installation, the bottom edge of the door under the driving force of the operator is to be against the floor when the door is fully closed.

(2) For operators other than those attached to the door, a solid object is not required to be located in line with the driving point of the operator. The solid object is to be located at points at the center, and within 1 foot of each end of the door.

(3) To test operators for compliance with requirements in paragraphs (a)(3), (f)(3), and (g)(3) of this section, § 1211.10(a)(6)(iii), and § 1211.13(c), a solid rectangular object measuring 4 inches (102 mm) high by 6 inches (152 mm) wide by a minimum of 6 inches (152 mm)long is to be placed on the floor of the test installation to provide a 4-inch (102 mm) high obstruction when operated from a partially open position.

*   *   *   *   *

(f)(1) An operator, using an inherent entrapment protection system that monitors the actual position of the door, shall initiate reversal of the door and shall return the door to, and stop the door at, the full upmost position in the event the inherent door operating "profile" of the door differs from the originally set parameters. The entrapment protection system shall monitor the position of door at increments not greater than 1 inch (25.4 mm).

(2) The door operator is not required to return the door to, and stop the door at, the full upmost position when an inherent entrapment circuit senses an obstruction during the upward travel.

(3) The door operator is not required to return the door to, and stop the door at, the full upmost position when a control is actuated to stop the door during the upward travel—but the door can not be moved downward until the operator reverses the door a minimum of 2 inches (50.8 mm).

(g)(1) An operator, using an inherent entrapment protection system that does not monitor the actual position of the door, shall initiate reversal of the door and shall return the door to and stop the door at the full upmost position. when the lower limiting device is not actuated

in 30 seconds or less following the initiation of the close cycle.

(2) The door operator is not required to return the door to, and stop the door at, the full upmost position when an inherent entrapment circuit senses an obstruction during the upward travel. When the door is stopped manually during its descent, the 30 seconds shall be measured from the resumption of the close cycle.

(3) The door operator is not required to return the door to, and stop the door at, the full upmost position when a control is actuated to stop the door during the upward travel—but the door can not be moved downward until the operator reverses the door a minimum of 2 inches (50.8 mm). When the door is stopped manually during its descent, the 30 seconds shall be measured from the resumption of the close cycle.

■ 3. Section 1211.10 is amended by revising paragraph (a)(1) and adding a new paragraph (a)(6) to read as follows:

§ 1211.10   Requirements for all entrapment protection devices.

(a) General requirements. (1) An external entrapment protection device shall perform its intended function when tested in accordance with paragraphs (a)(2) through (4) and (6) of this section.

*   *   *   *   *

(6)(i) An operator using an external entrapment protection device, upon detecting a fault or an obstruction in the path of a downward moving door, shall initiate reversal and shall return the door to, and stop the door at, the full upmost position.

(ii) The door operator is not required to return the door to, and stop the door at, the full upmost position when an inherent entrapment circuit senses an obstruction during the upward travel.

(iii) The door operator is not required to return the door to, and stop the door at, the full upmost position when a control is actuated to stop the door during the upward travel—but the door can not be moved downward until the operator has reversed the door a minimum of 2 inches (50.8 mm).

■ 4. Section 1211.13 is amended by adding a new paragraph (c) to read as follows:

§ 1211.13   Inherent force activated secondary door sensors.

(a) * * *

(b) * * *

(c) Obstruction test. For a door traveling in the downward direction, when an inherent secondary entrapment protection device senses an obstruction and initiates a reversal, a control activation shall not move the door researching, your updating is complete. **Figure 8.7** shows a sample entry for Title 16 of the C.F.R. from the Current List of CFR Parts Affected.

The chart in **Figure 8.8** summarizes the process of updating C.F.R. research with official sources, using the example of a regulation within Title 16 of the C.F.R. published on January 2, 2007, an LSA dated September 30, 2007, and the Current List of CFR Parts Affected dated October 15, 2007.

FIGURE 8.7   SAMPLE ENTRY FROM THE CURRENT LIST OF CFR PARTS AFFECTED

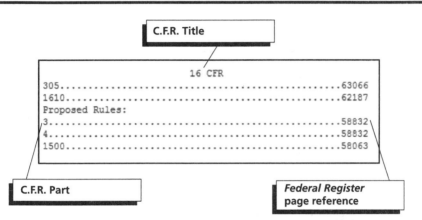

FIGURE 8.8   UPDATING C.F.R. RESEARCH USING OFFICIAL SOURCES

DATE	JANUARY 2, 2007	JANUARY 2, 2007– SEPTEMBER 30, 2007	OCTOBER 1, 2007– OCTOBER 15, 2007
Source	Title 16, C.F.R.	September 2007 List of CFR Sections Affected (LSA)	Current List of CFR Parts Affected (online) or CFR Parts Affected table in the print issue of the *Federal Register*
Use	Locate regulations in the C.F.R. Note the date of the C.F.R.	Use the latest monthly issue. Look up the Title and section number of the regulation. If it is listed, look up the page in the *Federal Register* to locate the change.	Use the current list online or the cumulative table in the back of the latest daily issue of the *Federal Register* in print. If the C.F.R. Part is not listed, no changes have taken place during the month to date. If the C.F.R. Part is listed, each page reference must be checked to see which individual sections have been affected.

D. CITING FEDERAL REGULATIONS

Citations to administrative materials are governed by Rule 19 in the *ALWD Manual* and Bluepages B6.1.4 and Rule 14.2 in the *Bluebook*. The citations are the same using either format.

A citation to the C.F.R. is very similar to a citation to a federal statute. It consists of the Title number, the abbreviation C.F.R., the pinpoint reference to the Part or section number, and a parenthetical containing the year. Here are two examples:

Title ←┐ ┌→ abbreviated name ┌→ year of the C.F.R. volume

16 C.F.R. pt. 1210 (2009).

abbreviation for Part ←┘ └→ Part number

Title ←┐ ┌→ abbreviated name ┌→ year of the C.F.R. volume

16 C.F.R. § 1210.2 (2009).

└→ section number

The preceding examples did not involve a regulation commonly known by name. If they had, the citation would have begun with the name of the regulation, pursuant to *ALWD Manual* Rule 19.1 and *Bluebook* Rule 14.2.

Citations to the *Federal Register* are also fairly simple and are the same using either the *ALWD Manual* or the *Bluebook*. They require the volume number, the abbreviation Fed. Reg., the page number, and a parenthetical containing the exact date.

volume ←┐ ┌→ abbreviated name ┌→ exact date

60 Fed. Reg. 7734 (Feb. 28, 1995).

└→ page number

If appropriate, you should also provide a pinpoint reference to the specific page or pages containing the cited material.

E. SAMPLE PAGES FOR FEDERAL ADMINISTRATIVE LAW RESEARCH

Beginning on the next page, **Figures 8.9** through **8.12** contain sample pages from the C.F.R. showing the process of researching regulations pertaining to safety standards for automatic garage door openers in GPO Access.

The first step is locating relevant regulations. You could use a subject index such as the CFR Index and Finding Aids, cross-references in statutory annotations, or a word search to locate relevant regulations. GPO Access allows you to view regulations in TEXT or PDF Format. Once you know the relevant part, you can use the outline of the Part to review the regulatory scheme.

FIGURE 8.9   16 C.F.R. PART 1211

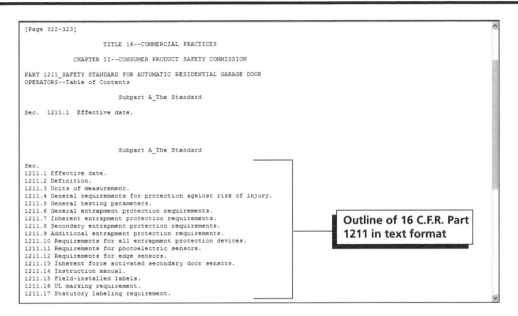

Outline of 16 C.F.R. Part 1211 in text format

The outline of the Part will direct you to specific regulations.

FIGURE 8.10   16 C.F.R. § 1211.14

```
               TITLE 16--COMMERCIAL PRACTICES

         CHAPTER II--CONSUMER PRODUCT SAFETY COMMISSION

PART 1211_SAFETY STANDARD FOR AUTOMATIC RESIDENTIAL GARAGE DOOR
OPERATORS--Table of Contents

                 Subpart A_The Standard

Sec.  1211.14  Instruction manual.

    (a) General. (1) A residential garage door operator shall be
provided with an instruction manual. The instruction manual shall give
complete instructions for the installation, operation, and user
maintenance of the operator.
    (2) Instructions that clearly detail installation and adjustment
procedures required to effect proper operation of the safety means
provided shall be provided with each door operator.
    (3) A residential garage door or door operator shall be provided
with complete and specific instructions for the correct adjustment of
the control mechanism and the need for periodic checking and, if needed,
adjustment of the control mechanism so as to maintain satisfactory
operation of the door.
    (4) The instruction manual shall include the important instructions
specified in paragraphs (b)(1) and (2) of this section. All required
text shall be legible and contrast with the background. Upper case
letters of required text shall be no less than \5/64\ inch (2.0 mm) high
and lower case letters shall be no less than \1/16\ inch (1.6 mm) high.
Heading such as ``Important Installation Instructions,'' ``Important
Safety Instructions,'' ``Save These Instructions'' and the words
``Warning--To reduce the risk of severe injury or death to persons:''
shall be in letters no less than \3/16\ inch (4.8 mm) high.
    (5) The instructions listed in paragraphs 1211.13(b)(1) and (2)
shall be in the exact words specified or shall be in equally definitive
terminology to those specified. No substitutes shall be used for the
word ``Warning.'' The items may be numbered. The first and last items
specified in paragraph (b)(2) of this section shall be first and last
```

```
respectively. Other important and precautionary items considered
appropriate by the manufacturer may be inserted.
    (6) The instructions listed in paragraph (b)(1) of this section
shall be located immediately prior to the installation instructions. The
instructions listed in paragraph (b)(2) of this section shall be located
immediately prior to user operation and maintenance instructions. In
each case, the instructions shall be separate in format from other
detailed instructions related to installation, operation and maintenance
of the operator. All instructions, except installation instructions,
shall be a permanent part of the manual(s).
    (b) Specific required instructions. (1) The Installation
Instructions shall include the following instructions:

[[Page 337]]

             Important Installation Instructions

    Warning--To reduce the risk of severe injury or death:
    1. Read and follow all Installation Instructions.
    2. Install only a properly balanced garage door. An improperly
balanced door could cause severe injury. Have a qualified service person
make repairs to cables, spring assemblies and other hardware before
installing opener.
    3. Remove all ropes and remove or make inoperative all locks
connected to the garage door before installing opener.
    4. Where possible, install door opener 7 feet or more above the
floor. For products requiring an emergency release, mount the emergency
release 6 feet above the floor.
    5. Do not connect opener to source of power until instructed to do
so.
    6. Locate control button: (a) within sight of door, (b) at a minimum
height of 5 feet so small children cannot reach it, and (c) away from
all moving parts of the door.
    7. Install Entrapment Warning Label next to the control button in a
prominent location. Install the Emergency Release Marking. Attach the
marking on or next to the emergency release.
    8. After installing opener, the door must reverse when it contacts a
```

You can update C.F.R. research in GPO Access using the electronic versions of the LSA, the Current List of CFR Parts Affected, and the *Federal Register*. You can also use the unofficial e-CFR to find regulatory changes.

FIGURE 8.11 e-CFR SEARCH SCREEN AND RESULTS

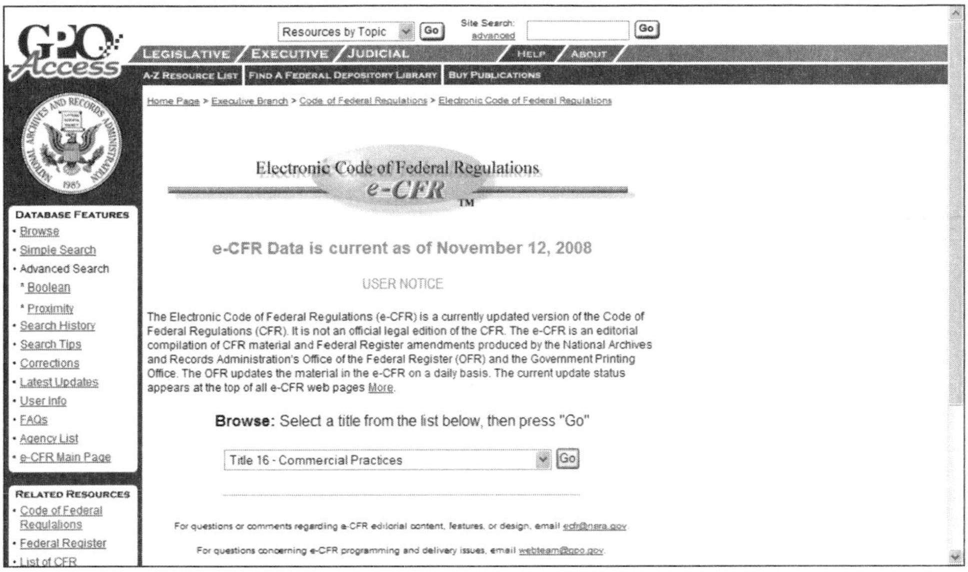

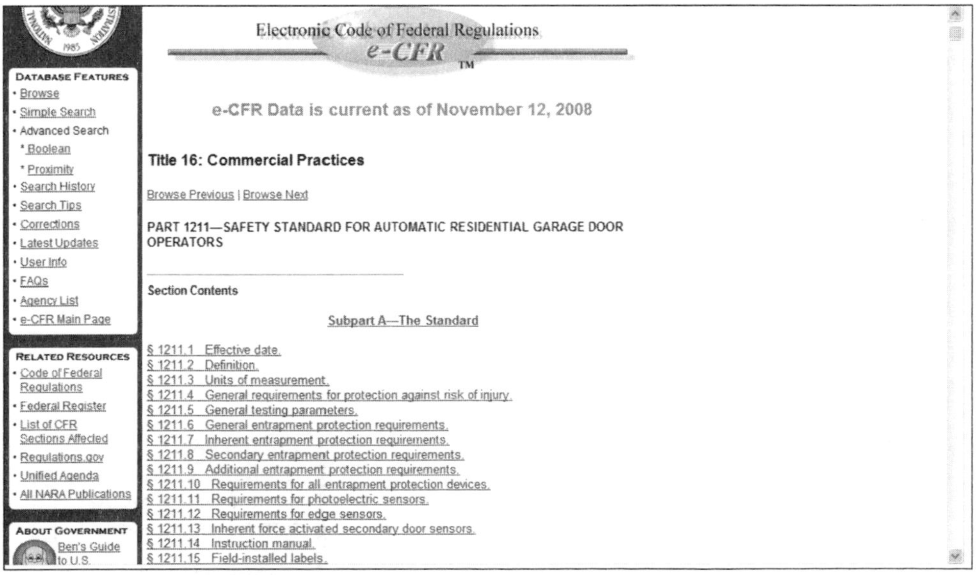

The regulation is displayed in textual form. At the end of the regulation, you will find a reference to the change to the regulation that appears in the *Federal Register*.

FIGURE 8.12   EXCERPT FROM THE e-CFR VERSION OF 16 C.F.R. § 1211.14

Federal Register reference indicating a change to the regulation on September 27, 2007

F. CHECKLIST FOR FEDERAL ADMINISTRATIVE LAW RESEARCH

1. LOCATE PERTINENT REGULATIONS

❏ Use the cross-references to the C.F.R. in the annotations in U.S.C.S. and U.S.C.A.

❏ Use a subject index, such as the CFR Index and Finding Aids.

❏ Use Westlaw to locate an annotated version of the C.F.R.

- Search by subject using an electronic index search with the RegulationsPlus index or by browsing the C.F.R. table of contents.
- Execute word searches in the database for the C.F.R. or specific subject areas.

❏ Use LexisNexis.

- Search by subject by browsing the table of contents.
- Execute word searches in the source for the C.F.R. or specific subject areas.

❏ Use GPO Access or other Internet sites to locate regulations by browsing the table of contents or executing word searches.

2. UPDATE GPO ACCESS RESEARCH WITH THE e-CFR

❏ Compare the official C.F.R. text with the e-CFR version to determine whether the regulation has been amended; locate *Federal Register* notices as necessary for an official citation or additional information.

3. UPDATE C.F.R. RESEARCH USING OFFICIAL SOURCES

❏ Use the same process to update official sources in print or electronically.

❏ To update from the date of the C.F.R. volume through the end of the prior month, look up the regulation in the most recent List of CFR Sections Affected (LSA) to locate page numbers in the *Federal Register* reflecting changes to the regulation.

- Look up the *Federal Register* page containing the change and read the information to see how it affects the regulation.

❏ To update from the end of the prior month to the present, use the cumulative Current List of CFR Parts Affected (electronically) or table of CFR Parts Affected (in the back of each print issue of the *Federal Register*).

- If the Part in which the section appears is listed, look up each page number referenced in the table to see if the section has been affected.

4. **CONTACT THE AGENCY FOR ADDITIONAL INFORMATION ON RECENT OR PROPOSED REGULATORY CHANGES**

5. **USE SHEPARD'S IN LEXISNEXIS OR KEYCITE IN WESTLAW TO LOCATE RESEARCH REFERENCES**

Subject-Matter Service Research

A. Introduction to subject-matter services

B. Researching subject-matter services in print, CD-ROM, and Internet formats

C. Subject-matter research in LexisNexis and Westlaw

D. Citing subject-matter services

E. Sample pages for subject-matter service research

F. Checklist for subject-matter service research

A. INTRODUCTION TO SUBJECT-MATTER SERVICES

Many research tools are organized by type of authority and jurisdiction. Some, however, are organized by subject. They may contain only one type of authority, such as cases, but include authority from many jurisdictions. Alternatively, they may collect multiple types of authority from multiple jurisdictions in a defined subject area. These services may also compile information not available in other sources, including cases not reported in general case reporters or news and analysis in the field not available elsewhere. As a consequence, if you are researching an area of law for which subject-matter services are available, complete research requires that you consult them.

Unlike the other chapters in this book, this chapter will not take you step-by-step through the process of using different types of subject-matter services. Subject-matter services are published by many different commercial publishers. As a consequence, no uniform method of organization or research process applies to all of them. Instead, each one contains its own explanation of how to use the service. This chapter, therefore, focuses on more general information about these resources, rather than on step-by-step instructions. The sample pages in Section E show the process for researching materials relating to the Americans with Disabilities Act so you can see how one of these services is organized.

1. OVERVIEW OF SUBJECT-MATTER SERVICES

Subject-matter research services are often called "looseleaf" services. This is because many of them are actually published in looseleaf binders. By putting the information in a binder, the publisher is able to update individual pages or sections as necessary. Not all services are published in binders, however. They are available in many formats, including bound print volumes, CD-ROMs, and Internet databases. Thus, this chapter refers to them as subject-matter services, rather than looseleaf services.

A subject-matter service may contain some or all of the following types of information:

- news or analysis of current events in the field
- statutory material, including
    federal statutes
    state statutes
    legislative history of pertinent statutes
- administrative materials, including
    federal regulations and agency decisions
    state regulations and agency decisions
- cases, including
    federal cases
    state cases

A few subject-matter services contain all of this information, but most contain some combination of these items. Some, but by no means all, of the areas for which subject-matter services are available include environmental law, tax, bankruptcy, government contracts, intellectual property, employment and labor law, and securities law. Some of the best known publishers of subject-matter services are the Bureau of National Affairs (BNA), CCH, Inc. (CCH), Clark Boardman Callaghan (CBC), Matthew Bender (MB), Pike & Fischer (P & F), and Research Institute of America (RIA).

The statutes, regulations, and legislative history documents contained in a subject-matter service could be located through other resources, such as an annotated code or LexisNexis Congressional. The advantage of the subject-matter service, however, is that it compiles all of this information in one place, which makes using it easier and more efficient than researching each item individually. This is especially true because many subject-matter services focus on complex, highly regulated areas of the law for which it might be difficult to compile all of the relevant information.

Many of the cases in a subject-matter service could also be located through digests or other general legal research resources, but again, the compilation of material from many different jurisdictions makes the subject-matter service easier to use. In addition, some of the opinions reported in the service may not be reported elsewhere, so the service may give you access to cases you would not have been able to locate in other sources.

In short, subject-matter services are portals to different types of authority in a defined subject area. Because they provide a single entry point for accessing multiple forms of authority and can include authority not published elsewhere, subject-matter services are an invaluable research tool.

2. LOCATING SUBJECT-MATTER SERVICES

Locating a subject-matter service is not unlike locating a treatise—it is much easier to find if you already know what you are looking for. The difficult part is figuring out whether a subject-matter service exists for your research issue when you have not previously conducted research in that area of law.

One quick place to check for subject-matter services is the *Bluebook*. Table T.15 contains an alphabetical list of some of the more commonly used services.

Another place to look is in a directory of subject-matter services. Two that are especially helpful are *Legal Looseleafs in Print* and *Directory of Law-Related CD-ROMs*, both of which are compiled and edited by Arlene L. Eis. These reference books list subject-matter services by publisher, title, and subject. Both of these publications, plus a third publication entitled *Legal Newsletters in Print*, are indexed electronically in a subscription service called LawTRIO. If your library subscribes to this service, you should be able to access it from the library's network. Once you identify a pertinent subject-matter service from one of these directories, you can locate it using your library's online catalog or network.

B. RESEARCHING SUBJECT-MATTER SERVICES IN PRINT, CD-ROM, AND INTERNET FORMATS

Although no uniform process applies to using subject-matter services, this section provides some general information that may help you get started with your research.

1. PRINT RESOURCES

In print form, most subject-matter services have a section at the beginning of the binder or in the front of a bound volume entitled "Overview" or "How to use this service." This section should first explain the scope of the service. Does it contain statutes, cases, news bulletins, or some combination of materials? Knowing the scope will help you determine how the service fits with your overall research strategy. This section should also explain how to find and update material within the service, and some contain sample research problems illustrating the research process. Subject-matter services that contain cases are often organized in a digest format similar to the format of West digests, although they do not use the West topic and key number system. Regardless of how they are organized, however, all subject-matter services have some type of indexing method that you can use to locate information.

2. CD-ROM AND INTERNET RESOURCES

Some subject-matter services are available in CD-ROM format. A growing number of publishers are also making their products available through subscriptions to databases available via the Internet.

Your library may have special terminals for using CD-ROM resources, or these services may be accessible through the library's network. Internet services should also be accessible through the library's network, although you may need a password to retrieve information. A reference librarian will be able to give you instructions for accessing the Internet version of any subject-matter service available at your library.

As with the print versions of these services, the CD-ROM and Internet versions vary in their scope, organization, and searching options. Like other electronic research tools, they require you to execute searches to retrieve information contained within the database. Chapter 10 explains general techniques that you can use to search effectively in CD-ROM and Internet subject-matter services. Accordingly, you may want to review Chapter 10 in conjunction with this chapter. Whenever you use a CD-ROM or Internet subject-matter service for the first time, you should plan to spend some time reviewing the search tips, FAQ, or help function to use the features of the service effectively.

C. SUBJECT-MATTER RESEARCH IN LEXISNEXIS AND WESTLAW

Both LexisNexis and Westlaw have databases devoted to subject areas of the law. You will find them in the LexisNexis source directory under "Area of Law—By Topic" and in the Westlaw directory under "Topical

Practice Areas." These databases allow you to search cases, statutes, regulations, secondary sources, and other materials in a subject area, instead of by jurisdiction. Once within the database for a subject area, you can limit your search to a particular jurisdiction. Thus, for example, if you were to select the database for Labor & Employment, you could search all jurisdictions in that subject area, or you could choose to search only materials for an individual state. In addition, some of the subject-matter services published by BNA, CCH, and other publishers are available in the LexisNexis and Westlaw subject-area databases.

D. CITING SUBJECT-MATTER SERVICES

Citations to subject-matter services contain the same elements using either the *ALWD Manual* or the *Bluebook*, although as noted below, abbreviations for some items within the citation will vary depending on which format you use. In the *ALWD Manual*, subject-matter service citations are governed by Rule 28, and in the *Bluebook*, they are governed by Rule 19.

A citation to a subject-matter service consists of six components: (1) the title of the item; (2) the volume of the service; (3) the abbreviated title of the service; (4) the abbreviated name of the publisher of the service in parentheses; (5) the pinpoint reference to the subdivision in the service where the cited item begins; and (6) a parenthetical containing the date and, for case citations, the jurisdiction and level of court deciding the case. The *ALWD Manual* always requires the exact date of the item. The *Bluebook* requires the exact date for items from a looseleaf service, but just the year for items from a bound service. When citing cases, be sure to refer to the rules for case citations, as well as those for subject-matter services.

The following example shows how to cite a case reported in *Americans with Disabilities Cases*, a subject-matter service, in *ALWD Manual* format.

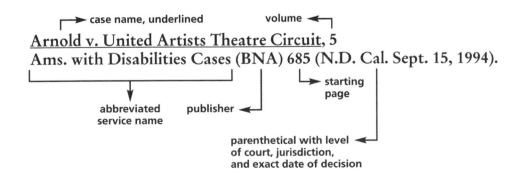

Determining the abbreviated name of the service requires you to use Appendix 3 in the *ALWD Manual*. For the example above, Appendix 3 abbreviates "American" (singular) as "Am." but directs you to add an "s" to form an abbreviation of the plural form of the word. Appendix 3 does not abbreviate any other words in the title of the service. Thus, the service is cited as Ams. with Disabilities Cases.

Using the *Bluebook*, the citation is similar, but not identical. The name of the service is abbreviated slightly differently. Also, because *Americans with Disabilities Cases* is a bound service, only the year is necessary for the date:

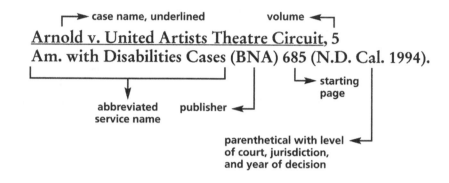

Determining the proper abbreviation for the name of the service requires you to use two Tables. Rule 19 refers you to Table T.15, which contains abbreviations for commonly used services. *Americans with Disabilities Cases* is not listed in Table T.15. If a publication does not appear in Table T.15, Rule 19.1 directs you to use the periodical abbreviations in Table T.13 to determine the abbreviation for the service. Table T.13 abbreviates "Americans" (plural) as "Am." Table T.13 does not abbreviate any other words in the title of the service. Thus, the service can be abbreviated as Am. with Disabilities Cases.

E. SAMPLE PAGES FOR SUBJECT-MATTER SERVICE RESEARCH

Figures 9.1 through **9.5** illustrate some of the features in an electronic subject-matter service, the Labor and Employment Law Library published by BNA. This service contains, among other items, news, federal labor and employment statutes, federal regulations, state labor and employment laws, practice tools, and labor and employment cases from federal and state courts and administrative agencies. You can retrieve authorities in this service's database from their citations.

You can also search the electronic index, browse by topic, or execute word searches to research any of these sources.

BNA publishes reporters devoted to labor and employment cases (such as *Americans with Disabilities Cases*, which BNA abbreviates as A.D. Cases) and has its own digesting system for organizing summaries of the cases by subject. BNA's subject headings are called "classifications," and each classification is assigned a number. Cases published in BNA labor and employment reporters have headnotes, and each headnote is assigned a classification number. Therefore, case research with this service is similar to West digest research. If you find a case on point, you can use the classification numbers in the headnotes to find additional cases. You can also search or browse the classification numbers. The Labor and Employment Law Library provides electronic access to the cases published in BNA reporters, as well as to the classification number system.

The sample pages that follow show some of the search options in the Labor and Employment Law Library, as well as the format of a case published in the A.D. Cases reporter.

The introductory screen for BNA's Labor and Employment Law Library shows the resources available and the search options.

FIGURE 9.1   INTRODUCTORY SCREEN, BNA LABOR AND EMPLOYMENT LAW LIBRARY

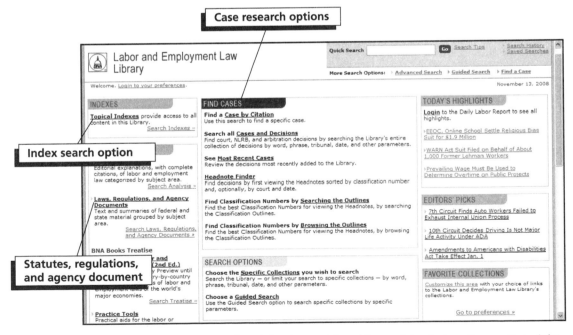

Reproduced with permission from *BNA's* Labor & Employment Law Library, Introductory Screen. Copyright 2008 by The Bureau of National Affairs, Inc. (800-372-1033), http://www.bna.com.

You can browse statutory and regulatory outlines and view the full text of relevant provisions. You can also locate technical assistance documents that explain the law.

FIGURE 9.2   EXCERPT FROM 49 C.F.R. 38.161 FROM BNA LABOR AND EMPLOYMENT LAW LIBRARY

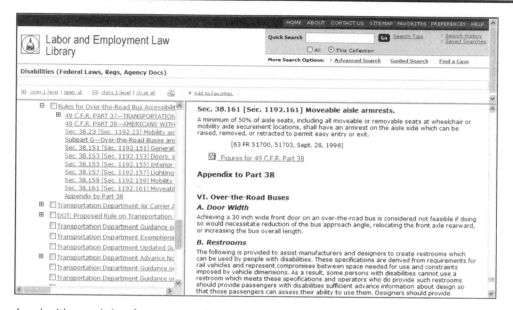

Reproduced with permission from *BNA's* Labor & Employment Law Library, excerpt from 49 C.F.R. 38.161. Copyright 2008 by The Bureau of National Affairs, Inc. (800-372-1033), http://www.bna.com.

FIGURE 9.3   EXCERPT FROM E.E.O.C. TECHNICAL ASSISTANCE FOR EMPLOYERS FROM BNA LABOR AND EMPLOYMENT LAW LIBRARY

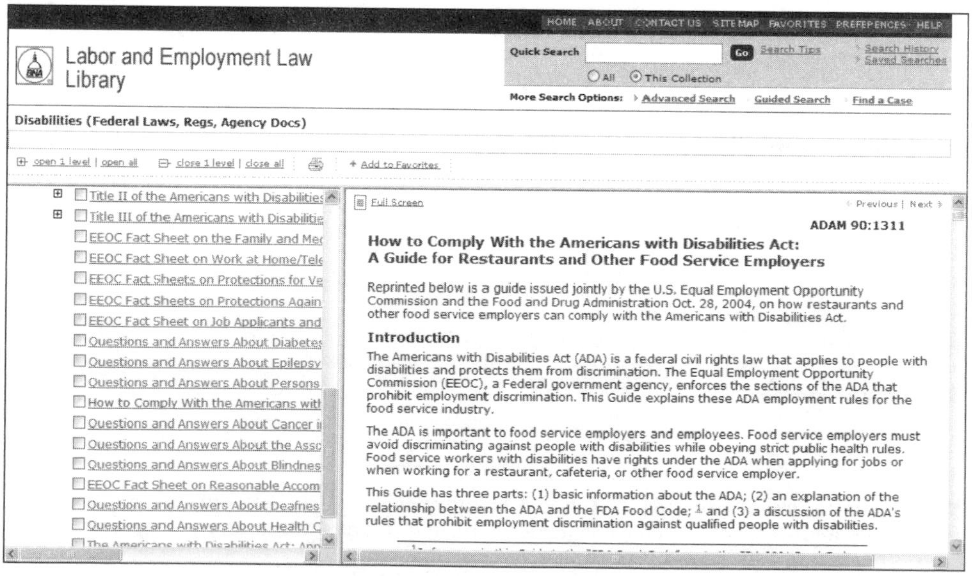

Reproduced with permission from *BNA's* Labor & Employment Law Library, excerpt from E.E.O.C. Technical Assistance for Employers. Copyright 2008 by The Bureau of National Affairs, Inc. (800-372-1033), http://www.bna.com.

You have several options for researching cases. One option is browsing the outline of classification numbers. Selecting a classification number retrieves summaries of relevant cases, and selecting a case retrieves the full text.

FIGURE 9.4   CLASSIFICATION NUMBER OUTLINE BY TOPIC FROM BNA LABOR AND EMPLOYMENT LAW LIBRARY

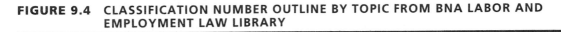

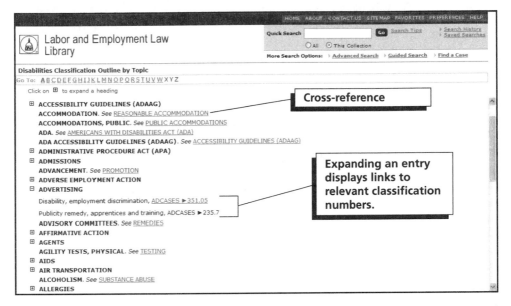

Reproduced with permission from *BNA's* Labor & Employment Law Library, Classification Number Outline by Topic. Copyright 2008 by The Bureau of National Affairs, Inc. (800-372-1033), http://www.bna.com.

FIGURE 9.5   CLASSIFICATION NUMBER DIGEST AND FULL TEXT OF A CASE FROM BNA LABOR AND EMPLOYMENT LAW LIBRARY

Reproduced with permission from *BNA's* Labor & Employment Law Library Classification Number Digest and Full Text of a Case. Copyright 2008 by The Bureau of National Affairs, Inc. (800-372-1033), http://www.bna.com.

F. CHECKLIST FOR SUBJECT-MATTER SERVICE RESEARCH

1. LOCATE A SUBJECT-MATTER SERVICE FOR YOUR RESEARCH ISSUE

❐ Look in Table T.15 in the back of the *Bluebook*.

❐ Check a reference source such as the LawTRIO database or print sources such as *Legal Looseleafs in Print* or *Directory of Law-Related CD-ROMs*.

❐ Locate subject area databases in LexisNexis and Westlaw.

2. DETERMINE HOW TO USE THE SERVICE

❐ In print services, look for the "Overview" or "How to use this service" section.

❐ In CD-ROM and Internet services, follow the service's instructions for locating information.

❐ In LexisNexis and Westlaw, execute word searches or use other available search options.

CHAPTER 10

ELECTRONIC LEGAL RESEARCH

A. Introduction to electronic legal research

B. Conducting effective electronic legal research

C. Additional electronic research resources

D. Citing authority obtained from electronic legal research services

E. Sample pages for electronic legal research

F. Checklist for electronic legal research

As Chapter 1 explains, legal research can be accomplished using both print and electronic research tools. Frequently, you will use some combination of these tools in completing a research project. Although print and electronic resources are often used together, this chapter introduces you to some search techniques unique to electronic research. Earlier chapters discussed both print and electronic research in the context of individual types of authority, such as cases or statutes. This chapter explains some of the basics of electronic searching that can be used effectively in a number of services, regardless of the type of authority you need to locate. In doing so, it focuses on research in Westlaw and LexisNexis, two of the most commonly available commercial services containing a wide variety of legal authority. Although Westlaw and LexisNexis are featured in this chapter, they are only two of many electronic research services available, and you should be able to adapt the techniques described here to other electronic research services.

This chapter describes electronic search techniques in general terms and provides few specific commands for executing them. Electronic research providers update their services regularly, thus making it impossible to describe commands with any accuracy. In fact, you will likely receive training through your law school on the use of at least Westlaw and LexisNexis, if not other electronic services, and those training sessions will cover the commands necessary to execute the functions in those services.

In addition, any electronic service you use will have a help function, search tips, or other instructions explaining how to execute search commands. A single instruction session on any electronic service cannot convey all of the nuances involved in researching with it, so you should plan to review additional instructional material for any electronic service you learn to use.

A. INTRODUCTION TO ELECTRONIC LEGAL RESEARCH

1. OVERVIEW OF ELECTRONIC LEGAL RESEARCH SERVICES

Electronic legal research services can be divided into three categories. Fee-based services charge individual users a fee every time the service is used. Subscription services charge the subscriber for access, but individual users ordinarily are not charged for researching with the service. Publicly available services are those available for free on the Internet. Appendix A contains the Internet addresses for a number of publicly available research sites, including those discussed in this chapter and elsewhere in this text. A brief overview of some popular electronic legal research services follows.

a. Fee-Based Services

WESTLAW AND LEXISNEXIS. As noted earlier, Westlaw and LexisNexis are two of the most commonly available electronic services for conducting legal research. Both of these services contain the full text of a broad range of primary and secondary authorities.

LOISLAW. Loislaw is similar to Westlaw and LexisNexis, in that it contains the full text of many legal authorities. It also contains treatises on a number of subjects and has its own citator service, GlobalCite. Although Loislaw has less comprehensive coverage than either Westlaw or Lexis-Nexis, it can be a cost-effective alternative to those services if it contains the information you need. Loislaw is available on the Internet.

VERSUSLAW. VersusLaw is similar to Loislaw. It also offers access to the full text of a range of legal authorities, and like Loislaw, it can be a cost-effective alternative to Westlaw and LexisNexis. As of this writing, however, its coverage is also less comprehensive than that of Westlaw and LexisNexis. VersusLaw is available on the Internet.

b. Subscription Services

INDEX TO LEGAL PERIODICALS AND LEGALTRAC. These are index services, meaning that they will generate lists of citations to authority. Although they primarily provide citations to legal periodicals, they also provide access to the full text of selected documents. These services are described in more detail in Chapter 3.

HEINONLINE. This service provides access to a wide range of authorities, including legal periodicals and other secondary sources; legislative documents, including compiled legislative histories; administrative materials, including the C.F.R. and *Federal Register*; and some international materials. HeinOnline's databases go back further in time than those of some other services. In addition, it provides access to documents in .pdf format. This service is described in more detail in Chapter 3, on secondary source research, and Chapter 7, on federal legislative history research.

LEXISNEXIS CONGRESSIONAL. This service is available at many law libraries. LexisNexis Congressional contains a wealth of legislative information, including federal statutes, congressional documents generated during the legislative process, administrative regulations, and news about activities taking place on Capitol Hill. This service is described in more detail in Chapter 7, on federal legislative history research.

SUBJECT-MATTER SERVICES. Chapter 9 discusses research in defined subject areas of the law using specialized subject-matter services. A number of subject-matter services are available electronically, either on the Internet or in CD-ROM format. The techniques for drafting searches described in this chapter can be used effectively in many electronic subject-matter services.

c. Publicly Available Services

WEB SITES OPERATED BY GOVERNMENT OR PRIVATE ENTITIES. Government web sites can provide access to local, state, and federal legal information. Some examples of useful sites for federal law include Thomas, which is maintained by the Library of Congress, and GPO Access, a site operated by the Government Printing Office. These services are described in Chapters 7 and 8. Many courts also maintain web sites where they publish the full text of opinions, local court rules, and other useful information. In addition, web sites operated by trade, civic, educational, or other groups may provide useful information in their specialized fields.

LEGAL RESEARCH WEB SITES. A number of Internet sites collect legal information, and these can be useful research sources. Examples of legal research web sites include FindLaw and American Law Sources Online. In addition, several law schools have developed "virtual law library" sites, such as Cornell Law School's Legal Information Institute.

INTERNET SEARCH ENGINES. A general search engine such as Google is not likely to be an effective tool for locating individual legal authorities. It may, however, help you locate government, educational, legal research, or other web sites with useful information. LawCrawler is a search engine that limits its searches to law-related web sites, and MetaCrawler searches multiple search engines simultaneously.

2. COMPARISON OF ELECTRONIC AND PRINT SEARCH TECHNIQUES

Before you undertake the process of electronic research, you need to assess the search options available to you. As Chapter 1 explains, three common research techniques are retrieving a document from its citation, searching by subject, and word searching. This section explains each of these search techniques in the context of electronic searching and compares them with analogous print research techniques.

If you have a citation to a document contained in an electronic service's database, you can retrieve it using its citation. There is not much difference from a process perspective between retrieving a document in print or electronically using its citation. Your decision about how to obtain the document will probably turn on other considerations. Print resources can be more economical to use and easier to read than electronic resources. In addition, many secondary sources are only available in print. By contrast, electronic resources can be more up to date than print materials and can give you access to documents unavailable in your library's print collection.

Most electronic search services offer a couple of options for subject searching. Browsing a publication's table of contents is one way to search by subject. Often you can follow links, or drill down, through a publication's table of contents to view the text of individual sections of the document. Table of contents searching usually is not available for every publication in a service's database, but statutory codes, regulations, and selected secondary sources can often be searched this way. Again, from a process perspective, there is not much difference between browsing a table of contents in print and browsing it electronically.

Another option for searching by subject is to use a directory of subject headings created by the service's editors. With this technique, you ordinarily select a subject from an alphabetical menu of topics and then select the source or type of authority that you want to search for information on the subject. To select a subject, you can drill down through menu options for general subjects to more specific subtopics. If you do not know which subject is most relevant to your research, many services will allow you to execute a search within the menu options to identify relevant subjects or subtopics. After you drill down through the menu options, you will often also have the choice of adding a word search to further refine the search. The print search technique most comparable to searching an electronic directory of subject headings is browsing digest topics. (Digests are explained in Chapter 4, on case research.) In fact, browsing digest topics online is a common form of electronic subject searching.

Using a directory of subject headings can be an effective search technique when you know the general subject area you want to search. In addition, you can often search several publications simultaneously online, whereas with print research you must search one publication at a time. You should be aware, however, that many services will not allow you to search for all types of authority in this way. You may be limited to searching for cases and selected secondary sources. Therefore, if you need to search for a type of authority that is not searchable through the subject directory, you will need to use a different search technique.

A third subject searching option is to use an electronic index. Of course, some services, such as the *Index to Legal Periodicals*, are simply electronic indices. Most full-text services do not provide access to indices, but electronic index searching for certain types of authority (such as statutes) is becoming more common. An index is usually more detailed than a table of contents and will provide cross-references if the information you need is listed under a different heading than one you have chosen. An index can also be a good way to find information on concepts that are too general to be useful as word searches. From a process perspective, there is little difference between print and electronic index searching.

Electronic word searching is available for virtually any source contained in an electronic service's database. Word searching differs from subject searching. Subject searching tools are organized around subjects or concepts, rather than individual words in a document, whereas word searches locate documents based on individual terms, rather than by subject. Obviously, there is a fair amount of overlap between subjects or concepts and the words used to express them, and some print index entries are generated from specific terms or key words within a document. Nevertheless, electronic word searching and subject searching are not identical. Word searching, of course, is available only electronically. If you want to locate documents that contain specific terms, you should use an electronic word search.

Successful researchers do not limit themselves either to print or electronic research to complete a research project. Understanding how print and electronic search techniques compare will help you determine the mix of research tools appropriate for your research project.

3. Overview of the Electronic Research Process

Electronic research, like print research, is a process. You need to follow an organized plan to research effectively using electronic research tools. Effective electronic searching usually involves the following four steps.

a. Selecting a Service

You want to choose the service or services most likely to contain the information you need. In addition, although you may not be concerned with the cost of research while you are in law school, in practice, selecting a cost-effective service is also an important consideration.

b. Selecting a Search Technique

Once you have selected a service, you will probably have several options for searching for authority, including citation, subject, and word searching. To search effectively, you must decide which method is most likely to retrieve the information you need. If you decide to use a word search, you will also need to construct a query that will retrieve the information you need.

c. Selecting a Database in Which to Execute a Search

After you select a search technique (and construct a word search if necessary), you are ready to sign on to a service and execute a search. Most of the time, you will not search through the entire contents of the service. The majority of services divide their contents into databases based on subjects, such as torts or criminal law, or on the sources of information they contain, such as federal cases or cases from an individual state. These databases may be called databases, but they may also have other names, such as sources, libraries, files, infobases, or something similar. To retrieve information, you will need to select a database in which to execute the search.

d. Reviewing the Search Results

Once you have executed a search, you will need to manipulate the results in a way that allows you to determine whether the search has been successful. You may need to view a list of documents retrieved, read the text of individual documents, find specific terms within a document, or use links to other documents. You may also need to refine the search to improve the search results.

Following these steps is not always a linear process. You might decide first on your search technique, which could influence the service you select. Even if you follow the steps in order initially, you may repeat some of them based on the search results. For example, after reviewing your search results, you might go back to the second step and select a different search technique. A single search is unlikely to retrieve exactly the desired information, except when you are retrieving a document you need from its citation. One provider offers the following explanation of the search process in the context of word searching:

> Searching is a process, not an event. This should be your mantra when using [electronic research services]. Searching . . . is not about spending time and mental energy formulating the "golden query" that retrieves your desired information in a single stroke. In practice, good online searching involves formulating a succession of queries until you are satisfied with the results. As you view results from one search, you will come across additional leads that you did not identify in your original search. You can incorporate these new terms into your existing query or create a new one. After each query, evaluate its success by asking:
>
> - Did I find what I was looking for?
> - What better information could still be out there?
> - How can I refine my query to find better information?
>
> Issuing multiple queries can be frustrating or rewarding, depending on how long it takes you to identify the key material you need to answer your research problem.[1]

Sections B and C below discuss the electronic research process in greater detail. Section B discusses how to conduct electronic research effectively. Section C discusses some additional electronic research tools that may be useful for specific types of electronic research.

B. CONDUCTING EFFECTIVE ELECTRONIC LEGAL RESEARCH

1. SELECTING AN ELECTRONIC LEGAL RESEARCH SERVICE

Because many electronic legal research services exist, you must determine which service or services you should consult for your research project. Two important considerations are scope and cost.

The scope of the service is clearly a paramount consideration. You want to be sure to choose a service that contains the type of material you need. The more you know about your research issue, the easier this will be. For example, if you know you need to retrieve a United States

---

[1]VersusLaw, Inc. Research Manual, Part 1, Electronic Searching Strategy, http://www. versuslaw.com; *select* FAQ/Help, Research Manual, Research Manual, Part 1—Search Basics (accessed June 28, 2008).

Supreme Court case from the last term, you could research in Westlaw, LexisNexis, Loislaw, VersusLaw, or a publicly available legal research site containing Supreme Court decisions. If you know you need to research federal administrative regulations, you could research in Westlaw, LexisNexis, Loislaw, VersusLaw, LexisNexis Congressional, or GPO Access. Conversely, if you do not know the precise jurisdiction or type of authority you need, you might limit yourself to Westlaw or LexisNexis because those services contain a broad range of authorities.

After you have identified services with the proper scope of information, you should consider the cost of use. The cost of electronic research is something you might not notice as a law student because most, if not all, of the cost is subsidized. In practice, however, cost is an important consideration. You cannot use research services for which your client cannot or will not pay. Even if your client is willing and able to pay for some electronic research, you may not have unlimited ability to use fee-based services.

Of course, just because a service is fee-based does not mean it is a bad research option. It can be less expensive to locate authority through a fee-based service than it is to purchase books that would rarely be used, and some tasks can be accomplished more quickly through electronic research. In those situations, increased efficiency can justify the cost of using a fee-based service. You should not shy away from fee-based services simply because using them costs money. You should, however, be aware of cost issues and select the most cost-effective research options for your client, whether they are print or electronic, fee-based or free of charge.

It is difficult to generalize about the cost of fee-based services because many pricing options exist. Generally speaking, use of Westlaw and LexisNexis will result in the most direct expense to your client. Some large organizations negotiate flat rates for use of these services. But rates are based on the amount of usage, and law firms still pass on the costs to clients. Charges can also be based on the amount of time spent online, the number of searches executed, or both. Premiums may be charged for accessing certain sources, especially those containing multiple types of authority, and separate charges for printing or downloading information also may apply. Loislaw and VersusLaw charge for use of their services as well, but their rates are generally lower than those for Westlaw and LexisNexis. Therefore, if the scope of information available in one of those services is sufficient to meet your research needs, you might choose one of them over Westlaw or LexisNexis.

Because pricing varies widely among fee-based services, it is important to investigate cost issues before you get online. Regardless of the method of billing, efficient searching can reduce the cost associated with the use of fee-based services. Cost-cutting strategies for searching efficiently in Westlaw and LexisNexis are discussed below. These strategies can be used when searching in other fee-based services as well.

Subscription and publicly available services are economical choices for your client if they will give you the information you need. Although charges for access to subscription services are usually paid by the subscriber, rather than the user, users can be charged for printing or downloading information. Publicly available services on the Internet are the least expensive option because they involve only the cost of access to the Internet.

If scope and cost do not dictate which service you should use, use the service with which you are most familiar. The more familiar you become with a service, the more comfortable you will feel using it and the more efficient you will be. Although you should try to gain experience using as many services as possible while you are in law school, you may find in practice that you gravitate toward those services that meet your research needs on a regular basis.

Once you have selected a service, you are ready to begin searching for information. As noted earlier, you can retrieve a document from its citation, search by subject, or execute a word search. If you search by subject, you may be able to refine your search by adding word search terms. Because word searching is the most technically complex way to search, it is discussed in detail below. To locate information using a word search, you will need to construct a search, select a database in which to execute the search, and review the results. The following sections discuss each of these steps. After the discussion of the steps necessary for effective word searching, you will find additional techniques for effective Westlaw and LexisNexis research.

2. CONSTRUCTING A WORD SEARCH

A word search searches for the terms in your query and retrieves documents containing those terms. Most electronic services recognize two types of word searches: Boolean searches (sometimes called terms and connectors searches) and natural language searches. **Figures 10.1** and **10.2** show the search screens from Westlaw and LexisNexis, respectively. The search features identified in these figures are explained in this section.

a. Boolean Searching

Boolean searching retrieves information based on the relationships among words in a document. Using specific commands, you can locate documents that contain certain words in defined relationships to other words. For example, you could search for documents that contain both the term "ice cream" and the term "sundae." Alternatively, you could search for documents that contain either the term "ice cream" or the term "sundae," but not necessarily both. In a Boolean search, the search identifies documents containing the precise terms you identify, in the precise relationships you request.

FIGURE 10.1   WESTLAW SEARCH SCREEN

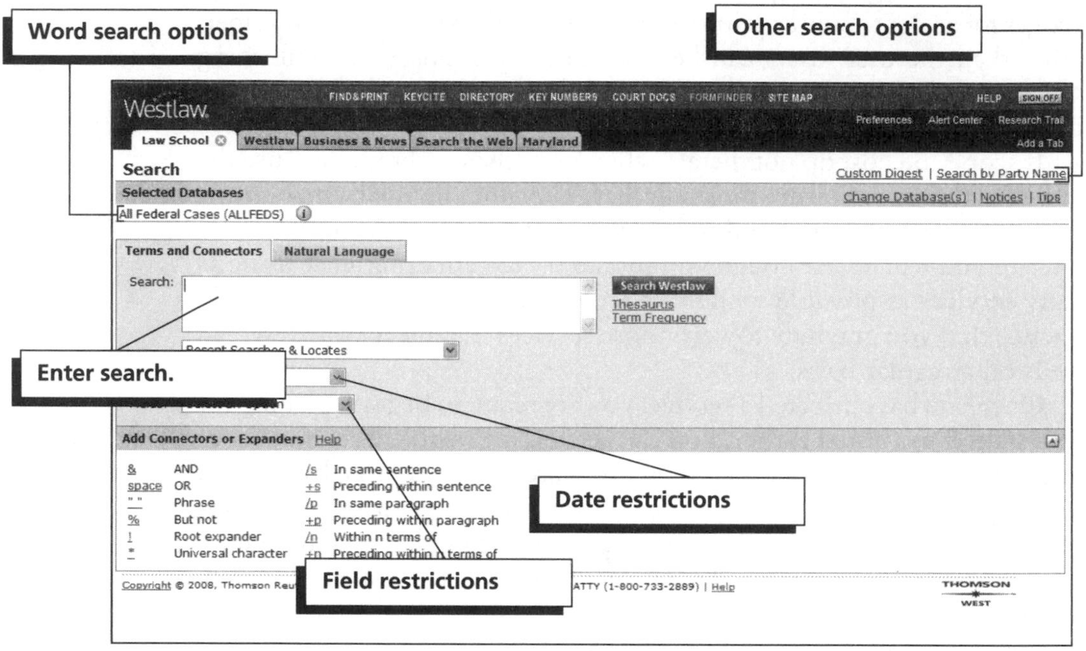

Reprinted with permission from Thomson Reuters/West, from Westlaw, search screen. © 2008 Thomson Reuters/West.

(1) Boolean search commands

In Boolean searching, you define the relationships among the terms in the search using "connectors." The most common connectors are AND and OR. AND retrieves documents containing all of the specified terms. OR retrieves documents containing any one of the specified terms. In addition to indicating relationships among words within the document as a whole, connectors can also indicate more specific relationships, such as terms appearing within a certain number of words of each other (/N), or within the same paragraph (/P) or sentence (/S). Some services use the connectors ADJ (for adjacent) or NEAR to indicate words in proximity to each other, instead of allowing you to specify the proximity. The help function or search tips section of the service should indicate how close adjacent or near terms have to be to be captured by the search. Connectors can also be used to exclude terms. For example, the AND NOT connector allows you to search for documents that include one term and exclude another. The chart in **Figure 10.3** shows some of the more common connectors.

You can search for individual terms within a Boolean search, or you can search for phrases. The way you indicate that terms should be searched together as a phrase will depend on the service you are using. In some services, such as LexisNexis, words in a sequence are automatically treated

FIGURE 10.2   LEXISNEXIS SEARCH SCREEN

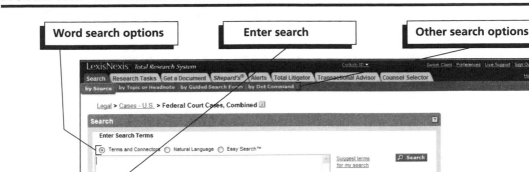

Reprinted with permission of LexisNexis, from LexisNexis, search screen.

as a phrase unless separated by a connector. In a search for ICE CREAM, therefore, LexisNexis would search for the phrase ICE CREAM as a single unit. Other services automatically treat words in a sequence as though they have a particular connector between them. Westlaw, for example, automatically applies the OR connector between words in a sequence. A Westlaw search for ICE CREAM operates as a search for ICE OR CREAM. Other services may automatically apply the AND, ADJ, or NEAR connectors between words in a sequence. In services that automatically apply a particular connector, you can usually create a phrase using quotation marks or some other type of punctuation. You can search for a phrase in Westlaw by placing the words in quotation marks: "ICE CREAM".

Most searches contain several terms and several connectors. When the search is executed, Boolean logic will process the connectors in a specific sequence. In Westlaw and LexisNexis, the OR connector is processed first, followed by the proximity connectors (/N, /P, /S), the AND connector, and finally, the exclusion connectors (AND NOT, BUT NOT). It is important to understand this hierarchy of connectors to create an effective search.

If you executed a search for ICE AND CREAM OR SUNDAE, the search for the terms CREAM OR SUNDAE would be processed first.

FIGURE 10.3   BOOLEAN SEARCH CONNECTORS

CONNECTOR OR COMMAND	WESTLAW	LEXISNEXIS	OTHER SERVICES OR SEARCH ENGINES
Search for terms as a phrase.	"Place phrase in quotation marks."	Create a phrase by joining words in sequence without a connector.	Options vary by service; single or double quotation marks are common ways to denote a phrase.
Segregate terms and connectors within a search.	(Place in parentheses.)	(Place in parentheses.)	Options vary by service; parentheses are often used to segregate parts of a search.
Search for terms in the alternative.	Connect terms with **or**; leave a space between terms.	Connect terms with **or**.	Connect terms with **or**; other options vary by service.
Search for, or exclude, terms in proximity to each other. (n = a specific number)	Term1 **+n** Term2 (Term1 appears a certain number of words before Term2.) Term1 **/n** Term2 (Term1 appears within a certain number of words of Term2; Term1 can occur before or after Term2.) Term1 **/s** Term2 (Term1 appears within the same sentence as Term2.) Term1 **/p** Term2 (Term1 appears within the same paragraph as Term2.)	Term1 **/n** Term2 (Term1 appears within a certain number of words of Term2; Term1 can occur before or after Term2.) Term1 **pre/n** Term2 (Term1 appears a certain number of words before Term2.) Term1 **not/n** Term2 (Term1 does not appear within a certain number of words of Term2.) Term1 **/s** Term2 (Term1 appears within the same sentence as Term2; can also be used to exclude terms, using **not /s**.) Term1 **/p** Term2 (Term1 appears within the same paragraph as Term2; can also be used to exclude terms, using **not /p**.)	Often, proximity is indicated with **/n**, **/s**, or **/p**, depending on the service. Some services use **adj** (for adjacent) or **near** (for nearby terms).
Search for all terms.	Connect terms with **and** or **&**.	Connect terms with **and** or **&**.	Connect terms with **and**; other options vary by service.
Exclude terms.	Connect terms with **but not** or **%**.	Connect terms with **and not**.	Options vary by service.

After documents with one or the other of those terms were identified, the search for the term ICE would begin. In effect, the query would be processed as a search for ICE AND CREAM OR ICE AND SUNDAE. This is probably not the intended search, and it could miss documents containing the terms you want or retrieve irrelevant documents.

Here, you probably intended to search for the phrase "ice cream" or the term "sundae." There are two ways you could have modified this search to achieve that result. One is by searching for "ICE CREAM" as a phrase, instead of connecting the words with AND. That would result in a search for the phrase "ICE CREAM" or the term "SUNDAE," which was the intended search.

Another way to vary the search would have been to segregate the ICE AND CREAM portion of the search. In Westlaw or LexisNexis, you can accomplish this by placing a portion of the search in parentheses: (ICE AND CREAM) OR SUNDAE. The terms within parentheses would be treated as a separate unit. Thus, the AND connector would apply only to the terms within the parentheses. In this example, adding parentheses would result in a search for the terms ICE AND CREAM as a unit, and then in the alternative, for the individual term SUNDAE. This again would achieve the intended search result. The chart in **Figure 10.3**, containing common connectors, lists them in the order in which they are processed in Boolean searches in Westlaw and LexisNexis.

The hierarchy of connectors, as well as the precise connectors and punctuation used to create a search, can vary in any given service. You should consult the help or search tips function when you are using a service for the first time to make sure you use the appropriate search commands.

(2) Constructing a basic Boolean search

Once you understand the concept of Boolean searching, your next task is creating an effective search that is tailored to find the information you need. Constructing a basic search involves three steps:

- developing the initial search terms
- expanding the breadth and depth of the search and adding wildcard characters
- adding connectors and parentheses to clarify the relationships among the search terms.

In developing the initial search terms, you should use the process described in Chapter 2. Think about the problem in terms of the parties, any places or things, potential claims and defenses, and the relief sought. You may recall the example factual scenario in Chapter 2, which involved the issue of whether a hotel operator is liable in negligence to a guest whose wrist was broken during a robbery that took place on the hotel premises. To develop a Boolean search on this issue, you might begin with the following words:

hotel negligence guest robbery

Having identified the relevant terms, your next step would be expanding the search. This can be done in two ways. First, unless you are searching for terms of art that need to appear precisely as written to be useful, you need to expand the breadth and depth of the search, as explained in Chapter 2. Expanding the breadth of the search involves generating synonyms and terms related to the initial search terms. Expanding the depth involves expressing the terms with varying degrees of abstraction. Recall that a Boolean search is limited to the exact terms you identify. If an object, idea, concept, or action is expressed in a document using different terminology, a Boolean search will not locate it. Therefore, it is especially important to expand your search terms with this type of searching.

The second way to expand your search is to use wildcard characters. Wildcard characters substitute for variable letters within a word. Westlaw and LexisNexis use two wildcard characters: the asterisk (*) to substitute for individual letters, and the exclamation point (!) to substitute for variable word endings. Thus, in the example above, you might change NEGLIGENCE to NEGLIGEN! to expand the search to include negligence, negligent, negligently, and any other variation on the word.

Although many services use wildcard characters, the functions of the characters are not standard. For example, the asterisk (*) in some services is used for variable word endings, not the exclamation point (!). You should review the search commands in any service with which you are unfamiliar. In addition, some services will not search for plurals, which means you need to use wildcard characters to capture them, e.g., hotel! for hotel or hotels, wom*n for woman or women. Both Westlaw and LexisNexis will search for plural forms of words automatically if they end in "s" or "es." Westlaw will also automatically search for irregular plurals, such as "mice" or "children," but LexisNexis will not.

The example search might be expanded in the following ways:

hotel motel inn! negligen!
guest visitor tourist robbery theft crim!

Now that a series of terms has been developed and expanded, the next step is identifying the appropriate relationships among the terms using connectors and, if appropriate, parentheses. The closer the connections you require among the terms, the more restrictive the search will be, and the broader the connections, the more open the search will be. For example, the AND connector, which requires only that both words appear somewhere within the same document, will retrieve more documents than a proximity connector such as /P, which requires the words to appear within the same paragraph. Parentheses should be used to group categories of terms that you want to search together.

In the example search, the terms might be connected as follows:

(hotel or motel or inn!) /p
negligen! /p (guest or visitor or tourist) and
(robbery or theft or crim!)

The parentheses group related terms together within the search. Thus, the terms relating to the premises (hotel, motel, inn, etc.) will be searched together, as will the terms relating to the injured party and the cause of the injury. The query will then proceed to the relationships among the groups of terms (within the same paragraph or document).

The /P proximity connector is used in the example search to connect the terms relating to the premises, the legal theory, and the injured party. Hotels can be involved in many types of claims, so requiring the premises terms to appear within the same paragraph as the legal theory (NEGLIGEN!) helps target cases involving hotel negligence. Because hotels can be subject to liability in negligence to many parties, requiring terms relating to the injured party to occur within the same paragraph also helps focus the search. By contrast, the terms relating to the act that caused the injury could occur anywhere within the document and still be relevant to the search. Therefore, the AND connector is used for that part of the search.

The example search is more complex than many Boolean searches you will execute. It is drafted to illustrate a range of Boolean search options. To be effective, a Boolean search does not have to use all or even most of the available search commands. The structure and complexity of any search will depend on the nature of the information you need.

(3) Constructing a more sophisticated search
In addition to allowing you to search for terms within the body of a document, many services will allow you to limit your search to individual components of the document, such as words in the title, the name of the author, or the date of the document. Although you will not always use this search option, it is an important feature to understand.

In Westlaw, the document components are called "fields"; in LexisNexis, they are called "segments." Both services will allow you to add field or segment restrictions using menu options or by typing commands into the search.

In the example search, the search results could be limited to cases from a particular jurisdiction or time period. In the hypothetical set out in Chapter 2, the hotel was located in Illinois. Therefore, you might want to limit your search to cases from courts in Illinois. You could do that in

Westlaw by choosing the option for "Court" under the "Fields" section on the search screen and typing the restriction in the parentheses. The same connectors and commands that apply to other Boolean searches also apply to field and segment searches.

As another example, you can search for a document by name or title by limiting the search to terms within the name or title. If you wanted to search for the United States Supreme Court case of *Roe v. Wade*, you could search in LexisNexis using the query ROE AND WADE. This search, however, would retrieve every case within the database that ever mentioned *Roe v. Wade*, which could be hundreds or even thousands of cases. The search would be more successful with a segment restriction. Using the menu of document segments, you could limit the search to cases in which the terms ROE and WADE both appear only in the name of the document.

b. Natural Language Searching

Boolean searching requires you to understand various commands and connectors, and as a consequence, can be challenging to master. Another way to execute a word search is to use what is called "natural language" searching. This is what many Internet search engines use as their default search option. It is also available in Westlaw, LexisNexis, and other electronic research services.

With natural language searching, you simply enter your search as a question, without concern for connectors, parentheses, or wildcard characters. The terms in the question are automatically converted into a search format to retrieve documents. In Westlaw and LexisNexis, natural language searching retrieves a fixed number of documents. You can manually increase or decrease that number by selecting "Preferences" from the top of the screen.

To construct a natural language search, you begin by developing the initial query. The example search might look like this:

> Is a hotel liable in negligence if a guest is injured
> during a robbery that occurs on the premises?

Like a Boolean search, a natural language search will be limited to the terms you specify. Therefore, the initial search must be expanded:

> Is a hotel, motel, inn, or innkeeper liable
> in negligence if a guest, visitor, or tourist is injured
> during a robbery, theft, or crime that occurs on the premises?

Both Westlaw and LexisNexis have additional options for refining a natural language search. For example, in both services, related terms should be placed in parentheses following the main term, e.g., hotel (motel, inn). Both services also allow you to specify certain terms as required or mandatory in the search results.

Natural language searching can be helpful if you are researching an area of law with which you are unfamiliar. If you know some relevant terms, but are uncertain about how to construct an effective Boolean query, you can use a natural language search as a starting point. If you have tried subject or Boolean searches without success, switching to a natural language search may yield better results. If the search retrieves relevant authorities, you can use them as an access point into other electronic search functions. For example, if the search retrieves a relevant case, you can use a citator or search by headnote number to find additional cases. Reading the authorities that the search retrieves can also give you enough knowledge about the subject to construct an effective Boolean search.

Many people gravitate toward natural language searching because it is similar to Internet searching. LexisNexis has developed an even simpler search option called Easy Search that is intended for short searches of two to three terms and that does not require you to use any search syntax. It is important to remember, however, that legal research is different from routine Internet searching. In daily life, natural language Internet searches are useful for finding a specific item of information (such as an address) or accessing sources that are at least somewhat interchangeable (such as sources for national news) or searching for information from a universe of options that are largely already known (such as which retailers are likely to carry an item for purchase). When you do these types of searches, you are able to assess the results fairly accurately; you know when you have found what you are looking for. As a consequence, natural language search functionality is sufficient to meet your needs.

That degree of functionality, however, may not be precise enough for accurate legal research, especially because comprehensive research ordinarily requires you to locate multiple authorities, not simply to find or choose just one. Natural language results can be inconsistent, especially because you do not specify the connectors used to define the relationships among the search terms. Boolean searching offers more flexibility in tailoring a word search to your needs. Therefore, natural language and other simplified search options should not be your only search strategies. Instead, they should be integrated into your repertoire of search techniques to be used when they will be most effective.

3. SELECTING A DATABASE IN WHICH TO EXECUTE THE SEARCH

Once you have constructed a word search, you are ready to execute it in the electronic service you have chosen to use. As noted earlier, most services divide their contents into databases based on subjects or on the sources of information they contain. Therefore, you will need to select the database in which to execute your search. Selecting *a* database is not difficult. What is more challenging is selecting *the best* database to obtain the information you need.

Generally speaking, you should select the narrowest database that contains all of the information you need. For example, if you were researching Maryland statutes online, you should not choose a database that contains statutes from all fifty states. Instead, if possible, search a database that contains only Maryland statutes. Searching in an overly broad database requires you to sort through information that is not relevant to your search, making it difficult to determine whether your search was successful. Choosing a database tailored to your research needs will improve the efficiency of your electronic searching.

4. REVIEWING THE SEARCH RESULTS

Sometimes when you execute a word search, the results may not be quite what you expected. Specifically, you may retrieve too many documents, not enough documents, or documents that simply are not useful in resolving your research issue.

If your word search does not retrieve useful information, consider the following options:

- searching in a narrower or broader database
- subtracting less essential terms or expanding the breadth and depth of the search
- excluding terms from the search (AND NOT or BUT NOT can be used as connectors in a Boolean search, and natural language search menus may allow you to exclude terms)
- subtracting or adding field or segment restrictions.

In a Boolean search, you have additional options for revising your search:

- making the proximity connectors more restrictive or less restrictive
- subtracting or adding wildcard characters

You may need to browse some of the documents you have retrieved to see why the search was not successful. For example, if you conducted a Boolean search for cases involving diving accidents and included the term DIV! in your search, you could be retrieving cases concerning divestiture of assets or diversity jurisdiction in addition to cases about diving and divers. Browsing can also help you identify additional terms that should be added to your search.

If the search seems completely off the mark, you might not be searching in an appropriate database or for the correct terms. In that case, you may need to consult secondary sources to obtain background information on your research issue, and subject searching may prove easier to use at this stage of your research. Chapter 3 discusses the use of secondary sources. In addition, Chapter 11, on creating a research plan, discusses ways to improve your research results if your initial efforts prove fruitless.

5. RESEARCHING EFFECTIVELY IN WESTLAW AND LEXISNEXIS

This section provides some information on how to retrieve and refine search results in Westlaw and LexisNexis. It also provides some techniques for cost-effective Westlaw and LexisNexis searching.

a. Search Options and Results in Westlaw

To search in Westlaw, you must first select a database. Westlaw offers more than one way to select a database. The database Directory provides the most complete listing. The Resources screen under the Law School tab provides a more abbreviated listing. If you do not find the type of authority you want to search through the Resources list, you may want to browse the Directory. Also, sometimes the search screen and options appear differently depending on how you access a database. If you do not see the search function you want to use from the search screen, try accessing the database a different way or using the Site Map to access a specific search function.

Once you select a database, you can execute a search. If you execute a word search, Westlaw will automatically display a list of documents retrieved. You can view the text of a document by selecting it from the list. The search terms will be highlighted within the documents.

The Term function provides another way to browse word search results. Term will move the cursor forward or backward to each occurrence of one of your search terms. Instead of browsing the full text of a document, you can use Term to jump to passages that are likely to have relevant information. Once you select a document, use the Term arrows at the bottom of the screen to jump to the search terms in the document.

After you have browsed your search results, you may want to refine your query, which you can do in a couple of ways. The first is to edit your query, which allows you to change or add terms or field restrictions to the search. If you edit the query, Westlaw will execute the edited search within the original database you selected. You can also choose to run the search in a different database. If the search has retrieved too many documents, another alternative is to use the Locate command. Locate allows

FIGURE 10.4   WESTLAW SEARCH RESULTS

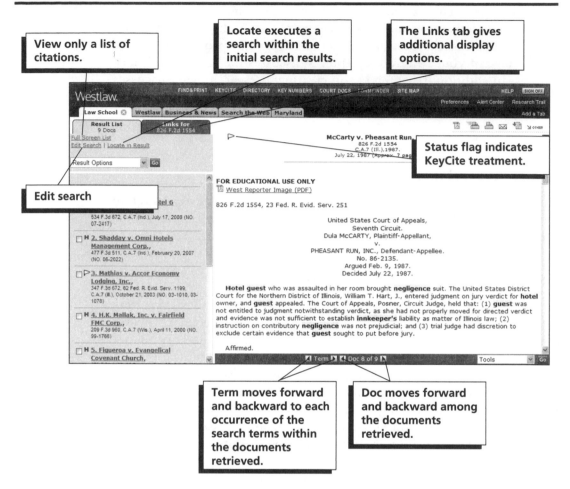

Reprinted with permission from Thomson Reuters/West, from Westlaw, search results display. © 2008 Thomson Reuters/West.

you to search for terms within the documents retrieved in the initial query. In effect, it operates as a search within a search. You can use Locate regardless of whether your initial search was a Boolean or natural language query, but the Locate query must be submitted in Boolean format. Once you have executed a Locate request, the citation list will show only the documents containing the Locate term(s), and the Term function will identify the Locate term(s). An example of a Westlaw search result screen appears in **Figure 10.4**.

b. Search Options and Results in LexisNexis

Searching in LexisNexis requires you to select a Source in which to search. After you select a Source, you will have several search options.

To execute a word search, you can use a Boolean, natural language, or Easy Search query.

Once you have executed a word search, LexisNexis offers several options for viewing the results: TOC (for statutes and regulations) Full, KWIC, Cite, and Custom. TOC displays the statutory on regulatory table Full retrieves the full text of each document. KWIC displays portions of the document containing your search terms, along with the immediately surrounding text. In both Full and KWIC formats, your search terms will be highlighted. When you are viewing a document in Full or KWIC, you can move to the previous or next document using the arrows above the title of the document, and you can use Term to move to each occurrence of one of your terms. Cite displays a list of citations to the documents retrieved by the search. From the citation list, you can view individual documents in Full or KWIC format by selecting a citation. Custom allows you to customize the information in the search results display.

LexisNexis offers several ways to refine your search results if necessary. One way is by editing the initial search. Another option is the FOCUS function, which is similar to Locate in Westlaw. By selecting FOCUS, you can search for new terms within the documents retrieved by the initial search.

LexisNexis also has a search function called More Like This. You may be familiar with this function from Internet search engines. This function creates a new search using terms within a document you have retrieved. Thus, if you found a document that was especially helpful, the More Like This function would allow you to specify key terms from the document and use them to conduct another search in the same or another Source. A related search option is More Like Selected Text. This option allows you to select terms from a document to use as a search in the same or another Source. An example of a search result screen displaying a document in Full format appears in **Figure 10.5**.

c. Cost-Effective Searching in Westlaw and LexisNexis

If you conduct research in Westlaw or LexisNexis, advance planning will allow you to take advantage of strategies to make your research as cost effective as possible:

- Construct word searches and plan your research path in advance.
- Use research assistance provided by Westlaw and LexisNexis.
- Execute your searches in a way that takes into account the way you are being billed.
- Determine charges for printing or downloading information.

The strategies discussed here can be applied to other fee-based services as well.

FIGURE 10.5   LEXISNEXIS SEARCH RESULTS

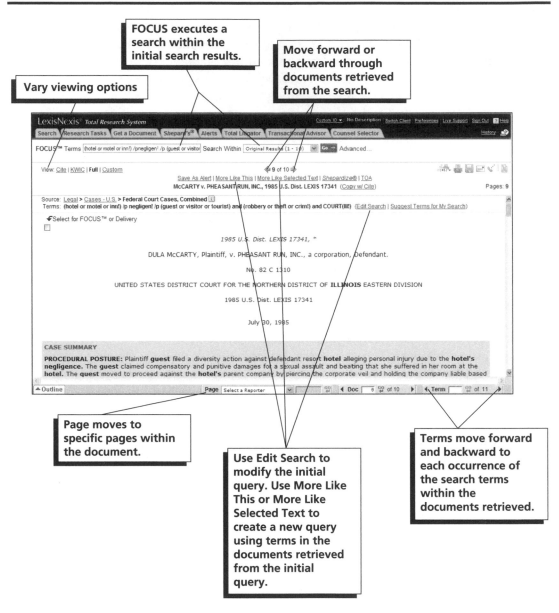

Reprinted with permission of LexisNexis, from LexisNexis, search results display.

(1) Construct word searches and plan your research path in advance

One of the best ways to cut costs is to draft your word searches and plan your research path before you get online. No matter how you are being billed, a thoughtful search strategy defined before you sign on is more likely to lead to useful results. This involves writing out your word searches and deciding which databases to search in advance.

Writing out your word searches in advance allows you to generate a list of terms and refine your search before you start incurring charges. Deciding in advance which databases you plan to search will also allow you to search quickly and efficiently. Recall that searching the narrowest database that meets your research needs makes evaluating your search results easier, which in turn reduces the amount of time you spend online. In addition, Westlaw and LexisNexis charge a premium for access to databases that contain multiple types of authority, such as those containing all federal or state cases. Deciding in advance which databases have the most appropriate information for your search, instead of automatically searching in the premium databases, will make your research more cost effective.

Advance planning also makes keeping notes of your search process easier. As noted in Chapter 11, on creating a research plan, it is important to keep track of your research process as you search for authority. If you have written out your word searches and intended research path, you will not have to keep as many notes while you are searching online. Of course, you may change your strategy based on what your searches retrieve, and you will need to keep track of your revised searches. At a minimum, however, you should begin with a search mapped out.

(2) Use research assistance

Another way to cut costs is to use the research assistance provided by Westlaw and LexisNexis. Both of these services employ research attorneys to provide assistance to users. You can obtain live help online or telephone assistance through their toll-free numbers. If you are unsure about whether your strategy is likely to be effective, you may want to contact the provider for assistance. The research attorneys will help you create word searches and select appropriate databases to search to maximize your search results.

(3) Execute searches to account for the billing structure

Once you have signed on to Westlaw or LexisNexis, some search options may be more cost effective than others. If you are being charged by the amount of time you spend online, you want to work as quickly as possible to minimize your costs. In that situation, it is especially important that you draft your planned word searches before you sign on because you do not want to spend time thinking up your search once you have started accruing charges. You also want to execute your searches quickly without spending a lot of time browsing documents. It is often more economical to print a list of the citations retrieved by your search so you can review the documents in hard copy off-line. If it turns out that your search was not effective, you can get back online to try again.

If you are being charged by the number of word searches you execute, you will often be able to modify your initial search at no additional cost. In that case, when you draft word searches in advance, you may want to devise relatively broad searches, along with potential narrowing modifications. You can then execute the broad searches, browse documents online, and execute modifications to narrow the results if necessary. This will allow you to maximize your search results at a lower cost than executing a series of new word searches.

(4) Determine charges for printing or downloading information

Regardless of the overall billing structure for use of Westlaw or Lexis-Nexis, it is often more cost efficient to photocopy materials from hard copy available in the library than it is to print or download information online. Even while you are in law school, there may be limits to the amount of printing you can do without charge. Therefore, whether you are at work or at school, be sure to investigate printing and downloading costs before you get online.

C. ADDITIONAL ELECTRONIC RESEARCH RESOURCES

1. ALERT OR CLIPPING SERVICES

Sometimes your work on a research project will be done in a few days, but other times it will extend over a longer period of time. In law school, you might work on a moot court brief or scholarly paper for several weeks or even an entire semester. In legal practice, work on individual cases often extends over months or years. When you are working on an issue over a period of time, one electronic resource that may be useful to you is an alert or clipping service. These services automatically run searches through electronic databases and notify you when relevant new information is added to a database. These services allow you to stay up to date on developments affecting your research while you are working on a project.

Many news services offer automatic updates on general news topics and current events. Providers of legal information also frequently offer alert or clipping services. Free services, such as Law.com, offer free daily updates on top legal stories. Fee-based services will often allow you to draft specific queries to update your research on a schedule you specify. You can specify the database(s) in which to run the search, the frequency with which the search is to be run, and the manner in which the search results will be delivered to you. Once you access the service, a menu of options will set out the choices available to you.

Westlaw offers several alert services. The two that are most likely to be of use to you in law school are KeyCite Alert and WestClip. KeyCite Alert, which is described in more detail in Chapter 5 on citators, notifies you when new information is added to the KeyCite entries for cases, statutes, federal regulations, or certain federal administrative agency decisions. WestClip allows you to draft a word search to be run periodically in the database(s) you specify and delivers the search results to you. After you run a search, you can create a WestClip entry by clicking on the "Add Search to WestClip" link at the top of the list of citations. You can access WestClip without first running a search using the Site Map. Note, however, that WestClip works only with Boolean (terms and connectors) searches, not natural language searches.

LexisNexis also has two alert services. Shepard's Alert® is similar to KeyCite Alert and is also described in more detail in Chapter 5. It notifies you when new information is added to the Shepard's entries for cases, statutes, or federal regulations. LexisNexis also has a service that is similar to WestClip. This service used to be called ECLIPSE but is now called simply Alert. It runs your search in specific Sources at specified intervals and delivers the search results to you. You must run a search before you can save it as an Alert entry. After you run a search, click on the "Save as Alert" link at the top of the screen. Like WestClip, the LexisNexis Alert service works only with Boolean (terms and connectors) searches, not natural language or Easy Search queries.

Other services also offer clipping services. Loislaw's clipping service is called LawWatch, and VersusLaw's service is called AdvanceLink. You should look for alert or clipping services in any electronic resource you use.

2. PUBLICLY AVAILABLE INTERNET SOURCES

Legal research used to be accomplished primarily, if not exclusively, in a limited universe of research sources produced by legal publishers. As more and more information becomes available via the Internet, however, the range of sources available for researching legal issues continues to grow. Government, educational, nonprofit, trade, and civic organizations that are engaged in public education efforts make useful information on many areas of the law available via their web sites. In addition, blogs are becoming an increasingly important source of information both in our culture as a whole and in legal research. A blog, as you are no doubt aware, is a web site on which the author posts information on a defined topic. Blogs on virtually every topic exist, including many legal topics. You can even find blogs on legal research. Law-related blogs are sometimes called blawgs.

Publicly available Internet sources are most likely to be useful to you when you are looking for information on a specific topic. If you find a relevant web site or blog, it may provide you with background information on the topic, references to significant legal authorities, news about legislative initiatives pending at the local, state, or federal level, and links

FIGURE 10.6   LEGAL RESOURCES, WRIGHTSLAW WEB SITE

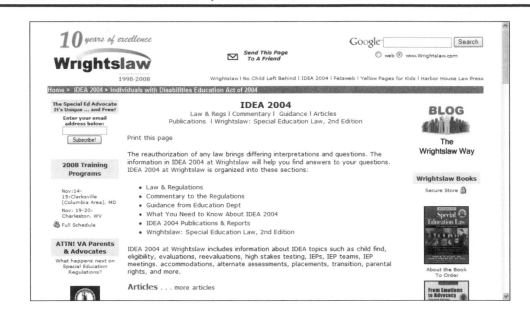

Reprinted with the permission of wrightslaw.com. IDEA 2004 Legal Information Resources from wrightslaw.com. ©1998-2008, Peter D. Wright and Pamela Dan Wright. All rights reserved.

to other sites with useful information. For example, if you were asked to research a problem involving the educational rights of children with disabilities, you might want to spend some time looking over the web sites for organizations devoted to educational or disability issues. The screen reproduced in **Figure 10.6** shows some of the kinds of legal information you find on the Wrightslaw site. If you were unfamiliar with educational laws as they apply to children with disabilities, this site might be a good starting point for familiarizing yourself with the topic.

As another example, if you were researching an issue regarding labeling requirements for herbal dietary supplements, you might want to locate a blog on alternative medicine. **Figure 10.7** shows a portion of an entry in CAMLaw, a blog devoted to legal issues in complementary and alternative medicine. If you located entries relevant to your research issue, they might provide useful information to familiarize you with the area of law and get you started on your research.

If you are following a number of blogs, either to research a specific issue or to stay up to date with developments in the field, you may want to use an RSS feed reader. An RSS feed reader delivers blog headlines to you along with links to the full articles so that you do not have to visit each blog in which you are interested to see if new, relevant information has been posted. In a sense, RSS feed readers act like alert services for blogs.

FIGURE 10.7   ENTRY FROM THE CAMLAW BLOG

Reprinted with permission from Complementary and Alternative Medicine Law Blog (CAMLaw Blog), www.camlawblog.com, © 2008, lexBlog, Inc.

Publicly available Internet sources are simply new types of secondary sources. When viewed this way, their role in legal research becomes clear. The caveats described in Chapter 3, on secondary source research in more traditional legal sources, also apply to publicly available web sites: Use them to obtain background information on an area of law and to obtain citations to primary authority. Do not rely on them as authoritative sources of legal rules or as official sources of primary authority.

To make sure you use publicly available Internet sources appropriately, you should plan to undertake four steps: (1) locate useful information; (2) assess the credibility of the source of the information; (3) save or print a copy of the information you are using; and (4) verify and update any legal authorities you locate through the source. In the following discussion of these four steps, you will find references to

Internet sites that may be useful to you. The web site addresses for all these sites appear in Appendix A at the end of this text.

To locate useful information, you could use a general search engine, such as Google, or a specialized search engine, such as Google Scholar for scholarly publications or LawCrawler for law-related web sites. You can also use a directory such as Blawg, a directory of law-related blogs.

Once you have located useful information, you must assess the credibility of the source. Anyone with the necessary equipment can post information on the Internet. Much information available on the Internet is inaccurate or out of date. Many individuals and groups post information on the Internet to advance their social or policy agendas. Therefore, you need to make a separate assessment of how much weight to give to information posted on an individual's or organization's web site. The sites you visit should contain information you can use to assess the sources' credibility. Most sites sponsored by organizations or entities include information about the group, such as its history and mission. The authors of many blogs will provide biographical information to help you assess their expertise.

If you find useful information on the Internet, be sure to save or print a copy of the page. Internet sites can change at any moment; the information most helpful to you could change or disappear altogether at any time. If you find that information you accessed earlier is no longer available, you can try to find it in an Internet archive, such as the Internet Archive Wayback Machine, which stores copies of sites for future reference. The University of North Texas library system also hosts the Cybercemetery of Former Federal Web Sites, which you can link to through GPO Access. Although these sites provide limited historical records of Internet sites, you cannot count on finding an archived version of a web page that has been changed, moved, or deleted. The better practice, therefore, is to save or print useful information as you locate it.

If you find references to legal authorities through publicly available web sites, the last step is verifying and updating your research. You should not assume that the authorities you have located are correct, complete, or up to date. Use the information you have found as a springboard into more traditional avenues of legal research to make sure that you have located all pertinent information and that the legal authority you cite is authoritative.

D. CITING AUTHORITY OBTAINED FROM ELECTRONIC LEGAL RESEARCH SERVICES

Much of the information you locate through electronic services will also be available in print format. Both the *ALWD Manual* and the *Bluebook* require that you cite the print format if possible. This is not as difficult as it might seem. Many electronic services provide all the information you need for a print citation, including page numbers. For cases, statutes, and other materials available only in electronic format, the following rules apply. This chapter does not contain complete explanations about citing cases, statutes, and other authorities. More information about citing each of these types of authority is included in the chapters devoted to those sources.

1. CASES

Citations to cases available only in Westlaw or LexisNexis are similar, but not identical, in *ALWD Manual* and *Bluebook* format. *ALWD Manual* Rule 12.12 provides that the citation must contain the following three components: (1) the case name; (2) the database identifier, including the year, the name of the database, and the unique document number; and (3) a parenthetical containing the jurisdiction and court abbreviations and the full date. A pinpoint reference can be provided with "at *" and the page number. Here is an example:

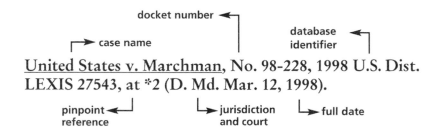

A *Bluebook* citation is the same, except that Bluepages B5.1.3 requires that the docket number for the case be included in the citation and that a comma appear before the pinpoint reference. Here is an example:

docket number ←
case name →   database identifier ←
United States v. Marchman, No. 98-228, 1998 U.S. Dist. LEXIS 27543, at *2 (D. Md. Mar. 12, 1998).
pinpoint ← reference   jurisdiction → and court   full date →

2. STATUTES

Statutory provisions retrieved from Westlaw or LexisNexis should be cited the same way print materials are cited, with additional information in the parenthetical indicating which electronic service was accessed and the date through which the service was updated. Electronic statutory citations are covered in *ALWD Manual* Rule 14.5 and *Bluebook* Rule

18.1.2. The examples in the *Bluebook* and the *ALWD Manual* use slightly different wording to convey the updating information. Also, the *Bluebook* examples show LEXIS in all capital letters, whereas the *ALWD Manual* does not. Otherwise, the citations are the same using either format. Here is an example in *ALWD Manual* format:

10 U.S.C.A. § 816 (West, Westlaw current through Pub. L. No. 110-247).

Here is an example in *Bluebook* format:

N.Y. Penal Law § 190.05 (McKinney, LEXIS through ch. 115, June 17, 2008).

3. MATERIALS AVAILABLE ON THE INTERNET

Both the *ALWD Manual* and the *Bluebook* discourage citations to information on the Internet if it is available in print form because of the transient nature of many Internet sites. If you are citing something available in both print and electronic form that you obtained from an electronic source, both the *ALWD Manual* and the *Bluebook* generally require that you provide the print citation, supplemented with additional information indicating the electronic source.

In the *ALWD Manual*, Rule 38 provides general guidance on citing electronic sources, and Rule 40 covers citations to information available only on the Internet. According to Rule 40, a citation to an authority available only via the Internet consists of up to five components: (1) the author of the item or owner of the web site; (2) the title of the item, underlined or italicized; (3) a pinpoint reference if one is available; (4) the URL; and (5) the date, which could be the date of the item, the date the site was updated, or the date you accessed the site, depending on the material you are citing. Here is an example of a citation to a news report in *ALWD Manual* format:

In the *Bluebook*, information on Internet citations appears in Rule 18.2. Rule 18.2.1 provides general guidance on citing information available on the Internet. The rest of Rule 18.2 (18.2.2-18.2.4) discusses how to construct different types of Internet citations. To cite a source available only via the Internet in *Bluebook* format, you must combine the requirements of Rule 18.2.1 with those in 18.2.2-18.2.4. The *Bluebook* does not provide specific formats for Internet citations to all forms of authority. In many cases, you will need to format the citation by analogizing to the rules applicable to similar print sources.

For example, an Internet news report is analogous to a print newspaper article. Applying the principles in Rule 18.2, as well as those for newspaper articles in Bluepages B9.1.4, you could cite the news report this way:

E. SAMPLE PAGES FOR ELECTRONIC LEGAL RESEARCH

Sample search screens for Westlaw and LexisNexis appear earlier in this chapter and throughout the text. Earlier chapters also contain sample search screens for several of the services outlined at the beginning of this chapter, including the *Index to Legal Periodicals*, LegalTrac, and Hein-Online (Chapter 3), Thomas and LexisNexis Congressional (Chapter 7), and GPO Access (Chapter 8). Therefore, the sample pages in **Figures 10.8** through **10.10** illustrate some of the services not highlighted elsewhere: FindLaw and Cornell Law School's Legal Information Institute.

FindLaw organizes legal information by category. You can search by type of authority, by jurisdiction, or by practice area. Selecting the option to search "Cases, Codes, Articles" reveals options
for searching for case summaries by topic and browsing material by jurisdiction.

FIGURE 10.8   SEARCH OPTIONS IN FINDLAW

Reprinted with permission. © 2008 Findlaw, a Thomson Reuters business, from Findlaw for Legal Professionals,
http://lp.findlaw.com.

Cornell Law School's Legal Information Institute site (LII) contains a variety of legal information.

FIGURE 10.9   INTRODUCTORY SCREEN, LEGAL INFORMATION INSTITUTE

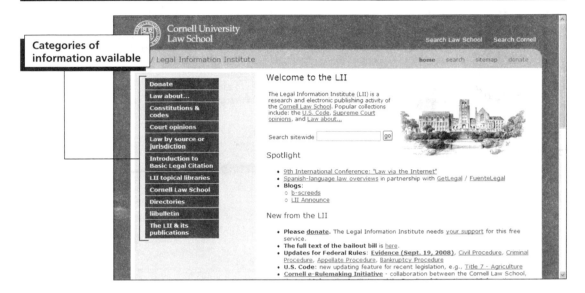

Reprinted with permission. © 2008 Cornell Law School, from http://www.law.cornell.edu.

For statutory research, LII provides free access to useful material such as a popular name table to the U.S. Code; selected uniform laws; and a directory of state statutes by topic, which indexes statutes from multiple jurisdictions by subject. You can also access an annotated version of the U.S. Constitution.

FIGURE 10.10   SEARCH OPTIONS IN LEGAL INFORMATION INSTITUTE

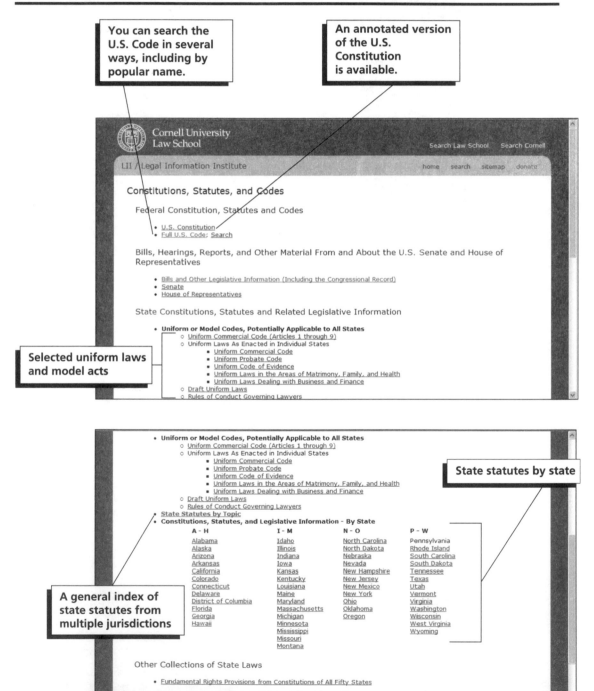

Reprinted with permission. © 2008 Cornell Law School, from http://www.law.cornell.edu.

F. CHECKLIST FOR ELECTRONIC LEGAL RESEARCH

1. SELECT AN ELECTRONIC RESEARCH SERVICE

❏ Consider the scope of coverage of the service.

❏ Consider the cost of the service.

2. SELECT A SEARCH TECHNIQUE

❏ Search techniques:

- Retrieve a document from its citation.
- Search by subject by browsing a publication's table of contents, searching the service's subject directory, or using an electronic index.
- Execute a word search.

❏ For word searches, construct an effective Boolean search:

- Develop the initial search terms.
- Expand the breadth and depth of the search and add wildcard characters.
- Specify the relationships among the terms using connectors and parentheses.
- Use a field or segment restriction to target useful authorities.

❏ Natural language searching may also be available.

3. SELECT A DATABASE TO SEARCH AND REVIEW THE RESULTS

❏ Search the narrowest database that contains the information you need.

❏ Browse documents or review a citation list to evaluate your search results.

❏ Refine word searches if necessary.

- Search in a narrower or broader database.
- Subtract or add terms.
- Make the proximity connectors more restrictive or less restrictive.
- Subtract or add wildcard characters.
- Subtract or add connectors that exclude terms.
- Subtract or add field or segment restrictions.

4. RESEARCH EFFECTIVELY IN WESTLAW AND LEXISNEXIS

❏ In Westlaw:

- Browse search results from the list of citations or using the Term function.

- Refine a word search by editing the search or using the Locate function.

☐ In LexisNexis:

- Browse documents in Full or KWIC using the Term function, view a list of citations in Cite, or customize the display using Custom.
- Refine a word search by editing the query or using the FOCUS, More Like This, or More Like Selected Text functions.

☐ In both services, search cost effectively.

- Construct word searches and plan your research path in advance.
- Use research assistance provided by Westlaw and LexisNexis.
- Execute searches to account for the billing structure.
- Determine charges for printing or downloading information.

5. USE ADDITIONAL TOOLS FOR EFFECTIVE ELECTRONIC RESEARCH

☐ Use an alert or clipping service to keep research up to date.

- In Westlaw, use KeyCite Alert and WestClip.
- In LexisNexis, use Shepard's Alert® and Alert.

☐ Use publicly available Internet sources.

- Locate useful sites to obtain background information on a topic or citations to primary authority.
- Assess the credibility of the source.
- Save or print copies of useful pages.
- Verify and update any legal authorities you locate.

DEVELOPING A RESEARCH PLAN

A. Introduction to research planning

B. Creating a research plan

C. Finding help

D. Sample research plans

E. Research checklists

A. INTRODUCTION TO RESEARCH PLANNING

When you get a research assignment, you might be tempted to begin the project by jumping directly into your research to see what authority you can find. In fact, searching for authority right away is not the best way to start. Thought and planning before you begin researching will help you in several ways. You will research more efficiently if you have a coherent research plan to follow. You will also research more accurately. Searching haphazardly can cause you to miss important authorities, and nothing is more disconcerting than feeling as though you came across relevant authority by accident. Following an organized plan will help ensure that you check all the appropriate places for authority on your issue and will give you confidence that your research is correct and complete.

B. CREATING A RESEARCH PLAN

Creating a research plan requires three steps: (1) obtaining preliminary information about the problem; (2) writing out a plan to follow as you research; and (3) working effectively in the library and online. Each of these steps is discussed in turn.

1. OBTAINING PRELIMINARY INFORMATION

When you first receive a research assignment, you might feel like you do not know enough to ask very many questions about it. While this might be true as far as the substance of the problem is concerned, you need to determine the scope of your project by obtaining some preliminary information from the person making the assignment. Specifically:

■ HOW MUCH TIME DO I HAVE FOR THIS ASSIGNMENT?

The amount of time you have affects your overall approach, as well as your time management with other projects you have been assigned.

■ WHAT FINAL WORK PRODUCT SHOULD I PRODUCE?

You should determine whether you are expected to produce a memorandum, pleading, brief, or informal report of your research results. To a certain extent, this also will be a function of the amount of time you have for the project.

■ ARE THERE ANY LIMITS ON THE RESEARCH MATERIALS I AM PERMITTED TO USE?

As a matter of academic integrity, you want to make sure you use only authorized research tools in a law school assignment. In practice, some clients might be unable or unwilling to pay for research completed with tools requiring additional fees, such as LexisNexis or Westlaw research.

■ WHICH JURISDICTION'S LAW APPLIES?

This is a question the person giving you the assignment might not be able to answer. There will be times when the controlling jurisdiction will be known. In other cases, it will be up to you to determine whether an issue is controlled by federal or state law, and if it is a question of state law, which state's law applies.

■ SHOULD I RESEARCH PERSUASIVE AUTHORITY?

Again, the person making the assignment might not be able to answer this question. You could be asked to focus exclusively on the law of the controlling jurisdiction to answer your research question, or you could specifically be asked to research multiple jurisdictions. If either of those requirements applies to your research, you certainly want to know that before you begin your research. What is more likely, however, is that you will simply be asked to find the answer to a question. If the law of the controlling jurisdiction answers the question, you might not need to go further. If not, you will need to research persuasive authority. Understanding the scope of the assignment will help you focus your efforts appropriately.

In your research class, there will be many parts of the assignment that your professor will expect you to figure out on your own as part of learning about the process of research. In a practice setting, however, you might also ask the following questions:

■ **DO YOU KNOW OF ANY SOURCES THAT ARE PARTICULARLY GOOD FOR RESEARCHING IN THIS AREA OF LAW?**

Practitioners who are experienced in a particular field might know of research sources that are especially helpful for the type of research you are doing, including looseleaf or other subject-matter services.

■ **WHAT BACKGROUND ON THE LAW OR TERMS OF ART SHOULD I KNOW AS I BEGIN MY RESEARCH?**

In a law school assignment, you might be expected to identify terms of art on your own. In practice, however, the person giving you the research assignment might be able to give you some background on the area of law and important terms of art to help you get started on your research.

■ **SHOULD I CONSULT ANY WRITTEN MATERIALS OR INDIVIDUALS WITHIN THE OFFICE BEFORE BEGINNING MY RESEARCH?**

Again, in law school, it would be inappropriate to use another person's research instead of completing the assignment on your own. In practice, however, reviewing briefs or memoranda on the same or a similar issue can give you a leg up on your research. In addition, another person within the office might be considered the "resident expert" on the subject and might be willing to act as a resource for you.

2. WRITING OUT A PLAN

Once you have preliminary information on your research project, you are ready to start writing out a plan to take you through the research process. The written plan should have the following components:

- an initial issue statement
- a list of potential search terms
- an outline of the sources you plan to consult, including the order in which you plan to consult them and whether you expect to use print or electronic tools for each source.

a. Developing an Initial Issue Statement and Generating Search Terms

The starting points for your written plan are developing an initial issue statement and generating possible search terms. The issue statement does not need to be a formal statement like one that would appear at the beginning of a brief or memorandum. Rather, it should be a preliminary assessment of the problem that helps define the scope of your research. For example, an initial issue statement might say something like, "Can the plaintiff recover from the defendant for destroying her garden?" This issue statement would be incomplete in a brief or memorandum because it does not identify a specific legal question and might not contain enough information about the facts. At this point, however, you do not know which legal theory or theories might be successful, nor do you know for certain which facts are most important. What this question tells you is that you will need to research all possible claims that would support recovery.

Alternatively, you might be asked to research a narrower question such as, "Can the plaintiff recover from the defendant *in negligence* for destroying her garden?" This issue statement again might be insufficient in a brief or memorandum, but for purposes of your research plan, it gives you valuable information. Your research should be limited to liability in negligence; intentional torts or contract claims are beyond the scope of this project.

Although this might seem like an exercise in the obvious, the discipline of writing out a preliminary issue statement can help you focus your efforts in the right direction. If you are unable to write a preliminary issue statement, that is an indication that you are not sure about the scope of the assignment and may need to ask more questions about what you should be trying to accomplish.

Once you have written your initial issue statement, you are ready to generate a list of possible search terms. Chapter 2 discusses how to do this, and the techniques described in that chapter should be employed to develop search terms in your research plan.

b. Identifying Research Sources

Once you have a preliminary view of the problem, the next step in creating an effective research plan is identifying potential research sources. First, you need to determine which research sources are likely to have relevant information. Then, you must determine the order in which you want to research those sources.

Chapter 1 discusses three general categories of authority: mandatory primary authority, persuasive primary authority, and secondary authority. You need to decide which of these categories of authority provides a good starting point for your research, and then, within each category, which specific authorities you should consult. The best way to do this is to begin with what you know, identify what you do not yet know, and determine the best ways to fill in the blanks.

For many research projects, your ultimate goal will be to produce a written document, such as a brief or memorandum, describing and applying primary mandatory authority relevant to the issue. If this type of authority does not exist or does not fully resolve the question, then you will also probably need to discuss primary persuasive authority, secondary authority, or both. Although this is not what you will be asked to do in every research project, this section will illustrate the process of writing a research plan based on this goal. As you will see, this process can be adapted for other types of research projects that you might be asked to complete.

The process of identifying what you know, identifying what you do not yet know, and determining how best to fill in the blanks can be applied to two components of the project: the search for primary mandatory authority, and the search for persuasive authority. You might not be able to write out a complete research plan for both components of the project before beginning your research. At a minimum, however, you should try to map out your search for primary mandatory authority. If a search for persuasive authority becomes necessary, you can then rework your plan to include those sources.

(1) Searching for primary mandatory authority
Beginning with the search for primary mandatory authority, the flow-chart in **Figure 11.1** illustrates the process you might undertake.

As you can see from the flowchart, there are several points at which you might consult secondary sources and several points at which you might make the jump into researching individual primary authorities, depending on how much information you have about your issue when you begin your research.

When you are ready to begin researching individual primary authorities, you need to decide the order in which to consult those sources. There are a couple of ways to do this. If you have consulted secondary sources, you should have a sense of whether the issue is a common-law issue governed by case law or an issue to which statutes, regulations, and other types of authority might apply. This information will help you determine the best starting point for researching individual primary authorities.

Once you have located some type of primary mandatory authority on the issue, whether through secondary sources or some other avenue, you can use that as a springboard to other primary authorities. As noted in the flowchart, for example, a case will contain headnotes that can lead you into the digest to locate other cases. The cases should also cite relevant statutory and regulatory provisions. Statutory annotations can lead you to legislative history, regulations, secondary sources, and cases. Of course, it is possible that the sources you consult initially will not lead you to other primary authorities. In that case, you might want to search independently in primary sources to make sure you have located all of the relevant authority.

FIGURE 11.1 FLOWCHART FOR DETERMINING YOUR RESEARCH PATH

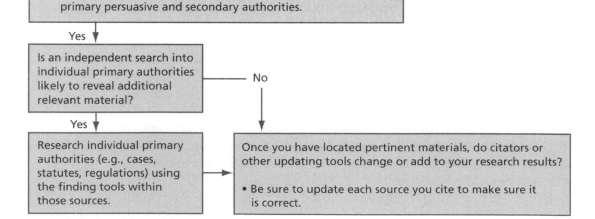

(2) Searching for persuasive authority

As you conduct your research, you might determine that you need to search for persuasive authority to analyze your research issue thoroughly. As in your search for primary mandatory authority, in your search for persuasive authority, you should begin with what you know, identify what you do not yet know, and determine the best ways to fill in the blanks.

The first thing you need to know is why you are searching for persuasive authority. Persuasive authority can serve a variety of purposes in your analysis of a research question. Here are four common reasons why you would want to research persuasive authority:

- When you want to buttress an analysis largely resolved by primary mandatory authority.
- When the applicable legal rules are clearly defined by primary mandatory authority, but the specific factual situation has not arisen in the jurisdiction. You might want to try to locate factually analogous cases from other jurisdictions.
- When the applicable rule is unclear and you want to make an analogy to another area of law to support your analysis.
- When the issue is one of first impression in the controlling jurisdiction for which no governing rule exists. In this case, you might want to find out how other jurisdictions have addressed the issue, or if no jurisdiction has faced the question, whether any commentators have analyzed the issue.

In each of these situations, you might want to research persuasive authority consisting of non-mandatory primary authority from within the controlling jurisdiction, such as cases or statutes in an analogous area of law; primary authority from other jurisdictions; or secondary authority analyzing the law.

Once you have determined why you need to research persuasive authority, you should review the material you have already located. In your search for primary mandatory authority, you might already have identified some useful persuasive authority. Secondary sources consulted at the beginning of your research could contain persuasive analysis or useful citations to primary persuasive authority. Secondary sources often identify key or leading authorities in an area of law, and that might be enough to meet your needs. A citator might also have identified useful persuasive authority. If the authorities you have already located prove sufficient, you should update your research to make sure everything you cite remains authoritative and, if appropriate, end your search for persuasive authority.

On the other hand, you might review the results of your research and determine that you need to undertake a separate search for persuasive authority. When you first reviewed secondary sources and used citators, it might not have been with an eye toward locating persuasive authority. Therefore, you might want to take a second pass at these sources. In addition, the persuasive authority you ran across early in your research might not be the best material for you to cite; a more focused research effort could yield more pertinent material.

If you determine that you need to conduct a separate search for persuasive authority, your next step will be deciding the best research path to follow. The flowchart in **Figure 11.2** illustrates several research avenues for locating persuasive authority. Your research path will vary according to a number of factors, including the amount of time you have, the resources available to you, and the type of work product you are expected to produce. Therefore, the flowchart is intended simply to illustrate options that would be available to you, not to establish a definitive path for locating each type of authority.

One thing you might notice as you review the flowchart is that secondary sources play an important role in locating persuasive authority. Unless you know the precise jurisdiction from which you plan to cite persuasive authority, and the precise type of authority you need to locate (cases, statutes, etc.), beginning your search for persuasive authority in primary sources is not likely to be efficient in most cases. Secondary sources are key to determining which jurisdictions are likely to have relevant authority and which types of authority are likely to be helpful to you.

c. Deciding Between Print and Electronic Sources

One additional decision you will need to make in formulating a research plan is whether to conduct your research using print research tools, electronic tools, or both. For many research projects, a combination of the two will be necessary for complete, accurate, and efficient research. Some sources can be accessed more easily in one format or the other. In addition, if an initial search for a particular type of authority is unfruitful, you might want to switch from print sources to electronic, or vice versa. For purposes of this discussion, electronic sources include LexisNexis and Westlaw, as well as CD-ROM and Internet resources.

Generally speaking, you will want to use print research sources in the following circumstances:

■ **WHEN YOU ARE SEARCHING FOR MATERIAL NOT AVAILABLE ONLINE.** For example, although a number of secondary sources are available in electronic form, many others are not. Many treatises and hornbooks and a number of legal periodicals are not included in electronic research services. LexisNexis and Westlaw in particular do not include all legal periodicals in their databases, and their coverage is limited to articles published after 1980.

FIGURE 11.2 FLOWCHART FOR RESEARCHING PERSUASIVE AUTHORITY

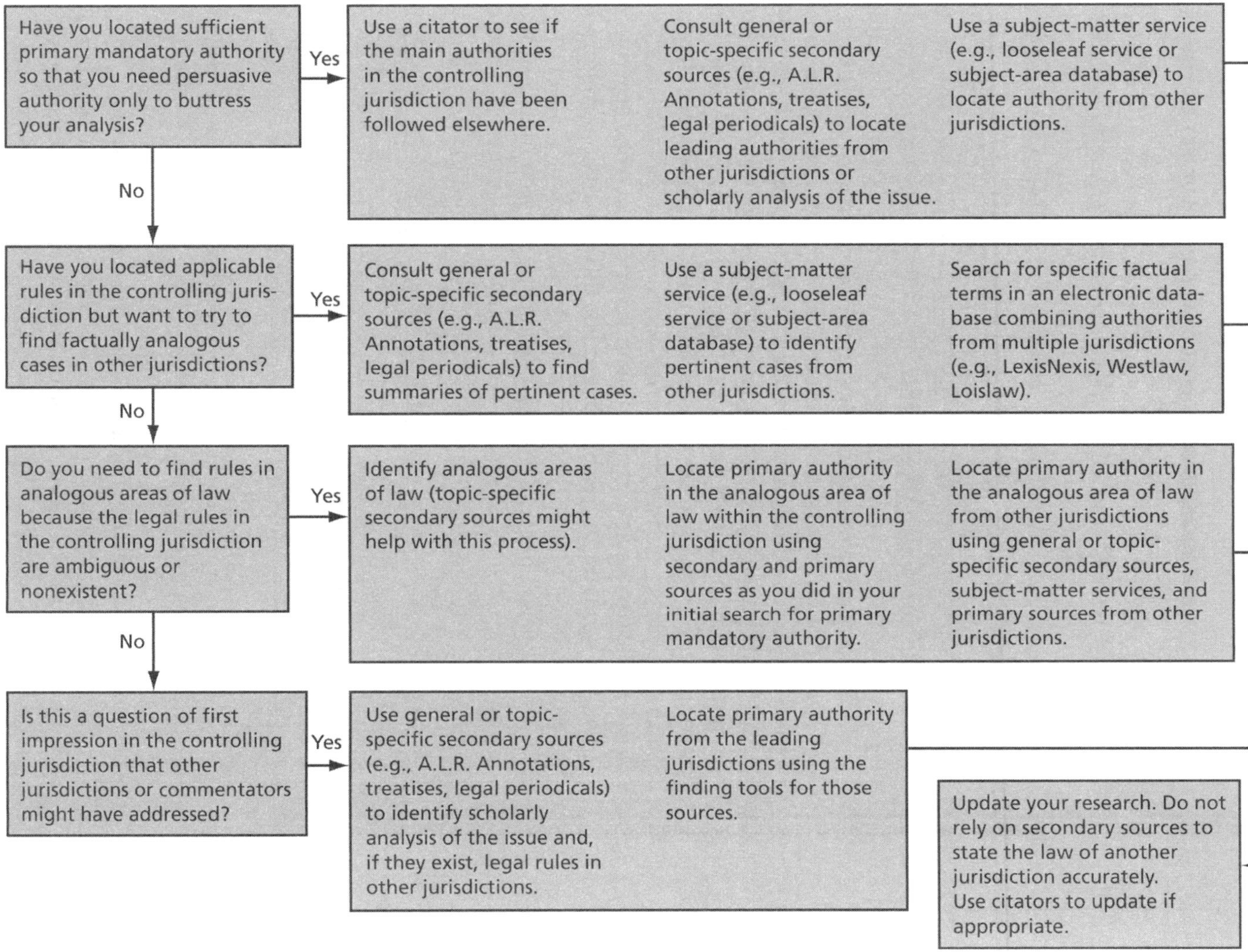

Have you located sufficient primary mandatory authority so that you need persuasive authority only to buttress your analysis?

No →

Yes →
- Use a citator to see if the main authorities in the controlling jurisdiction have been followed elsewhere.
- Consult general or topic-specific secondary sources (e.g., A.L.R. Annotations, treatises, legal periodicals) to locate leading authorities from other jurisdictions or scholarly analysis of the issue.
- Use a subject-matter service (e.g., looseleaf service or subject-area database) to locate authority from other jurisdictions.

Have you located applicable rules in the controlling jurisdiction but want to try to find factually analogous cases in other jurisdictions?

No →

Yes →
- Consult general or topic-specific secondary sources (e.g., A.L.R. Annotations, treatises, legal periodicals) to find summaries of pertinent cases.
- Use a subject-matter service (e.g., looseleaf service or subject-area database) to identify pertinent cases from other jurisdictions.
- Search for specific factual terms in an electronic database combining authorities from multiple jurisdictions (e.g., LexisNexis, Westlaw, Loislaw).

Do you need to find rules in analogous areas of law because the legal rules in the controlling jurisdiction are ambiguous or nonexistent?

No →

Yes →
- Identify analogous areas of law (topic-specific secondary sources might help with this process).
- Locate primary authority in the analogous area of law within the controlling jurisdiction using secondary and primary sources as you did in your initial search for primary mandatory authority.
- Locate primary authority in the analogous area of law from other jurisdictions using general or topic-specific secondary sources, subject-matter services, and primary sources from other jurisdictions.

Is this a question of first impression in the controlling jurisdiction that other jurisdictions or commentators might have addressed?

No →

Yes →
- Use general or topic-specific secondary sources (e.g., A.L.R. Annotations, treatises, legal periodicals) to identify scholarly analysis of the issue and, if they exist, legal rules in other jurisdictions.
- Locate primary authority from the leading jurisdictions using the finding tools for those sources.
- Locate primary authority in the analogous area of law from other jurisdictions using general or topic-specific secondary sources, subject-matter services, and primary sources from other jurisdictions.

→ Update your research. Do not rely on secondary sources to state the law of another jurisdiction accurately. Use citators to update if appropriate.

■ **WHEN YOU NEED GENERAL INFORMATION ON A TOPIC ABOUT WHICH YOU ARE UNFAMILIAR.**

It is difficult to draft an effective word search if you have little or no information about your topic, and electronic subject searching is not available in all services or for all types of authority. Searching by subject in print resources may be more effective in this situation.

■ **WHEN YOUR SEARCH TERMS ARE GENERAL OR THE SUBJECT OF YOUR RESEARCH INVOLVES BROAD CONCEPTS.**

A word search for terms such as "negligence" or "equal protection" will probably retrieve too many documents to be useful because it will retrieve every document in the database that contains those terms. By contrast, these general topics could be useful search terms in a print index. The print index may subdivide these general topics into subtopics so that you can target pertinent authorities. It may also limit its references to key authorities under the topic, rather than referring you to every authority containing those terms.

■ **WHEN YOU ARE CONDUCTING STATUTORY OR REGULATORY RESEARCH.**

There are two reasons why researching statutes and regulations can be difficult to do online. First, an electronic word search will search only for the terms you specify. A word search that does not include the precise statutory or regulatory language will not be effective. A print index, by contrast, is organized by subject and will contain cross-references that can help direct you to the correct terms or concepts. Second, you will often need to review the complete statutory or regulatory scheme to analyze your research issue. This can be difficult to do through piecemeal research into individual code sections or regulations done electronically, although it has become easier to do through search functions that allow you to see outlines and tables of contents. Nevertheless, statutory and regulatory research can be easiest to accomplish in print.

■ **WHEN YOU NEED TO READ AUTHORITIES LOCATED THROUGH OTHER MEANS.**

It can be difficult to read material on a computer screen. Although it is possible to print material retrieved electronically, cost considerations could make that a poor choice, and the format of the electronic version of a document might not be as easy to read as the print version.

By contrast, electronic research is most likely to be effective under the following circumstances:

■ **WHEN THE MATERIAL YOU NEED IS NOT AVAILABLE IN PRINT.**

The scope of the print collection will vary from library to library; thus, some material you need might only be available in electronic form. In addition, some subject-matter services are available only in CD-ROM format or on the Internet. Even if material is available in print in your library, some material might be easier to access in electronic form. For example, legislative history research is often easier to conduct via the Internet using LexisNexis Congressional or Thomas than in the microfiche format available in many libraries.

■ WHEN YOU HAVE UNIQUE SEARCH TERMS OR ARE SEARCHING FOR PROPER NAMES.

If you have unique search terms, electronic sources can be a good search option because electronic word searches will search for the precise terms you need, whereas print sources organized by subject might not index those terms. Searches for proper names can also be accomplished effectively in electronic resources.

■ WHEN YOU NEED TO UPDATE YOUR RESEARCH.

Not all electronic resources are more up to date than print resources, but many are. Updating your research can often be quickly and efficiently accomplished using electronic sources.

When these circumstances do not apply to your research, you will have a choice between print or electronic sources. The amount of time you have for your research, cost considerations, and your level of comfort with the research tools available will inform your choice about which resources to use. Chapter 10, on electronic research, compares several print and electronic search techniques. You may want to review that material when deciding between print and electronic research.

3. WORKING EFFECTIVELY

a. Keeping Track: Effective Note Taking

Once you have created your research plan, you are ready to begin your search for authority. Keeping effective notes as you work is important for several reasons. It will make your research more efficient. You will know where you have already looked, so you can avoid repeating research steps. This is especially critical if you will be working on the project for an extended period of time or if you are working with other people in completing the research. You will also have all of the information you need for proper citations. Moreover, if it happens that your project presents novel or complex issues for which there are no definitive answers, careful note taking will allow you to demonstrate that you undertook comprehensive research to try to resolve those issues.

Note taking is an individualized process, and there is no single right way to do it. Your personal preferences will largely dictate the method you use. Some people use binders, folders, or pads of paper. Others take notes electronically by creating files and folders on a computer or taking notes with a PDA. Having said that, however, many people find their notes easiest to follow if the notes are organized around topics or issues, rather than by type of authority or individual source. Then within each topic or issue, specific information on each authority can be noted. Regardless of the method you use for keeping notes, you should try to keep each of the following items of information on each source you use:

Source or database

Citation This does not need to be in proper citation form, but enough information for a proper citation should be included here.

Method of locating the source This could include references to a secondary source that led you to this authority or the search terms you used in an index or electronic database.

Summary of relevant information This might be a few sentences or a few pages, depending on the source and its relevance; specific page or section numbers should be noted, and all quotations should be marked clearly here to avoid inadvertent plagiarism later, especially if you are cutting and pasting from electronic sources.

Updating information Note whether the source has been updated and the method of updating. If you are researching in print, you might note the date of any pocket part or supplement. For electronic research, you should note the updating date for the source. If appropriate, you should also note which citator you use to verify the validity of the source.

This might not be the only information you need to note. For example, in case research, you might also want to note separately the topics and key numbers in the most important cases. At a minimum, however, you should keep track of these pieces of information. Once you find a method of note taking that is effective for you, you might be able to create a form or template that you use for each source you locate.

As you work through your research plan, be sure to keep notes of the steps you follow both in print and electronically. With electronic research, it is easy to follow a series of links until you lose track of where you have gone. Both LexisNexis and Westlaw will save your research trails so you can retrace your steps later, but they do not save this information indefinitely, and other electronic research services may not save this information at all. Although most web browsers will give you at least limited ability to retrace your steps, your computer might not save this information in a useful format. Therefore, it is important to keep notes on your electronic research while you are doing it.

There is a constant tension as you are researching between keeping written notes on the material you locate and photocopying, printing, or downloading the material itself. Most people print more than they need, and many students use printing as a procrastination technique, promising themselves that they will read the information later. Excessive downloading, printing, or copying will not improve your research. Certainly, having access to key authorities is important for accurate analysis, quotation, and citation. Facing a huge, disorganized stack of paper, however, can be demoralizing, especially because most of the information will probably prove to be irrelevant in the end if you have not made thoughtful choices about what to copy or print.

The fact is that you will not know for certain at the beginning of your research which sources should be saved and which should not. Only as you begin to understand the contours of the legal issue will the relevance (or irrelevance) of individual legal authorities become apparent to you. Therefore, you should conduct some research before you begin saving material, and as you delve into the research, you might find that you need to go back and obtain copies of materials you bypassed originally. If you copy or print material or cut and paste material from electronic sources, make sure all of the necessary information for a proper citation is included, and make a note at the beginning indicating why you saved the item and any steps you took to update the source.

b. Deciding When to Stop

Deciding when your research is complete can be difficult. The more research you do, the more comfortable you will be with the process, and the more you will develop an internal sense of when a project is complete. In your first few research assignments in law school, however, you will probably feel uncertain about when to stop because you will have little prior experience to draw upon in making that decision.

One issue that affects a person's sense of when to stop is personal work style. Some people are anxious to begin writing and therefore stop researching after they locate a few sources that seem relevant. Others put off writing by continuing to research and research, thinking that the answer will become apparent if they just keep looking a little bit more. Being aware of your work style will help you determine whether you have stopped too soon or are continuing your research beyond what is necessary for the assignment.

Of course, the amount of time you have and the work product you are expected to produce will affect the ending point for your research. If you are instructed to report back in half an hour with your research results, you know when you will need to stop. In general, however, you will know that you have come full circle in your research when, after following a comprehensive research path through a variety of sources, the authorities you locate start to refer back to each other and the new sources you consult fail to reveal significant new information.

The fact that a few of the sources you have located appear relevant does not mean it is time to stop researching. Until you have explored other potential research avenues, you should continue your work. It might be that the authorities you initially locate will turn out to be the most relevant, but you cannot have confidence in that result until you research additional authorities. On the other hand, you can always keep looking for one more case or one more article to support your analysis, but at some point, the benefit of continuing to research will be too small to justify the additional effort. It is unlikely that one magical source exists that is going to resolve your research issue. If the issue were clear, you probably would not have been asked to research it. If you developed a comprehensive research strategy and followed it until you came full circle in your research, it is probably time to stop.

C. FINDING HELP

Even if you follow all of the steps outlined in this chapter, from time to time, you will not be able to find what you need. The two most common situations that arise are not being able to find any authority on an issue and finding an overwhelming amount of information.

1. WHAT TO DO IF YOU ARE UNABLE TO FIND ANYTHING

If you have researched several different sources and are unable to find anything, it is time to take a different approach. You should not expect the material you need to appear effortlessly, and blind alleys are inevitable if you approach a problem creatively. Nevertheless, if you find that you really cannot locate any information on an issue, consider the following possibilities:

■ **MAKE SURE YOU UNDERSTAND THE PROBLEM.**
One possibility is that you have misunderstood a critical aspect of the problem. If diligent research truly yields nothing, you might want to go back to the person who gave you the assignment to make sure you correctly noted all of the factual information you need and have understood the assignment correctly.

■ **RETHINK YOUR SEARCH TERMS.**
Have you expanded the breadth and depth of your search terms? You might be researching the right concepts but not have expressed them in a

way that yields information in print indices or electronic databases. Expanding your search terms will allow you to look not only more widely for information, but also more narrowly. For example, if you have searched unsuccessfully under "moving vehicles" for authority involving transportation equipment, you might need to move to more concrete terms, such as "automobiles" or "cars."

In addition, you might need to rethink search terms directed to applicable legal theories. If you have focused on a theory of recovery for which you have not been able to locate authority, you might need to think about other ways to approach the problem. Try not to become so wedded to a legal theory that you pursue it to the exclusion of other viable claims or defenses.

■ **GO BACK TO SECONDARY SOURCES.**

If you did not consult secondary sources originally, you might want to take that route to find the information you need. The material on the issue might be scattered through many digest topics or statutory sections so that it is difficult to locate without secondary sources that compile the relevant information. In addition, the search terms that seemed applicable when you started your research might, in fact, not be helpful. Secondary sources can help point you in the right direction.

Another difficulty is that you might be looking for the wrong type of authority. Are you sure this is a question of state law? Might statutes as well as cases apply to the situation? Secondary sources can help you determine what type of primary authority is likely to be relevant to the situation.

Finally, secondary sources can help you determine whether you are facing a question of first impression. If the controlling jurisdiction simply has not faced this question yet, secondary sources should direct you to jurisdictions that have. If no jurisdiction has resolved the issue, legal periodicals might direct you to arguments and analogies that could be made.

2. WHAT TO DO IF YOU FIND AN OVERWHELMING AMOUNT OF MATERIAL

The same research options that will help you if you are unable to find any material will also help you if you find an overwhelming amount of material. Making sure you understand the problem, of course, is critical. Rethinking your search terms to narrow your approach can also help. If you located information primarily using electronic word searches, you might want to try searching by subject, using either print or electronic research tools, because searching by subject instead of by terms in the document might help you focus on relevant authority. Consulting secondary sources, however, is probably the most useful strategy.

Synthesizing large amounts of authority is difficult. Secondary sources can help you identify the key authorities and otherwise limit the scope of the information on the issue.

Another consideration here is the scope of your research. If much of the authority you have located is secondary authority or primary persuasive authority, you might need to refocus on primary mandatory authority from the controlling jurisdiction. If the controlling jurisdiction has a sufficient amount of authority for thorough analysis of the issue, you might not need to cite persuasive authority. You might also need to narrow your scope by limiting the legal theories you are considering. If some are clearly more viable than others and you already have an overwhelming amount of authority, you might want to focus on the theories that seem to provide your client with the best chances of prevailing.

D. SAMPLE RESEARCH PLANS

The research plans in **Figures 11.3** through **11.6** are intended to help you develop a coherent research strategy for four common types of research: state common-law research, state statutory research, federal statutory research, and federal and state procedural research. These plans are representative samples of how you could approach the research process and may provide a useful starting point for your own research planning.

1. STATE COMMON-LAW RESEARCH

FIGURE 11.3 FLOWCHART FOR STATE COMMON-LAW RESEARCH

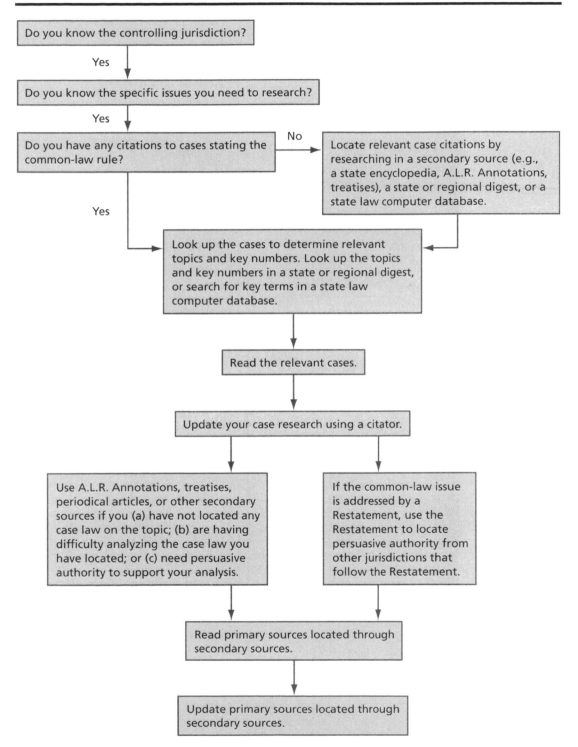

2. State Statutory Research

FIGURE 11.4   FLOWCHART FOR STATE STATUTORY RESEARCH

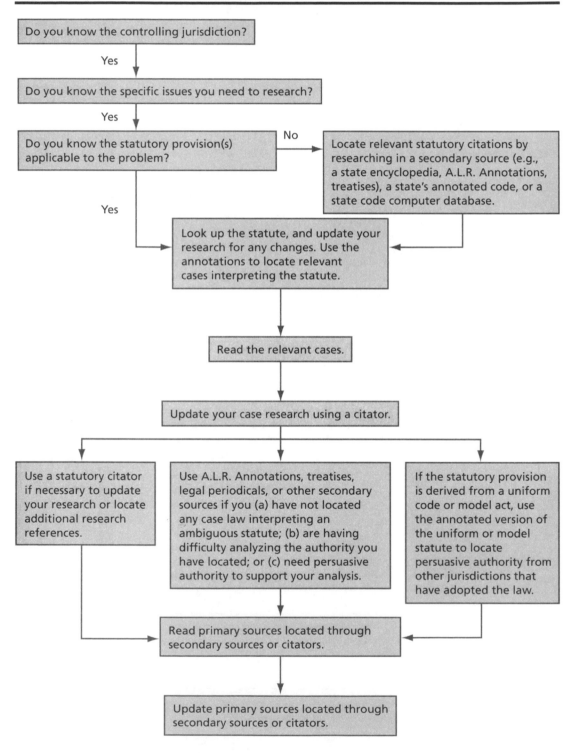

3. FEDERAL STATUTORY RESEARCH

FIGURE 11.5 FLOWCHART FOR FEDERAL STATUTORY RESEARCH

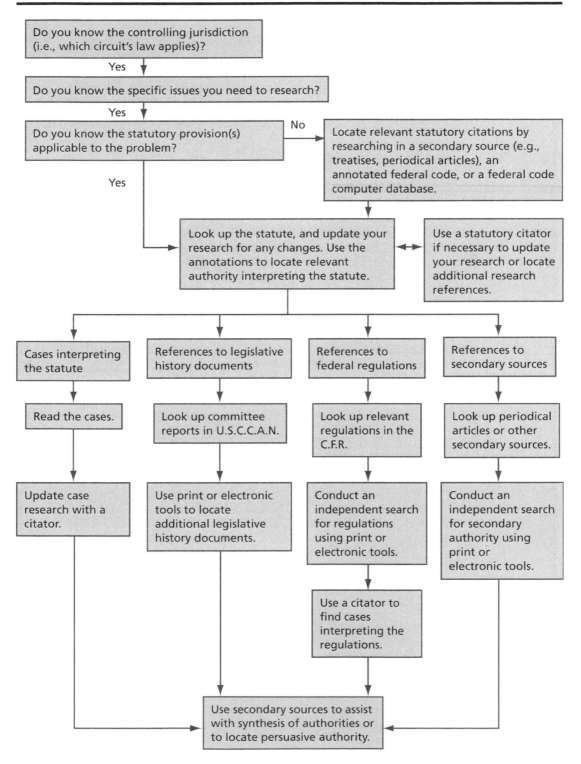

4. FEDERAL OR STATE PROCEDURAL RESEARCH

FIGURE 11.6   FLOWCHART FOR RESEARCHING RULES OF PROCEDURE

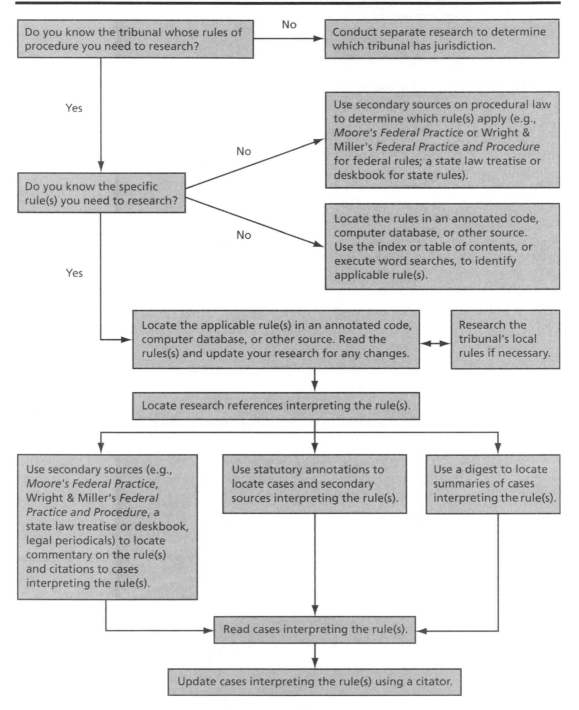

E. RESEARCH CHECKLISTS

1. CHECKLIST FOR DEVELOPING AN EFFECTIVE RESEARCH PLAN

1. OBTAIN PRELIMINARY INFORMATION ON THE PROBLEM

❑ Determine the due date, work product expected, limits on research tools to be used, controlling jurisdiction (if known), and whether persuasive authority should be located (if known).

❑ If permitted, find out useful research tools, background on the law or terms of art, and whether other written materials or individuals with special expertise should be consulted.

2. WRITE OUT A PLAN

❑ Develop a preliminary issue statement.

❑ Generate a list of search terms.

❑ Identify the type and sequence of research sources to consult by identifying what you know, what you do not yet know, and how best to fill in the blanks.

  ■ Locate primary mandatory authority first.
  ■ Locate persuasive authority later, if necessary:

    ■ to buttress an analysis largely resolved by primary mandatory authority
    ■ to locate factually analogous cases from other jurisdictions
    ■ to make an analogy to another area of law when the applicable rule is unclear
    ■ to locate commentary or applicable rules from other jurisdictions on an issue of first impression.

  ■ Determine the best mix of print and electronic research tools for your research project.

3. WORK EFFECTIVELY

❑ Keep effective notes.

❑ Stop researching when your research has come full circle.

❑ Find help if you need it.

  ■ If you are unable to find anything or find too much material, make sure you understand the problem, rethink your search terms, consult secondary sources, and reevaluate the legal theories you are pursuing.

2. MASTER CHECKLIST OF RESEARCH SOURCES

The following is an abbreviated collection of the research checklists that appear at the end of the preceding chapters in this book. This master checklist may help you develop your research plan. It may also be useful to you while you are conducting research.

Secondary Source Research

1. LEGAL ENCYCLOPEDIAS

❏ Use for very general background information and limited citations to primary authority, but not for in-depth analysis of a topic.

❏ Locate information in print by using the subject index or table of contents, locating relevant sections in the main volumes, and updating with the pocket part.

❏ Use word or table of contents searches in LexisNexis and Westlaw to access Am. Jur. 2d.; use Westlaw to access C.J.S.

2. TREATISES

❏ Use for an in-depth discussion and some analysis of an area of law and for citations to primary authority.

❏ Locate treatises in print through the online catalog; locate information within a treatise by using the subject index or table of contents, locating material in the main volumes, and updating with the pocket part.

❏ Use word or table of contents searches in LexisNexis and Westlaw to access selected treatises.

3. LEGAL PERIODICALS

❏ Use for background information, citations to primary authority, in-depth analysis of a narrow topic, or information on a conflict in the law or an undeveloped area of the law.

❏ Use the LegalTrac and ILP electronic indices to locate citations to periodical articles and full text of selected articles.

❏ Use LexisNexis and Westlaw to access periodical articles.

❏ Use HeinOnline to locate the full text of legal periodicals in .pdf format.

❏ Selected periodicals may be available on the Internet.

4. *AMERICAN LAW REPORTS*

❏ Use A.L.R.3d, A.L.R.4th, A.L.R.5th, A.L.R.6th, A.L.R. Fed., or A.L.R. Fed. 2d for an overview of an area of law and citations to primary authority.

❏ Locate material in A.L.R. by using the A.L.R. Index, locating material in the main volumes, and updating with the pocket part.

❏ Use Westlaw to locate A.L.R. Annotations.

5. RESTATEMENTS

❏ Use for research into common-law subjects and to locate mandatory and persuasive authority from jurisdictions that have adopted a Restatement.

❏ Locate information within a print Restatement by using the subject index or table of contents to find Restatement sections in the Restatement volumes, locating case summaries in the noncumulative Appendix volumes, and updating the Appendix volumes with the pocket part.

❏ Use LexisNexis and Westlaw to access Restatement rules and case annotations.

6. UNIFORM LAWS AND MODEL ACTS

❏ Use to interpret a law adopted by a legislature and to locate persuasive authority from other jurisdictions that have adopted the law.

❏ Locate in print using *Uniform Laws Annotated, Master Edition* (ULA).

❏ Locate information in the ULA set by using the *Directory of Uniform Acts and Codes: Tables and Index*, locating relevant provisions in the main volumes, and updating with the pocket part.

❏ Use LexisNexis and Westlaw to access selected uniform laws and model acts.

Case Research

1. SELECT A PRINT DIGEST

❏ Use federal, state, regional, or combined digests.

2. LOCATE TOPICS AND KEY NUMBERS IN A PRINT DIGEST

❏ Work from a case on point, the Descriptive-Word Index, or the topic entry.

3. READ THE CASE SUMMARIES IN THE PRINT DIGEST

❏ Use the court and date abbreviations to target appropriate cases.

4. UPDATE PRINT DIGEST RESEARCH

❑ Check the pocket part and any cumulative or noncumulative interim pamphlets.
❑ If necessary, check the closing table and mini-digests.

5. ELECTRONIC CASE RESEARCH

❑ Locate cases by subject.

- In Westlaw, use the West Key Number Digest Outline (Custom Digest) function to search by digest topic and key number or the KeySearch function to search by subject.
- In LexisNexis, use the Topic or Headnote search function to search by subject.

❑ Locate cases with word searches in Westlaw and LexisNexis.
❑ Selected cases may be available on the Internet.

Research with Citators

1. USE SHEPARD'S IN LEXISNEXIS

❑ Access Shepard's from the Shepard's tab or from a relevant case.
❑ Interpret the entry.

- Direct history appears first, followed by citing cases organized by jurisdiction and secondary sources.
- Use history and treatment codes and headnote references to identify the most relevant citing cases.
- Customize the display to focus on the most relevant information.

2. USE KEYCITE IN WESTLAW

❑ Access KeyCite from the KeyCite link or from a relevant case.
❑ Interpret the entry.

- View the Full History of the original case to see direct history and negative indirect history or the Direct History (Graphical View) to see the history of the original case in chart form.
- View the Citing References to see indirect history and citing sources; negative cases appear first, followed by positive cases (divided by depth of treatment and then by jurisdiction) and citing sources.
- Use the descriptions of the history and treatment and headnote references to identify the most relevant cases.
- Customize the display to focus on the most relevant information.

Statutory Research

1. LOCATE A STATUTE

❐ Use a subject index, popular name table, or for federal statutes, the conversion tables in print.

❐ Use LexisNexis and Westlaw to access state and federal statutes electronically using word, table of contents, or popular name searches; in Westlaw, use the statutory index.

❐ On the Internet, locate statutes on government or general legal research web sites.

2. READ THE STATUTE AND ACCOMPANYING ANNOTATIONS

3. UPDATE YOUR RESEARCH

❐ With print research, check the pocket part accompanying the main volume and any cumulative or noncumulative supplements accompanying the code.

■ In U.S.C.A., update entries to the popular name and conversion tables with the noncumulative supplements.

■ In state codes, check for additional updating tools.

❐ With state or federal statutory research, update your research or find additional research references using a statutory citator such as Shepard's in LexisNexis or KeyCite in Westlaw.

❐ With Internet research, check the date of the statute and update your research accordingly; consider using a statutory citator to update your research and find additional research references.

Federal Legislative History Research

1. IDENTIFY THE SCOPE OF YOUR RESEARCH

❐ Determine whether you need to find the history of a particular statute or material on a general subject.

2. LOCATE A COMPILED LEGISLATIVE HISTORY

❐ Use the library's online catalog; Johnson, *Sources of Compiled Legislative Histories*; or *Reams, Federal Legislative Histories*.

3. LOCATE COMMITTEE REPORTS IN U.S.C.C.A.N.

❐ Use annotations in U.S.C.A. to locate cross-references to U.S.C.C.A.N.

4. LOCATE COMPLETE LEGISLATIVE HISTORIES IN THE CIS MICROFICHE SET

❒ Use the Legislative Histories volumes or Index and Abstracts.

5. LOCATE FLOOR DEBATES IN THE *CONGRESSIONAL RECORD* USING PRINT SOURCES

❒ Use the *Congressional Record* index to search by subject or bill number.
❒ Locate references to floor debates using the CIS Legislative Histories volumes or reports reprinted in U.S.C.C.A.N.

6. SEARCH FOR LEGISLATIVE HISTORY ELECTRONICALLY

❒ Use Hein Online, LexisNexis, and Westlaw to locate compiled legislative histories.
❒ Use LexisNexis Congressional for electronic access to the CIS legislative histories.
❒ Use Westlaw, LexisNexis, Thomas, and GPO Access to locate a range of legislative documents.

Federal Administrative Law Research

1. LOCATE PERTINENT REGULATIONS

❒ Use statutory cross-references or a subject index to locate federal regulations in the C.F.R. in print.
❒ Use LexisNexis, GPO Access, or other Internet sites to locate unannotated C.F.R. provisions electronically using word or table of contents searches.
❒ Use Westlaw to locate an annotated version of the C.F.R. using word, table of contents, or index searches.

2. UPDATE GPO ACCESS RESEARCH WITH THE e-CFR

3. UPDATE C.F.R. RESEARCH WITH OFFICIAL SOURCES

❒ Update from the date of the C.F.R. volume through the end of the prior month by using the most recent LSA to find *Federal Register* references affecting the regulation.
❒ Update from the end of the prior month to the present by using the cumulative Current List of CFR Parts Affected (electronically) or table of CFR Parts Affected (in the most recent print issue of the *Federal Register*).

4. CONTACT THE AGENCY FOR ADDITIONAL INFORMATION ON RECENT OR PROPOSED REGULATORY CHANGES

5. **USE SHEPARD'S IN LEXISNEXIS OR KEYCITE IN WESTLAW TO LOCATE RESEARCH REFERENCES**

Subject-Matter Service Research

1. **LOCATE A SUBJECT-MATTER SERVICE FOR YOUR RESEARCH ISSUE**

   ❐ Use Table T.15 in the back of the *Bluebook*, a reference source such as the LawTRIO database or print sources such as *Legal Looseleafs in Print* or *Directory of Law-Related CD-ROMs*, or subject area databases in LexisNexis and Westlaw.

2. **DETERMINE HOW TO USE THE SERVICE**

   ❐ In print services, look for the "Overview" or "How to use this service" section.

   ❐ In CD-ROM and Internet services, follow the service's instructions.

   ❐ In LexisNexis and Westlaw, execute word searches or use other available search options.

Electronic Legal Research

1. **SELECT AN ELECTRONIC RESEARCH SERVICE**

   ❐ Consider the scope of coverage and cost.

2. **SELECT A SEARCH TECHNIQUE**

   ❐ Search techniques: retrieving a document from its citation; searching by subject using a table of contents or index; conducting a word search.

   ❐ For word searches, construct an effective Boolean search by developing the initial search, expanding the breadth and depth of the search, using connectors and parentheses, and using a field or segment restriction.

   ❐ Natural language searching may also be available.

3. **SELECT A DATABASE TO SEARCH AND REVIEW THE RESULTS**

   ❐ Search the narrowest appropriate database.

   ❐ Browse documents or review a citation list to evaluate your search results.

   ❐ Refine the search if necessary.

4. **RESEARCH EFFECTIVELY IN WESTLAW AND LEXISNEXIS**

   ❐ In Westlaw, browse documents using the list of citations or Term function; refine word searches by editing the search or using the Locate function.

❑ In LexisNexis, browse documents in Full or KWIC using the Term function, view a list of citations in Cite, or customize the display using Custom; refine word searches by editing the query or using the FOCUS, More Like This, or More Like Selected Text functions.

❑ In both services, use search strategies for cost effectiveness.

5. USE ADDITIONAL TOOLS FOR EFFECTIVE ELECTRONIC RESEARCH

❑ Use an alert or clipping service to keep research up to date.

❑ Use publicly available Internet sources by locating useful sites, assessing the credibility of the source, saving or printing copies of useful pages, and verifying and updating legal authorities.

SELECTED INTERNET RESEARCH RESOURCES

FEDERAL GOVERNMENT WEB SITES

GPO Access
http://www.gpoaccess.gov
> Contains congressional bills, hearings, and reports, as well as a weekly compilation of Presidential documents. The *Code of Federal Regulations, Federal Register*, and *United States Code* are also included. An archive of federal web sites is also accessible through the Cybercemetery of Former Federal Web Sites.

Library of Congress
http://www.loc.gov
> Search the online catalog of the Library of Congress, and locate a wealth of legal and general information.

Thomas
http://thomas.loc.gov
> The Library of Congress's online source for legislative information. This site contains committee reports, the *Congressional Record*, and other legislative history documents.

United States House of Representatives
http://www.house.gov
> The site for the House of Representatives. This site contains an electronic version of the United States Code.

United States Senate
http://www.senate.gov
> The site for the Senate.

United States Supreme Court
http://www.supremecourtus.gov
> The site for the U.S. Supreme Court.

USA.gov
http://www.usa.gov
> The U.S. government's official portal to a wide range of government resources.

United States Courts of Appeals
http://www.ca[identifier].uscourts.gov
> Each federal circuit court of appeals has its own web site; insert the number of the circuit as the identifier in the web address above to access a numbered circuit's site, e.g., ca1 for the First Circuit; ca2 for the Second Circuit, etc. For the Federal Circuit, use the abbreviation cafc, and for the District of Columbia Circuit, use cadc.

The White House
http://www.whitehouse.gov
> The site for the White House.

STATE GOVERNMENT WEB SITES

National Center for State Courts
http://www.ncsconline.org
> The National Center for State Courts (NCSC) provides links to the web site for each state's judicial branch in the "Information" section of the NCSC web site.

Every state government has a portal that provides access to a wide range of legal information for the state. You can locate state-specific web sites using a search engine or through the library web sites listed below.

LIBRARY WEB SITES

These sites can be used to search for a wide range of legal authorities, including state and federal cases and statutes, administrative materials, secondary sources, and legal news.

Cornell Law School's Legal Information Institute
http://www.law.cornell.edu

The University of Michigan Documents Center, State Legal Resources on the Web
http://www.lib.umich.edu/govdocs/statelaw.html

Washburn University School of Law WashLaw Legal Research on the Web
http://www.washlaw.edu

General Legal Research Web Sites

Like the law library web sites, these sites provide access to a wide range of legal materials. Some can be accessed free of charge; others are fee-based services.

Free Services

All Law
http://www.alllaw.com

American Bar Association: The Lawlink Legal Research Jumpstation
http://www.abanet.org/lawlink/home.html

American Law Sources On-line
http://www.lawsource.com

FindLaw
http://lp.findlaw.com

HG.org
http://www.hg.org

LawGuru
http://www.lawguru.com

LLRX.com
http://www.llrx.com

Megalaw.com
http://www.megalaw.com

Rominger Legal
http://www.romingerlegal.com

Fee-based Services

LexisNexis
http://www.lexis.com

Loislaw
http://www.loislaw.com

VersusLaw
http://www.versuslaw.com

Westlaw
http://www.westlaw.com

INTERNET SEARCH ENGINES

You undoubtedly know of many general search engines. Those listed here are specialized search engines.

Google Scholar
http://www.scholar.google.com
    Searches scholarly literature.

LawBot
http://www.megalaw.com
    Searches for legal web sites.

MetaCrawler
http://www.metacrawler.com
    Allows you to excute a search through multiple search engines simultaneously.

OTHER WEB SITES OF INTEREST

ALWD Citation Manual
http://www.alwdmanual.com
    Contains updates and information on the *ALWD Citation Manual*.

Blawg
http://www.blawg.com
    Contains a directory of law-related blogs.

Bluebook
http://www.legalbluebook.com
    Contains the electronic version of the *Bluebook*, along with tips and updates available without a subscription.

Introduction to Basic Legal Citation
http://www.law.cornell.edu/citation
    Provides tips on using the *Bluebook* and *ALWD Citation Manual*.

Internet Archive Wayback Machine
http://www.archive.org
    Contains archived web pages. To see what a web site displayed on a date in the past, enter the URL for the site, and select the date.

Law.com
http://www.law.com
> Contains legal news, employment listings, and other legal information.

LawyersUSA
http://www.lawyersweeklyusa.com
> Contains legal news, classified advertisements, and selected court opinions.

Martindale-Hubbell
http://www.martindale.com
> Search for individual lawyers, firms, or government agencies employing attorneys.

Social Science Research Network (SSRN)
http://www.ssrn.com
> Provides full-text access to articles on a variety of subjects, including economics, law, and political science. To locate articles on legal topics, select the option to search the Legal Scholarship Network (LSN).

Subscription Services

This list of subscription services does not include their web addresses because individual users cannot access these services' search features from their web sites. Your library may subscribe to the services listed below. If so, you may be able to access them through the library's network.

Casemaker
> A service providing full-text access to a range of primary authorities that is available through some state bar associations.

HeinOnline
> A service providing full-text access to legal periodicals, legislative history documents, and other publications.

Index to Legal Periodicals
> A periodical index that also provides full text of selected articles.

LegalTrac
> A periodical index that also provides full text of selected articles.

LexisNexis Congressional
> A service that provides full-text access to federal legislative history documents.

Index

Bold page numbers indicate reprinted examples.

Abandoned and lost property (research
example)
   case summaries, **87**, **114–115**
   Descriptive-Word Index (DWI), **92**,
      109–111
   digest volume, pocket part, **116**
   interim pamphlets, noncumulative,
      117–118
   key number outline, **112–113**
   mini-digests, **119**
   topic entry for, **86**
A.D. Cases. *See Americans with*
     Disabilities Cases
ADA. *See* Americans with Disabilities
     Act (research example)
Administrative agencies, 237–240, 258
Administrative law research. *See* Federal
     administrative law research
Administrative Procedure Act (APA), 238
AdvanceLink, 293
Agency staff members, regulation
     research via, 241, 258
Alert (LexisNexis), 293, 304
Alert or clipping services, 138–139, 145,
     182, 292–293, 304. *See also*
     KeyCite Alert; Shepard's Alert
A.L.R. *See American Law Reports*
ALWD Manual: A Professional System of
     Citation, 19–22
   abbreviations (Appendices 1, 3, 4, & 5),
      18, 20–21

A.L.R. Annotations (Rule 24), 54, 57
appendices, 20–21
case citations, 105–108
   case names (Rule 12.2 &
      Appendix 3), 106–107
   electronic legal research services, 297
   parentheticals (Rules 12.6-12.7 &
      Appendixes 1 & 4), 106, 107–108
   primary sources by jurisdiction
      (Appendix 1), 20–21
   print, 105–108
   reporters (Rules 12.3-12.5 &
      Appendix 1), 106, 107
   rules governing, 106
   Westlaw or LexisNexis (Rule 12.12),
      297
electronic legal research services,
     296–299
   cases, 297
   Internet materials (Rules 38 & 40),
      298
   statutes (Rule 14.5), 297–298
Fast Formats, 21
federal administrative publications
     (Appendix 8), 21
federal legislative history (Rule 15),
     222–224
Federal Register (Rule 19), 252
federal taxation materials
     (Appendix 7), 21
index, 19, 20

legal encyclopedias (Rule 26), 54–55
legal periodicals (Rule 23), 54, 56–57
local court rules (Appendix 2), 21
memorandum (Appendix 6), 21
model acts (Appendix 3), 54, 58–59
overview, 15, 19–22
periodical abbreviations
        (Appendix 5), 57
regulations (Rule 19), 252
Restatements (Rule 27), 54, 58
secondary sources (Rules 22-24, 26,
        27 & Appendix 5), 53–59
Sidebars, 20
statutes
    citing in print (Rule 14 &
        Appendix 1), 184–186
    electronic legal research services
        (Rule 14.5), 297–298
    subject-matter service research (Rule 28 &
        Appendix 3), 263–264
table of contents, 19, 20
text of citation rules, 19, 20
treatises (Rule 22), 55–56
uniform laws & model acts (Rule 27),
        54, 58–59
web site, 21
Am. Jur. 2d. *See American Jurisprudence,*
        Second Edition
American Jurisprudence, Second Edition
    checklist, legal encyclopedias, 74, 326
    citation to, 54–55
    described, 32–33
    electronic research, 50
    false imprisonment (research example),
        34–36
    index, **34**
American Law Reports, 40–41
    annotations
        citations, 54, 57–58
        index, **60**
        later page, **43**
        sample pages, **60–68**
    checklist, 75, 326–327
    electronic research, 50, 138
    false imprisonment (research example),
        60
    index, **60, 62**
    pocket parts, **67–68**
American Law Sources Online, 271
Americans with Disabilities Act (research
        example), **264–267**
Americans with Disabilities Cases
        (A.D. Cases), 265

case example, **267**
classification numbers, 265, **267**
Annotated codes, 159, 161, 166. *See
        also* United States Code
        Annotated (U.S.C.A.);
        United States Code Service
        (U.S.C.S.)
APA (Administrative Procedure Act), 238
Association of Legal Writing Directors
        Citation Manual. *See ALWD
        Manual*
Authority, generally
    electronic sources, 12–15
    print products, 13–14
    types of, 4–9
        distinguishing among, 5
        mandatory vs. persuasive authority,
            4–9, 10
        primary vs. secondary authority, 4–5
        relationships among, 8–9, 10
        research path, planning, 11
    weight of, 5–9
        jurisdiction of court, 8–9
        level of court, 6–9
        persuasive, 5–9, 10
        primary, 5–9
        secondary, 5, 10
Automatic residential garage door
        operator, safety standards for
        (research example)
    Code of Federal Regulations (CFR),
        239–240, 254
    e-CFR, **255–256**
    index entry, **253**
    List of CFR Sections Affected (LSA),
        249, **255–256**
    Federal Register, **248, 250**
    GPO Access, **255**
    United States Code Service (U.S.C.S.),
        243

Bills, passage of, 200–202, **201**
Blawg (directory of law-related
        blogs), 296
*The Bluebook: A Uniform System of
        Citation,* 15–19
    abbreviations, 18, 19
    A.L.R. Annotations (Rule 16.6.6), 54,
        57–58
    Bluepages and Bluepages tables, 16
    capitalization (Bluepages B13), 57, 58,
        185–186, 222

case citations, 105–108, 106
 case names (Bluepages B5.1.1 &
  Tables T.6 & T.10), 106–107
 court names (Table T.7), 107–108
 parentheticals (Bluepages B5.1.3 &
  Table T.1), 106, 107–108
 reporters (Bluepages B5.1.2, B5.1.3, &
  Table T.1), 106, 107
 Westlaw and LexisNexis (Bluepages
  B5.1.3), 297
electronic legal research services, 296–299
 cases, 297
 Internet materials, 298–299
 statutes, 297–298
electronic version, 18–19
federal legislative history (Bluepages
 B6.1.6 & Rule 13), 222–224
Federal Register, 252
finding tools for rules, 18
index, 18, 19
inside covers, 18
Internet citations (Rule 18.2), 298–299
legal encyclopedias (Bluepages B8), 54–55
legal periodicals (Bluepages B9), 54,
 56–57
model acts (Rules 12.8.4 & 12.8.5),
 54, 58–59
newspaper articles (Bluepages B9.1.4),
 299
overview, 12, 15
periodical abbreviations (Table T.13),
 57, 264
quick reference examples, 18, 19
regulations (Bluepages B6.1.4 &
 Rule 14.2), 252
Restatements (Bluepages B6.1.3), 54, 58
secondary sources, 53–59
statutes
 citing (Bluepages B6 & Table T.1),
  184–186
 electronic legal research services,
  297–298
steps for using, 19
subject-matter service research
 (Rule 19), 261, 263–264
 abbreviations for (Table T.15),
  261, 264
table of contents, 18, 19
tables, 17–18, 19
text of citation rules, 17
tips and updates, 18–19
treatises, 54, 55–56
typeface, briefs and memoranda, 19

uniform laws & model acts (Rules
 12.8.4 & 12.8.5), 54, 58–59
BNA. *See* Bureau of National Affairs
Boolean searching, 277–284
 basic search, 281–283
 connectors, 278–281
 constructing search, 277–284
  basic search, 281–283
  sophisticated search, 283–284
 fields, **278**, 283–284
 flexibility of, 285
 reviewing search results, 286
 search commands, 278–281
 segments, **279**, 283–284
 sophisticated search, 283–284
Branches of government
 legal rules and, 2
 relationships, 3–4
Bureau of National Affairs (BNA)
 Americans with Disabilities Cases
  (A.D. Cases), 265, **267**
  classification numbers, **267**
 Labor and Employment Law Library,
  265–267
  classification number, 265, **267**
  digest and full text of case, **267**
  E.E.O.C. Technical Assistance for
   Employers, **266**
  introductory screen, **265**
  outline, **267**
  statutory and regulatory outlines in,
   266
 subject-matter service research, 260, 263

CAMLaw (blog), 294, **295**
Canons of construction, 200
Case history, 132
Case reporters, 13, 77–80, **81–82**
 citations, 105–108
Case research, 77–127
 case name, 106–107
 case summaries
  checklist, 126
  reading, 91, 93
  sample research example, **114–115**
 checklist, 126–127, 327–328
 citators. *See* Citators
 citing cases, 105–108
 court opinions. *See* Court opinions
 digests, 84–98. *See also* Digests
 electronic research, 99–105. *See also*
  Electronic research

interim pamphlets, 94
    closing table, **95, 118**
    sample research example, **117–118**
key numbers
    locating, 89–91, 126, 327
    outline, sample research example,
        112–113
methods of locating cases, 83–84
mini-digests, research example, **119**
municipal courts or local agencies, 105
non-precedential opinions, 83
party name, search by, 84
pocket parts, 93–94, **116**
    Descriptive-Word Index (DWI), **111**
precedential opinions, 83
print digest
    sample pages, **108–125**
    selection of, checklist, 126, 327
print research, 84–98
research plan, developing, 327–328
Shepard's Citations. *See* Shepard's
        Citations
update print digest research, checklist,
        126, 328
Case summaries
    checklist, 126
    reading, 91, 93
    sample research example, **114–115**
CBC (Clark Boardman Callaghan), 260
CCH, Inc. (CCH), 260, 263
CD-ROM
    overview, 13
    subject-matter service research, 260,
        262, 268, 271
        directory, 261
CFR. *See Code of Federal Regulations*
Checklists
    American Law Reports, 75, 326–327
    case research, 126–127, 327–328
    electronic research, 326
        case research, 126–127, 328
        federal legislative history, 234
        KeyCite, 155–156
        regulations, 257–258
        research plan, developing, 331–332
        reviewing search results, 303
        Shepard's Citations, 155, 328
    federal administrative law research,
        257–258, 330–331
    federal legislative history, 233–235,
        329–330
    key numbers, locating, 126, 327
    legal periodicals, 326
    model acts, 75, 327

print digest, selection of, 126, 327
research plan, developing, 325–332
Restatements, 75, 327
scope of research, identifying, 233
secondary source research, 74–75
Shepard's Citations, 155, 328
sources for research, 326–332
statutory research, 198, 329
subject-matter service research, 268, 331
topics, locating, 126, 327
uniform laws, 75, 327
update print digest research, 126, 328
CIS. *See* Congressional Information
        Service
Citations. *See also ALWD Manual;*
        The Bluebook; Citators
    A.L.R. Annotations, 54, 57–58
    case name, 106–107
    case research, 105–108
    committee reports, 222–223
    defined, 13
    electronic legal research services, 296–299
    federal legislative history, 222–224
        committee reports, 222–223
        floor debates, 224
        U.S.C.C.A.N., 222–223
    Internet materials, 298–299
    introduction to, 15–22
    legal encyclopedias, 54–55
    legal periodicals, 54, 56–57
    model acts, 54, 58–59
    parallel, 78
    parentheticals, 106, 107–108, 184–185
    regulations, 252
    reporters, 106, 107
    Restatements, 54, 58
    secondary sources, 53–59
    Shepard's. *See* Shepard's Citations
    statutes, 184–186
        electronic legal research services,
            184–186, 297–298
        subject-matter service research,
            263–264
    treatises, 54, 55–56
    uniform laws, 54, 58–59
    U.S.C.C.A.N., 222–223
    use in legal research, 13
Citators, 129–156. *See also* KeyCite;
        Shepard's Citations
    checklists, 155–156
    choosing among, 130–131
    introduction to, 129–132
    purpose of, 129–130
    regulations, 258

statutory research, 174
terms and procedural concepts used in citator research, 131–132
Cite function, LexisNexis, 289
C.J.S. *See Corpus Juris Secundum*
Clark Boardman Callaghan (CBC), 260
Clipping or alert services, 138–139, 145, 182, 292–293, 304. *See also* KeyCite Alert; Shepard's Alert
Closing tables
    digests, 94–96, **95, 118**
    interim pamphlets, 94–96, **95, 118**
Code of Federal Regulations (CFR)
    citators, using for research of, 244, 258
    e-CFR, 246–247, **255–256,** 257, 330
    electronic research, 241–242, 244–251, **246,** 246–247, **248–251,** 258
    GPO Access, introductory screens for research, **246**
    index entry, **253**
    LexisNexis, 245
    List of CFR Sections Affected (LSA), 243–244, 247–248, **248–249, 251,** 257–258
    methods of locating, 241–242, 258
    official sources, updating through, 247, **251,** 257
    official sources, updating with, **251**
    print research, **239–240**
        cross references, 242–243, **243**
        generally, 238
        updating process, 243–244
    Westlaw, 245
Codes. *See also* Statutory research
    annotated vs. unannotated, 138, 159, 161
    defined, 157
    federal laws. *See* Statutory research; United States Code Annotated (U.S.C.A.); United States Code Service (U.S.C.S.); United States Code (U.S.C.)
    official vs. unofficial, 159, 161
    regulatory. *See Code of Federal Regulations* (CFR)
    state codes, 172, 179, 180, 182–183
    statutes
        codified within federal code, **160**
        defined, 2
    subject matter organization of, 158–159
Combined digests
    described, 85, 87, 89
    when to use, 90
Committee reports
    citations, 222–223

locating, checklist, 233
overview, 204
Common-law rules
    court and legislature, relationship between, 3–4
    defined, 2
    Restatements and, 42, 44
    state common-law research, 321
Computer word searching, 27–28, 272–273, 277–285. *See also* Electronic research
    Westlaw and LexisNexis, 99, 100
Congressional Information Service (CIS), 207–208, 210, **211**
    described, 207–208, 210
    electronic research, 214
    entries, **211**
    floor debates, 206, 208
    Four-Year Cumulative Indices, 208
    Index, 208, 210
    Legislative Histories volume, 208, 210, **211,** 212–213
    LexisNexis Congressional, 207, 215, 219, **221, 230–232,** 260, 271, 276, 299, 315, 330
        search options, **230–232**
    overview, 206
Congressional Record
    daily edition, 210–212, **213**
    described, 210, 212–214
    electronic research, 214–215, 221, **232**
    floor debates, 203, 210, 224
        locating using print resources, 210, 212–214, 234
    GPO Access, 216, 219
    index, 212, 214
    LexisNexis Congressional, **232.** *See also* LexisNexis Congressional
    overview, 206
    permanent edition, 212
Connectors, Boolean searching, 278–281
Constitutions
    defined, 2
    state, 3, 6
    U.S., 3, 6
Conversion tables, statutory research, 168, 170–172, **171**
Cornell Law School, Legal Information Institute, 183, 271, **301–302**
Corpus Juris Secundum (C.J.S.)
    checklist, legal encyclopedias, 74, 326
    citation to, 54–55
    secondary source, 32–33, 53–54

Cost-effective searching, electronic research, 289–292
Court opinions, 77–84
  case reporters, 13, 77–80, **81–82**. *See also* Reporters
  citators. *See* Citators
  components of, 80, **81–82**
  defined, 2
  federal courts of appeals, geographic boundaries, 9
  published opinions, 78, 80
  reporters, generally, 13
  structure of court system, 7, 77
  syllabus, 80
  unpublished opinions, 78, 80, 83
Courts-martial (research example)
  statute codified within federal code, **160**
  supplementary pamphlets, updating research using, **191**
  United States Code Annotated (U.S.C.A.)
    annotations accompanying, **167, 189–190**
    chapter outline, excerpt, **188**
    code section, **160, 188**
    index entry, **165, 187**
    pocket part update, **169**
Currency
  print products, legal authority, 13
  secondary sources, 30
Current Law Index, 38, 40
Custom Digest, Westlaw, 99, 101, 126
Cybercemetery of Former Federal Web Sites, 296

Descriptive-Word Index (DWI), 90–91, **92**
  research example, **109–111**
Deskbooks, 173
Digests, 84–98
  case on point, working from, 90
  case summaries, reading, 91, 93
  closing tables, 94–96, **95**, 118
  combined digests, 85, 87, 89
    when to use, 90
  defined, 83
  Descriptive-Word Index (DWI), 90–91, **92, 111**
  electronic case research, Westlaw, 99, 101
  federal digests, 85, 87, 88
    when to use, 90

interim pamphlets, 94
  noncumulative, **117–118**
key numbers, locating, 89–91
locating correct set, 85, 87, 89
mini-digest, **119**
pocket parts, 85, 93–94, **116**
  Descriptive-Word Index (DWI), **111**
print research, 84–98
regional digests, 85, 87, 88
  when to use, 90
relevant topics, going directly to, 91
research process, 85–96
state digests, 85, 87, 88
  when to use, 90
subject-matter service research compared, 261
Table of Cases, 96–97, **97**
topics, locating, 89–91
  checklist, 126, 327
updating digests research, 93–96
Words and Phrases, 97, **98**
Direct case history, 132
Directory of Law-Related CD-ROMs (Eis), 261
Directory of Uniform Acts and Codes: Tables and Index, 47, 75
Disabled individuals. *See* Americans with Disabilities Act (research example)
Downloading, 317
DWI. *See* Descriptive-Word Index

Easy Search, 285
e-CFR *(Electronic Code of Federal Regulations),* 246–247, **255–256,** 257, 330
ECLIPSE, 293
Eis, Arlene, 261
Electronic Code of Federal regulations (e-CFR), 246–247, **255–256,** 257, 330
Electronic research, 269–304. *See also specific services*
  accounting for billing structure, 291–292
  additional resources, 292–296, 304
  advance planning, 290–291
  Alert (LexisNexis), 293, 304
  alert or clipping services, 138–139, 145, 182, 292–293, 304
  authority, 12–15
  blogs, 293–296, **295,** 304

Boolean searching, 277–284. *See also*
    Boolean searching
case research, 99–105
    electronic case research, 126–127
    formats, Westlaw and LexisNexis, 99,
        100, 101–102, **103–104**
    Internet, 104–105, 127
    LexisNexis, 101–102, **103–104**
    subject searching, Westlaw and
        LexisNexis, 99–104
    Westlaw, **100**, 105
    word searching, Westlaw and
        LexisNexis, 99–104
checklists, 326
    additional tools, using, 304
    alert and clipping services, 304
    blogs and publicly available Internet
        sources, 304
    case research, 328
    federal legislative history, 234
    research plan, developing, 331–332
    selection of service, 303
citing electronic legal research services,
    296–299
    cases, 297
    Internet materials, 298–299
    statutes, 184–186, 297–298
conducting effective, 275–292
Congressional Record, 214–215, 221,
    232
constructing search, 277–285. *See also*
    Boolean searching
    checklist, 303–304
    LexisNexis, 277–285, **279**
    natural language searching, 284–285
    sophisticated search, 283–284
    Westlaw, 277–285, **278**
cost-effective searching, 289–292
database, selection of, 274, 285–286, 303
downloading information, charges, 292
ECLIPSE, 293
federal legislative history, 214–221
    United States Statutes at Large, 214
fee-based services, 270, 276
full-text services, 14, 219, 221
generally, 269–270
HeinOnline
    administrative material, 271
    legislative history, 206–207, 219, **220**,
        234, 235, 271
    secondary sources, 51–52, **52**
Internet sources. *See* Internet sources
introduction to, 270–275

KeyCite Alert, 145, 292–293, 304
LawTRIO, 261
legal research web sites, 271
LexisNexis. *See* LexisNexis
natural language searching, 284–285
print, comparison between, 272–273
printing information, charges, 292
process, overview, 273–275
publicly available services, 271–272,
    277, 293–296, **294–295**, 304
regulations, 244–247, **246**, **248–251**
    checklist, 257–258
research assistance, 291
research plan, developing, 312, 314–315
    checklist, 331–332
reviewing search results, 274–275, 286–287
    checklist, 303
sample pages, **294–295**, **299–302**
search techniques, 269–270
    constructing search, 277–285
    database, selecting, 274, 285–286, 303
    effective research, 298–292, 303–304,
        331–332
    overview, 272–273
    reviewing search results, 274–275,
        286–287, 303
    selecting, 274, 303–304
    service, selecting, 274, 275–277, 303
    subject searching, 272–273
    table of contents, browsing, 175–178,
        272
    word searching, 272–273, 277–285
secondary sources, electronic search of,
    50–53, 138, 142
selection of service, 274, 275–277
    checklist, 303
services, overview, 270–272
    alert or clipping services, 138–139,
        145, 182, 292–293, 304
    blogs, 293–296, **295**, 304
    fee-based services, 270, 276
    publicly available services,
        271–272, 277, 293–296,
        294–295, 304
    subscription services, 270–271, 277
Shepard's Alert, 138–139, 182, 293, 304
Shepard's Citations, 155, 328, 329
statutory research, 174–183
    LexisNexis, 179–182, **181–182**
    Westlaw, 175–179, **176–177**, **179**
subject-matter service research,
    262–263, 271
subscription services, 270–271, 277

techniques, overview, 272–273
United States Statutes at Large, 214
updating, 269
virtual law library sites, 271
West Clip, 292–293, 304
Westlaw. *See* Westlaw
Electronic sources. *See* Electronic
    research
Eleventh Decennial Digests (West), 87, 89
Enabling legislation, 237
Executive branch of government, 2, 3

FACE Act, 168, **170, 171**
False imprisonment (research example)
    American Jurisprudence, Second
        Edition
        citations to, 55
        index entry, **34**
        main volume entry, **35**
        pocket part entry, **36**
    American Law Reports, index, **60**
    *Index to Legal Periodicals and
        Books,* **39**
    legal periodicals, **39–40**
    Restatement (Second) of Torts, **69–73**
    treatises, **37**
Family and Medical Leave Act, 238
Fast Formats, *ALWD Citation Manual,* 21
Federal administrative law research,
    237–258
    administrative agencies, 237–240, 258
    checklists, 257–258, 330–331
    GPO Access, **246,** 246–251
    regulations, researching
        electronic research, 244–251
        print, 238–240, 242–244, 257
        sample pages, **252–256**
        Shepard's for CFR, 244
Federal Appendix (Fed. Appx. or
    F. App'x), 78, 79, 83
Federal digests, 85, 87, 88
    when to use, 90
Federal government web sites. *See*
    Government web sites
*Federal Legislative Histories: An
    Annotated Bibliography and
    Index to Officially Published
    Sources* (Reams), 207, 233, 329
Federal legislative history, 199–235
    ALWD Citation Manual, 222–224
    bills, 203
        laws, passage of, **201**

The Bluebook, 222–224
checklists, 233–235, 329–330
citations, 222–224
    committee reports, 222–223
    floor debates, 224
committee reports, 204, **209**
    citations, 222–223
    locating, checklist, 233
compiled legislative histories, 206–207
    checklist, 233
complete histories, CIS microfiche set,
    233–234
definition of, 200
electronic research, 214–221
    checklist, 233–235
    Internet sources, 216–219, **217, 218,**
        219–221, 271
    LexisNexis, 215–216, 219, 221
    United States Statutes at Large, 214
    Westlaw, 215
floor debates, 203–204, 210
    citations, 224
    locating in *Congressional Record,*
        using print resources, 234
full-text searches, 219, 221
hearings, 203
HeinOnline, 206–207, 219, **220,** 234, 235
Internet sources
    full-text searches, 219, 221
    GPO Access, 216, **218,** 219, 234, 235,
        246, 246–251, 330
    LexisNexis Congressional, 207, 215,
        219, **221, 230–232,** 235, 260, 271,
        276, 299, 315, 330
    subscription services, 219–221,
        220–221
    Thomas, 216, **217,** 219, **228–229,** 234,
        271, 330
laws, enactment of, 200–202
    bills, passage of, **201**
LexisNexis, 215–216, 219, **221**
methods of locating, 204–205
print, researching, 206–214
    CIS. *See* Congressional Information
        Service
    compiled legislative histories,
        206–207, 233–234
    U.S.C.C.A.N. *See United States
        Code Congressional and
        Administrative News*
research strategies, 204–205
research summary for, 235
sample pages, **224–232**

sources of, 202–204
  bills, 203
  committee reports, 204, 233
  floor debates, 203–204, 210, 224, 234
  hearings, 203
subscription services, 219–221, **220–221**
Westlaw, 215
Federal or state procedural research, 324
Federal Practice and Procedure (Wright & Miller), 173
Federal Practice Digests (West)
  closing table, 94–96, **95**
  described, 85, 87, 88
  research example, **86–87**
Federal procedural research, 324
Federal Register
  generally, 238
  government sources, 246–251
  Internet, 244–251
  LexisNexis, 245
  List of CFR Sections Affected (LSA), 243–244, 247–248, **248–249, 251,** 257–258
  new or amended regulations, 243–244, 246–251, **250, 255–256**
  Parts Affected table, 244, **246,** 246–247, **248–251, 255–256**
  Westlaw, 245
Federal regulations. *See* Regulations
Federal Reporter, 78, 79, **81–82**
  research example, **120–125**
Federal Rules Decisions (F.R.D.), 78, 79
Federal Rules of Civil Procedure, 78, 173
Federal Rules of Criminal Procedure, 78
Federal statutory research, 323. *See also* Statutory research
Federal Supplement
  reporter, 78, 79
Federal Supplement mini-digest, **119**
Fee-based electronic research services, 270, 276
FindLaw, 271, **300**
Floor debates
  citations, 224
  locating in *Congressional Record,* using print resources, 212–214
  locating in *Congressional Record,* using electronic resources, 214–221
  overview, 203–204, 210
  sources for, 206
FOCUS function, LexisNexis, 138, **139,** 289
Freedom of Access to Clinic Entrances Act (FACE Act), 168, **170, 171**
FULL function, LexisNexis, 289

Full-text services, 14, 219, 221
General Digests (West), 87, 89
  Eleventh Decennial Digests, 87, 89
GlobalCite, 130, 270
Google, 272, 296
Google Scholar, 296
Government Printing Office (GPO)
  GPO Access, 216, **218,** 219, 234, 235, **246,** 246–251, **248, 255,** 271, 276, 296, 330
    C.F.R. research, introductory screens, **246, 248**
    Cybercemetery of Former Federal Web Sites, 296
    search options, **246, 248**
  Thomas site, 216, **217,** 219, **228–229,** 234, 330
Government web sites, 216, 271
GPO. *See* Government Printing Office
GPO Access. *See* Government Printing Office

Hearings, generally, 203
HeinOnline
  administrative material, 271
  legal periodicals, 51–52, **52**
  legislative history, 206–207, 219, **220,** 234, 235, 271
  subscription service, 271
House Judiciary Committee Report
  Thomas site, **229**
  United States Code Congressional and Administrative News (U.S.C.C.A.N.), **209, 227**

ILP. *See Index to Legal Periodicals and Books*
Index
  ALWD Citation Manual, 19, 20
  American Jurisprudence, Second Edition, **34**
  American Law Reports, 60, **62**
  The Bluebook, 18
  Congressional Information Service (CIS), 208, 210–212, 221
  Congressional Record, 212, 214
  Descriptive-Word Index (DWI), digests, 90–91, **92**
  electronic indexes, 14–15, 38, 40
  Index to Legal Periodicals and Books, entry, **39**
  print, researching regulations, 242–243

secondary sources, 31, **34**
state statutory code, **193**
United States Code Annotated
(U.S.C.A.), 163–164, **165, 187**
United States Code Service (U.S.C.S.),
172, 242–243
United States Code (U.S.C.), 171
Indexing services, 38
Index to Legal Periodicals and Books, 38,
40, 270–271
electronic citation list, **39**
Indirect case history, 132
Intangible concepts, generating search
terms, 26
Interest in freedom from confinement
(research example), **45–46**
Interim pamphlets
closing tables, 94–96, **95, 118**
digests, 94
noncumulative, **117–118**
Internet Archive Wayback Machine, 296
Internet sources
ALWD Citation Manual, 21
archives, 296
blogs, 293–296, **295,** 304
case research, 104–105, 127
citations, 298–299
federal legislative history
GPO Access, 216, **218,** 219, **255,**
271, 330
LexisNexis Congressional, 207, 215,
219, **221, 230–232,** 235, 260, 271,
299, 315, 330
Thomas, 216, **217,** 219, **228–229,** 234,
271, 330
LawTRIO, 261
legal periodicals, 52–53
overview, 12–15
publicly available, 271–272, 277,
293–296, **294–296,** 304
regulations, 244–251
GPO Access, **246,** 246–251, **248**
research trails, saving, 316–317
RSS feed reader, 294
search engines, 272
secondary sources, 52–53
statutory research, 182–183, 198
subject-matter service research, 261,
262–263, 268
checklist, 268, 331

Johnson, Nancy P., 206, 207, 219, 233,
234, 329

Journal articles. *See* Legal periodicals
Judicial branch of government, 2, 3–4
Jurisdiction, 8–9, 306

KeyCite, 140–145
accessing and interpreting, 140–144,
155–156
case research, 140–145
checklist, 328
when to use in, 130
checklists, 155–156, 328
choosing among citators, 130–131
customizing options, 144–145, 156
described, 130, 138, 140–145
electronic research, checklist, 328
entry excerpt, **141, 143, 151–154**
full history entry, **141, 151**
Graphical KeyCite display, 141–142, **142**
legislative history, 215
limited display options, 144–145, **145,**
152–153
purpose of, 130
regulations, using for research of, 244,
245, 258
sample pages, **151–154**
star categories, definitions of, 144
status flags, 140
statutory research, 174, 178–179, **179,**
198, 329
terms and procedural concepts used in
citator research, 131–132
KeyCite Alert, 145, 292–293, 304
Key numbers
locating, 89–91
checklists, 126, 327
outline, case research, **112–113**
KeySearch, Westlaw, 101, 126
KWIC function, LexisNexis, 138,
148–150, 289

Law.com, 292
LawCrawler, 272, 296
Law reviews and journals. *See* Legal
periodicals
Laws. *See* Legislation
LawTRIO, 261
LawWatch, 293
Legal encyclopedias, 32–33, **34–36**
checklist, 74, 326
citations, 54–55
Legal Information Institute. *See* Cornell
Law School

Legal Looseleafs in Print (Eis), 261
Legal Newsletters in Print (Eis), 261
Legal periodicals
  checklist, 74–75, 326
  citations, 54, 56–57
  false imprisonment (research example),
      39–40
  HeinOnline, 51–52, **52**
  indices, 14–15
  Internet resources, 52–53
  as secondary sources, 36, 38–40
Legal research, 1–23
  defined, 1
  introduction to process of, 9–12
  strategies overview, 12–15
Legal system, introduction to, 2–9
LegalTrac, 38, 40, 270–271
  citation list, **40**
Legislation. *See also* Federal legislative
      history; Statutory research
  enabling legislation, 237
  enactment of laws, 200–202
    bills, passage of, 200–202, **201**
  federal legislative history. *See* Federal
      legislative history
Legislative branch of government, 2, 3–4
Legislative history. *See* Federal legislative
      history
LexisNexis. *See also* Electronic research
  Alert, 293, 304
  American Jurisprudence, Second
      Edition, 50
  "Book Browse" function, 180, **181**
  case research, example, **103–104**
  choice of research source, 276
  Cite function, 289
  commercial database, 14
  constructing search, 277–285, **279**
    segments, **279,** 283–284
  cost-effective searching, 289–292
  cost of, 276
  Easy Search, 285
  ECLIPSE, 293
  electronic case research
    checklist, 126–127
    formats, 101–102, **103–104**
    Internet research compared, 105
    subject searching, 83–84, 99–104
    word searching, 102, 104
  electronic research, 179–181, **181–182**
  federal legislative history, 215–216
  FOCUS function, 138, **139,** 289
  FULL function, 289

generally, 270
  Headnotes, 102–104, **103**
  HeinOnline compared, 51–52
  KWIC function, 138, **148–150,** 289
  More Like This search function, 289
  natural language searching, 284–285
  regulations, 244
  regulations, research of, 245
  research plan, creation of, 306
  research trails, saving on, 316
  Restatements, 51
  search options, 102–104
  search results, 288–289, **290**
  search techniques, 274–292, 303–304,
      331–332
  secondary sources, 50–51
  Shepard's Alert, 138–139, 293, 304
  Shepard's Citations, 132–139, 182
    accessing, 132–133, **148–150**
    customizing options, 138–139,
      139, 155
    entries, sample, **133–134**
    FOCUS function, 138, **139**
    interpreting entries, **133–135,**
      133–138, 155
    KWIC function, 138, **148–150**
    legislative history, 216
    signals, 133, 135
    statutes, 174, 182, **183,** 198
  Source, 180
  statutory research, 174, 179–182,
      181–182
  subject-matter service research,
      262–263, 268
LexisNexis Congressional, 271, 276
  abstracts entries, **231**
  CIS, 207, 221, 330
  legislative history, 215, 219, **221,** 234,
      235, 271, 315, 330
  search options, **221, 230–232**
  selection of electronic databases,
      276, 299
  subject-matter research compared, 260
Liability of Attorney for Abuse of Process
  sample A.L.R. Annotation, **61–68**
  sample A.L.R. index entries, **62**
Library of Congress, Thomas, 216, **217,**
      219, **228–229,** 234, 271, 330
List of CFR Sections Affected (LSA),
      243–244, 247–248, **248–249,** 251
  checklist, 257–258
Local court rules, 21, 173
Locate request, Westlaw, 287–288, 289

Loislaw, 130, 270, 276, 293
Looseleaf services. *See* Subject-matter
  service research

Mandatory authority. *See also* Primary
    mandatory authority
  defined, 5
  determining, 5–9, 10
Matthew Bender, 260
MetaCrawler, 272
Microfiche, locating legislative histories,
    233–234
Mini-digests, **119**
Model acts, 47
  checklists, 75, 327
  citations, 54, 58–59
Model Penal Code, 47, 58–59
Moore's Federal Practice, 173
More Like This search function,
    LexisNexis, 289
Municipal courts or local agencies,
    opinions of, 105

National Reporter System, 78, 79
Natural language searching, 284–285
Negligence, rules of, 3–4
Newspaper articles, citation of (Bluepages
    B9.1.4), 299
Noncumulative pamphlets, U.S.C.A., 164,
    168, 170–171, 172, **191, 197**, 198
Non-precedential opinions, 83

Official codes, 159, 161

Pamphlets. *See* Interim pamphlets;
    Noncumulative pamphlets;
    Supplementary pamphlets
Parallel citations, 78
Parentheticals, citations, 106, 107–108,
    184–185
Parts Affected table, CFR, 244, **246**,
    246–261, **248–251, 255**
Party name, search by, 84
Persuasive authority
  defined, 5, 10
  determining, 5–9, 10
  research plan and
    flowchart, **313**
    preliminary information, 306–307
    writing out plan, 308–309, 311–312, **313**

P & F (Pike & Fisher), 260
Photocopying, 316
Pike & Fisher (P & F), 260
Places involved in problem, generating
    search terms, 26
Pocket parts
  American Law Reports, **67–68**
  described, 14
  digests, 93–94, **116**
    Descriptive-Word Index (DWI), **111**
  Restatement (Second) of Torts, **72–73**
  secondary sources, 32, **36**
  state statutory code example, **197**
  United States Code Annotated
      (U.S.C.A.), 164, 168, **169,**
      191–192
Popular name tables, statutory research,
    168, 170–172, **171,** 175, 178, 180
Potential claims and defenses, generating
    search terms, 26–27
Primary authority. *See also* Primary
    mandatory authority; Primary
    persuasive authority
  no authority found in search, 30
  secondary authority vs., 4–5
  too much authority found in search, 30
Primary mandatory authority, 5–9, 10, 11,
    12, 308–309, 310
  flowchart, 310
Primary persuasive authority, 12
  determining, 5–9, 10
  research path, planning, 11, 308–309,
    311–312, **313**
  secondary sources used to find, 30,
    311–312
Print resources
  digest, selection of, checklist, 126, 327
  electronic search techniques compared,
    272–273
  legal authority, 12–14
  researching regulations. *See* Print
    resources, researching
    regulations
  research plan, developing, 312, 314–315
  secondary authority, 31–49
  Shepard's Citations. *See* Print
    resources, Shepard's Citations
    used
  subject-matter service research, 262, 268
Print resources, researching regulations,
    238–240, 242–244
  annotated code, use of, 242–243
  index, use of, 242–243

List of CFR Sections Affected (LSA),
    243–244
  checklist, 257
locating regulations, 242–243
  checklist, 257
updating regulations, 243–244
  checklist, 257
Print resources, Shepard's Citations used,
    130, 145–147
  citators, examples of, **147**
  correct set of books, locating, 146
  entries, 146, *147*
  interpreting entries, 146, **147**
  what your library should contain, 146
Procedure rules, research of, 172–173, 324
Process of legal research
  electronic legal research, 273–275
  introduction, 9–12
  preliminary steps, 10–11, 12
Procrastination, 317
Products liability
  statutory research example, **193–197**
Public accommodations. *See* Americans
        with Disabilities Act (research
        example)
Public laws. *See also* Statutory research
    example of Public Law 103-416,
    157–158
Publicly available electronic research
        services, 271–272, 277, 293–296,
        295–296, 304
Published opinions, 78, 80

Reams, Bernard D., 207, 233, 329
Regional digests, 85, 87, 88
  when to use, 90
Regulations
  agency staff, research via, 241, 258
  citator, using for research of,
        244, 258
  citing, 252
  described, 3, 237–240
  electronic research, 244–251
    checklist, 257
  email, research via, 241, 258
  Internet sources, 244–251
  LexisNexis, 244, 245
  methods of locating, 241–242, 258
  official sources, updating with, **251**
  print, researching, 238–240, 242–244
    annotated code, use of, 242–243
    index, use of, 242–243

List of CFR Sections Affected (LSA),
    243–244, 257
  locating regulations, 242–243, 257
  updating regulations, 243–244, 257
  research plan, developing, 314
  telephone, research via, 241, 258
  Westlaw, 244, 245
Relief sought by complaining party
  search terms, generating, 27
Reporters, **81–82.** *See also* West; specific
        reporters
  citations, 106, 107
  described, 77–80
  non-precedential opinions, 78, 80, 83
  official reporter, 78, 80
  overview, 13
  regional reporters, 78
  unofficial reporter, 80, 83
Research assistance, electronic
        research, 291
Research Institute of America
        (RIA), 260
Research plan, developing, 305–332
  authorities located through other
        means, 314
  case research, checklist, 327–328
  checklists, 325–332
  costs, 306
  determining research path, 11
  downloading, 317
  effective research plan, checklist for
        developing, 325
  electronic sources
    checklist, 331–332
    deciding on, 312, 314–315
  federal administrative law research,
        checklist, 330–331
  federal or state procedural
        research, 324
  federal statutory research, 323
  final product, determining, 306
  flowcharts for research, 310, **313,**
        320–324
  general search terms, 314
  help, finding, 306, 318–319
  jurisdiction, 306
  master checklist of research sources,
        326–332
  materials not available in print, 314–315
  materials not available online, 312
  note taking, 315–317
  overwhelming amount of material,
        finding help, 319–320

persuasive authority
    decision to research, 306–307
    searching for, 308–309, 311–312, **313**
photocopying, 317
preliminary steps, 306–307
    checklist, 325
primary mandatory authority
    research path, planning, 11, 12,
        308–309, 310
    searching for, 308–310
printing, 317
print sources, deciding on, 312, 314–315
procrastination, 317
reason to create plan, 305
regulatory research, 314
sample research plans, 320–324
search terms
    generating, 25–28, 307–308
    rethinking, 318–319
    unique, 315
secondary sources, 319
Shepard's Citations, 328, 329
sources, identifying, 308–312, **313**
state common-law research, 321
state statutory research, 322
statutory research, 314
    checklist, 329
steps in creating plan, 305–318
stopping, 317–318
subject-matter service research,
    checklist, 331
terms of art, 307
time constraints, 306
understanding problem, 318
unfamiliar topics, getting information
    on, 314
unique search terms, 315
updating research, 315
working effectively, 315–318
    checklist, 325
    deciding when to stop, 317–318
    keeping track of material, 315–317
    note taking, 315–317
writing out plan, 307–315
    checklist, 325
    initial issue statement, 308–309
    persuasive authority, searching for,
        308–309, 311–312, **313**
    primary mandatory authority,
        searching for, 308–310
    sources, identifying, 308–312
Restatements, 41, 44–47, **45–46**. *See also
    Restatement (Second) of Torts*

appendix volumes, 44, **46, 72–73**
checklists, 75, 327
citations, 54, 58
common-law rules, determination, 43, 44
rules volume, **45**
sample pages, **69–73**
Restatement (Second) of Torts, 44
    appendix to, 44, **46, 72–73**
    example of section, **45–46**
    false imprisonment (research example),
        69–73
    table of contents, **69**
Reviewing search results. *See* Electronic
    research
RIA (Research Institute of America), 260
RSS feed readers, 294
Rules of procedure, statutory research,
    172–173

Searching, electronic research
    techniques. *See* Electronic
    research
Search terms, generating, 25–28
    categories of information, based
        on, 25–27
    computer searching, 27–28
    expanding initial search, 27–28
    general search terms, 314
    intangible concepts, 26
    parties involved in problem, 25–26
    places involved in problem, 26
    potential claims and defenses, 26–27
    relief sought by complaining party, 27
    research plan, developing, 308–309
    rethinking terms, 318–319
    synonyms, 27–28
    tangible objects, 26
    unique search terms, 315
Secondary sources, 29–75
    American Law Reports, 40–41, **42,
        43,** 138
        Annotations, **61–68**
        checklist, 75, 326–327
        citations, 57–58
        index, **60, 62**
    checklists for research, 74–75
    citations to, 30–31, 53–59
    currency, 30
    electronic indices, 38, 40
    electronic research of, 50–53, 138, 142
    HeinOnline, 51–52, **52**
    how to use, 31–75

index, 31, **34**
legal encyclopedias, 32–33, **34–36**
    checklist, 74, 326
    citations, 54–55
legal periodicals, 36, 38–40
    checklist, 74–75
    citations, 54, 56–57
    false imprisonment (research
        example), **39–40**
    HeinOnline, 51–52, **52**
    Internet resources, 52–53
methods of locating, 31
model acts, 47
    checklists, 75, 327
    citations, 54, 58–59
no authority found in primary
        sources, 30
pocket parts, 32, **36**, **67–68**
primary authority vs., 4–5, 10
primary persuasive authority, as aid to
        find, 30, 311–312
print resources, 31–49
process of legal research, 11, 12
research plan, developing, 319
Restatements, 41, 44–47, **45–46**. *See also*
        Restatements
rules for citing, 54
sample pages, **59–73**
state legal encyclopedias, 32
table of contents, 31
too much authority found in primary
        sources, 30
treatises. *See* Treatises
undeveloped area of law,
        researching, 30
unfamiliarity with area of law, 29
uniform laws, 47, **48–49**
    checklists, 75, 327
    citations, 54, 58–59
when not to use, 30–31
when to use, 29–30
Shepardizing. *See* Shepard's Citations
Shepard's Alert, 138–139, 293, 304
Shepard's Citations, 132–139
    accessing, 132–133, **148–150**
    case example, **147**, **148–150**
        case history codes, 133, 135–136,
            146, **147**
        customizing options, 138–139,
            139, 155
        headnote, tracing, 136–138, **137**
        interpreting entries, **133–135, 147,** 155
        treatment codes, 133, 135, 146, **147**

case research, 130, 132–139, 145–147,
        328
    checklist, 155, 328
    when to use in, 130
checklist, 155
checklists, 155, 328
choosing among citators, 130–131
Code of Federal Regulations (CFR),
        244, 258
customizing options, 138–139,
        139, 155
described, 130, 132–139, 145–147
electronic research, checklist, 155, 328
FOCUS function, 138, **139**
headnote, tracing, 136–138
history of, 129–130
interpreting entries, **133–135**, 133–138,
        146, **147**, 155
KWIC function, 138, **148–150**
legislative history, 216
LexisNexis, 132–139
    accessing, 132–133, **148–150**
    customizing options, 138–139,
        139, 155
    entries, sample, **133–134**
    FOCUS function, 138, **139**
    headnote, tracing, 136–138, **137**
    interpreting entries, **133–135,**
        133–138, 155
    KWIC function, 138, **148–150**
    signals, 133, 135
    statutes, 174, 182, **183**, 198
print, 130, 145–147
    correct set of books, locating, 145–147
    entries, **147**
    entry for case within each volume,
        locating, 146–147
    interpreting entries, 146, **147**
    what your library should
        contain, 146
purpose of, 130
regulations, using for research of,
        244, 258
research plan, developing, 328
sample pages, **148–150**
Shepard's Alert, 138–139, 293, 304
signals, 133, 135
statutes, 174, 182, **183**, 198
terms and procedural concepts used in
        citator research, 131–132
types of citators available, 146
Shepard's Federal Citations, 146
Shepard's Indiana Citations, 146

Shepard's North Eastern Citations, 146
Sources of Compiled Legislative Histories: A Bibliography of Government Documents, Periodical Articles, and Books (Johnson), 206, 207, 219, 233, 234, 329
Sources of law, 2–4
State codes, statutory research, 179, 322
  products liability example, **193–197**
    pocket part, **197**
State common-law research, 321
State constitutions, 3
State courts
  decisions, reporters, 78, 80
  jurisdiction, 8–9
  regional reporters, 78, 79, 80
  systems, structure, 7
State digests, 85, 87, 88
  when to use, 90
State legal encyclopedias, 32
State procedural research, 173, 324
Statutes. *See* Codes; State codes, statutory research; Statutory research
Statutes at Large. See United States Statutes at Large
Statutory research, 157–198
  checklist, 198
  citators, 174, 198
  citing statutes, 184–186
    electronic legal research services, 297–298
  codification, 158
  conversion tables, 168, 170–171, **171**
  electronic research, 174–183, 198
    Internet sources, 182–183, 198
    LexisNexis, 179–182, **181–182**
    Westlaw, 175–179, **176–177, 179**
  federal statutes
    codification of, 158, **160**
    legislative history. *See* Federal legislative history
    publication of, 157–158, **159**
      annotated vs. unannotated, 161
      official vs. unofficial, 161
      publication process, **159**
    research, 163–171, 323
    title and subject-matter organization of, 158–159
  introduction to, 157–163
  location of statute, checklist, 198
  methods of locating, **160,** 162–163
  popular name tables, 168, 170–171, 172, 175, 178, 180

print, research in, 163–174
products liability example, **193–197**
publication of statutory law, **159**
  codified within federal code, 158, **160**
publication process for statute, 157–158, **159**
public laws, 157–158, 163, **170, 171,** 198, 206
reading statute, checklist, 198
research plan, developing, 314
  checklist, 329
  federal statutory research, 323
  state statutory research, 322
rules of procedure, 172–173
sample pages, **186–197**
Shepard's, 174, 182, **183,** 216, 329
slip laws, 158
state codes, 163, 172, 179, 180, 182–183, 322
  example, **193–197**
    index, **193**
    pocket part, **197**
  publication of, 151
    annotated vs. unannotated, 159, 161
    codification, 159, 161
    official vs. unofficial, 157, 161
    subject matter organization, 159
    title organization, 159
    title and subject-matter organization of, 159
title and subject-matter organization of codes, 158–159
uniform laws and model acts, 173–174
update print research, checklist, 198
U.S. codes. *See specific publications starting with "United States"*
Structure of court system, 7, 77
  federal and state courts, 7
  federal courts of appeals, geographic boundaries, 9
Subject-matter service research, 259–268
  annotated codes, 260
  CD-ROM, 260, 262, 268, 271
    directory, 261
  checklists, 268, 331
  citations, 263–264
  electronic research, 262–263, 271
  generally, 259–261
  how to use, determination, 268

Internet sources, 261, 262–263, 268
  checklists, 268, 331
LawTRIO, 261
LexisNexis, 262–263, 268
locating, 261
  checklists, 268, 331
overview, 260–261
print resources, 262, 268
research plan, creation of, 307
sample pages, **264–267**
Westlaw, 262–263, 268
Subject searching
  electronic research, 272–273
  legal research, 13, 14
  secondary sources, 31
  Westlaw and LexisNexis, 99–104
Subscription electronic research services,
  270–271, 277
Supplementary pamphlets
  United States Code Annotated
    (U.S.C.A.), 164, 168, **191**
  United States Code Service (U.S.C.S),
    172
  United States Code (U.S.C.), 171
Supreme Court Reporter, 78, 79
Syllabus, 80
Synonyms as search terms, 27–28

Table of contents
  ALWD Citation Manual, 19, 20
  The Bluebook, 18, 19
  browsing, electronic research, 14, 272
  Restatement (Second) of Torts, **69**
  secondary sources, 31
  statutes, 175–178
Tables
  The Bluebook, 16, 17–18, 19
  cases, digests, 96–97, **97**
Tangible objects, generating search
    terms, 26
Term function, Westlaw, 287–288
Terms of art, 307
Thomas, 216, **217,** 219, **228–229,** 234,
    271, 330
Thomson West. *See* West
Topics, locating, 126, 327
Treatises
  checklist, 74, 326
  citations, 54, 55–56
  described, 33, 36
  false imprisonment (research
    example), **37**

ULA. *See Uniform Laws Annotated,*
    Master Edition
Unannotated codes, 159, 161
Undeveloped area of law, researching, 30
Unfamiliarity with area of law, 29
Uniform Commercial Code, 47
Uniform laws, 47
  checklists, 75, 327
  citations, 54, 58–59
Uniform Laws Annotated, Master Edition
    (ULA), 47, **48–49,** 75, 174
Uniform Single Publication Act (research
    example), **48–49**
Unique search terms, 315
United States Code Annotated (U.S.C.A.),
    163–171
  annotations accompanying, 164, 166,
    167, 189–190, 225–226
  chapter outline, excerpt, **188**
  code section in, **160, 188**
  conversion tables, 168, 170–171, **171**
  defined, 161
  differences from other codes,
    161, 172
  general index, 163–164, **165, 187**
  information contained in annotations, 166
  locating statutes, 163–171
  noncumulative pamphlets, 164, 168,
    170–171, 172, **191, 197**
  pocket parts, 164, 168, **169, 191–192**
  popular name and conversions tables,
    168, **170–171**
  public law number, **226**
  regulations, 242–243
  researching in, 163–171
  sample pages, **186–192**
  statute codified within federal
    code, **160**
  supplementary pamphlets, updating
    research using, 164, 165, 168,
    170–171, **191**
  unofficial code, 161
United States Code Congressional and
    Administrative News
    (U.S.C.C.A.N.)
  annotations in U.S.C.A., **208**
  citation, 222–223
  committee reports, 207, 212, 214
  Congressional Record references, 212
  House Judiciary Committee Report,
    209, 227
  legislative histories, 206, 207
  locating statute, **227**

United States Code Service (U.S.C.S.), 172
  annotations, content of, 215–216
  defined, 161
  index, 242–243
  regulations, 242–243, **243**, 245
  unofficial code, 161
United States Code (U.S.C.)
  defined, 161
  statutory research, 171
United States Courts of Appeals, 6, 7, 8, 9,
  78, 79
United States District Courts, 6, 7, 8, 9,
  78, 79
United States Statutes at Large
  electronic research, 214
  legislative history, 205
  overview, 158
  popular name and conversion tables,
    168, **170–171**
  Shepard's and, 172
United States Supreme Court
  Internet research, 105
  mandatory authority, as, 6, 7, 8, 9
  primary authority, as, 4
  reporters, 78, 79
University of North Texas archive web
  site, 296
Unofficial codes, 159, 161
Unpublished opinions, 78, 80, 83
U.S. Constitution, 3
U.S.C. *See United States Code*
U.S.C.A. *See United States Code
  Annotated*
U.S.C.C.A.N. *See United States Code
  Congressional and
  Administrative News*
U.S.C.S. *See United States Code Service*

V.Cite, 130
VersusLaw, 130, 270, 276, 293

War Crimes Act of 1996 (research
    example)
  Congressional Information Service
    (CIS)
    entry, **211**
    Legislative Histories entry, **211**
  Congressional Record, **213**, **232**
    LexisNexis Congressional, **232**
  federal legislative history, sample pages,
    224–232

House Judiciary Committee Report
  Thomas, **229**
  *United States Code Congressional
    and Administrative News*
    (U.S.C.C.A.N.), **209**, **227**
LexisNexis Congressional
  abstracts entries, **231**
Thomas, **228–229**
*United States Code Congressional and
  Administrative News*
  (U.S.C.C.A.N.)
  annotations in U.S.C.A. to, **208**
  House Judiciary Committee Report,
    209, **227**
  locating statute, **227**
Web sites. *See* Internet sources
West. *See also* Westlaw
  Atlantic Reporter example, **147**
  digest system, 85
    abandoned and lost property
      (research example), **86–87**
    characteristics of, summary, 88–89
    features of, **86–87**
  Federal Practice Digests
    closing table, 94–96, **95**
    described, 85, 87, 88
    research example, **86–87**
  Federal Reporter, 78, **81–82**
  Federal Supplement
    research example, **120–125**
  General Digests, 87, 89
  headnotes, 80, 90, 99
  regional reporters, 78
  reporters, 78, 80, **81–82**
    components of, 80, **81–82**
    editorial enhancement, 80
  state court decisions, 78, 80
  U.S.C.C.A.N. *See United States Code
    Congressional and
    Administrative News*
West Clip, 292–293, 304
Westlaw. *See also* Electronic research
  American Jurisprudence, Second
    Edition, 50
  case research, 100
  choice of, 276
  commercial database, 14
  constructing search, 277–285, **278**
    fields, **278**, 283–284
  cost-effective searching, 289–292
  cost of, 276
  Custom Digest, 99, 101, 126
  electronic case research

checklist, 126–127
    formats, 99, **100**
    Internet research compared, 105
    subject searching, 99–101
    word searching, 99, 101
federal legislative history, 215
generally, 270
HeinOnline compared, 51–52
KeyCite. *See* KeyCite
KeySearch, 101, 126
Locate request, 287–288, 289
natural language searching, 284–285
regulations, research of, 244, 245
research plan, creation of, 306
research trails, saving on, 316
Restatements, 51
search options, 99–101, 287–288
search results, 287–288, **288**

search techniques, 274–292, 303–304,
    331–332
secondary sources, 50–51
statutory research, 175–179, **176–177, 179**
subject-matter service research,
    262–263, 268
Term function, 287–288
West Clip, 292–293, 304
Words and Phrases, digests, 97, **98**
Word searching
    electronic research, 13, 15, 272–273,
    277–285
    search terms. *See* Search terms,
        generating
    Westlaw and LexisNexis, 99, 101, 102, 104
Writing out research plan. *See* Research
    plan, developing
Wrightslaw (web site), **294**